NEW HISTORICAL LITERARY STUDY

NEW HISTORICAL
LITERARY STUDY

ESSAYS ON REPRODUCING TEXTS,
REPRESENTING HISTORY

Edited by
Jeffrey N. Cox and Larry J. Reynolds

PRINCETON UNIVERSITY PRESS   PRINCETON, NEW JERSEY

Library of Congress Cataloging-in-Publication Data

New historical literary study : essays on reproducing texts,
representing history / edited by Jeffrey N. Cox and Larry J. Reynolds.
p.   cm.
Includes index.
ISBN 0-691-06990-5 — ISBN 0-691-01546-5 (pbk.)
1. English literature—History and criticism—Theory, etc.
2. American literature—History and criticism—Theory, etc.
3. American literature—Criticism, Textual.   4. English literature—
Criticism, Textual.   5. Literature and history.   6. Historicism.
I. Cox, Jeffrey N.   II. Reynolds, Larry J.
PR25.N48   1993   820.9—dc20   92-42580

Contents

Illustrations

Acknowledgments

THIS COLLECTION OF ESSAYS represents moments not only in the intellectual lives of each of the contributors but also in the ongoing intellectual life of the Interdisciplinary Group for Historical Literary Study (IGHLS) at Texas A&M University. Some of these essays were presented as part of the IGHLS conference on "(Re)producing Texts/(Re)presenting History" held September 27–29, 1989; some were delivered as papers during other IGHLS events, such as the symposium "Wordsworth and the Age of English Romanticism" and the lecture series "Writing and Rewriting Literary History." This volume would not have been possible had it not been for the collective efforts of the Interdisciplinary Group, and thus it is to IGHLS that the editors wish to dedicate the collection.

During the period that IGHLS sponsored this work, the following were IGHLS Fellows: David Anderson, Mark B. Busby, W. Bedford Clark, Donald R. Dickson, Margaret J. M. Ezell, Terence A. Hoagwood, Craig Kallendorf, Barbara Johnstone, Janet P. McCann, Clinton J. Machann, David G. Myers, Robert D. Newman, Patricia Phillippy, Kenneth M. Price, E. Cleve Want, and Stephen R. Yarbrough. We thank them for their support and all their hard work.

The 1989 conference on text production and literary history was a defining moment for IGHLS, and essays from that conference form the backbone of this volume. This conference was organized by Katherine O'Brien O'Keeffe, who is also one of the founding members of IGHLS and has served on its Steering Committee since its formation in 1986; this volume would not have existed without Katherine. Support for the conference, and thus indirectly for this volume, came from the Moody Foundation, the Westinghouse Corporation, and the College of Liberal Arts, the Department of English, the Department of Political Science, and the Interdisciplinary Program in Women's Studies at Texas A&M University. Teri Lathum and Harvey Tucker were instrumental in arranging for this support. We also want to thank Mark Lussier for organizing the 1988 IGHLS symposium on Wordsworth, funded by the Texas Committee on the Humanities.

IGHLS was founded and has prospered during the term of Daniel Fallon as Dean of Liberal Arts at Texas A&M. Dean Fallon had the vision to support the Interdisciplinary Group from its conception, and we want to thank him for his years of help and encouragement. We also want to thank William H. Mobley, President of Texas A&M, who has been a friend to IGHLS and participated in our 1989 conference. This volume was planned when Hamlin Hill served as Head of the Department of English at Texas A&M; it is being completed while J. Lawrence Mitchell serves in the same capacity. Both have been strong supporters of IGHLS, offering intellectual leadership, administrative help, and financial aid. We owe a great debt to both of them.

This volume, and particularly the work of the editors, has benefited from conversations with all IGHLS Fellows, past and present, and all those who have visited with the Interdisciplinary Group. This list of friends and colleagues is too long to include here, but we do want to single out G. Douglas Atkins, J. Douglas Canfield, Moira Ferguson, Kevin Kiernan, and Susanne Woods for their gracious help in making this volume possible. A number of our contributors, as well as the readers for Princeton University Press, and our colleague Howard Marchitell made useful suggestions for the Introduction to this volume. Susan Egenolf, who also helped with the Introduction, has served as a valuable editorial assistant for the project. We also want to thank Jan Want, and Robert Brown and the staff of Princeton University Press. Finally, we thank Carol and Amy for all their support.

Contributors

JANET E. AIKINS, Associate Professor of English at the University of New Hampshire, is the author of articles on eighteenth-century literature in such journals as *Studies in English Literature, The University of Toronto Quarterly*, and *Papers in Language and Literature*

LAWRENCE BUELL, Professor of English and American Literature at Harvard University, is author of *Literary Transcendentalism: Style and Vision in the American Renaissance* (1973) and *New England Literary Culture: From Revolution through Renaissance* (1986) and is coeditor of *The Morgesons* by Elizabeth Stoddard (1984).

RALPH COHEN, Kenan Professor of English at the University of Virginia, edits *New Literary History* and is Director of the Commonwealth Center for Literary and Cultural Change. He is editor of and contributor to *Studies in Historical Change* (1992).

JEFFREY N. COX, Associate Professor of English at Texas A&M University and codirector of the Interdisciplinary Group for Historical Literary Study, is the author of *In the Shadows of Romance: Romantic Tragic Drama in Germany, England, and France* (1987) and is the editor of *Seven Gothic Dramas 1789–1825* (1992).

MARGARET J. M. EZELL, Professor of English at Texas A&M University, is the author of *The Patriarch's Wife: Literary Evidence and the History of the Family* (1987) and *Writing Women's Literary History* (1993) and is the editor of *The Poetry and Prose of Mary, Lady Chudleigh* (1993); she is a member of the Women Writers Project.

STEPHEN GREENBLATT, Class of 1932 Professor of English at the University of California, Berkeley, is the author of such books as *Renaissance Self-Fashioning* (1980), *Shakespearean Negotiations: The Circulation of Social Energy in Renaissance England* (1988), and *Marvelous Possessions* (1991) and is the coeditor of *Representations*.

TERENCE ALLAN HOAGWOOD, Professor of English at Texas A&M University, is the author of *Prophecy and the Philosophy of Mind: Traditions of Blake and Shelley* (1985), *Skepticism and Ideology: Shelley's Prose and Its Philosophical Context from Bacon to Marx* (1988), and *Byron's Dialectic: Skepticism and the Critique of Culture* (forthcoming).

JEROME J. McGANN, Commonwealth Professor of English at the University of Virginia, is the author of such books as *The Romantic Ideology* (1981),

Social Values and Poetic Acts: The Historical Judgment of Literary Work (1988), and *The Textual Condition* (1991) and is the editor of the seven-volume *Complete Poetical Works of Byron* (1980–1992).

ROBERT D. NEWMAN, Associate Professor of English at Texas A&M University, is the author of *Understanding Thomas Pynchon* (1986) and *Transgressions of Reading: Narrative Engagement as Exile and Return* (1993) and is the coeditor of *Joyce's Ulysses: The Larger Perspective* (1987).

KATHERINE O'BRIEN O'KEEFFE, Professor of English at the University of Notre Dame, is the author of *Visible Song: Transitional Literacy in the Reading and Writing of Old English Verse* (1990) and is the editor of *The Anglo-Saxon Chronicle Manuscript MS C* (forthcoming 1993); she is former codirector of the Interdisciplinary Group for Historical Literary Study.

LEE PATTERSON, Professor of English at Duke University, is the author of *Negotiating the Past* (1986) and *Chaucer and the Subject of History* (1991) and is the editor of *Literary Practice and Social Change in Britain, 1380–1530* (1990).

LARRY J. REYNOLDS, Thomas Franklin Mayo Professor of English at Texas A&M University, is the author of *James Kirke Paulding* (1984) and *European Revolutions and the American Literary Renaissance* (1988) and is the co-editor of *"These Sad But Glorious Days"* by Margaret Fuller (1991); he is codirector of the Interdisciplinary group for Historical Literary Study.

MICHAEL ROGIN, Professor of Political Science at the University of California, Berkeley, is the author of such books as *Fathers and Children: Andrew Jackson and the Subjection of the American Indian* (1975), *Subversive Genealogy: The Politics and Art of Herman Melville* (1983), and *"Ronald Reagan," the Movie and Other Episodes in Political Demonology* (1987).

EDWARD W. SAID, University Professor and Chair of the Doctoral Program in Comparative Literature at Columbia University, is the author of such books as *Orientalism* (1978), *The World, the Text, and the Critic* (1983), *Musical Elaborations* (1991), and *Culture and Imperialism* (forthcoming).

HORTENSE J. SPILLERS, Professor of English at Emory University, is the author of *In the Flesh: A Situation for Feminist Inquiry* (forthcoming) and is the coeditor of *Fiction and Literary Tradition* (1985).

NEW HISTORICAL LITERARY STUDY

or "return to
history" (p.5)

The Historicist Enterprise

JEFFREY N. COX AND LARRY J. REYNOLDS

THIS BOOK is about the production and interpretation of cultural texts. Its various contributors explore how historical forces—social, economic, political, biographical, psychological, sexual, aesthetic—interact with these productive and interpretive processes. The historical and worldly interests of these essays, along with their attempt to move beyond formalist, essentialist, and ahistorical notions of truth, reveal their strong ties to the celebrated "Turn toward History" that has occurred within American literary studies in the past decade. Several of our contributors, in fact, have played leading roles in this "Turn," which has produced a body of criticism given a number of names, including "the new history," "critical historicism," "historical-materialist criticism," "cultural poetics," and especially "the New Historicism."[1] Though initially identified with studies in the Renaissance and Romanticism, new historicism now involves all areas of literary study (thus, we will not capitalize the term as we use it in this general sense).

To attempt to identify this heterogeneous body of criticism is a formidable task. One of our contributors Lee Patterson has observed, "No single label can be usefully applied to the historicist enterprise as a whole, least of all the already assigned, hotly contested, and irredeemably vague 'New Historicism.'"[2] Moreover, a number of those engaged in the enterprise, including some contributors to this volume, reject the "new historicism" label, while others have appeared as both its practitioners and critics. There are clearly sharp differences between the concerns and practices of various new historicists, as we will show; nevertheless, the enterprise has discernible features, and many scholars would agree with Walter Cohen's observation that when new historicism came to prominence at the beginning of the 1980s, "it represented something new in North America in its combination of theory, criticism, and historical scholarship, all of them informed by a vaguely leftist sensibility."[3] Its theoretical indebtedness to Marx, Foucault, and Bakhtin seems clear, as does its anxious relationship to deconstruction, especially the work of Paul De Man.[4] In terms of critical practice, it also owes much to the politically committed historical criticism of feminists, ethnic minorities, third-world critics, and those engaged in American Studies.[5] Benefiting from the archival work of so-called "old" historicists, drawing upon the reading practices of poststructuralists, and using forms of ideological critique developed by Marxists, new historicism at its best tends toward an open, sophisticated, and liberating practice of cultural criticism.

For the most part, new historicism can be distinguished from "old" historicism by its lack of faith in "objectivity" and "permanence" and its stress not upon the direct recreation of the past, but rather the processes by which the past is constructed or invented. Unsettling, transgressive, at times contradictory, new historicism tends to regard texts in materialist terms, as objects and events in the world, as a part of human life, society, the historical realities of power, authority, and resistance; yet at the same time, it rejects the idea of "History" as a directly accessible, unitary past, and substitutes for it the conception of "histories," an ongoing series of human constructions, each representing the past at particular present moments for particular present purposes. In other words, new historicism seeks to ally a cultural materialist understanding of history with the poststructuralist understanding of textuality. Or, in Louis Montrose's well-known formulation, the new orientation to history in literary studies may be characterized as a reciprocal concern with the historicity of texts and the textuality of history.[7] Of course, for some, this balancing formulation masks an unresolved tension; for others, it blurs the lines between the "literary" and the "historical" (the "fictional" and the "actual") in productive yet under-theorized ways. The best new historicist work, though, clearly recognizes that texts exist within particular historical contexts and that these contexts come to us through a variety of signifying practices subject to all the problematics associated with the interpretive process.

I

Perhaps one can best begin to chronicle the emergence of the historicist enterprise in the 1980s by citing certain key texts. Raymond Williams's *Marxism and Literature* (1977), though situated within British "cultural materialism," anticipated and in part inspired the rehistoricization of literary studies in America.[8] Similarly, Edward Said's *Orientalism* (1978) gave an impetus to what has become the widespread historicist critique of Eurocentric cultural discourse, bringing into question not only the concept of "Western" but also the preeminence of the "Western" literary canon.[9] Frank Lentricchia's *After the New Criticism* (1980) provided a timely indictment of the teleological and totalizing conceptions of "History" found in the dominant formalist theories of the 1960s and 1970s and made a persuasive argument for recognizing "resisting forces of heterogeneity, contradiction, fragmentation, and difference."[10]

At the beginning of the 1980s, a definably new historicism arose within

Renaissance studies, particularly in Stephen J. Greenblatt's *Renaissance Self-Fashioning* (1980), which directed attention to the problematics of "representation" and argued that self-fashioning involved not self-creation but submission to absolute power—"God, a sacred book, an institution such as church, court, colonial or military administration"—as well as conflict with a threatening Other—"heretic, savage, witch, adulteress, traitor, Antichrist"—who must be discovered or invented.[11] Greenblatt's introduction to *The Forms of Power and the Power of Forms in the Renaissance* (1982) provided the new historicism with its name, and in his later works, *Shakespearean Negotiations* (1988), *Learning to Curse* (1990), and *Marvelous Possessions* (1991), he has continued to refine his ideas on power relations in Renaissance culture.[12]

In 1982, the founding of the journal *Representations* by Greenblatt and others at Berkeley gave strong encouragement to the production of new historicist scholarship in a number of periods and fields, and the work of members of *Representations'* editorial board did as well, especially in the area of American literature. Michael Paul Rogin's *Subversive Genealogy* (1983) and Walter Benn Michaels's *The Gold Standard and the Logic of Naturalism* (1987), to cite two examples, provided influential sociohistorical analyses of the relations between American politics, economics, and culture in the nineteenth century.[13] During the 1980s, other Americanists used new historicist methods to produce strong reinterpretations of American literary history.[14] Sacvan Bercovitch has been regarded as the leading figure of this group (labeled "New Americanists" by Frederick Crews), and the collection *Ideology and Classic American Literature* (1986), edited by Bercovitch and Myra Jehlen, showcased some of the best of this work. Arguably the most important book-length study to appear in the 1980s, however, was Lawrence Buell's massive literary history, *New England Literary Culture* (1986), which drew upon archival research, new literary theory, and overlapping socioeconomic, ideological, and generic analyses to narrate a new history of creative work in New England from 1770 to 1865.[15]

In the 1980s, British Romantic studies also came to be marked by a strong return to history, led by the example of Jerome J. McGann.[16] McGann's *The Romantic Ideology* (1983) consolidated his powerful critique of Romantic criticism and its uncritical acceptance of Romantic self-representations and ideologies. The book marked the beginning of McGann's five-part project for establishing a new self-conscious historical methodology for literary criticism, a project he has continued in *A Critique of Modern Textual Criticism* (1983), *The Beauty of Inflections* (1985), *Social Values and Poetic Acts* (1988), and *Towards a Literature of Knowledge* (1989).[17]

At the 1983 Modern Language Association Convention, Said, Herbert Lindenberger, and Jonathan Culler all emphasized the importance of "history" to "The Future of Criticism" (the title of their session),[18] and in his

1986 Presidential Address to the Modern Language Association the eminent deconstructionist J. Hillis Miller lamented that "literary study in the past few years has undergone a sudden, almost universal turn away from theory in the sense of an orientation toward language as such and has made a corresponding turn toward history, culture, society, politics, institutions, class and gender conditions, the social context, the material base."[19] Despite resistance such as Miller's, the last half of the 1980s and the beginning of the 1990s saw even more scholars engaged in the "Turn toward History," including Miller himself,[20] and as this book goes to press controversy about the new historical criticism continues. In fact, at times it seems there are more discussions of new historicism than actual examples of it.[21] In his afterword to the collection *The New Historicism*, for example, Stanley Fish points out, "For the most part . . . these essays are not doing New Historicism, but talking about doing New Historicism, about the claims made in its names and the problems those claims give rise to."[22] The essays in the present volume, however, while often theoretical and metacritical, move beyond talk about the new historicism to offer important new historicist work.

Still, it should come as no surprise that a historicist criticism provokes and participates in historizations of itself, nor that what emerges are multiple, conflicting accounts. For some, the new historicism can be explained within the special history of literary criticism, as a story about the transformation of literary theory and academic writing. In such an account, literary criticism moves from the "Reign of the New Criticism" to the "Dominance of Theory"—in particular deconstruction—then makes the "Turn toward History."[23] In this account, formalism declines when its perception of texts as isolated cultural icons is repeatedly questioned by readings that break down the boundaries between the literary and the nonliterary, that find the strands within texts connecting into webs of larger structures—linguistic, mythological, psychological, sociohistorical. This process of connecting the text into synchronous systems culminates in deconstruction, which looks at language and sees not meaning, but rather its instability or absence, caused by aporias within each text which cannot be spanned without mystifying the text and the supposed "reality" to which it refers. With each new theoretical move made in the name of going beyond formalism, the "Turn toward History" can be seen as an attempt to demystify, circumscribe, or escape deconstruction itself as one more text-based interpretive method.

The escape from deconstruction, however, often proves problematic in some versions of this account. Joseph Litvak has argued that new historicism in fact does not solve the problem raised by deconstruction of language's undecidability, but instead tells a story in which deconstruction turns into new historicism's belated and marginal effect. According to Gregory S. Jay, new historicism's separation from deconstruction is misguided and only when the two remain joined does penetrating cultural interpretation occur.

see
Montrose
"Professing"
p. 23

In the current volume, Lee Patterson similarly decribes the relations between deconstruction and historicism as necessarily close, and he presents
deconstruction itself as a historicizing theory. McGann, on the other hand,
has distanced new historicism from deconstruction by focusing upon "the
scandal of referentiality" (the missing actual world), which in his view deconstruction tries to hide.[24] Simply put, this new historicist argument is that
there are many forms of mediation besides "language," such as modes of
production, social customs, patriarchal practices, generic forms, state institutions, and political events, all of which affect the symbolic discourse of
texts. One thus liberates "history" and culture from the prison of intertextuality by assuming the existence of historical reality and regarding texts not as
indeterminate linguistic abstractions but as dynamic, worldly, constitutive   — x
events occurring within this reality. As Said has put it, "Words and texts are
so much of the world that their effectiveness, in some cases even their use,
are matters having to do with ownership, authority, power, and the imposition of force."[25] In this account, studies of formal features, linguistic patterns,
the play of signifiers give way to questions of context, representation, and
ideological activity.[26]   —

Another version of the new historicism situates it not in the history of
criticism, but in the history of the American academy, particularly of the Left
in the academy during and after the 1960s. This history of the Left has been
written from the Left—the 1960s taught us that criticism had to be committed and thus gave rise to a politically, historically aware scholarship—and
from the Right—the Left, which lost politically at the end of the 1960s, as
Nixon became president to make way for Reagan and Bush, retreated to the
academy where it could continue its battles by other subversive means.
Again, this history can be a story of continuity and gain—historical, political
criticism is a continuation of the "audacity of the politics of the 1960s,"[27] a
reflection of "a general increase in countercultural activity"[28]—or of loss and
compensation: "As the academy continues to be isolated from the centers of
economic and political power, and as postmodern aesthetic production becomes fully appropriated by capitalist commodity production as a whole,
literary studies seeks to recover a sense of cultural wholeness by establishing
the idea of social totality as a privileged instrument of analysis."[29] The question of whether the Left remains impotent or becomes empowered through
its historicist strategies remains debatable, though all agree its work has
provoked considerable reaction outside the academy.[30]

Another narrative of the historicist enterprise could be constructed drawing not upon such macrohistories of the modern academy but upon the lives
of individuals. That is, one can argue that the new historicist emphasis in
criticism arises from the existential realities of life in the academy. If one
wanted to be cynical, one could figure the seductions of the "new," as well
as institutional demand for its production into this account.[31] More charita-

bly, one could argue that if the new historicism emphasizes the powers of institutions, it is perhaps in part because literary scholars, especially feminists, ethnic minorities, and Marxists are so aware of the shaping and at times oppressive power of the institutions of which they are a part. And, if some historicists have emphasized the impact of readers, editors, compositors on the final creation of any literary text as a social product, it may reflect the time academics spend interacting with colleagues, outside readers, journal editors, copy editors, and others involved in the publication process.

Finally, we might explain the rise of new historicism in broader cultural terms, as Louis Montrose has, "as a compensation for that acceleration in the forgetting of history which seems to characterize an increasingly technocratic and future-oriented academy and society,"[32] or, conversely, as a sympathetic response to the concern for history among contemporary writers and artists. We might notice that modern drama, from Brecht to Shaffer and Brenton, treats historical themes; that the postmodern novel as constructed by Pynchon, DeLillo, Marquez, and Vargas Llosa is deeply involved in history; that postmodern architecture quotes from historical styles; and that even minimalist music—surely the least referential, the least representative of art forms—draws upon history in works such as *Einstein on the Beach*, *Nixon in China*, and *Different Trains*. Of course, this deep historicist commitment within modern culture can likewise be viewed as compensation for the "forgetting of history" in contemporary society.

What these differing accounts of the "Turn toward History" finally tell us is what we know as historicists: that the creation of cultural objects—including scholarly works—is embedded in multiple, complex, intersecting pasts, a set of conceptually separable but interlocking histories, one of which might be called literary tradition or discourse, one political history, one ideological development, another biography, another technological change, and so on. In other words, the histories of the new historicism will be no less complex, diverse, and various than the histories that the new historicism offers of past cultural moments.

This volume, which brings together a group of key practitioners of historicist criticism, occupies its own historical moment, of course, linked to a complex network of histories, some institutional, some disciplinary, some ideological. Perhaps the simplest history of this volume would be the story of its development within a particular institution. In 1986 a group of fifteen scholars employed in the Department of English at Texas A&M University, a large public institution, a land-grant university with a conservative past, found that they shared an interest in the conjunction between theory and historical scholarship and a willingness to rethink and cross national, period, and disciplinary boundaries in the search for new knowledge and power. With support from the College of Liberal Arts at Texas A&M, they formed the Interdisciplinary Group for Historical Literary Study (IGHLS), which invited to campus for formal lectures and informal discussions a series of eminent scholars engaged in new historicist approaches to literary study. IGHLS sponsored colloquia, lecture series on "Writing and Rewriting Literary History" and "The Use and Abuse of the New Historicism" as well as two conferences, one on Katherine Anne Porter and Texas and the other on English Romanticism. In the fall of 1989, IGHLS held a major conference, "(Re)producing Texts/(Re)presenting History," and this volume features work presented at that conference and other IGHLS events.

In a number of ways we see the work of IGHLS and the publication of this volume as oppositional, that is, as part of an ongoing critique of the conventional canon, of reactionary values, of state power and its cultural apparatuses. All of the essays we have collected here may be read as politically left to one degree or another in that they side with victims, with those who have been hurt, silenced, dominated, excluded. We are well aware of the irony of presuming to occupy an oppositional position as employees of one of the state's most powerful ideological apparatuses and as beneficiaries of institutional support. The irony of our predicament is not unique, however, despite its extremity; in fact, its prevalence is a key insight of much new historicist scholarship. Power, consolidation, subversion, contestation, containment, appropriation, agency, and exchange are all issues addressed in the essays in this volume. And, as the essays turn to the past to explore the negotiations between power, subversion, and containment, as they investigate the tangled relations between the world, the text, and the critic, they help illuminate the present, making self-consciousness of our acts, values, and negotiations both a possibility and a necessity. In such self-consciousness lies the beginning of the liberation we believe to be the goal of historicist scholarship.

While this volume may appear oppositional in its institutional context, we also see it as affirmative and consolidating within the more circumscribed context of literary scholarship. While there is always a tendency among scholars to stress differences and divisions (to provide more rigorous accounts of particularities of thought and to accentuate individual achievements), one goal of this volume is to consolidate and showcase some of the best new historicist work being done today on text production and literary history.

The essays included here, considered separately, illuminate particular topics, texts, and literary periods, but we believe the volume as a whole reveals the multiple, contestatory issues, interests, and commitments at stake across the spectrum of historicist criticism. In commenting on each essay, we will focus on what seem the most important of these. First, though, we should point out that following Ralph Cohen's wide-ranging lead essay, the contributions are arranged chronologically, each focusing on a different literary period. It is partly a matter of chance that the volume came to have one essay dealing with Anglo-Saxon literature, one with later medieval culture, one with Renaissance texts, and so on; but it was obviously our choice to arrange the essays according to conventional notions of period and national (that is, American and British) tradition. Historicist scholarship, of course, has mounted strong challenges to the notions of period and nation (Said's essay in this volume, for example, raises crucial questions about the usefulness of the nation as a category in literary history); nevertheless, the concept of period—like that of the canon—has been and continues to be useful, if only as a site of contestation. As McGann has pointed out, "The significance, effect, and hence the full reality of [literary] periods remain a perpetual human interest and endeavour."[33] Moreover, periodization seems central to historical consciousness/for every historical vision provides a division, a break, a period—even if it is only between present and past. Without period, there is no pastness of the past, no historical change; everything is merely absorbed into the present. While we would surely wish to argue with conventional boundaries and the grounds upon which they have been drawn, we acknowledge the need for periodization and recognize that historicist scholarship will begin with the old periods even as it subjects them to critique. In a sense, the chronological order of the volume sketches in the background of the "old" historicism from which all new historicisms must develop.

II

While the essays here can be surveyed in various ways, perhaps the most useful is to begin with examples of work in the two most visible areas of literary study today: Renaissance new historicism and Romantic new historicism. Alan Liu has claimed that "where Romanticism in the '60's and '70's was the premiere field of literary studies grounding the explosion of new theories and methodologies, now Renaissance studies carries on the flame."[34] Feminists, Americanists, and a host of others would surely disagree, but such a view brings into focus the work of two of our contributors: Stephen Greenblatt, most often cited as the exemplar of Renaissance new historicism, and Jerome McGann, the most prominent new historicist in Romantic studies.[35] Both, of course, shun the new historicist label, but a comparison of their concerns, methods, and goals can tell us much about the enterprise this volume illuminates, as long as we remember that these two critics and their practices serve a heuristic purpose here and are not being used to arrive at "essential" notions of historicist scholarship.

A key way in which McGann and Greenblatt are representative of the new historicist enterprise as a whole is in their problematic relations with Marxism. One widely discussed attack on the new historicism has called it "a kind of 'Marxist criticism' "[36] and although the characterization lacks precision,[37] it is true that Marxism provides many of the critical concepts—ideology, class struggle, means and modes of production—used by a number of new historicists in their work. The simple reason for this is that the Marxist tradition represents an extraordinarily rigorous and sustained analysis of history and culture. Marxism with its master narrative of class struggle, with its clear causal theory of historical change, with its various theories of the relationship between cultural artifacts and the social, political, economic, and material world provides a strong model for historicist criticism, which, in the hands of a Raymond Williams or a Fredric Jameson can offer a total contextual understanding of the literary text and a total program for the literary scholar committed to social change.[38] In McGann's words, Marxism is "a powerful and dynamically coherent tradition of critical inquiry."[39] Nevertheless, most American historicists (including Greenblatt, McGann, Said, Buell, and Patterson) distance themselves from Marxism in one way or another, believing that its total vision (its insistence that parts can only be understood in relation to the whole) is reductive, totalizing, even totalitarian.[40]

Like most of our contributors, both Greenblatt and McGann borrow from the Marxist tradition and would ally themselves with Marxists against opponents on the Right; both have strong affinities with British cultural materialism and share a debt to Bakhtin and the Frankfurt school, especially the work of Benjamin and Adorno.[41] Nevertheless, both finally refuse to subscribe to Marxism as a theoretic. Like Edward Said, they see themselves as independent of any "ism" and strive to proceed heuristically as opposed to deductively in their criticism.[42] Greenblatt has responded to the Marxist charge that he evades political commitment by declaring, "It's true that I'm still more uneasy with a politics and a literary perspective that is untouched by Marxist thought, but that doesn't lead me to endorse propositions or embrace a particular philosophy, politics or rhetoric, *faute de mieux*."[43] Greenblatt has acknowledged his self-dividedness with regard to Marxism, and the same is true of McGann, who has both attacked and defended his own work in Marxist terms. Referring to McGann's writings, a speaker in one of McGann's dialogues declares, "They don't *change* anything essential in the way the academy goes about its business," and another speaker answers the charge—"But they make change possible."[44] This self-reflexive, self-critical feature of McGann's work (evident in the dialogue included in this volume) serves not only to make/answer the Marxist demand for commitment, but also to ground his own critique of Marxist literary criticism, which, he claims, "fails to take account of its own investment in the Ideological State Apparatuses which we operate within—indeed, which we all serve."[45] McGann, in other words, uses Marxism against itself.

Greenblatt's stance on the issue of political commitment is less clearly political, and it has perhaps best been articulated by Catherine Gallagher who has argued (from a new historicist perspective) that critical practices are not simply politics in disguise, that they seldom contain their politics as an essence; rather, they "occupy particular historical situations from which they enter into various exchanges, or negotiations, with practices designated 'political.' "[46] One strong rebuttal to this argument has been expressed by Patterson, who has accused the new historicism of "unintended conservatism," and asserted "if you do not have an explicit politics—an ideology—then one will certainly have you."[47] The matter of "explicitness" is key, of course. "I am certainly not opposed to methodological self-consciousness," Greenblatt has recently said, "but I am less inclined to see overtness—an explicit articulation of one's values and methods—as inherently necessary or virtuous."[48]

Though more closely allied with Marxism than Greenblatt and willing to grant it a dialectical force, McGann has expressed dissatisfaction with its preemptiveness and its tendency to sacrifice existential particularity to a priori concepts. In his view, as in Sartre's, "the scope of its pretensions can easily weaken its pragmatic grip upon what is local and immediate, both at the level of theory and at the level of fact."[49] He thus chooses to incorporate Marxism into a larger project, a heteroglossia of historicism, formalism, deconstruction, and Marxism, and to argue for dialectical freedom. Although Greenblatt's commitment to "cultural poetics" is clearly indebted to studies in cultural anthropology, especially to the work of Clifford Geertz and the practice of synchronic "thick description,"[50] and although Geertz insists upon a nonevaluative conception of ideology as a system of interacting symbols, a pattern of interworking meanings,[51] as opposed to the Marxist conception of ideology as false consciousness, it is nevertheless an Althusserian version of ideology ("a 'Representation' of the imaginary relationship of individuals to their real condition of existence")[52] that at times emerges in Greenblatt's work as it does in McGann's. In fact, according to his critics, Greenblatt often depicts Renaissance culture in Althusserian (and Foucauldian) terms—as a place where human agency and resistance are overpowered by ideological apparatuses that relentlessly transform individuals into subjects.[53] His more recent work, however, eludes the charge.

If at times Greenblatt appears to view history and political life as overdetermined by power relations, if he seems to reduce the power of the text in order to dominate it, he also turns our attention to the concept of *wonder*, "the art work's capacity to generate in the spectator surprise, delight, admiration, and intimations of genius";[54] or he shows us the possibility of an authorial understanding that can take possession of a politically contested subject, giving it new form and power outside the political sphere, as he does here in his essay on Shakespeare and witchcraft.[55] Similarly, if McGann at times seems to accept the pervasiveness of ideology, if at times he seems to suggest that a text is overdetermined by sociohistorical forces, then he introduces the idea of the *incommensurate*: "details, persons, events which the work's own (reflected) conceptual formulas and ideologies must admit, but which they cannot wholly account for."[56] The incommensurate, he argues, assures historical contextuality its independence from textuality—perhaps even from ideology—allowing the past reconstituted in the present to critique the present and thus enable future change.

These tensions in McGann's and Greenblatt's work map the contours of divisions within the historicist enterprise as a whole. Historicist scholars must all balance between the particularity of texts or individuals and explanatory frames that offer some way of linking abstracted components, such as texts or individuals, to historical wholes. When the frame dominates, the critic is accused of being reductive, totalizing; when the component is given precedence, the critic is found to be sliding back toward formalism. The most general formulation of this tension has already been noted—the relation of text to context—but the tension is also found in debates over the relation between hegemonic power and local resistance or over the role of ideological articulation versus the role of unique aesthetic expression; it could also be stated as a tension between the theoretical power of Marxism and the convincing textual tactics of various formalisms from New Criticism to deconstruction. To simplify greatly, the historicist scholar works to reconnect text and context, without either allowing the text to exist transhistorically apart from the world, or reducing the text to a mere falsification of a reality that precedes it; that is, the text must be conceived as a material *fact* but the power of *fiction* must not be reduced to the ability to lie about social realities. One of the reasons that Greenblatt and McGann—along with others in this volume such as Said, Cohen, Patterson, Rogin, Buell, and Spillers—have been such influential scholars, spurring other scholars to new, historical work, is that they are able to create a tactical, tactful alliance between text and context.

The slightly different methods of distancing themselves from Marxism adopted by McGann and Greenblatt point to a larger difference between McGann's new historicism and Greenblatt's. McGann seeks a new systemized conception of literature, a dialectical, historicist theory of knowledge, while Greenblatt embraces an antitheoretical pragmatism committed to estrangement, "the project of making strange what has become familiar, of demonstrating that what seems an untroubling and untroubled part of ourselves . . . is actually part of something else, something different."[57] This project resembles McGann's Othering of the past, with the difference that it is grounded in individual rather than collective experience. Although the influences upon the two men may be the same and their values similar, their projects move in different directions—McGann's toward theoretical consolidation and social change, Greenblatt's toward critical destabilization and personal insight. In other words, we find in the differences between these two scholars the debate between theory and practice given prominence by Walter Benn Michaels and Steven Knapp and taken up by Stephen Mailloux and Stanley Fish,[58] and in this volume by Ralph Cohen, Lawrence Buell, and Margaret Ezell.

This distinction between Greenblatt's and McGann's work is not a simple opposition, for in certain ways their respective styles, the genres they adopt, obscure this difference, making it seem the opposite of what it is. At first glance or telling, Greenblatt seems still to believe in narrative, still to long for the stories that would make sense of things, while McGann eschews narrative, turning instead to the open-ended dialogue as one of his main forms. ("When critical discourse assumes a narrative format," McGann has said, "the analysis generates a structure of self-confirmation."[59]) Greenblatt's narratives, however, are actually anecdotes, that is, mini-narratives that disturb and complicate understanding and lead most immediately to synchronic interpretation rather than diachronic explanation.[60] Greenblatt's historicism is an archeological (and Foucauldian) exploration of a particular layer in time, not a grand narrative of change over time (though some of his more recent work in *Learning to Curse* begins to trace diachronic stories such as the ties between psychoanalysis and the Renaissance notion of the self). McGann, on the other hand, while giving up narrative as his organizing device, is centrally interested in the diachronic. His programme for historical criticism involves investigation of the textual history of a work and the history of its reception, stopping at certain moments on this double helix to analyze the interactions between the two histories.[61] Put simply, we can see in these two scholars' work the tension between the semiotic and the historical; that is, first, the pull toward synchronous "thick description" and the attempt to allow the past moment to stand on its own, in all its strangeness and wonder, and, second, the tug of the diachronic and the desire to track and explain historical movement and change. These conflicting attractions arise from new historicism's desire, on one hand, to avoid the simple, linear, progressive models of past histories and its recognition, on the other, that to be historical means to be able to plot the movement from one past to another and from the past to the present.

Greenblatt and McGann have come to define the field of new historicism for many because their differing bodies of work help to outline the features of that field and the pressures that shape those features. They also share a similar conceptual move (or, perhaps, it is a value) that is even clearer in the work of feminists and scholars of ethnicity: all are concerned with Othering. Greenblatt seeks to increase our wonder—even our horror—at cultural objects from the past to show us something that is Other, something that can extend our personal experience and understanding. McGann locates the otherness of the past to unlink our admiration—our wonder—of past texts from our unself-conscious reproduction of their value systems. Feminists seek to explore Otherness, difference across gender lines; scholars of ethnicity, across the boundaries of race and nation. When we consider the role of the Other in Lacanian psychoanalysis, of the long philosophical history of the battle between self and other from Hegel to Heideigger and Sartre, of the theologically informed notion of "altarity" in the work of Mark Taylor, we begin to see the pervasiveness of this concept. In the current volume, we might note in particular the interest in gendered others in the essays by Aikins, Ezell, and Spillers; the notion of exile in Said, Newman, Spillers, and Cohen; the importance of race to the pieces by Spillers and Rogin. The notion of Otherness is essential to historicism, for the historical imagination exists only when one can conceive of a time, a place, a people, a culture different from ours, only when the past becomes something other than a mirror image of our concerns and interests.

Though Renaissance and Romantic studies have provided the most widely discussed examples of new historicist work, other periods and fields exemplified in this volume have made important contributions to the historicist enterprise. As we have already indicated, the work of Buell and Rogin is related to the older and now revitalized historicist project in American Studies. The feminist criticism engaged in by Aikins, Spillers, and Ezell also predates and informs much new historicism. Feminist and minority scholars have long been engaged in revealing that what were accepted in the past as universal ahistorical truths are actually contingent, political, and historically situated. These scholars have necessarily examined the social and political contexts that produced the cultural texts of interest to them, and they have been deeply involved in the attempt to map out new and alternative literary histories to complement the expanded (or perhaps exploded) canon that their work necessitates. Some observers have seen the new historicism and feminism as opposed and others have argued that the new historicism originates with feminism's insights. As Judith Newton has put it, "Feminist politics and feminist theory . . . along with the black liberation movement and the new left, have helped generate the 'post-modern' assumptions about 'objectivity,' the construction of the subject, and the cultural power of representation currently identified with 'new historicism,' but they have articulated those assumptions in ways which are significantly different from what have become the more dominant, more fashionable, and the less politicized articulations."[62] Few new historicists would disagree, though two of our contributors, Ezell and Spillers, have opposed what they see as the dominative mode of some feminist work. Ezell challenges the assumptions and practices of standard feminist literary histories in the name of a stronger feminist historical theory; Spillers, believing that the experience of the black American female remains unspoken in feminist discourse, seeks a new feminist hermeneutics.

Cultural criticism, which is closely allied to much feminist and African-American criticism, also represents an important area of the contemporary historicist project. Edward Said's international and comparativist work has been particularly effective in unsettling the views of many by revealing the constructedness of cultural truths previously regarded as absolute. Through his historicizing methods and polemical power, Said has illuminated "the vast domains commanded by . . . gigantic caricatural essentializations" such as the "Orient," "Islam," "Communism," and the "West." He has examined historical/political categories in the same way that feminists have examined gendered categories and that scholars of ethnicity have examined racial ones. Within literary studies, Said's more particular goal has been to explode the categories of national literature, generic purity, and the isolated author. His call for a global and oppositional criticism resembles McGann's call for a critical imagination, and when he speaks of the contamination of literature, of its hybrid quality, he draws attention to important extraliterary issues. Like Greenblatt, Said appreciates the continual negotiations that occur between culture and power, and he has been a keen analyst of the uses and abuses of our cultural heritage. Like McGann, he also insists that writing and reading are social acts with public consequences, and that as citizens of the Euro-American cultural empire we are obligated to discover "the illusions of our knowledge and the realities of what we do not know."[63]

III

The kinds of new historicism being practiced in the academy today are obviously heterogeneous. Despite their differences, though, these critical engagements with history and culture remain part of the same theoretical moment, a moment bound up with new understandings of text production and literary history, which are the subjects of this volume. Although many of the essays raise large questions about the relationship of literature and history, one will not find here—nor does one find elsewhere in current historicism—many scholars who seek to plot or theorize the transitions, the shifts in literary history. Ralph Cohen has been one of the few, and in his lead essay, "Generating Literary Histories," he addresses many of the issues we have raised about the historicist enterprise. Cohen in his position as editor of *New Literary History* has promoted key theoretical developments affecting the genre of literary history during the years of formalism's ascendancy, and in his essay here he offers a wide-ranging meditation upon the "generation" of literary histories. He investigates the rise of the new historicism within Renaissance studies, turning in particular to the work of Greenblatt and Montrose. He touches briefly upon the issues raised by the kind of textual materialism found in critics such as McGann. He tackles the ties between the new historicism and Marxism. And he places at the center of his discussion of historicism the work being done by African-American and feminist scholars.

Cohen makes the important observation that a conflict exists between the work of new historicists seeking to dispense with the canon and to negate the idea of a unitary literary history and the attempt of many African-American and feminist literary historians who essentially seek to create a canon and a literary history that can compete with—and thus imitate—the conventional canon and traditional histories. In Cohen's words, it is impossible to "generate a new history without being contaminated by the language and genre of the old." Cohen thus raises a key problem treated elsewhere in the volume, in Ezell's attempt to re-vision women's literary history, for example, or in Said's suggestion that the idea of "contamination" is essential to any literary history that will move beyond the old boundaries and formulas.

Cohen also examines the debates between literary history and literary theory, and he discusses the use of autobiographical material in women's literary history. Of course, at the core of Cohen's argument—and at the heart of so much of his work—is the issue of genre. He seeks to bridge what has been perceived as the gap between theory and history by discussing them as genres that can join in various combinations and permutations; genre becomes a mediating term between autobiography, theory, and social aims and ideology. His generic account of literary history is one of the most useful approaches to the current debate on historicist issues just as his account of literary, cultural variation through generic transformation is one of the few theories of change we have available.

Whereas Cohen's concern is with the theory informing literary history, Katherine O'Brien O'Keeffe examines the production of texts upon which such history is based. Her focus is upon the editing of Old English verse, and she offers a critique of two complementary analytical strategies characterizing past editorial methods: first, one that aims to recover a text which, if not "authorial" or "original," is at least anterior to the text's surviving manuscript record; second, one that translates Old English verse into a print array far removed from the visual conventions of its manuscripts. Both editorial strategies, O'Keeffe shows, alienate the poetic work from its own history by trying to create an ideal text, in the process obscuring the text's essential material existence in manuscript. McGann has stated that "an encounter with the concrete particulars of an aesthetic object—an experience of the objectivity of 'the text' in all its rich and various determinations—is fundamental to the *experience* of literary texts (or works) as well,"[64] and O'Keeffe shows the relevance of this idea to medieval text editing. Like McGann, she argues that a manuscript is properly regarded not as a vehicle for transmitting a transcendent text, but rather a physical encoding of the poetic work, a materialization of the circumstances of the text's production, and a witness to the conditions of its reception.

O'Keeffe argues persuasively that existing conventions of text editing reflect and constitute a "literate ideology" that blinds us to how early readers of Old English read verse. This argument is an extension of the thesis in her book *Visible Song: Transitional Literacy in Old English Verse* (1990), which demonstrated that the workings of this "literate ideology" stemmed from the visual dominance of our own thought processes and hid the importance of orthographic redundancy, graphic cues, and variant readings in the production and reproduction of Old English verse. In the concluding chapter of *Visible Song*, O'Keeffe raises the question: "In scholarly editions, how may printing conventions be extended to accommodate the developing visual significances of scribal practice in order to present Old English verse in its fullest historical dimensions?"[65] In her essay here, she provides an answer; she concludes that the fullest historical criticism must seek to present *realized* texts as they exist in the world. Such texts, she believes, are poetic *works* in the sense that they are the product of labor, at some points authorial, at others certainly scribal, and in many circumstances, productive of future labor by readers. She sees the development of a strategy to present and to balance both modes of editing as a crucial goal for historical textual criticism.

The eminent medievalist Lee Patterson also brings new historicist theory to bear upon the practice of "old" historicist scholarship in medieval studies. Patterson has expressed high regard for "the New Historicism that now flourishes in Renaissance studies," yet he has also been highly critical of it, perhaps because of the contiguity of the Renaissance to his area of study, perhaps because of the unavoidable influence of Stephen Greenblatt, the "major domo of New Historicism," as Patterson has called him.[66] Greenblatt and other Renaissance critics, Patterson has argued, treat the Middle Ages as a rejected object, an alien Other whose historical existence must be suppressed in order to establish the modernity of their own enterprise. In *Negotiating the Past* (1988), Patterson criticizes Greenblatt's version of new historicism for being totalizing, conservative, and quietistic. In his view, it fails as an enterprise by allowing the effacement of the human subject and discouraging political action and change. "To deprive the human agent of any purchase upon the social whole is to signal the end of a politics we desperately need,"[67] he declares. In his introduction to the collection *Literary Practice and Social Change in Britain, 1380–1530* (1990), however, which appeared as volume 8 in Greenblatt's "The New Historicism" series, Patterson indicates a shift in his thinking by crediting the return to historicism with mounting a profound political challenge to the world at large: "The public reaction to the rehistoricization of literature has served to remind the academy that, like it or not, it does play a central role in the world of political action."[68]

In the essay included in this volume, Patterson continues his project of renovating medieval studies through the use of historicist methods of analysis and critiquing those very methods. His concern remains, on the one hand, to challenge assumptions that alienate the Middle Ages from us and to reveal continuities between the medieval past and the present; and on the other hand, to challenge theoretical preconceptions, here the assumed disjunction between deconstruction and historicist thought. In his richly documented contextual study for this volume entitled "Making Identities in Fifteenth-Century England: Henry V and John Lydgate," he makes a deliberate attempt to connect literature and history by examining the ideology of poetry in the royal court of late medieval England. He finds both Lydgate and Henry engaged in practices of self-fashioning; Henry in particular is revealed as anticipating the manipulation of images for absolutist purposes usually associated with Renaissance rather than medieval monarchs. Patterson argues that Henry and Lydgate practiced complementary forms of absolutism—a poetics of identity and a politics of identity, as he calls them. Focusing on Lydgate's *Siege of Thebes* (1421–1422), the essay shows that the poem expresses, almost against its will, an opposition to Henry's annexation of the French crown in 1420. In working through the intricate play of poetics and politics within the court, Patterson finds that its forms of absolutism finally unravel, undone by differences that counter the totalizing impulses of poet and ruler. In tackling the notions of opposition and containment and in addressing the relations between deconstruction and historicism, Patterson treats issues at the heart of all historicist scholarship.

Stephen Greenblatt's essay in this volume, "Shakespeare Bewitched," can be read in part as an answer to those critics who, like Patterson, have attacked his previous work for regarding Renaissance culture as devoid of human agency and thoroughly controlled by the malign principle of power. Here the issue under examination is Shakespeare's handling of the contestatory subject of witchcraft. Greenblatt's interest in the permeable boundaries between life and art is again in evidence; yet the power of church and state seems diminished, while the power and freedom of the playwright seem greater. Though Shakespeare's representation of witches, Greenblatt argues, makes him a participant in the contemporary witchcraft controversy, he rises above or stands apart from the contest through his "undisguised theatrical opportunism," his following "out the inner imperatives of the genres in which he is working." Greenblatt, of course, has been charged with mesmerizing his readers by the strange stories he tells and the wonderful way he tells them; here he grants Shakespeare similar occult powers, as one who redistributes the phantasmagorical horror of witchcraft across the field of the play, yet without placing himself on one side or the other of the serious debate about how witches should be conceived. Many would question whether such a neutral, uncontaminated place to stand actually exists, and the issue obviously relates to the contemporary debate about political commitment discussed above. Can aesthetics be separated from politics? For Greenblatt, the answer is that the two cannot be collapsed into one another. Art is not autonomous, but the gaps between social practice and literary endeavor are real. "I think it important," he declares, "in the interest of preserving the small breathing space of the imagination, to resist the recent tendency to conflate, or even to collapse into one another, aesthetics, ethics, and politics." Greenblatt marks here an important moment in the development of his own criticism.

The following essay, Margaret Ezell's "Re-visioning the Restoration," shares the double focus of historicist work on past and present. Ezell's particular subject is women writers of the past that feminists in the present have overlooked or excluded in their constructions of feminist anthologies and histories. Ezell, whose historiography owes a debt to Peter Laslett and the Cambridge Group for the History of Population and Social Structure, has been concerned in all of her work with the uses of literary evidence in history and in the construction of literary history. For example, her *Patriarch's Wife: Literary Evidence and the History of the Family* (1987) questioned the way in which literary evidence has been used as if it directly reflected social attitudes and practices; she sought to reveal that behind our totalizing view of the seventeenth-century family as a patriarchal institution there were women who resisted and wrested power, that beyond our accounts of the silencing of early women writers there existed a thriving women's manuscript culture and coteries of women writers. Ezell's work is an instructive example of how much literary historians have to learn from social historians and how careful social historians must be in using literary evidence.

In her essay in the current volume, Ezell seeks to re-vision the writing of women's literary history. While noting the importance of current versions of women's literary history that serve the vital function of providing the texts and historical framework for women's studies, she is concerned that these histories have been "contaminated" (to use Cohen's and Said's word) by the structures and attitudes of the very patriarchal histories in opposition to which they have been written. Her essay offers an examination of the ways in which early women's writings have been unconsciously obscured by the very theoretical models that seek to preserve and promote women's writing. Ezell recognizes the power of our current model of women's literary history, a model that emphasizes the silencing of early women writers and that traces the "progress" of women's writing as it develops toward the great women novelists of the nineteenth and twentieth centuries; but she is concerned that this model which celebrates some, silences others who do not fit within this tradition or who adopt differing literary practices or genres. Ezell notes, for example, the large body of material produced by seventeenth-century Quaker women. Her call, then, is for a more thoroughly feminist literary history, one that allows us to hear all of the voices of women in the past, even those that conflict with our constructed histories or who contest our notions of feminism.

Janet Aikins shares Ezell's feminist orientation, and in her essay on "Representing the Body in *Pamela II*" this combines with a materialist approach to books and questions of text production. Like O'Keeffe and McGann, Aikins regards the book as a concrete reality in the world. Tracing the history of the production of Richardson's sequel to *Pamela*, she argues that in this book the commissioned illustrations and the text work together to reflect upon the processes of representation and upon the status of the book as a physical artifact. Aikins reminds us about the actual illustrated construction of the novel as it was originally produced and not as it has been reproduced in modern editions and reveals how the novel's visual and verbal images would have been read by eighteenth-century readers. Thus, she skillfully returns the text to its actual material incarnation and its own historical moment. Reflecting upon the many senses of representation—from the sequel's re-presenting the characters of *Pamela* to the various visual representations of Pamela's body in the text to self-reflective representations within the novel of books as objects—Aikins contributes to the ongoing discussions of representation and of the links between texts and images. Aikins's essay has obvious connections with Rogin's later discussion of images of blacks in American film, and it also anticipates many of the questions about the female body as text that Spillers explores in her essay.

If O'Keeffe and Aikins join McGann in their concern with the physique of the book, Terence Hoagwood is indebted to McGann's analysis of ideology, particularly the Romantic ideology. His essay on "Fictions and Freedom: Wordsworth and the Ideology of Romanticism" follows McGann's polemical correction to much of the work done by earlier Romanticists. Hoagwood wishes to correct two particular misconceptions. First, he demonstrates that the romantic concern with the imagination does not mark an inward turn to some isolated, abstract psychological space; instead, there is, he argues, a direct connection for them between mental structures and social institutions, imagination and society, poetry and politics. Second, he disputes the long-standing position—stated in even stronger terms by critics such as Marjorie Levinson and James Chandler—that Wordsworth (as well as Coleridge) after his radical youth experienced a Tory "apostacy" that involved a rejection of politics for pietistic quietism. Hoagwood argues that Wordsworth is always involved in the political, the ideological, though the valence of his ideology may change; moreover, the structure of Wordsworth's analysis of ideology remains the same throughout his work, so that his later poetry does not so much abandon his earlier revolutionary hopes as reconfigure them in a symbolic discourse that keeps alive Wordsworth's dreams of freedom and equality. To make this argument, Hoagwood analyzes a romantic conception of the fictionality—the constructedness—of reality.

Jerome McGann's essay "Beyond the Valley of Production; or, *De factorum natura*" responds in rather explicit ways to criticism that has been directed at his version of new historicism. Here one of his speakers, Anne Mack, after admiring McGann's detailed historicist criticism of Pound's *Hugh Selwyn Mauberley*, critiques this work as merely "the consumption and reproduction of our institutionalized literary codes," arguing, in the spirit of Stanley Fish, that criticism such as McGann's has no consequences, it merely "offers a way to expand the range of institutionalized hermeneutics." In response to Mack's Marxist insistence upon social change and her charge that the literary profession merely conserves larger social formations, the speaker Georg Mannejc argues that some aspects of these formations are perhaps worth conserving and that the absolute distinction between "interpreting" and "changing" reifies an illusion. The speaker J. J. Rome adds to this argument the historicist point that scholarship and literary studies are politically neutral in and of themselves; they only become reactionary, conservative, liberal, or radical when particular choices are made about how and where the past is engaged.

In her second consideration of McGann's Pound criticism, Anne Mack makes the point that Pound's text alters during its various reproductions, each bringing its own ideological visions into contradiction. The radical self-alienation of a text, according to Mack, is the means by which "imaginative work escapes the happy valley of production and consumption," that is, becomes more than just a producer of determinate meanings which can be consumed and reproduced endlessly. (Mack's opposition to a restricted economy seems to constitute a veiled criticism of Greenblatt's notion of the circulation of social energy within a mimetic economy; the closed nature of this circulatory system obviously conflicts with McGann's commitment to dialectical openness.) The speakers Rome and Mannejc extend Mack's point about self-contradictions and the escape they offer, Mannejc discussing the importance of "facts," Rome discussing the importance of the "thickness" of the facts (with both conditions obviously related to what McGann elsewhere calls *incommensurates*). Mack rejects the accommodation of her co-speakers, however, and ends by turning again to Pound's poem and pointing out its ambiguous and unstable features that lie outside criticism's powers of interpretation. In McGann's system, in other words, at least as articulated by Anne Mack, literature successfully resists the domination of criticism.

Lawrence Buell as critic and literary historian has also been attracted to Marxism's sensitivity to absent causes and socioeconomic determinants, yet it is a Geertzean rather than Marxist notion of ideology he subscribes to: "I take as axiomatic," he has written, "the propositions of Marxist aesthetics that 'aesthetic form is to be conceived of as ideological' and that the 'artistic process . . . should be regarded as a form of *ideological praxis*,' but I gloss the term *ideology* in the neutral sense of 'implicit value system' rather than in the pejorative sense of 'false consciousness.' "[69] Like the New Englanders he studies, Buell attaches considerable cultural importance to moral and religious values yet takes a pragmatic approach to the problems he addresses as a scholar and critic. His belief in the power of genre study as a means to critical understanding aligns his work with that of Ralph Cohen; yet, like Greenblatt, he is more a neo-pragmatist than a theorist, even though all that he does is richly informed by theory. Buell was one of the first Americanists to challenge New Criticism's dominance in American literature study with his highly regarded *Literary Transcendentalism* (1973), in which he argued for the importance of genres such as the conversation, the essay, the sermon, the literary travelogue, the diary, and the autobiography, all of which fell outside New Criticism's privileged order of poetry, drama, and prose fiction. In his *New England Literary Culture*, (1986), Buell adds Marxist and feminist methods of analysis to his revisionary formalist ones and continues to depend most heavily upon genre as a principle of organization.

In his essay here, "Literary History as a Hybrid Genre," Buell draws upon his own experience as literary historian to address the question of how literary historical discourse negotiates between a model of interpretive criticism and a model of empiricist historiography. To answer the question, he examines textbook codifications of American national literary history, specifically the three most important twentieth-century compendia to date. He shows how all three, in their readings of a particular literary work, Twain's *Connecticut Yankee*, employ the same basic structure, the most fundamental analytic convention in literary historiography: the encapsulated formulation of a work's significance as historical artifact and national product. Buell calls this formulation a "sociogram" (a term he coins) and shows that the three literary histories deploy the sociogram using framing, chronology, proportion, and précis. He concludes by considering the question of the future of literary histories, whether they have been made obsolete by new theoretical conceptions of history or whether they will continue to be reproduced because of pedagogical and market necessities.

The four essays that conclude this volume all deal with twentieth-century culture, and each in its different way is engaged in rethinking historicism in relation to the contemporary historical moment. Michael Rogin's essay initiates another stage in his provocative exploration of the American psyche. In his books *Fathers and Children: Andrew Jackson and the Subjugation of the American Indian* (1975) and *Subversive Genealogy: The Politics and Art of Herman Melville* (1983), Rogin drew upon the insights of Marx and Freud to reveal the underlying socioeconomic-psychohistorical determinants of racism, expansionism, and imperialism in nineteenth-century America. In his essay for this volume, Rogin directs his attention to the beginning of the twentieth century and relations between Jews and blacks as structured through foundational moments in film. Like his colleague Greenblatt, Rogin has long been fascinated by the interpenetrations of life and art, of fantasy and reality, discussed most tellingly and frighteningly in his book "*Ronald Reagan," the Movie and Other Episodes in Political Demonology* (1987). Here that fascination comes into play as he illuminates the way in which the founding movie of Hollywood sound, *The Jazz Singer* (1927), shows the Jew, by putting on blackface, acquiring access to white fantasies and black achievements, especially jazz, at the expense of blacks, who remain silenced and excluded.

Rogin's larger argument is that "just as the frontier period in American history generated the classic literature (beginning with captivity narratives), so American film was born from the conjunction between southern defeat in the Civil War, black resubordination, and national reintegration; the rise of the multiethnic, industrial metropolis; and the emergence of mass entertainment, expropriated from its black roots, as the locus of Americanization." D. W. Griffith's *The Birth of a Nation* (1915), "the single most important American movie ever made," according to Rogin, celebrated the Ku Klux Klan's suppression of black political and sexual revolution; *The Jazz Singer*, in Rogin's analysis, takes as its subject that which lies hidden in *The Birth of a Nation*, that the interracial double is not the exotic Other but the split self, the white in blackface. Whereas the earlier film makes war on blacks in the name of the fathers, *The Jazz Singer*'s protagonist adopts a black mask and kills his father. This process frees the son not only from the Jewish father but also from the black pariah, the Jew's stigmatized self. Whereas in nineteenth-century classic American literature the white man uses Indians to establish an American identity against the Old World, so the jazz singer in the classic movie of Hollywood sound uses blacks for the same purpose.

Hortense Spillers, in the essay included here and in her other work, has taken a keen interest in the appropriation of blackness by whites, especially as it involves the denial of black female experience. "The minstrel's blackened face," she writes, "not only parodies the African person, but actually erases him or her as a human possibility." Whereas Rogin, as a "graybearded Jewish son," is interested in the ways blackface exteriorizes Jewishness, Spillers, as a black female, is interested in the *interior* dynamics of alterity, the way in which "race" is "an *outcome*, rather than an originary source of power relations." Spillers's cultural criticism owes more to Foucault, Roland Barthes, Kenneth Burke, and reader-response theorists than it does to Marx or Freud. History, however, particularly as it involves the ordeals of African-Americans, always looms large for her as it does for Rogin, and she, like Ezell, works both in and against the feminist tradition to create a broader, egalitarian feminist hermeneutic. Spillers's project can be seen as the creation of a multivoiced, multivalent criticism within a single reading—a literary theory that would be the worthy complement to multiculturalism in canon and curriculum formation. Unlike much liberal criticism, however, her work maintains a radical, insurgent thrust to it, one resistant to assimilation and cooptation. Spillers has written with passion and anger about past and present injustices inflicted upon the black female, not just the torture of her body during slavery, but the "unthinkably vast and criminal fraud" that made her into an exotic and transformed her history "into a pathology turned back on the subject in tenacious blindness." This "fraud" she attributes not just to "patriarchy," but rather to a "dominative mode" practiced by white men and white women.[70] Today as in the past, women—including feminists—remain silent and exclusionary when it comes to the black American female; "history has divided the empire of women against itself," she writes, so that "when we say 'feminist' we mean white women."[71] Her goal is to bring into being a sense of kinship between black and white women at the same time maintaining the particular nuances of black female experience. "Just as we duly regard similarities between life conditions of American women—captive and free—we must observe those undeniable contrasts and differences so decisive that the African-American female's historic claim to the territory of womanhood and 'femininity' still tends to rest too solidly on the subtle and shifting calibrations of a liberal ideology."[72]

Though Spillers's immediate text in this volume is Paule Marshall's *The Chosen Place, The Timeless People* (1969), her larger project is the creation of a new hermeneutic for black women's writing. Here the female character from the novel's "Carnival" section that she analyzes forces us into new modes of reading, for through her we discover that "Otherness"—whether of gender, race, or class—cannot be contained, that (to return to Cohen's and Said's term) the "Other" contaminates the "I" or the "we." Put simply, Spillers's powerful and parabolic theory argues that we must learn to recognize that what we locate as "present" in a text is not only a function of an author or an act of language but of the reader's social positionality—one's gender, class, race, sexual practice, relation to power; we need to recognize this because too often our acts of reading are acts of colonization, tyrannies of the (reading) self over the (written) other that arise from the self's unacknowledged involvement in systems of oppression and repression that surround all cultural objects. For Spillers, it is imperative we find a criticism that situates "itself not only 'against' the expectations of critical behavior, but also the self-service to one's own ideological investments." When we write against these involvements, when we seek multiplicity in a single reading—the "Black, White, and In Color" of her title—we may discover a feminist hermeneutic of difference. For Spillers self-consciousness offers a possible liberation from ideology and from the violence of power, a project whose utopian goal she recognizes. In a feminist, multicultural hermeneutic, we may discover freedom from hegemonic power, may liberate the imagination from ideology. If so, we thereby make a place for the African-American female, a place where her "particular and vivid thereness" of experience can be expressed and heeded. "In doing so," she declares, "we are less interested in joining the ranks of gendered femaleness than gaining the *insurgent* ground as female social subject." From this ground, she speculates, one "might rewrite after all a radically different text for a female empowerment."[73]

Many of the central concerns of Spillers's essay—the Other, the quest for a new hermeneutic, the concern with the contemporary, the immediate—are also discovered in Robert D. Newman's "Exiling History: Hysterical Transgression in Historical Narrative," an essay which links current psychoanalytic theory to historicist scholarship. Newman has a postmodernist's skepticism of grand historical narrative. He is interested in the narratives each text—whether fictional, historical, or scientific—creates and in the narratives that each reader recreates through the acts of reading and interpretation. In a sense, Newman relocates some of the larger tensions that mark historicist theory (and that Spillers seeks to resolve) within the text and the reader. If historicist theory balances between theoretical models and the drive to particularize, Newman finds that the act of reading moves from a rational metanarrative that organizes the text to textual particularities that escape any framing device. Newman reconceptualizes the relations between text and context through his discussion of memory: every text must evoke a context because memory is always at play. Many have noted new historicism's interest in the strange, the fantastic, even the grotesque; Newman argues that an interplay between fascination and repulsion is always engaged in reading as he treats Ariel Dorfman's troubling novel *Mascara*, Freud's troubled *Moses and Monotheism*, and the terrifying events at Jonestown as recounted by James Reston, Jr.

At the center of Newman's discussion is the idea of exile, developed in part from the work of Said (it is interesting to note how often issues of exile arise within this volume—in Cohen, Said, and Spillers as well as Newman). Newman finds in the dynamics of homeland (its loss, exile, desired return, and its impossibility) a key to interactions within texts, between texts and readers, and ultimately between us and the past we attempt to read. His provocative account of the reading process of exile serves to highlight certain difficulties in the phenomenology of the historical imagination: We may long for the past as a kind of lost home, but that past/homeland could only be regained/returned to by an apocalyptic destruction of the present, of our current position; put differently, to possess the past immediately, transparently we would need to destroy all the mediations, the opacities that configure our own moment and selves. While Newman at times evokes an erotics of reading, his is finally a tragic account in which the past-home-other can be won only through a suicide of the self, or perhaps less dramatically, through an embrace of the hysterical.

Said's concluding essay offers another persuasive meditation on exile. Cohen in his essay speaks of the importance of place, of deconstruction's connection to Jacques Derrida's exilic condition, for example, and one could attribute Said's highly influential cultural criticism to the same exilic status. In an interview with Imre Salusinszky, Said has talked about the series of displacements and expatriations he has experienced, concluding, "I would say that's the single strongest strand running through my life: the fact that I'm always in and out of things, and never really *of* anything for very long."[74] The essay he presents here, "Figures, Configurations, Transfigurations," harks back to his earlier study *Covering Islam* (1981), yet attempts to go beyond that book. Focusing on the expanded use of English throughout the contemporary world, due in part to the international media system, Said argues that an untutored national/religious consciousness, along with the world-system map, articulates and produces culture, including such constructions as "Islam" and the "West." Written and given as a lecture before the war in the Persian Gulf, Said's essay is prophetic, warning of falling prey to these constructed extra-historical and extra-world agencies and pointing out that "compared to the way in which the four major Western news agencies operate, or the mode by which television journalists from CNN or NBC select, gather and rebroadcast pictorial images from India or Ethiopia . . . we not only have in the media system a fully integrated practical network, but there also exists within it a very efficient *mode of articulation* knitting the world together." As for the critic and his or her role in the world, which is Said's true subject, he says we must seek a ground of our own, unattached, unbiased.

In many ways, Said's essay responds to the unasked question that all engaged in historical literary criticism face, that is, how to avoid becoming part of a new orthodoxy, how to avoid the totalizing impulse that seems to impel any established critical method or approach. This is not unrelated to the spectre of Political Correctness currently disturbing the Right in the United States. Elizabeth A. Meese has addressed her fellow feminists on the issue, saying, "As we forge a new criticism, our theories and assumptions must stay clear of a hegemonic role reversal that results from unending deconstruction of oppositions like male/female and insider/outsider, where the second term simply replaces the first in an infinite regression within an economy of oppression."[75] Said's solution to this problem, which resembles that of others in our volume, calls for an oppositional, contestatory critical method that questions essences and fabricated identities and creates a separate space for itself as unaffiliated interrogator. He appreciates "the contestatory force of a historical method whose material is made up of disparate, but intertwined and interdependent, and above all, overlapping streams of historical experience." In opposition to "the State with its borders, customs, ruling parties, and authorities," he posits a critic operating from outside the borders, as an exile. A number of new historicists would include self-critique as part of this oppositional criticism. As Don Wayne has argued, "Those of us identified as new historicists have a special responsibility to articulate the relationship between our construction of the past and our present situation."[76] Greenblatt has expressed agreement with this sentiment, adding that the self-consciousness need not be overt in order to be effective. McGann's self-criticism is not only overt, but at the center of his dialectical mode of criticism. In one way or another, all of the contributors to this volume find themselves seeking means of liberating both the texts they admire and the texts they would produce from powerful historical forces—generic, political, economic, mythic, and psychological—that would limit those texts and those that read them.

If one were to select a single topic under which to unify the historicist enterprise represented by this volume, it might be power and freedom. All of these essays are interested, in one way or another, in the role of power in culture: the power of court life in Patterson, of demagogues in Newman, of men over women in Spillers and Aikins, of nations in Said; or again of the power of intellectual constructs and academic institutions in Buell, Ezell, O'Keeffe, McGann. All of these essays help us to explore the fact that between the world and the text, between reality and its representation in culture, falls the shadow of power. This has been called the politicization of culture, though it is in fact merely a realization that culture is made by particular human beings within particular contexts with particular means and for particular ends; for some, it has seemed defeatist, as monolithic power seems to be able to shape everything—even cultural revolution—to its hegemonic vision. But the power investigated by these essays is a destroyer and a preserver; it is "The still and solemn power of many sights, / And many sounds, and much of life and death."

The presence of power can distort culture, as we can see in the productions of Fascist and Stalinist art. But it is also power—material, political, intellectual—that presents the possibility of there being culture. Culture is one of power's presents, one of the gifts that might redeem the many tragedies of power which collectively we call history. Culture, as our contributors from Cohen to Greenblatt to Rogin, Spillers, and Said have shown, cannot escape its deep alliance with power; but as these same critics have revealed, this alliance grants culture its own transforming force, its own ability to resist, to destroy, and to create. Though culture cannot be "liberated" from power, criticism at times can trace power's presence, its meanings and workings, good and ill; in doing so, criticism makes us self-conscious responders to powerful cultural objects rather than merely their reproducers. The great project of historicist criticism is liberation, and only through its work in the world—its interpretation of culture and its critique of power's presence—will it become not a discipline but a gift, one of power's presents.

NOTES

1. These terms have been offered as names in, respectively, Herbert Linden-berger, "Toward (and After) a New History in Literary Study," chap. 9 in his *The History in Literature: On Value, Genre, Institutions* (New York: Columbia University Press, 1990), pp. 189–210; Howard Horwitz, "I Can't Remember: Skepticism, Syn-thetic Histories, Critical Action," *South Atlantic Quarterly* 87 (Fall 1988): 787–820; Robert Weimann, "Towards a Literary Theory of Ideology: Mimesis, Representation, Authority," in *Shakespeare Reproduced: The Text in History and Ideology*, ed. Jean E. Howard and Marion F. O'Connor (New York and London: Methuen, 1987), pp. 265–72; Stephen J. Greenblatt, "Towards a Poetics of Culture," chap. 8 in his *Learn-ing to Curse: Essays in Early Modern Culture* (New York: Routledge, 1990); and Stephen J. Greenblatt, "Introduction" to *The Forms of Power and the Power of Forms in the Renaissance*, special issue of *Genre* 15 (Spring 1982): 3–6.

2. Lee Patterson, "Introduction: Critical Historicism and Medieval Studies," in *Literary Practice and Social Change in Britain, 1380–1530*, ed. Lee Patterson (Berke-ley: University of California Press, 1990), p. 1.

3. Walter Cohen, "Political Criticism of Shakespeare" in *Shakespeare Repro-duced*, ed. Jean Howard and Marion O'Connor, p. 33.

4. For insight into new historicism's relationship to deconstruction and De Man, see, in particular, Jerome J. McGann, *Social Values and Poetic Acts: The Historical Judgment of Literary Work* (Cambridge, Mass. and London: Harvard University Press, 1988), pp. 1–10, 95–131, and Joseph Litvak, "Back to the Future: A Review-Article on the New Historicism, Deconstruction, and Nineteenth-Century Fiction," *TSLL* 30 (1988): 120–49. Litvak stresses that one of the foremost anxieties of new historicism "is an anxiety about becoming trapped inside the aporias and rhetorical blind alleys that deconstructive critics have specialized in mapping" (123). See also, Fredric Jameson, *The Prison-House of Language* (Princeton: Princeton University Press, 1972); and Michael Ryan, *Marxism and Deconstruction* (Baltimore: Johns Hopkins University Press, 1982).

5. For an account of feminism's role in the development of new historicism, see Judith Newton, "History as Usual? Feminism and the 'New Historicism,' " *Cultural Critique* 9 (Spring 1988): 87–121. Janet Todd, *Feminist Literary History* (New York: Routledge, 1988), pp. 98–99, discusses the relationship between feminist literary history and new historicist criticism. The anticipation of new historicism by British Marxists and those working in women's studies, ethnic studies, African-American studies, and American literary studies is pointed out by Carolyn Porter in "Are We Being Historical Yet?" *South Atlantic Quarterly* 87 (1988): 743–86. For excellent summaries of the development of American Studies and its historicization, see Giles

"Gunn, American Studies as Cultural Criticism" in his *The Culture of Criticism and the Criticism of Culture* (Oxford: Oxford University Press, 1987), pp. 147–72; Christopher P. Wilson, "Containing Multitudes: Realism, Historicism, American Studies," *American Quarterly* 41 (September 1989): 466–95; and Robert F. Berkhofer, Jr., "A New Context for a New American Studies?" *American Quarterly* 41 (December 1989): 588–613. Gerald Graff plots the politicization and historicization of American literary studies in "American Criticism Left and Right," in *Ideology and Classic American Literature*, ed. Sacvan Bercovitch and Myra Jehlen (Cambridge: Cambridge University Press, 1986), pp. 91–121.

6. A survey of "old" historicism can be found in Wesley Morris, *Toward a New Historicism* (Princeton: Princeton University Press, 1972), pp. 3–13. For comparisons of "old" and "new" historicism, see Greenblatt, "Introduction," *The Forms of Power and the Power of Forms in the Renaissance*: 3–6; Lindenberger, *The History in Literature*, pp. 2–19, 82–83; Brook Thomas, "The New Historicism and other Old-fashioned Topics," in *The New Historicism*, ed. H. Aram Veeser (New York and London: Routledge, 1989), pp. 182–203; Thomas's updated and expanded version of this essay as chap. 2, "The New Historicism in a Postmodern Age," in his *The New Historicism: And Other Old-Fashioned Topics* (Princeton: Princeton University Press, 1991), pp. 24–50; and Marjorie Levinson, "The New Historicism: Back to the Future," in *Rethinking Historicism: Critical Readings in Romantic History* (Oxford and New York: Basil Blackwell, 1989), pp. 20–22, 24–34.

7. Montrose explains, "By *the historicity of texts*, I mean to suggest the cultural specificity, the social embedment, of all modes of writing—not only the texts that critics study but also the texts in which we study them. By *the textuality of history*, I mean to suggest, firstly, that we can have no access to a full and authentic past, a lived material existence, unmediated by the surviving textual traces of the society in question—traces whose survival we cannot assume to be merely contingent but must rather presume to be at least partially consequent upon complex and subtle social processes of preservation and effacement; and secondly, that those textual traces are themselves subject to subsequent textual mediations when they are construed as the 'documents' upon which historians ground their own texts, called 'histories' " ("Professing the Renaissance: The Poetics and Politics of Culture," in Veeser, *The New Historicism*, pp. 15–36, p. 20).

The new historicist conception of "the textuality of history" arises from the work of historiographers such as Hayden White. See especially his *Metahistory: The Historical Imagination in Nineteenth-Century Europe* (Baltimore: Johns Hopkins University Press, 1973) and his *Tropics of Discourse: Essays in Cultural Criticism* (Baltimore: Johns Hopkins University Press, 1978).

Some critics of new historicism have stressed the contradiction involved in accepting the poststructuralist textualization of history yet insisting on a material historical reality. Stanley Fish, for example, writes, "The implicit claim of the materialists to be more immediately in touch with the particulars of history cannot be maintained, because all accounts of the past (and, I might add, of the present) come to us through 'some kind of natural or technical language' (297) and that language must itself proceed from some ideological vision"; "Commentary: The Young and the Restless," in *The New Historicism*, p. 305. (Fish is quoting Hayden White, "New Historicism: A Comment" also in *The New Historicism*, pp. 293–302.) Alan Liu makes a similar point when he observes that "to argue as Montrose does repeatedly that texts are historical, and history textual . . . is to draw yet another version of the hermeneutic circle"; "The Power of Formalism: The New Historicism," *ELH* 56 (Winter 1989): 721–71, p. 755.

8. Carolyn Porter points this out in "Are We Being Historical Yet?" 747. Williams developed "cultural materialism" as "a theory of the specificities of material cultural and literary production within historical materialism." See especially his *Marxism and Literature* (New York: Oxford University Press, 1977).

A slightly earlier book that provided an influential Marxist theory of literary history is Robert Weimann, *Structure and Society in Literary History: Studies in the History and Theory of Historical Criticism* (Charlottesville: University Press of Virginia, 1976). Weimann offers a penetrating critique of the underlying ideology and assumptions of formalism in America and posits a theory of literary history that situates writing and reading within sociohistorical contexts. In an expanded edition (Baltimore and London: Johns Hopkins University Press, 1984), Weimann adds a chapter entitled "Text and History: Epilogue, 1984," in which he discusses how recent criticism (especially that associated with Derrida and Foucault) "has attempted to redefine (or obliterate) the relationship of text and society in literary history and criticism" (270).

9. Edward W. Said, *Orientalism* (New York: Random House, 1978). For the importance of this book, see Lindenberger, *The History in Literature*, p. 209. Said, in a later influential study, *The World, the Text, and the Critic* (Cambridge, Mass.: Harvard University Press, 1983), sought to answer the question "What does it mean to have a critical consciousness if . . . the intellectual's situation is a worldly one and yet, by virtue of that worldliness itself, the intellectual's social identity should involve something more than strengthening those aspects of the culture that require mere affirmation and orthodox compliancy from its members?" (24).

10. Frank Lentricchia, *After the New Criticism* (Chicago: University of Chicago Press, 1980), p. xiv. Lentricchia, it should be added, has become a harsh critic of "new historicism in its strong Foucauldian vein." See his *Ariel and the Police: Michel Foucault, William James, Wallace Stevens* (Madison: University of Wisconsin Press, 1988), pp. 89–101. He focuses his attack on the work of Stephen Greenblatt.

11. Stephen J. Greenblatt, *Renaissance Self-Fashioning: From More to Shakespeare* (Chicago: University of Chicago Press, 1980), p. 9. An important earlier example of new historicist work in Renaissance studies was Stephen Orgel's *The Illusion of Power* (Berkeley: University of California Press, 1975), which stressed the theatrical dimensions of Renaissance culture. Others whose work has come to be associated with Renaissance New Historicism include Jonathan Dollimore, Alan Sinfield, Kiernan Ryan, Lisa Jardine, Leah Marcus, Louis Montrose, Jonathan Goldberg, Steven Mullaney, Don E. Wayne, Leonard Tennenhouse, and Arthur Marotti; see Jean E. Howard, "The New Historicism in Renaissance Studies," *ELR* 16 (1986): 13–43.

12. Commentators on Greenblatt's early work accused him of worshiping power and creating a totalitarian model of Renaissance culture in which all forms of resistance were futile. See, for example, Jonathan Goldberg, "The Politics of Renaissance Literature: A Review-Essay," *ELH* 49 (1982): 514–42. In the first chapter of *Shakespearean Negotiations* (Berkeley: University of California Press, 1988), Greenblatt indicated the following development in his thinking:

"I had tried to organize the mixed motives of Tudor and Stuart culture under the rubric *power*, but that term implied a structural unity and stability of command belied by much of what I actually knew about the exercise of authority and force in the period.

"If it was important to speak of power in relation to Renaissance literature—not only as the object but as the enabling condition of representation itself—it was equally important to resist the integration of all images and expressions into a single master discourse" (2–3).

Although *Shakespearean Negotiations* treats power relations, its focus is upon the circulation of "social energy" by and through the Renaissance stage. This social energy is "not part of a single coherent, totalizing system." It is "partial, fragmentary, conflictual," and takes the forms of "power, charisma, sexual excitement, collective dreams, wonder, desire, anxiety, religious awe, free-floating intensities of experience" (19).

In *Learning to Curse: Essays in Early Modern Culture* (New York and London: Routledge, 1990), Greenblatt further clarifies his position with regard to charges that his new historicism is deterministic and totalizing: "Agency is virtually inescapable," he acknowledges, adding, "Inescapable but not simple: new historicism, as I understand it, does not posit historical processes as unalterable and inexorable, but it does tend to discover limits or constraints upon individual intervention. Actions that appear to be single are disclosed as multiple; the apparently isolated power of the individual genius turns out to be bound up with collective, social energy; a gesture of dissent may be an element in a larger legitimation process, while an attempt to stabilize the order of things may turn out to subvert it" (164–65). He insists that he "did not propose that all manifestations of resistance in all literature (or even in all plays by Shakespeare) were coopted." For him, "some are, some aren't" (165). His new essay on *Macbeth* in this volume should be read as his latest treatment of this issue.

13. Rogin's *Subversive Genealogy: The Politics and Art of Herman Melville* (New York: Knopf, 1983) focuses on the relations between Melville's family history, his work, and certain features of American capitalist culture, such as imperialist expansionism and racial exploitation, at midcentury. Walter Benn Michaels's *The Gold Standard and the Logic of Naturalism: American Literature at the Turn of the Century* (Berkeley: University of California Press, 1987) traces the parallel representations of American market capitalism and literary culture at the turn of the century.

14. For an account of this development, see Gerald Graff, "The Promise of American Literature Studies," chap. 13 in his *Professing Literature: An Institutional History* (Chicago and London: University of Chicago Press, 1987), pp. 209–25. Others whose work has come to be associated with new historicism in American literature studies include Jonathan Arac, Nina Baym, Sacvan Bercovitch, Lawrence Buell, Richard Brodhead, Gillian Brown, William E. Cain, Michael Colacurcio, Cathy Davidson, Wai-chee Dimock, Ann Douglas, Philip Fisher, Michael T. Gilmore, T. Walter Herbert Jr., Howard Horwitz, Gregory S. Jay, Myra Jehlen, Annette Kolodny, Frank Lentricchia, Steven Mailloux, John McWilliams, Susan Mizruchi, Donald E. Pease, Larry J. Reynolds, John Samson, Ivy Schweitzer, Eric Sundquist, Brook Thomas, Jane Tompkins, Priscilla Wald, and Michael Warner.

15. *Ideology and Classic American Literature*, ed. Sacvan Bercovitch and Myra Jehlen (Cambridge: Cambridge University Press, 1986); Lawrence Buell, *New En-*

gland Literary Culture: From Revolution Through Renaissance (Cambridge: Cambridge University Press, 1986). For a discussion of Bercovitch's importance, see Emily Miller Budick, "Sacvan Bercovitch, Stanley Cavell, and the Romance Theory of American Fiction," *PMLA* 107 (January 1992): 78–91. For strong accounts of the importance of Buell's volume to the new historicism in American literature studies, see Giles Gunn, "The Kingdoms of Theory and the New Historicism in America," *Yale Review* 77 (1988): 207–36; and Philip F. Gura, "Toward New History of the American Renaissance," *ESQ* 32 (1st Quarter 1986): 68–78.

Frederick Crews's derogatory account of the "New Americanists" appeared in his review article "Whose American Renaissance?" *New York Review of Books*, 27 October 1988, 68–81. For a rebuttal, see Donald E. Pease, "New Americanists: Revisionist Interventions into the Canon," in *New Americanists: Revisionist Interventions into the Canon*, ed. Donald E. Pease, special issue of *boundary 2* 17 (1990): 1–37. For an impressive recent collection of essays by New Americanists, see *The New American Studies: Essays from "Representations"*, ed. Philip Fisher (Berkeley: University of California Press, 1991).

16. Scholars other than McGann whose work has come to be associated with Romantic new historicism include John Barrell, Alan Bewell, David Bromwich, Marilyn Butler, Julie Carlson, James Chandler, Jerome Christensen, Laurence Goldstein, Heather Glen, Paul Hamilton, Gary Harrison, Kurt Heinzelman, Mary Jacobus, Kenneth Johnston, Theresa Kelley, Jon Klancher, Karl Kroeber, Marjorie Levinson, Alan Liu, Peter Manning, David Simpson, and Olivia Smith. See, Alan Liu, "Review of David Simpson, *Wordsworth's Historical Imagination*," *The Wordsworth Circle* 19 (1988): 172–82; p. 180; and Marjorie Levinson, "The New Historicism," p. 55, n. 3.

17. Jerome J. McGann, *The Romantic Ideology: A Critical Investigation* (Chicago and London: The University of Chicago Press, 1983); *A Critique of Modern Textual Criticism* (Chicago: University of Chicago Press, 1983); *The Beauty of Inflections: Literary Investigations in Historical Method and Theory* (New York: Oxford University Press, 1985); *Social Values and Poetic Acts* (Cambridge, Mass.: Harvard University Press, 1988); and *Towards a Literature of Knowledge* (Chicago: University of Chicago Press, 1989).

18. See Lindenberger, *The History in Literature*, p. 204.

19. J. Hillis Miller, "Presidential Address 1986. The Triumph of Theory, the Resistance to Reading, and the Question of the Material Base," *PMLA* 102 (1987): 281–91; p. 283. For new historicist responses to Miller, see Louis A. Montrose, "Professing the Renaissance," pp. 15–16, and Alan Liu, "The Power of Formalism," 770. Liu detects in Miller's essay "a haunting tone of embattled isolation solaced by meditative loneliness."

20. See J. Hillis Miller, *Hawthorne and History: Defacing It* (Cambridge: Blackwell, 1991).

21. Donald Pease has noted that at the 1988 Modern Language Association Convention there were "more than thirty papers in which the new historicism figured in the title." "Toward a Sociology of Literary Knowledge: Greenblatt, Colonialism, and the New Historicism" in *Consequences of Theory: Selected Papers from the English Institute, 1987–1988*, ed. Jonathan Arac and Barbara Johnson (Baltimore and London: Johns Hopkins University Press, 1991), pp. 108–53; p. 149, n. 20.

For informed discussions of new historicism, see the essays by Goldberg, Horwitz, Levinson, Lindenberger, Liu, and Litvak cited above plus A. Leigh DeNeef, "Recent

Studies in the English Renaissance," *Studies in English Literature* 27 (1987): 141–71; Jonathan Dollimore, "Introduction: Shakespeare, Cultural Materialism and the New Historicism," in *Political Shakespeare: New Essays in Cultural Materialism* (Ithaca: Cornell University Press, 1985), pp. 2–17; Catherine Gallagher, "Marxism and The New Historicism," in *The New Historicism*, pp. 37–48; Geoffrey Galt Harpham, "Foucault and the New Historicism," *American Literary History* 3 (Summer 1991): 360–75; Jean E. Howard, "The New Historicism in Renaissance Studies," *English Literary Renaissance* 16 (1986): 13–43; Louis A. Montrose, "Renaissance Literary Studies and the Subject of History," *English Literary Renaissance* 16 (Winter 1986): 5–12; and Don E. Wayne, "Power, Politics, and the Shakespearean Text: Recent Criticism in England and the United States," in *Shakespeare Reproduced*, pp. 47–67.

For critiques of new historicism, see the essays by Cohen, Fish, Newton, Pease, Porter, and Thomas cited above, plus Lentricchia, *Ariel and the Police*, pp. 89–101, Lee Patterson, *Negotiating the Past: The Historical Understanding of Medieval Literature* (Madison: University of Wisconsin Press, 1987), pp. 57–74, and Edward Pechter, "The New Historicism and Its Discontents: Politicizing Renaissance Drama," *PMLA* 102 (May 1987): 292–303.

22. Fish, "Commentary: The Young and the Restless," p. 303.

23. Murray Krieger plots a similar history in his introduction to *The Aims of Representation: Subject/Text/History*, ed. Murray Krieger (New York: Columbia University Press, 1987), pp. 1–22. According to Krieger, "the three terms in the subtitle—in the order in which they appear—represent, in brief, the focal points in the sequence of theoretical movements in recent years: the subject as controlling author of the literary work, then the work seen as produced by and absorbed within the larger textuality, and then that textuality seen as produced by and absorbed within power-driven historical forces. Subject, text, and history, in other words, can be seen as reflecting the consecutive dominance, respectively, of the criticism of consciousness, of deconstruction—whether Lacanian or Derridean—and of what we might call theories of social power, Foucaultian and/or Marxian" (2).

24. Litvak, "Back to the Future," 127–28; Gregory S. Jay, *America the Scrivener: Deconstruction and the Subject of Literary History* (Ithaca and London: Cornell University Press, 1990), especially pp. 236–54; McGann, "The Scandal of Referentiality" in *Social Values and Poetic Acts*, pp. 115–31.

25. Edward W. Said, *The World, the Text, and the Critic* (Cambridge, Mass.: Harvard University Press, 1983), p. 48. Said observes, for example, that "texts of such a length as *Tom Jones* aim to occupy leisure time of a quality not available to just anyone" (45). McGann similarly insists that "the price of a book, its place of publication, even its physical form and the institutional structures by which it is distributed and received, all bear upon the production of literary meaning, and hence all must be critically analyzed and explained" (*Social Values and Poetic Acts*, p. 117).

26. In an epilogue to this account, however, the new historicism becomes for some "a new kind of formalism" and "the newest academic orthodoxy" (see Vincent P. Pecora, "The Limits of Local Knowledge" in *The New Historicism*, p. 272, and Montrose "The Poetics and Politics of Culture, p. 18).

The story Alan Liu tells to emphasize the return to formalism of new historicism goes as follows: "If, very crudely, the New Criticism was an embarrassed subsumption of the Civil War and of the dominantly plural (and industrial) society that followed, and if deconstruction is an inheritor of New Criticism, then the New Historicism is Reconstruction—or, rather, a highly fastidious and inhibited version of reconstruction" ("The Power of Formalism," 742).

27. Don E. Wayne, "Power, Politics, and the Shakespearean Text," p. 57.

28. David Simpson, "Literary Criticism and the Return to 'History,'" *Critical Inquiry* 14 (Summer 1988): 721–47; p. 722.

29. Patterson, "Introduction: Critical Historicism and Medieval Studies," p. 13.

30. The charges made by conservatives in the Reagan and Bush administrations, in the media, and in the academy itself that leftist academics have politicized higher education in the United States and are destroying Western civilization are so well known and tiresome that they need not be rehearsed here. For thoughtful commentary on the charges, see Montrose, "The Poetics and Politics of Culture," pp. 27–31 and Gallagher, "Marxism and The New Historicism," pp. 45–48. For a polemical response, see H. Aram Veeser, "Introduction," in *The New Historicism*, pp. ix–xvi.

31. David Simpson articulates this explanation when he writes that "a profession which requires for itself a ritual of radical change must now search for a new source of energy. Suddenly it is sexy to plead for referentiality, and fashionable even to be called a Marxist, so long as one does not insist on too close a relation between practice and preaching by 'misbehaving' on university property" ("Literary Criticism and the Return to 'History,'" 722).

32. Louis Adrian Montrose, "Renaissance Literary Studies and the Subject of History," p. 11.

33. McGann, *The Beauty of Inflections*, p. 8.

34. Alan Liu, "Review of Simpson," 180.

35. Liu provides a brief comparison of Renaissance and Romantic new historicisms, pointing out that the latter is more diverse, less visible and aligned along three major axes of Marxism, intellectual history, and formalist or deconstructive method, resulting in a plurality of approach, whereas the "Foucauldian or Geertzian hyperspace" of Renaissance studies "fuse materialist, formalist, and history-of-ideas approaches." Liu acknowledges "the vitality, freshness, and sheer fullness" of Renaissance materials and readings, concluding, "At the present time, Romantic New Historicism has nothing to match it; and even if this were to change, it is unlikely that Romantic New Historicism will match the *collective* presence of its Renaissance counterpart" ("Review of Simpson," 180–81).

36. Pechter, "The New Historicism and Its Discontents: Politicizing Renaissance Drama," 292.

37. See Porter, "Are We Being Historical Yet?" 743–48.

38. See Williams's *Marxism and Literature* and Jameson's *The Political Unconscious*. Other major contributions to the Marxist tradition as it impinges upon the new historicist enterprise include Pierre Machery, *A Theory of Literary Production*, trans. Geoffrey Wall (London: Routledge and Kegan Paul, 1978 [1966]), Louis Althusser, "Ideology and Ideological State Apparatuses," in *Lenin and Philosophy and Other Essays*, trans. Ben Brewster (New York: Monthly Review Press, 1971), pp. 123–73, and Terry Eagleton, *Criticism and Ideology: A Study in Marxist Literary Theory* (London: New Left Books, 1976).

39. McGann, *Social Values and Poetic Acts*, p. 116. Lawrence Buell and Lee Patterson have been similarly positive about the Marxist tradition. Buell has expressed

admiration for the cohesiveness of Marxism as a model for literary history and its success "in accounting for how social forces condition literary language and the production of texts." He explains that this "is because Marxist theory envisages language not merely as a relational system that conditions discourse, and thereby threatens to collapse social reality back into text, but also as 'articulated social *presence*,' itself the creature of the social reality it textualizes" (*New England Literary Culture*, p. 10).

Patterson has praised Marxist historicism for its ability to resist totalizing positivistic historiographical practices and the monolithic, untheorized conceptions of history they offer: "In a world and a profession that persistently seeks to suppress the political, Marxist criticism has traditionally been—and remains—the most tenacious voice to insist upon its inescapability.... Instead of the methodologism and empiricism that foreclose theoretical reflection on the historiographical practice of history, Marxism diligently, even relentlessly, theorizes the problematic of historical-textual relations." Patterson also credits Marxism for refusing to allow the lover of art and literature "to evade the gross and painful social inequalities that make such pleasures possible" (*Negotiating the Past*, p. 46).

40. We do not find such distancing in the British historicists, of course, such as Janet Wolff, Terry Lovell, Terry Eagleton, Tony Bennett, Alan Sinfield, Jonathan Dollimore, and Graham Holderness. For astute comparisons of American new historicism and British cultural materialism, see Wayne, "Power, Politics, and the Shakespearean Text," pp. 52–60, and Jonathan Dollimore, "Introduction: Shakespeare, Cultural Materialism and the New Historicism," pp. 2–17.

Relevant to this issue is a point made by Edward Said in an interview: "I just came back from England, where I did a day-long conference with Raymond Williams, and we were talking together about the different social contexts in which we did our work. It's very striking that within an English context one *can* talk about Marxism, or at least socialism, as a tradition having a real presence. You cannot talk about that in America, where there is no socialist tradition of any consequence" (Imre Salusinszky, *Criticism in Society: Interviews with Jacques Derrida, Northrop Frye, Harold Bloom, Geoffrey Hartman, Frank Kermode, Edward Said, Barbara Johnson, Frank Lentricchia, and J. Hillis Miller* [New York: Methuen, 1987], p. 147).

For an account of the effects of American "exceptionalism" on Marxist cultural study of the United States (a tradition that features work by our contributors Michael Rogin and Lawrence Buell), see Michael Denning, " 'The Special American Conditions': Marxism and American Studies," *American Quarterly* 38 (1986): 356–80.

For excellent discussions of Marxist totalization, see Martin Jay, *Marxism and Totality: The Adventures of a Concept from Lukacs to Habermas* (Berkeley: University of California Press, 1984) and Patterson, *Negotiating the Past*, pp. 46–52.

41. For selections and a bibliography of the work of the Frankfurt school, see Andrew Arato and Eike Gebhardt, eds., *The Essential Frankfurt School Reader* (New York: Urizen Books, 1978).

42. "The history of thought, to say nothing of political movements, is extravagantly illustrative of how the dictum 'solidarity before criticism' means the end of criticism," Said has declared (*The World, the Text, and the Critic*, p. 28).

43. Greenblatt, *Learning to Curse*, p. 147. Greenblatt has also stated that "it is possible in the United States to describe oneself and be perceived as a Marxist literary critic without believing in the class struggle as the principal motor force in

history; without believing in the theory of surplus value; without believing in the determining power of economic base over ideological superstructure; without believing in the inevitability, let alone the imminence, of capitalism's collapse" (*Learning to Curse*, p. 3).

44. Anne Mack and J. J. Rome, "Marxism, Romanticism, and Postmodernism: An American Case History," *South Atlantic Quarterly* 88 (Summer 1989): 605–32; p. 626.

45. McGann, *The Romantic Ideology*, p. 158.

46. Gallagher, "Marxism and The New Historicism," 37.

47. Lee Patterson, *Negotiating the Past*, p. 70. Marjorie Levinson has astutely discussed the basic hermeneutic binds involved in binary approaches to the politics of texts, pointing out that "this kind of thinking (in the text [essentialism]/outside the text [pragmatism]: passive reflecting, elucidating/active politicizing, use) is predialectical and therefore not the task of a Marxist or any other criticism today" ("The New Historicism," p. 21).

48. Greenblatt, *Learning to Curse*, p. 167.

49. McGann, *Social Values and Poetic Acts*, pp. 112–13. Cf. Jean-Paul Sartre, *Search for a Method*, trans. Hazel E. Barnes (1963; repr., New York: Vintage Books, 1968), pp. 35–84.

50. See Geertz, "Thick Description: Toward an Interpretive Theory of Culture," *The Interpretation of Cultures* (New York: Basic Books, 1973), pp. 3–30. For a critique of Geertz's work and his influence upon new historicism, see Vincent Pecora, "The Limits of Local Knowledge," in *The New Historicism*, pp. 243–76.

51. See Geertz, *The Interpretation of Cultures*, p. 207.

52. Louis Althusser, "Ideology and Ideological State Apparatuses," in *Lenin and Philosophy and Other Essays*, trans. Ben Brewster (London: New Left Books, 1971), p. 162. For some excellent observations on the differences between Geertzean and Althusserian theories of culture, see Michael Ryan, *Politics and Culture: Working Hypotheses for a Post-Revolutionary Society* (Baltimore: Johns Hopkins University Press, 1989), pp. 10–11.

53. See note 12 above. A similar charge has been made against Said's work. See Dominick LaCapra, *Rethinking Intellectual History: Texts, Contexts, Language* (Ithaca and London: Cornell University Press, 1983), p. 43, n. 15.

54. Greenblatt, *Learning to Curse*, p. 180.

55. Louis Montrose has commented on Greenblatt's own attempt "to situate himself as a neo-pragmatist in relation to two totalizing discourses," Marxism and poststructuralism. "Greenblatt suggests that the practice of cultural poetics involves a repudiation of cultural politics," Montrose writes. "My own conviction is that their separation is no more desirable than it is possible" ("The Poetics and Politics of Culture," pp. 32–33).

56. McGann, *Social Values and Poetic Acts*, p. 128.

57. Greenblatt, *Learning to Curse*, p. 8.

58. See *Against Theory: Literary Studies and the New Pragmatism*, ed. W. J. T. Mitchell (Chicago: University of Chicago Press, 1985). Walter Benn Michaels and Steven Knapp's essay "Against Theory," which is reprinted in this volume along with responses by E. D. Hirsch, Jr., Mailloux, Fish, and others, originally appeared in *Critical Inquiry* (Summer 1982).

59. McGann, *Social Values and Poetic Acts*, p. 144.

60. See *Learning to Curse*, p. 5. For an extended discussion of the role of the anecdote in history and new historicist criticism, see Joel Fineman, "The History of the Anecdote: Fiction and Fiction," in *The New Historicism*, pp. 49–76. One of Fineman's points is that the anecdote *"lets history happen* by virtue of the way it introduces an opening into the teleological, and therefore timeless, narration of beginning, middle, and end" (61). For an opposing view, see Porter, who views the anecdote as indicative of a "totalized vision of history." For Porter the anecdote might be described as "colonial formalism," for it appropriates "the 'strange things' to be found outside the 'literary,' while effacing the social and historical realm that produced them, at once plundering and erasing the discursive spaces to which the argument appeals" ("Are We Being Historical Yet?" 779).

Lee Patterson has commented on the "relentlessly synchronic" nature of New Historicist criticism, arguing that "the result is both an enlightening extension of the range of materials to be brought to bear upon a text . . . and yet a weakening of explanatory force" (*Negotiating the Past*, pp. 67–68).

61. See McGann, "Theory of Texts," *London Review of Books*, 18 February 1988, 21. This programme has obvious affinities with Robert Weimann's "theory of tradition" and Hans Robert Jauss's "aesthetics of reception"; see Weimann's *Structure and Society in Literary History* and Jauss's *Toward an Aesthetic of Reception*, trans. Timothy Bahti (Minneapolis: University of Minnesota Press, 1982).

62. Newton, "History as Usual?" 99.

63. See McGann's *Social Values and Poetic Acts*, p. 114 and p. 259 n. 42., which refers the reader to Said's *Orientalism* and his "Orientalism Reconsidered," *Cultural Critique* 1 (1985): 89–107.

64. McGann, *The Beauty of Inflections*, p. 96.

65. O'Keeffe, *Visible Song: Transitional Literacy in Old English Verse* (Cambridge: Cambridge University Press, 1990), p. 193.

66. See Patterson, "On the Margin: Postmodernism, Ironic History, and Medieval Studies," *Speculum: A Journal of Medieval Studies* 65 (January 1990): 87–108; p. 99.

67. Patterson, *Negotiating the Past*, pp. xi, 72.

68. Patterson, ed., *Literary Practice and Social Change*, p. 13.

69. *New England Literary Culture*, p. 17.

70. See Spillers, "Interstices: A Small Drama of Words," in Carol S. Vance, ed., *Pleasure and Danger: Exploring Female Sexuality* (Boston: Routledge, 1984), pp. 73–100.

71. Ibid., p. 79.

72. Spillers, "Mama's Baby, Papa's Maybe: An American Grammar Book," *diacritics* 17 (Summer 1987): 65–81; p. 77.

73. Ibid., p. 80.

74. Salusinszky, *Criticism in Society*, p. 128.

75. Elizabeth A. Meese, "Sexual Politics and Critical Judgment," in *Twentieth-Century Literary Theory: A Reader*, ed. K. M. Newton (New York: St. Martin's Press, 1988), p. 275.

76. Wayne, "Power, Politics, and the Shakespearean Text," p. 60.

CHAPTER ONE

Generating Literary Histories

RALPH COHEN

MY AIM here is to inquire why and how some recent literary histories have come to be written or rewritten. I consider this inquiry important because it challenges us to understand our own desire for historicity, our sense of our own mortality; not only because we are conscious of a nuclear possibility, but because in this century we have become conscious of the readiness of human beings to end the lives of others. We live with the consciousness of what has been repressed, and despite our desire to expose the repressed, there always remains a remnant that eludes us. This compels us to recognize that our version of history, while it inevitably exposes that which has been repressed, nevertheless leaves us with incomplete knowledge of history and ourselves as historians.

I can but illustrate this point by offering you a biographical—not autobiographical—sketch of an author who, in our time, has developed a revised conception of literary history, a philosopher who has urged a new history based upon the concept of decentering linear texts, of arguing that textual boundaries must be made unbounded, that texts which have repressed social, political, and philosophical views should be deconstructed to reveal the repressions.

Jacques Derrida, whose views I am describing, is an Algerian Jew, born in a former French colony, a marginalized figure from a marginalized country. It seems to me no historical accident that his geographical image of boundary crossing should assert the democratization of what in previous criticism was considered bounded and fixed. His arguments for decentering texts and for attending to their repressive aspects of language seem, at least in part, to stem from a colonial environment. And I believe his argument for the indeterminacy of the text rests on rejection of the localization and stabilization of place, a rejection of any one place as the origin or center of commitment.

I speak with considerable reservation in analogizing personal experience to theoretical arguments. But such speculation is not foreign to Derrida's own way of thinking, and it can help to explain why the notion of the play of signifiers becomes important in reconceptualizing philosophy. He is, after all, an outsider encountering or discounting or reconstruing the assumed fixed play of the insiders.

Whatever phenomenological assumptions may govern his theory of writing, I want to suggest that we cannot ignore the sense of alienation, perhaps even of personal oppression, that has bred resentment from actual situations and social practices. For state practices of colonization or deprivation of the rights of minorities or the denial of economic and social equality to women are not forms of imaginary subordination.

Social movements which arise to resist these injustices have, in our time, fostered resistance to received histories, including literary history. They have resulted in histories and theories marked by opposition to exclusion and marginalization. The most obvious of such histories are those of the feminists and the black critics. They are generating histories out of an economic, legal, social, and educational awareness of injustice and deprivation. The problem facing the writers of the new histories is that generation implies that prior generations have established the language and genre of history writing. It is thus impossible to generate a new history without being contaminated by the language and genre of the old.

The complicity of writing a history even in opposition to that which has been received becomes apparent in Henry Louis Gates's effort to generate a black literary theory that will empower a black literary history. The problem is to create a distinctive theory to serve the needs of a black audience.

> We must redefine "theory" itself from within our own black cultures, refusing to grant the racist premise that theory is something that white people do, so that we are doomed to imitate our white colleagues, like reverse black minstrel critics done up in white face. We are all heirs to critical theory, but we black critics are heir to the black vernacular critical tradition as well. Our task now is to invent and employ our own critical theory, to assume our own propositions, and to stand within the academy as politically responsive parts of a social and cultural African-American whole.[1]

Gates seeks to create a distinctive black literary history, but to do this, he must establish a body of black writing about which a history can be written. In order for this to happen, he must turn to bibliographical research and urge others to do so in order to provide necessary texts. We can thus note that the writing of a black literary history involves the following assumptions: the repression, ignoring, disregarding a realm of texts by white historians. The history to be written will involve an exposure of texts that have been unknown or excluded from study and thus have not created a black literary consciousness. Such texts have to be uncovered, and black historians have to locate the texts for which a history can be written. Black historians are therefore involved in bibliographical studies pertinent to history no less than they are in expanding the notion of "text" to include oral as well as written expressions. And a black literary history must distinguish itself from a white history, despite the fact that they become entangled.

This distinction results in special problems for black theorists in proposing literary histories. They need to distinguish their history from that written for and by historians of the white majority. Yet such historians are often supporters and sometimes even leaders in opposing prejudice and oppression. Black critics who wish to establish a history of their own literature—with or without support from white critics—do so either by establishing a tradition within slavery or beyond national boundaries to a majority culture in Africa. This tradition can then be used to provide a continuity within the actual national history that is constructed.

Black historians and critics have to place this tradition within a history; they have to historicize tradition in contrast to T. S. Eliot and his followers who separate tradition from history. T. S. Eliot in "Tradition and the Individual Talent" defines tradition as a continuity that is changed by each great work—whatever such a work might be. History in no way impinges upon tradition, for the tradition transcends history. And the development of national historical conditions which alter the nature of writing does not result in altering judgments of literary value. But this separation of tradition from history and making the individual writer the continuator of the tradition no longer describes the condition governing either traditions or history.

For traditions do not exist in some transcendental realm but in genres which explain, as Eliot's essay does, what a specific tradition is. And as a kind of writing it inevitably carries ideological implications. For Eliot, it is tradition that involves the "historical sense."

> It involves, in the first place, the historical sense, which we may call nearly indispensable to any one who would continue to be a poet beyond his twenty-fifth year; and the historical sense involves a perception, not only of the pastness of the past, but of its presence; the historical sense compels a man to write not merely with his own generation in his bones, but with a feeling that the whole of the literature of Europe from Homer and within it the whole of the literature of his own country has a simultaneous existence and composes a simultaneous order. This historical sense, which is a sense of the timeless as well as of the temporal and of the timeless and of the temporal together, is what makes a writer traditional. And it is at the same time what makes a writer most acutely conscious of his place in time, of his own contemporaneity.[2]

Eliot's description of tradition begins by insisting on a historical sense that a writer must possess, a feeling that the "whole of the literature of Europe from Homer and within it the whole of the literature of his own country has a simultaneous existence and composes a simultaneous order." The historical sense is both timeless and temporal, and it is a sense of the "whole" of literature whether of Europe or one's own country. It is not necessary to point to this Eurocentric view of tradition, nor is it necessary to indicate that new works are seen as conforming—though individually—to a tradition. What is important to note is that, for Eliot, a literary historical sense is never oppositional, nor does he see an opposition between alterity and contemporaneity or tradition and history. Tradition is the archetypal linear development.

Eliot's essay is not, however, without its oppositional function. But what he wishes to attack is not an exclusion but a mistake, one about the personality of the poet. For the "poet has, not a 'personality' to express, but a particular medium, which is only a medium and not a personality . . . " (p. 9). How this medium is generated has to do with a psychological theory, not the historical nature of discourses in society. Eliot's argument is far removed from a society divided by different discourses—political, social, philosophical—and by texts that resist the view of a single tradition. Far removed from Gates's need to find an appropriate language to develop a literary history that can empower it. Ideologically, Eliot's tradition transcends history. Eliot's severing of the "medium" from "personality" shrewdly separates the language of a text from the writer, but it continues to conceive of this medium as a single, unified entity.

I should point out that Eliot conceives of "generation" as the entire body of individuals born and living at about the same time. The historical sense functions as a coherent responsiveness, and we know that, in our country for example, this coherence no longer applies to the writings of males and females nor to the writings of minority authors.

I have been discussing the problems that black theorists and historians have had in generating distinctive literary histories. I have noted their search for a tradition that would serve as a basis for differentiation while making it possible for them to link a national literary history to African traditions. And it is this linkage that created the problem of the language of literary history, one that would distinguish it from a white history. But this posed a dilemma for literary theorists and historians: For whom was this history to be written and what language or languages would be appropriate for it? The histories that are being generated bear the marks of divided authority with regard to the language, audience, and the ideological procedures that define "oppositional" literary history.

"Oppositional" literary history is not one phenomenon. One need only consider the writing of the new historicists and the feminists. It is not even unified within each of these groups. For the new historicists "oppositional" means not only an attack on a history that has suppressed texts or writers, but also an attack on an ideology that views history as a unity, as a harmony. The generation of new historicisms stems from opposition to received views of the relation of literary texts to society, especially the works of Shakespeare and other Renaissance writers. The so-called new historicists deny the validity of formalist or new critical analyses of Renaissance works and condemn the approaches that posit a unified Elizabethan world picture that explains literature as a direct reflection of a stable society.

The new historicists are themselves responding to a historical moment of dissention, disaffection, and deconstruction in our society and in our discipline. This disaffection has led them to emphasize subversions in literary texts and to see such texts as unstable arenas of power conflicts. This is not, it should be noted, the attitude of black critics to black writing. Renaissance studies have become the chief areas of new historicists' inquiry because our greatest writer—Shakespeare—has been our authorized canonical author— and if his texts can be shown to represent ideological, that is, political power, conflicts, a case can be made for reconceiving the entire English canon. Thus these critics pose a challenge to all other scholars to reconsider their historical concepts and practices.

I do not believe that the "generation" of new historicists can be identified with any one practice, but it is possible to identify the naming of this group. In 1982 Stephen Greenblatt introduced a selection of essays by stating that "many of the present essays *give voice*, I think, to what one may call the New Historicism, set apart from both the dominant historical scholarship of the past (in Renaissance Studies) and the formalist criticism that partially displaced this scholarship after World War II."[3] The *voices*, as Louis Montrose has pointed out, are less a choral movement than a symphonic orchestration, less a movement than an orientation. Those who are called or who call themselves "new historicists" often operate with diverse, sometimes even contradictory, hypotheses.

But all new historicists are intent on abandoning the historical procedures in Renaissance studies developed by Eustace Tillyard, by Douglas Bush, by Helen Gardner, by Lily Bess Campbell and to substitute historical procedures that characterize society as unstable and disunified by power struggle. As Montrose has pointed out, "In Renaissance literary studies, 'history' has traditionally meant the literary and intellectual histories that, in combination with the techniques of close reading . . . misrecognize[s] the dominant ideology of the Tudor-Stuart society [defining it] . . . as a stable, coherent, and collective Elizabethan world picture, a picture lucidly produced in the canonical literary works of the age."[4]

Montrose and Greenblatt find that Renaissance literature indicates an unstable society, revealing explicit or implicit strategies of subversion, conflicts, struggles for power. For them literary texts are not mere reflections of historical facts but highly complex social products related to other forms of social production. Literary texts have aesthetic possibilities but these are linked to the "complex network of institutions, practices, beliefs that constitute the culture as a whole." Above all, new historicists seek to erode the assumed stable ground of literary works by treating them as places of dissention and shifting interests, occasions for the jostling of orthodox and subversive impulses.

Renaissance writers and critics make no special distinction between a literary and a nonliterary language. Thus, history or philosophy, religious sermons or tracts, poems and plays can be referred to in similar terms. As is sometimes noted, the word "literary" came into use late in the eighteenth century as referring to writings distinguished by their form. But even as late as the 1785 edition of Johnson's *Dictionary*, "literary" is defined with reference to learning: "Respecting letters; regarding learning. *Literary History* is an account of the state of learning and of the lives of learned men. *Literary* conversation is talk about the questions of learning."[5] And "literature" is defined as "learning; skill in letters." It thus seems reasonable to assume that "literature" through the eighteenth century retained its meaning as a part of culture and included what we now identify as nonliterary works.

The new historicists are prepared to grant that for different centuries we need different "histories"; they are even prepared to argue that there is no one history for Renaissance studies but many histories. But what precisely do they take "history" to be? Although there is no one view of "history" that all new historicists espouse, most agree that texts are produced at a particular time by particular authors using genres that are socially and culturally conditioned. With regard to social conditioning, disagreement occurs even among new historicists, because the views that they espouse are drawn from diverse sources. Some new historicists see texts as emphasizing "the possibilities of subversion of the dominant ideology";[6] others emphasize the hegemonic capacity of the dominant ideology to contain and control subversive moves.

This notion of different histories for different times is not an issue for black historians since their desire is to create a history in which traditions can have some continuity. The question whether a different kind of history is necessary for slave narratives or the Harlem Renaissance seems an irrelevant question since no critic would deny that this period created writings that differ from earlier kinds. But such differences do not erase the dominance of similarities.

New historicists draw upon the ideological studies of members of the Marxist revisionist Frankfurt school, draw upon the works of established Marxists and anthropologists. Stephen Greenblatt, in his seminal historical study—*Renaissance Self-Fashioning* (1980)—entitles one of his chapters "The Work of God in the Age of Mechanical Reproduction" after Walter Benjamin's essay, "The Work of Art in the Age of Mechanical Reproduction." The influential study, *Dialectic of Enlightenment*, by Adorno and Horkheimer, indicts the ideological premises of the Enlightenment for subverting the practices of reason that it sought to defend.

Some new historicists derive their views of history from Foucault's studies of power. Others derive their views of contradictions within a text from Derrida. But it is the Marxist works of Raymond Williams—especially *Marxism and Literature* and *The Country and the City*—and those of Fredric Jameson that have proved especially valuable in shaping the historical views of the new historicists. Still, it is only appropriate to note that, while

Greenblatt and Montrose are not dependent upon a theory of class struggle, the Marxists are. Not only does Jameson insist on his slogan "Only Historicize!" but in his essay on *Paradise Lost* he urges that "we must learn to read theological discourse and discursive production related to it, such as Milton's Christian epic, in terms of class struggle."[7] These views seem more appropriate to the writings of Jonathan Dollimore and Alan Sinfield—British Marxist scholars often called new historicists (they prefer the name "cultural materialists")—than to the writings of the Americans.

It is simple enough to suggest that the British historicists write in opposition to a government policy that has seriously damaged the prospects of humanities education in universities. The turn to Marxist hypotheses can deliberately challenge the stability of such a society by suggesting that no society is stable, not even that of Shakespeare. But American new historicists have quite other sources for the generation of their histories. They write in opposition to the modernist separation of literary language from ordinary language. Their argument is that so-called literary texts are expressed in language that characterizes the language of politics and the state. They resist modernist aesthetic criteria and find in religious and political texts aesthetic functions previously disregarded. They are against views of textual holism and in this respect align themselves with Foucault and Derrida. But they are not ready to become complete relativists since they would then have to assume that their own discourses are as unstable as those of Renaissance writers.

Montrose offers as a new historical chiastic slogan—"The Historicity of Texts and the Textuality of History."[8] For him this formulation emphasizes the "dynamic, unstable, and reciprocal relationship between the discursive and the material domains." What this means for the study of Renaissance texts is that the critic draws attention to the reciprocal and unbalanced relations within a text and relates them in sophisticated ways to imbalances, oppressions, and division within the social order. However, both Greenblatt and Montrose eschew imposing generalizations about class struggle, preferring to argue that subversive moments are often coopted into the dominant ideology. In this respect Montrose shrewdly notes the possibility that the new historicism may itself be coopted into the dominant academic ideology, and that academic discussions will domesticate new historicism either by demonstrating that we already have it or that it can readily be appropriated merely as another point of view. He writes that "predictably, English (British) 'cultural materialism' ... remains a marginal academic discourse, whereas American 'New Historicism' is on its way to becoming the newest academic orthodoxy—not so much a critique as a subject of academic appropriation."[9]

No one in our time can neglect the irony of Montrose's remark that the academy can readily coopt any oppositional theory or history into the dominant academic ideology. Gates has made his own view clear in this regard, although it remains a paradox. And most feminist critics and historians are themselves institutionally based and this delimits both their vocabulary and their contribution to the larger nonacademic audiences they wish to change. This paradox is nowhere more obvious than in the university classroom where students are confronted by different literary perspectives and vocabularies. In such an environment, oppositional critics often find themselves welcomed into mainstream departments and find that some of their oppositional vocabulary is appropriated by theorists and historical critics who do not see themselves as oppositional.

I have been describing the generation of some contemporary literary histories and I have been trying to indicate the reasons for the generation of the new historicists. But it is necessary to raise the questions about the relation of theory to literary history especially since the new historicists have, as yet, no full-fledged theory of history. What function does theory serve in the generation of literary history? I have given an example of theory generating black history and the generation of literary history from political dissent by the new historicists, and I shall be talking about the generation of literary history by feminist historians. However, the audiences for these histories are in the academy, and this is the arena at present for a debate between those who believe that literary history inevitably involves theory and those who deny that literary theory is of significance in the writing of literary history. Gerald Graff argues for theory as follows:

> Whatever a teacher says about a literary work, or leaves unsaid, presupposes a theory—of what literature is or can be, of which literary works are worth teaching and why, of how these works should be read and which of their aspects are most worth being noticed and pointed out.[10]

And this *resistance* to theory, to altering received formulations or practices is also found among art historians. Rosalind Krauss notes this resistance:

> Art historians are shy of theory, rarely enunciating the ones they must undoubtedly have in order to be able to work at all. Theories of historical change. Theories of continuity. Theories of representation. Theories of the role of form. Theories of referentiality. Theories of function. And most important, theories of verification. For art history is proud of its roots in the German soil of *Wissenschaft*, even before that of *Geschichte*.[11]

What is meant by the statement that "whatever a teacher says about a literary work, or leaves unsaid, presupposes a theory"? Does theory need to be an overt constituent of history writing or is it that the making of statements about literature presupposes some theory about such statement-making? Is the *consciousness* of theoretical statements necessary for the writing of literary history? The very fact that some literary and art historians do not include theorizing in their essays, as these quotations make clear, does not invalidate the statements they make. The selection of texts to discuss in class may be the result of an established curriculum that may or may not have had conscious theorizing behind it.

When Rosalind Krauss remarks that art historians rarely enunciate the theories they "must undoubtedly have in order to be able to work at all," she is implying that their theories ought to be enunciated. But such demands of historians raise questions about the nature of history writing. Must a *necessary* component of history-writing be a consciousness of the grounds of history writing? Not if we realize that we are dealing with a generic problem. History is a kind of writing and so, too, is theory. There is no reason why theory should not be a component of history or history of theory since all genres are combinational. What we wish to know, is whether histories *must* include theoretical discourses. After all, history was combined with romance in the seventeenth century and with biography in the eighteenth—as witness *The History of Tom Jones.*

Literary histories are altered by the introduction of different discourses within them. Feminist discussions of literary history can include autobiographical statements, assumptions about race, gender, and class, about ideology and value. History writing has not only come to include ideological components, but personal statements as well. Since the generation of current histories is my subject, I want to suggest that genre and gender have generated conceptions of history that are ideologically connected with political and sexual theories. For example, Jane Tompkins's version of this history is polemical rather than self-assured, assertive about the need to resurrect feminine texts excluded from American literature. She writes not only in opposition to patriarchal history but to received views of literary value as well. In writing about "*Uncle Tom's Cabin* and the Politics of Literary History," she declares:

> Expressive of and responsible for the values of its [*Uncle Tom's Cabin*] times, it also belongs to a genre, the sentimental novel, whose chief characteristic is that it is written by, for, and about women. In this respect, *Uncle Tom's Cabin* is not exceptional but representative. It is the *summa theologica* of nineteenth-century American religion of domesticity, a brilliant redaction of the culture's favorite story about itself—the story of salvation through motherly love. Out of the ideological materials they had at their disposal, the sentimental novelists elaborated a myth that gave women the central position of power and authority in the culture; and of these efforts *Uncle Tom's Cabin* is the most dazzling exemplar.[12]

In reading *Uncle Tom's Cabin* "as a political enterprise, half way between sermon and social theory, that both codifies and attempts to mold the values of its time," she introduces a combinatory regeneration of the novel form that makes it a model for the kind of history she is writing. She writes with fervor, and anger, and she has generated other feminist histories. If history writing is a genre, then it is obvious that members of this genre will add or omit components from preceding histories. What identifies it as history is that it tells a story of actual events in a structure that resembles prior versions of such storytelling. Thus, when Tompkins seeks to displace the literary history of F. O. Mathiessen, her history is more like his than it is like *Uncle Tom's Cabin* about which she writes. She introduces into her discussion elements from sermons and household texts—not discussed by Mathiessen—to demonstrate that Little Eva's death, for example, "enacts the drama of which all the major episodes of the novel are transformations, the idea, central to Christian soteriology, that the highest human calling is to give one's life for another." Her history is generated not merely by her sense of the deprivation resulting from the exclusion of feminist writing from the canon, but from her disagreement with some of the assumptions of the received historical genre in which she continues to write.

I want to argue the resistance to the received view of a genre generates alterations within it. It is not merely personal resentment or social and economic or literary exclusion or the class opposition, but the omission or addition of components that lead to alterations of writing. This conflict within a genre, this expansion of literary history to include sermons and popular literature also establishes new relations among the genres. Clifford Geertz notes that histories have begun to include equations and tables and law court testimonies and are thus ceasing to be straightforward narratives. Reflecting on the generic changes in anthropological treatises in which theoretical arguments by Lévi-Strauss are set out as travelogues (*Tristes Tropiques*), Geertz believes that a refiguration of knowledge is taking place, a change in what it is we want to know. But genre has never been the fixed form Geertz and others have taken it to be. The extension of literary history by conflicts within the genre and with other genres for primacy has begun to diminish the significance of theory even by those who include it; and theory itself as a genre has come in the work of Richard Rorty to be narrativized as fiction. What these regenerated genres do is to make us question the generic combinations we have come to accept, and our consciousness of history as a given. In fact, one of the most prominent examples of regeneration in history writing is Hayden White's. For him history becomes a form of literary history. His argument is as follows:

> It is because historical discourse utilizes structures of meaning-production found in their purest forms in literary fictions that modern literary theory, and especially those versions of it oriented towards tropological conceptions of language, discourse, and textuality, is immediately relevant to contemporary theory of historical writing.[13]

White points out that theorists of historical discourse cannot ignore literary theorists' new conceptions of language, speech, and textuality because these have "reproblematized an area of inquiry which, in historical theory at least, had for too long been treated as having nothing problematical about it." The new views of language in literary theory are far from definitive, involving disagreements about the indeterminacy of language, the nature of its acculturation, the interaction between grammar and rhetoric, the distinction between literary and nonliterary language.

But insofar as literary theory is a discourse about discourses, it inevitably analyzes the discourses of history and is, therefore, for White a theory of history as well as of literature. In White's terms, "modern literary theory must of necessity be a theory of history, historical consciousness, historical discourse, and historical writing." The different components of literary theory extend like a web through White's version of history which obviously is at the opposite pole from those historians who resist theory in history writing.

White conceives of history as narrative and takes for granted that no unmediated—objective—history exists. As a narrative it involves a plot and falls into one of the four types of plots that White envisions. White interprets history writing as a literary structure since the narrative is composed of facts. Insofar as these are imaginatively plotted, they deny both the objectivity of history and its arbitrariness. It is apparent, however, that White's narratives are coherent rather than examples of aporias. But there is no reason to assume that history as literary history need be one single discourse. It can be structured with intersections from psychoanalytic or Marxist narratives.

What does this story of generic generation have to say about the role of literary history in our understanding of past texts? It compels us to see literary history as a series of transformations derived from generic intersections, conflicts, and oppositions. It provides an awareness of literary history as necessarily involving ideological conflicts since genres as they change nevertheless have some continuous elements. These are ideologically discontinuous with the additions that literary history includes. One might say that the different discourses in literary history are often at odds with each other. But more problematic is White's claim that history is a fictional genre. A history of the French revolution is indeed like a history of the novel. But both histories are more like other histories than like poems, plays, or acts of violence. Literary history, therefore, can contain selections from the interpretations of fictive genres but these are subservient to the ends of history.

The generations of literary history that I have been describing, the shifting conceptions of genre, compel us to ask as Geertz does what such formulations imply. Literary history as genre is obviously connected with social change, as in the effort to provide blacks with pride in their tradition, women with a new view of the importance of feminine bonding, minority readers with a consciousness of their exploitation, majorities with a sense of shame and guilt for their exploitation of others. These social aims are linked to identifying new relations among texts, including texts that have never been considered worthy of study. Oral texts are part of literary history including the lyrics of ballads and of contemporary songs by the various rock groups. Literary history includes the study of publishing practices, editors' revisions of manuscripts, the selection of books to print for profit, the incorporation of publishing into conglomerates that produce books, oil, and cereals. The commodification of books in our time has led critics to recognize ideology where previously was found individual creativity. The varieties of literary history, whether by contending black critics or feminist critics or Marxist critics or psychoanalytic critics, reveal how exclusive has been the literary history we have been teaching, for the audiences for literary history are primarily to be found in the institutions of learning where new histories and old histories still exist door by door.

It is sad to read that our most eminent historian of literary criticism, René Wellek, surveying his own work and the current scene, sees "The Fall of Literary History."

> The new literary history promises only a return to the old one: the history of tradition, genres, reputations, etc., less atomistically conceived as in older times, with greater awareness of the difficulties of such concepts as influence and periods but still the old one.
>
> Possibly, this is a good and right thing. The attempts at an evolutionary history have failed. I myself have failed in *The History of Modern Criticism* to construe a convincing scheme of development. I discovered, by experience, that there is no evolution in the history of critical argument, that the history of criticism is rather a series of debates on recurrent concepts, on "essentially contested concepts," on permanent problems in the sense that they are with us even today. Possibly, a similar conclusion is required for the history of poetry itself. "Art," said Schopenhauer, "has always reached its goal." Croce and Ker are right. There is no progress, no development, no history of art except a history of writers and institutions or techniques. This is, at least for me, the end of an illusion, the fall of literary history.[14]

But the assumption that literary history was teleological in an evolutionary sense was a mistake to begin with. The discourses of literary history as a genre should compel us to extend our understanding of what is at stake in the shifting components of a genre. We realize now how inadequate a conception of literature is that takes no account of paintings that include writing or illustrate writing, that disregards the music in sung prayers and oratorios, that sees no relation between Descartes's *Meditations* and the meditative poem or Shaftesbury's and Mandeville's dialogues and the development of the novel, between the narratives of criminals and the parodies of affairs of state.

When we consider the mixed media of fiction and television that no longer privilege words but connect them with images of the body and of the environment and with music, we realize how exclusive our histories of literature have been in ignoring the body in writing. No user of word processors can ignore the physiological role one feels in writing or in the order that appears on the screen shielding the disorder of one's thoughts. The generation of new literary histories opens for us the multiform nature of generation: a literary history possesses vestiges of past histories in a contemporary narrative, a narrative that is knowledgeable about past histories; knowledgeable about such generic practices as the ingestion of other genres for ideological purposes, their borrowings or claims to be what they are not to make the unacceptable respectable, the undermining of social practices by romance strategies. Interrelations revealed by past work result in literary genres shaping the consciousness of readers by avoiding or ignoring authors' autobiographical statements about their aims or ideological strategies such as inset stories or sermons or sermonic procedures. Generating such literary histories makes us conscious that while much of history is unrecoverable much remains to be discovered. But this discovery may need to be done, if it is to reach beyond the classroom, to a history that includes sounds and sights.

I conclude by returning to the generation of this essay, to the theories of the Algerian Jew that I related to place, exclusion, and colonization. No single statement about ideology or theory or tradition can adequately account for a literary history linked with genres that complicate social aims with autobiographical memories and generic competitions. I ask you to listen to the voice of another Algerian Jew, Hélène Cixous, describing a history of her writing. I do this to illustrate that her history is not one of alienation or resentment, but of love of words, place, and gender. Her writing became intertwined with herself and the Other; it became part of her body, her family, her culture, her ethnic identity, her gender, her sense of alienation, and her awareness of mysteries beyond language. Hers is an autobiographical literary history that reveals to us the possibilities we have missed and the opportunities we have before us.

> My writing was born in Algeria out of a lost country of the dead father and the foreign mother. Each of these traits which may seem to be chance or mischance became the causes and opportunities of my writings.
>
> I have had the luck to have foreignness, exile, war, the phantom memory of peace, mourning and pain as the place and time of my birth. At the age of three I knew, among the flowers and their scents, that one could kill for a name, for a difference. And I knew that uprooting existed. But also good uprooting. I should give you a date as well, 1940 for instance. I saw that human roots know no borders and that under the earth, at the very bottom of the ladder of the world, the heart was beating.
>
> My first others were the Arabs, the scarabaei, the French, the Germans. My first familiars were the hens, the rabbits, the Arabs, the Germans, etc.

And the tongue that was singing in my ears? It was languages: Spanish, Arabic, German, French. Everything on this earth comes from far off, even what is very near. I listened to all the languages. I sang in German. I also cackled with the hens. I lost myself often within the city of my birth. I was a veiled woman: it was a signifier. It was ORAN. I had everything:

OR–AN – HORS EN – ORAN–JE

(Golden-year) (Outside-in) (Oran-I: Orange)

The first of my treasures was the same of my native city which was Oran. It was my first lesson. I heard the name Oran and through Oran I entered the secret of language. My "sortie" occurred through entrance. I discovered that my city meant *fruit* through the simple addition of me. *Oran–je—Orange*. I discovered that the word held all the mystery of fruit. I will let you unravel to infinity the composition, decomposition of this name. Then I lost Oran. Then I recovered it, white, gold and dust for eternity in my memory and I never went back. In order to keep it. It became my writing. Like my father. It became a magic door opening onto the other world.[15]

NOTES

1. Henry Louis Gates, Jr., "Authority, (White) Power, and the (Black) Critic; or, it's all Greek to me," in *The Future of Literary Theory*, ed. Ralph Cohen (New York: Routledge, 1989), p. 344.

2. T. S. Eliot, "Tradition and the Individual Talent," in *Selected Essays of T. S. Eliot* (New York: Harcourt, Brace, and World, 1964), p. 4.

3. Stephen J. Greenblatt, "Introduction" to *The Forms of Power and the Power of Forms in the Renaissance*, special issue *Genre* 15 (Spring 1982): 1–2.

4. Louis Montrose, "Renaissance Literary Studies and the Subject of History," *English Literary Renaissance* 16 (1986): 6.

5. Samuel Johnson, *A Dictionary of the English Language* (London, 1755).

6. Montrose, "Renaissance Literary Studies and the Subject of History": 10. Montrose is discussing the work of Jonathan Dollimore and Alan Sinfield.

7. Fredric Jameson, *The Political Unconscious* (Ithaca: Cornell University Press, 1981), p. 9; and "Religion and ideology: a political reading of *Paradise Lost*," in *Literature, Politics and Theory: Papers from the Essex Conference 1976–1984*, ed. Frances Barker, Peter Hulme, Margaret Iversen, and Diana Loxley (London: Methuen, 1986), p. 39.

8. Montrose, "Renaissance Literary Studies and the Subject of History": 8. Montrose has expanded his discussion in "Professing the Renaissance: The Poetics and Politics of Culture," in *The New Historicism*, ed. H. Aram Veeser (New York: Routledge, 1989), pp. 15–36.

9. Montrose, "Renaissance Literary Studies and the Subject of History": 7, n4. Montrose is contrasting the work of American new historicists such as himself and Stephen Greenblatt with the work of British cultural materialists such as Jonathan Dollimore and Alan Sinfield who owe a major debt to Raymond Williams.

10. Gerald Graff, "The Future of Theory in the Teaching of Literature," in *The Future of Literary Theory*, p. 250.

11. Rosalind Krauss, "The Future of an Illusion," in *The Future of Literary Theory*, p. 281.

12. Jane Tompkins, *Sensational Designs: The Cultural Work of American Fiction 1790–1860* (New York: Oxford University Press, 1985), pp. 124–25.

13. Hayden White, " 'Figuring the nature of the times deceased': Literary Theory and History Writing," in *The Future of Literary Theory*, p. 36.

14. René Wellek, "The Fall of Literary History," in *The Attack on Literature and Other Essays* (Chapel Hill: University of North Carolina Press, 1982), p. 77.

15. Hélène Cixous, "From the Scene of the Unconscious to the Scene of History," in *The Future of Literary Theory*, p. 2.

CHAPTER TWO

Texts and Works:
Some Historical Questions on the Editing
of Old English Verse

KATHERINE O'BRIEN O'KEEFFE

"Every image of the past that is not recognized by
the present as one of its own concerns threatens to
disappear irretrievably."
(Walter Benjamin, Illuminations*)*

MODERN SCHOLARSHIP in Old English literature has had as its object the recovery of a body of mainly pre-Conquest vernacular texts and the creation of a context within which to understand them. In these twin endeavors, its predominant methodological focus may be broadly described as "historical," with boundaries, interests, and limitations determined by the critical procedures under which such researches are carried out.[1] The historical situation of Old English scholarship itself has been marked by a number of scholars. The political programs of the scholarship of earlier ages—the Renaissance (and later) interest in an Anglo-Saxon church and an English Protestant theology, the eighteenth-century American desire for roots in an authentic Anglo-Saxon democracy, the nineteenth-century use of Anglo-Saxon materials in the creation of nationalistic and romantic myths—now may appear transparent to us, though the ideological formations behind current scholarship in Old English are less apparent because more with us.[2] My interest in this essay is not the historical content or strategic limitations of current criticism as such, but rather the body of procedures on which any criticism of Old English verse texts necessarily depends—the editing practices which present those texts.

The philosophical and literary criticism of the last twenty years has urged us to consider, and sometimes painfully, that no text is innocent, no criticism objective, and that our encounters with the worlds of the present and of the past are mediated through ideologies. Acknowledging these difficult lessons, I should like to look at that element of the Old English enterprise which has made the fullest claim to objectivity—the scholarly edition. A scholarly edition may be properly understood as an articulation of a discursive system, and such an edition is generally evaluated by the scholarly community on the degree to which the edition conforms to the rigors of that system. Lying behind any evaluation of an edition is a set of answers to the question, "What do we expect (or wish) to see in this edition?" For members of that scholarly community and practitioners of that scholarly discourse it is at times difficult to remember as well that an edition functions doubly—it presents what we cannot help seeing (because the limit of information in an edition is determined by what the scholarly community has set out to find) and it hides what we are blinded from seeing (because some information may be deemed "uninteresting," or "unimportant," or, for various historical reasons, may be unthinkable). This double function suggests the importance of a continuing review of the goals and methods of scholarly editions.

In their monumental Anglo-Saxon Poetic Records, now the standard editions of Old English verse, George P. Krapp and Elliott Van Kirk Dobbie adopted a highly conservative posture toward the manuscript evidence. As Krapp wrote in his introduction to volume I, "The texts of the poems in this edition are kept as free as possible of scholarly intrusions, paleographical, typographical, grammatical, or otherwise illustrative and editorial, and the necessary machinery of exposition and interpretation is placed in the introduction and in the notes, where it seems more properly to belong. The two main duties of an editor, that of preserving a faithful record of the manuscript and that of taking account of all significant contributions to the understanding of the manuscript, it is hoped will be satisfactorily met in this way."[3]

The array of the text produced in this way is very clean: emendations are deliberately few, and the apparatus is limited to presenting either the original manuscript reading, when the text has been emended, or recording instances of scribal correction or physical damage. In the cases of illegibility or loss, no restoration is attempted, and missing letters are simply indicated by points within brackets.[4] Abbreviations are expanded without comment. As is now standard in the modern editing of Old English verse, the lineation, capitalization, punctuation, and placement of accents in the manuscript are silently replaced by practices of modern print conventions. The poetry is printed in verse lines, with an extended space to mark a caesura between "half-lines"; syntax is interpreted through modern punctuation and capitalization. Capitals, accents, and so-called sectional divisions of the manuscripts are collected in tables as part of the prefatory matter, and marks of punctuation are briefly described.[5]

Krapp notes in his preface (thinking perhaps of the tasks facing the editors of classical texts) that much of the job of an editor of Old English verse is simplified by the fact that most Old English poetry is preserved in only one manuscript version. However, for those poems which are attested multiply, the ASPR reveals a variety of procedures underlying the establishment of the text.[6] These may be most pointedly illustrated in the editing of two very different kinds of poem, Caedmon's *Hymn* and *Solomon and Saturn I*.

For Caedmon's *Hymn*, one of the best attested poems in Old English, the ASPR prints two texts.[7] In the first instance Dobbie uses Cambridge, University Library Kk. 5. 16 (M, ca. 737?) as the base text for the M–L version.[8] In the second, the base text is taken from Oxford, Bodleian Library, Tanner 10 (T, s. x[1], for the text of the *Æ version). Dobbie does not print a text for the version occurring in a third group (*Z), those West-Saxon descendants of the older Northumbrian version, because, in his view, its readings lack interest.[9]

The two printed, and now canonical, versions of Caedmon's *Hymn* owe their separate existences to an interest in early dialect forms: the oldest and the earliest Northumbrian state of the text is represented by M, the oldest West-Saxon state of the text by T.[10] While the reasoning behind such choices may be defended on the basis of the philological importance of the material being edited, the gain for philology necessarily leads to the loss of other useful information. According to Dobbie, the crucial difference between the versions of Caedmon's *Hymn* lies in the variation on line 5b—*aelda barnum* (M)/*eorðan bearnum* (T)—which in his view must have occurred early.[11] And although he regards *ælda* as the "more probable" candidate for the reading in "the original Northumbrian text," *eorðan* is preserved as a result of the ASPR's commendably conservative treatment of manuscript witnesses.[12] Yet Dobbie's single edition of the "West Saxon Version" from Tanner 10 effectively suppresses the interesting fact that the core of the semantically, syntactically, and metrically appropriate variants in the *Hymn* occur in *Æ, those five manuscripts where the *Hymn* is transmitted as part of the West-Saxon translation of the *Historia ecclesiastica*.[13] Their variety must raise serious questions about how meaningful the term "West Saxon Version" can be, beneath its imprimatur of uniformity and authority. Indeed, scribal variation from such a version is routinely inferred to be the result of error or incompetence, and with such a judgment Dobbie writes off the variations in the other group of West Saxon texts, *Z.[14] The variations in *Æ receive no separate consideration beyond a record in the textual apparatus.

Even as the ASPR seeks to follow an editing methodolgy scrupulously faithful to the manuscript record, it is less faithful than one might think. While *Soul and Body*, which is transmitted with significant variations in both the Exeter Book and the Vercelli Book, appears in separately edited texts (a strategy to preserve the integrity of the individually edited manuscripts which comprise volumes I–V of the ASPR),[15] *Solomon and Saturn I*, a poem transmitted in part by two manuscripts, is printed as a composite text.[16] Cambridge, Corpus Christi College 41 (B) transmits only the first ninety-four lines of the poem. Cambridge, Corpus Christi College 422 (A) transmits considerably more, but is illegible for lines 1–30. In Dobbie's words, "By putting the evidence of the two manuscripts together, we have a fairly complete text."[17] The first thirty lines of the text in the ASPR then is based on CCCC 41, a mid-eleventh-century copy, and the rest on the version in CCCC 422, copied in the late tenth century. Such an editorial procedure is not unusual, but in this case, it produces a synthetic modern composition, which does more than simply raze the differences between the two witnesses to a lowest common denominator.

Quite apart from orthographic differences, copying errors, and differing graphic practices, the sixty-three lines of *Solomon and Saturn I* attested by both manuscripts (lines 30–94a) contain as well ten pairs of truly alternate readings between which there is no clear choice.[18] For the shared lines, Dobbie prints the version from A only, and the readings from B are relegated to the apparatus. Even if we choose to ignore the implication of such a placement—that these readings are of small consequence—we are still presented with logical difficulties. Since it is unlikely that so high a number of lexically appropriate variants between the two versions would be restricted to lines 30–94a, the chances are very good that lines 1–30 in the ASPR edition, those lines supplied from B, contain a number of variants from the lines now illegible in A.

The textual consequences of such operations are significant. The relegation of the important lexical variants in B to the apparatus interprets any variation as damage or error insofar as it deviates from a postulated authorial text. Yet against the validity of such an interpretation stand the many significant variants in the transmissions of Caedmon's *Hymn*, *Soul and Body*, Exeter Riddle 30 (A and B), *The Battle of Brunanburh*, as well as in *Solomon and Saturn I*. The richness of such variants bespeaks a participatory transmission, where the scribe becomes a partner in presenting the text to the world. The production of an authoritative edition, however, hides such evidence of alternate forms of literacy in reading and copying, reception and reproduction, leveling medieval textual reproduction to our own benchmarks of accuracy and uniformity. Ironically, the consequence of the editorial "recovery" of the text of *Solomon and Saturn I* is the production of a modern redaction which conflates two distinct moments in the history of this poem. These edited texts of volume VI wander far indeed from "a faithful record of the manuscript."

The reduction of variety in the appearances of Caedmon's *Hymn* and the production of a composite text for *Solomon and Saturn I* are editorial maneuvers which presuppose the absolute separability of the text from the manuscript. Such a presupposition also permits the editor to disregard the poem's various manuscript formats. The *Hymn*'s status as a gloss in the M–L and *Z version barely receives notice, and the widely varying use of capitals and points in the different versions is simply ignored.[19] Similarly, while Dobbie notes that CCCC 41 transmits a number of Latin and Old English texts in the margins of the Old English translation of Bede's *Historia ecclesiastica*, he does not discuss the textual array of *Solomon and Saturn I*, nor its interesting use of capitals, nor its points.[20]

The manuscript of a poetic text subject to an editor's operations seems always to be a disappointment, never being either old enough nor accurate enough, because it is not a holograph.[21] Subject to corruption by its stay in the world, the poem requires some degree of rehabilitation in the process of editing to restore it as far as possible to a state close to authorial. The twin dissatisfactions underlying these editorial postures—the desire for an original (originary?) manuscript and authorial voice and the general disregard of manuscript formatting—are hallmarks of two ideological formations standing behind the editing of Old English. The first two are traceable to the nineteenth-century heritage of Old English studies and are products of the modern reflex of romantic ideology.[22] The impulse to transcend the worldly appears in any idealist attempt to recover the original and the authorial, but flight from the material world is only partly responsible for the general disregard of scribal format. The latter is more nearly the result of what may be termed a "literate ideology," in which assumptions inherent in our own literacy blind us to forms of literacy other than our own.

The most distinguishing hallmark of literate ideology is the unspoken assumption that literacy is a unitary phenomenon whose shape is defined by the *modern* conditions of literacy. The ideology functions by excepting literacy from the operations of history. Thus some assumptions, at first blush, quite modest—that the ability to write implies literacy as we understand it; that reading and writing are naturally conjoint skills; that "word" is a verbal unit expressed by letters bounded on each side by a space; that hierarchies of information are expressed graphically and spatially—are, in fact, highly problematic in editing texts of the early Middle Ages. Literacy is a phenomenon with a discernible historical development which is culture and time specific.[23] Evidence for the praxis of literacy—and an important index of its development—lies in the writing of the manuscripts. The details of scribal usage: the plasticity of "word," the graphic significance of space, the developing codification of punctuation, significant variation, copying slips, are more than simply background to our reading. They are the material condition for the presentation of Old English verse. They ground the poem in the world.

The functional reduction of variety in modern printed media (from regular orthography through the uniformity of fonts and spacing) and the ubiquity of print make books appear unremarkable, writing appear the transparent medium through which we encounter another's thoughts. Our own literacy fosters the illusion that the material aspects of writing are insignificant and all but dispensable. Barthes's separation of text from work (among other things a flight from the material object) may thus be understood as symptomatic of the development of literate ideology in the twentieth century.[24] And one might similarly read literate ideology as the ground of Derrida's spectacular subversion of "phonocentrism."[25] In medieval studies, work on early texts which presupposes a binary opposition between orality and literacy shows as well the operation of literate ideology.[26]

When, as the manuscripts persistently demonstrate, the actual praxis of literacy in the early Middle Ages was significantly different from our own, by what warrant does a textual editor describe and then dismiss the layout, lineation, capitalization, and punctuation of a manuscript, other than by the assumption that the physical details of a manuscript are of small importance relative to the text being transmitted? Such a move necessarily implies that the text is fully separable from the reality which the transmitting manuscript assured it. The flight from history underlying this position unites the operation of literate ideology with the romantic impetus to find an origin and to seek the authorial. Ironically, in a discipline so thoroughly wedded to history, the operations of these ideologies prevent the coherent integration of historical considerations in the presentation of an edition of Old English verse.

The modern blindness to issues of layout, capitalization, lineation, and punctuation is at work in the earliest attempts to present Old English verse to a modern audience. Although John Conybeare did not live to see his groundbreaking 1826 edition of Old English verse through the printing process, his brother, William, completed the task as editor of the volume.[27] In an addendum considering questions of verse form, William Conybeare discusses the rationale behind the presentation of the edition:

> Some discussion has taken place on the continent whether these short metrical systems should be regarded as entire lines, or hemistichs only; the remaining half of the alliterative couplet being included, in order to complete the full line: i.e. whether we ought to arrange the following lines thus:
>
>> Fæȝe Feollon
>> Feld dynode
>> Secȝa Swate
>> Siððan Sunne up
>> on Morȝan tid
>> Mære tuncȝol
>> Glad ofer Grundas
>> Godes candel beorht

Eces Drihtnes
oððæt sio AEðele ʒesceaft
Sah to Setle.

or thus:

Fæʒe feollon . feld dynode
Secʒa swate . siððan sunne up
On morʒen tid . mære tuncʒol
Glad ofer ʒrundas . Godes candel beorht
Eces Drihtnes . oððæt seo æðele ʒesceaft
sah to setle.

   To me the whole question appears to belong to the typographer rather than
the critic: whichever mode be adopted, the internal structure of the verse is
altogether unaffected; and our decision may be safely regulated by the convenience of the press. So far as use and authority are concerned, however, these
are clearly in favour of the division into shorter lines: but it must be allowed that
the second method would have the advantage of rendering the alliteration more
prominent, and illustrating the identity of the Saxon metre and that of Piers
Plowman, which is always thus printed.[28]

William Conybeare's argument is a fascinating example of the workings of
literate ideology. That information may be contained in the manuscript's
format, spacing, and punctuation is never entertained. While he has no alternative but to use space and typography to advance his argument about the
possibilities for presenting verse editorially, he simultaneously asserts that
neither space nor typography is significant to interpretation. To all appearances, a reader simply transcends such details of presentation as capitalization, lineation, and punctuation—matters sufficiently trivial to be relegated
to the production end of an edition.[29]

   Conybeare, the third Rawlinson Professor of Anglo-Saxon at Oxford, directed important scholarly attention to Old English verse, and this interest
would be quickly continued and developed by John Mitchell Kemble and
Benjamin Thorpe. Thorpe responded directly to Conybeare's posthumous
extracts from the Junius Manuscript in an effort to correct numerous "in-
accuracies, both editorial and typographical" in Conybeare's edition.[30]
Thorpe's 1832 edition was the first work published by the Society of Antiquaries of London in its series devoted to "Anglo-Saxon and Early English
Literary Remains." Thorpe presents the texts of the Junius Manuscript (plus
Azarias from the Exeter Book) in hemistichs with "corrected" scribal punctuation and in a typeface designed to imitate the letter forms of Anglo-Saxon
Square Minuscule: insular æ, d, f, g, r, s, t, ð, þ, w, dotted y, as well as
abbreviations for *ðæt* and *ond*.[31] A facing English translation is provided.

   John Mitchell Kemble's comparative study of the Solomon and Marculf

legend, ready for the printer in 1835, had to wait thirteen years to be published as numbers 8, 13, and 14 by the newly formed Aelfric Society in
1848.[32] Although the Aelfric Society used the same press as the Society of
Antiquaries, the typeface in the two editions differed considerably. Kemble's is most nearly a "modern" edition. Though still arrayed in hemistichs,
Kemble's *Solomon and Saturn I*, a composite edition with CCCC 422 as the
base text, is printed in the modern conventions of typeface, with insular
characters limited to æ, ð, and þ.[33] Although accents in the manuscript are
printed, punctuation and capitalization are silently modernized.

The dissonances I have been highlighting show a difference between two
concepts of a poem and its presentation. The standard concept, with its roots
in the romantic period, seeks an ideal text, untouched by the world. The
other concept pursues the historical, actual text, present in the matrix of
social production. It is certainly possible to conceive of an "idealist" text.
Such an idea necessarily refers to a product of the mind and intention of an
author unmarked by existence in the world. In the world, this ideal text is
necessarily subject to change by damage, error, corruption, and, most subtly,
by interpretation. (There thus will be a problem even with the author's writing a text down because at that point the "ideal" text leaves his or her control.) A *realized* text, on the other hand, is that object which is written down,
transmitted, understood, changed, improved, corrupted, and which also
changes, improves, affects, corrupts as it becomes known and used. Realized
texts situate us in the world: they are *works* in the sense that they are the
product of labor, at some points authorial, at others certainly scribal, and in
many circumstances, are productive of future labor by readers. The work
fixes the abstraction "text" in time and space. This fixing locates a realized
text temporally and geographically (as a manuscript may be dated and
placed). Its writing embodies a discourse well after its author no longer exists, fixing it spatially in conventional arrays which encode a meaning completely destroyed by translation to print. The production of an ideal text is
always an exercise in translation and interpretation. As such, it is an interesting and legitimate process, but its end product may hide as much as it reveals about the text in question. In the work, the text is made real and given
a history.[34]

In the light of this distinction, the options available for producing editions
of Old English verse require examination. The preeminent classical editorial
methods, inherited variously from the traditions of Lachmann and Greg,
offer a textual reconstruction which transcends the "merely" historical in the
recovery of a text by "scientific" means. Greg's "calculus" of variants for
printed texts presupposed a nineteenth-century confidence in the adequacy
of scientific (=evolutionary?) reconstruction, and the resulting creations
were usually given authorial status. However, the objectivity of this process
is plainly open to question. And that mode of editing which would temper

the simple logical calculus with "taste" or "experience" or "knowledge of the author's style" is, despite Lee Patterson's impressive arguments, probably impossible to defend from the charge of eclecticism or solecism.[35] These modes of editing presume to incarnate an idealist abstraction, yet the resulting "authorial" text is invariably remade, hybrid, stripped of its context, spatial arrangements, and visual conventions. This edited text, by privileging an *idea* of composition over actual, *realized* texts (i.e., those records surviving in manuscript) hides from the modern reader the condition of early literacy. Equally flawed are the traditional diplomatic editions, which are open to the charge of naive empiricism. And there is much merit to such a charge, particularly when even a diplomatic edition necessarily produces a visual array which conceals historically important visual information encoded in the manuscript.[36]

The methods of Lachmann and Greg were marked by genius and certainly advanced editing as a discipline well beyond their own times. Krapp and Dobbie too were giants, given the task they set out to accomplish in the Anglo-Saxon Poetic Records. Indeed, without the nineteenth-century concept of textual editing as backdrop, we would not have the rigorous philological method which gives us our knowledge of Old English. Nonetheless, a knowledge of the historical particulars of vernacular textual transmission and a respect for the manuscripts as witnesses ask us to question the theory behind the editing currently done.

No matter what the particulars of its practice, the general discourse of medieval editing bespeaks the persistent specter of an "authorial" text which seeks recovery from the world. This desire for the "authorial" is embedded in the axioms of each style of editing. It is as present in George Kane's conjecturalist principles that "the editor of a major poet must begin with a presumption of the excellence of his author; he is also governed by an axiom that texts, including archetypal texts, are corrupt,"[37] as it is in G. P. Krapp's highly conservative posture:

> It is scarcely necessary for a modern editor to be a greater purist in spelling than an eleventh century professional scribe, especially one so conscientious and capable as the scribe of the Vercelli Book appears to have been. It is to be regretted that the present state of Anglo-Saxon scholarship does not permit more positive convictions with respect to authorship and date of composition of the Anglo-Saxon poetical monuments, with respect also to the methods of composition and construction employed by Anglo-Saxon poets, or to the metrical principles according to which they wrote, or to the mixture of linguistic forms, dialectal or otherwise, which appear in the recorded texts. If a sceptical attitude towards all these questions still seems necessary after so many years of study, the hope nevertheless remains that further examination, and from new angles, will bring more certain results.[38]

Because most Old English poems are anonymous, and as products of a period of transitional literacy, changed in various ways during their transmission, modern-literate assumptions about an invariate, authorial text are misleading when applied to early literate cultures. In a limited transmission when it is logically impossible to recover an "authorial" reading, what does it mean to speak of the *Beowulf* poet, for example, save to long for an origin which ensures (by definition) "authority" for a reading of which we approve?

Finally, whichever the approach (whether an idealist or even a semidiplomatic edition), the manuscript text is translated into modern graphic array. Current editions break Old English verse spatially into lines and half-lines, although these visual conventions never appear in the manuscripts. Editors add modern spacing between words, modern capitalization, and modern punctuation, even when these twentieth-century conventions force an interpretation or level ambiguity.[39] The romantic and literate ideologies underlying the desire for a single, supposedly authorial text divert attention from what the manuscripts of poems in multiple copies tell us: that the copying of Old English verse was a participatory transmission, that semantically appropriate, metrically correct variants are legitimate parts of the history of these texts, and that the manuscripts as cultural objects preserve *realized* works which had a documented existence in history.

What, then, remains hidden in all styles of editions? The "authorial" suppresses the scribal, the ideal suppresses the actual, the text suppresses the work. The "actual" in this schema is the text-in-the-world, that is, the textual, material object, the manuscript which encodes a reading, an understanding, an attitude, a time, and a place. Scribal execution (and I am speaking *particularly* here of the circumstances of Old English verse) gives us at once production, reproduction, reading, participation. It *realizes* the text, and that realized text offers an entrée into a world of perception.

Current methods of editing, while admirable in their various strengths, nonetheless set rigid limits on the recuperation of literary production in its fullest cultural and social dimensions. This limitation will not be addressed by replacing an emphasis on the author as the privileged creator of a text with an equally distorting emphasis on that text as an articulation of a larger Discourse. In light of the compelling reasons for viewing a surviving Old English poetic text as a social production, I argue that a poem's material condition and its situation in the world require recognition and representation in an edition. No less important than the producer of a poetic text are the reproducers of those texts, the scribes, without whom the work would no longer exist. This is especially the case for verse, where the evidence of transmission suggests participatory reading.

The goal of a modern scholarly edition of an Old English poem is a version of the poem which is both responsible and readable. In an important sense, any edited text is yet one more reproduction of the poem in question, taking its place in the historical sequence of the poem's appearances in the world. It is an approximation to the text of the poem, not the poem itself. Its construction is also part of a social matrix where methods of editing are determined by agreed-upon scholarly procedures, choice of format determined by modern literate print conventions.

Countering the operations of romantic and literate ideologies in our apprehension of Old English verse must begin at the most fundamental level of editing. I do not propose an alternative *method* of editing (for we have methods enough) but rather wish to suggest an alternative *strategy* to produce a historically self-conscious edition. If the production of a scholarly edition requires editorial intervention in the form of emendation, punctuation, and format to achieve readability, it also demands responsibility to the historical situation of the poem in its realized manuscript text. These twin goals of modern readability and historical responsibility may be approached by a specific kind of facing edition where the poem, whether attested singly or in multiple manuscripts, is presented in an edited version faced by a scrupulously archaeological mapping of the manuscript in print.[40] Such a format permits what is in effect a dialectical approach to surviving textual evidence, allowing the production of a readable edition which at the same time acknowledges itself as both an approximation to and an interpretation of the edited poem. The historical self-consciousness of such a text is made possible by the facing "diplomatic" printing of a manuscript version as each recovery of the text comments on the other.

The juxtaposition of these two modes of editing will underscore the nature and number of visual and author-based assumptions made in standard editorial procedure and will help the modern reader to avoid anachronistic readings based on modern spatial assumptions. Such an edition not only stresses the partnership which the modern editor shares with the scribe, but through its mode of presentation (incorporated on the page and evoked in the strategy for using the page) prevents both the fetishizing of the work *as* manuscript text and the idealizing of the text as a formalist icon. It recognizes as well that the poetic text so produced is a social product irrevocably marked by the interests and ideologies of our time. And when, in the case of a multiply-attested poem, it must provide a mapping of one manuscript version, it admits that no edition of a multiply transmitted poem is final or authoritative.

I offer this editorial strategy as one possible way around the difficulties, limitations, and, at times, logical contradictions inherent in the single use of current modes of editing. The social and material nature of textual production I have been arguing may well be demonstrated by the immediate reservations which I suspect this proposal will call forth: that it is impractical, that no press would touch it, that it would be too expensive to produce and buy. Considerations of these sorts remind us of the social, economic, the *material* existence of literary production in the world. The simple exercise of making this proposal is itself revelatory of the degree to which the visual and the material are constituents of textual meaning. And there is a pleasant irony in the idealism behind proposing such an edition (given market and publishing constraints) in order to bring into balance the material nature of medieval text production.

Clearly in Old English, codicological as well as literary matters are valued and studied. What I suggest, however, is that they be studied materially, formally, and practically together, that textual criticism and codicological criticism work hand in hand to present to the modern reader of Old English verse a work which reveals more than it hides.

NOTES

1. On traditional philology in medieval studies see Stephen G. Nichols's introduction to *The New Philology*, "Philology in a Manuscript Culture," in *Speculum* 65 (1990): 1–18 at 2–7. See also the remarks of Paul Zumthor, *Speaking of the Middle Ages*, trans. Sarah White (Lincoln, Nebr. and London: University of Nebraska Press, 1986), pp. 48–50. For a critique of both exegetic and formalist methods see Lee Patterson, *Negotiating the Past* (Madison: University of Wisconsin Press, 1987), pp. 18–39.

2. See Michael Murphy, "Antiquary to Academic: The Progress of Anglo-Saxon Scholarship," in Carl T. Berkhout and Milton McC. Gatch, eds., *Anglo-Saxon Scholarship: The First Three Centuries* (Boston: G. K. Hall, 1982), pp. 1–17; Stanley R. Hauer, "Thomas Jefferson and the Anglo-Saxon Language," *PMLA* 98 (1983): 879–98 at 880; Allen J. Frantzen and Charles L. Venegoni, "An Archeology of Anglo-Saxon Studies," *Style* 20 (1986): 142–55.

3. George Philip Krapp, ed., *The Junius Manuscript* ASPR I (New York, 1931), p. v.

4. The exception is vol. 4, *Beowulf and Judith*, the last to be edited in the series. Here Dobbie offers in square brackets conjectural restorations. See Elliott Van Kirk Dobbie, ed., *Beowulf and Judith*, ASPR IV (New York, 1953), p. vi.

5. The regular metrical punctuation of the Junius Manuscript is discussed in ASPR I, pp. xxii–xxiii. N. R. Ker offers important corrections to this discussion in his *Catalogue of Manuscripts Containing Anglo-Saxon* (Oxford: Clarendon Press, 1957), p. 408. ASPR vols. II–V each discusses punctuation and accents in general. Volume 6, as a miscellaneous collection, omits to discuss the finer points of individual manuscript presentation.

6. These include Caedmon's *Hymn*, Bede's *Death Song*, the Leiden Riddle, *Soul and Body*, Exeter Riddle 30, the Metrical Preface and Epilogue to Alfred's *Pastoral Care*, the verse of the Anglo-Saxon Chronicle, *Solomon and Saturn I*. For a general critique of assumptions in the editing of Old English verse see Wilhelm G. Busse, "Assumptions in the Establishment of Old English Poetic Texts: P. J. Lucas's Edition of 'Exodus,' " *Arbeiten aus Anglistik und Amerikanistik* 6 (1981): 197–219. See also Michael Lapidge, "Textual Criticism and the Literature of Anglo-Saxon England,"

Bulletin of the John Rylands University Library of Manchester, 73 (1991): 17–45, esp. 38–45.

7. The ASPR prints three texts for Bede's *Death Song*, a Northumbrian (St. Gallen, Stiftsbibliothek 254), a West-Saxon (Oxford, Bodleian Library, Digby 211), and a mixed version, (Hague, Koninklijke Bibliothek, 70. H. 7) in ASPR VI. The Leiden Riddle is printed in its Northumbrian version (from Leiden, Rijksuniversiteit, Voss. Lat. Q. 106) in ASPR VI and in its West-Saxon version (Exeter, Cathedral 3501) in ASPR III.

8. Leningrad, Saltykov-Schedrin Public Library, Q. v. I. 18 (L) is conceivably the older manuscript. See M. B. Parkes, *The Scriptorium of Wearmouth-Jarrow*, Jarrow Lecture, 1982 (Jarrow 1982), pp. 5–6. For a stemma of the surviving manuscripts see Elliott Van Kirk Dobbie, *The Manuscripts of Cædmon's Hymn and Bede's Death Song* (New York: Columbia University Press, 1937), p. 48. He identifies three groups of manuscripts copied in England: M-L, *Æ and *Z. Two late continental manuscripts form the *Y group.

9. See Dobbie, ASPR VI, p. xcix.

10. Dobbie produces a single text of the the multiply-attested poems of the Anglo-Saxon Chronicle under similar rubrics. As he notes in his preface to *The Battle of Brunanburh*, he follows Alistair Campbell (ed., *The Battle of Brunanburh* [London: W. Heinemann and Co., 1938], p. 13) in using Cambridge, Corpus Christi College 173 as the base text, in order to offer the poem in its earliest dialect state, although he emends from later manuscript versions.

11. Dobbie, ASPR VI, p. c.

12. A. H. Smith, ed., *Three Northumbrian Poems* (London: Methuen, 1933), pp. 39 and 41, uses Oxford, Bodleian Library, Hatton 43 (a *Z manuscript with the reading *ylda*) as his base text for the West-Saxon version. J. C. Pope, ed., *Seven Old English Poems*, 2d ed. (New York: Norton, 1981), prints a normalized West-Saxon translation of the *ælda*-version to supplement his edition of the text in CUL Kk. 5. 16.

13. See Katherine O'Brien O'Keeffe, *Visible Song: Transitional Literacy in Old English Verse* (Cambridge: Cambridge University Press, 1990), pp. 39–40.

14. ASPR VI, p. xcix.

15. For Exeter Riddle 30, Krapp and Dobbie print the two versions in the same order as they occur in the Exeter Book. (See ASPR III, pp. 195–96 and 224–25.)

16. Volume 6 edits in similar fashion the poems of the Anglo-Saxon Chronicle and the Metrical Preface and Epilogue to Alfred's translation of the *Regula pastoralis*.

17. Dobbie, ASPR VI, p. liii.

18. These are: 32b, *feohgestreona* (A)/*fyrngestreona* (B); 35a, *ungelic* (A)/ *ungesibb* (B); 44a, *dream* (A)/ *dry* (B) (Dobbie emends to *dreor*); 59a: *gemenged* (A)/ *geondmenged* (B); 60b, *dreosed* (A)/ *dreoged* (B); 62b, *hædre* (A)/ *hearde* (B); 78b, *dumbra* (A)/*deadra* (B); 82a, *and wyrma [w]elm* (A)/ *wyrma wlenco* (B); 85a, *sodice* (A)/ *smealice* (B); 86b, *gæst* (A)/ *gesid* (B). For an analysis of these variations see O'Keeffe, *Visible Song*, pp. 64–66.

19. Even Dobbie's "diplomatic" edition of the individual versions (*Manuscripts*, pp. 13–28 and 38–42) prints the versions with modern lineation and word division.

20. Robert J. Menner, ed., *The Poetical Dialogues of Solomon and Saturn* (New York: Modern Language Association of America, 1941), prints facing texts of *A* and *B* for the shared lines of *Solomon and Saturn I*. His apparatus provides a scrupulous record of both manuscripts.

21. See, for example, David N. Dumville's and Simon Keynes's editors' preface to Janet M. Bately, ed., *The Anglo-Saxon Chronicle: MS A*, The Anglo-Saxon Chronicle: a Collaborative Edition 3 (Cambridge: D. S. Brewer, 1986), p. ix: "Yet despite the great importance of MS. A as the oldest surviving manuscript of the *Chronicle*, it would be hazardous to give too much weight to its particular readings against those of the other manuscripts or to attach too much significance to its particular physical features (for example, as reflexions of the earliest stages in the compilation of the text), for even MS. A is by no means as close as we should like to the lost original in textual authority or date."

22. See Jerome J. McGann, *The Romantic Ideology: A Critical Investigation* (Chicago and London: University of Chicago Press, 1983), p. 13.

23. For example, the circumstances of developing literacy in Carolingian France differed significantly from those in Anglo-Saxon England. See Rosamond McKitterick, *The Carolingians and the Written Word* (Cambridge: Cambridge University Press, 1989).

24. Roland Barthes, "From Work to Text," in his *The Rustle of Language*, trans. Richard Howard (New York: Hill and Wang, 1986), pp. 56–64, at 57 (originally published in *Revue d'esthétique*, 1971).

25. Jacques Derrida, *Of Grammatology*, trans. G. C. Spivak (Baltimore: Johns Hopkins University Press, 1976), pp. 30–73.

26. On the possibilities of a transitional literacy see Jack Goody, *The Interface between the Written and the Oral* (Cambridge: Cambridge University Press, 1987), p. 106.

27. John Josias Conybeare, *Illustrations of Anglo-Saxon Poetry*, ed. William Daniel Conybeare (London: Harding and Lepard, 1826). On Conybeare's role in the "rediscovery" of Old English poetry in the romantic period see Richard C. Payne, "The Rediscovery of Old English Poetry in the English Literary Tradition," in Berkhout and Gatch, eds., *Anglo-Saxon Scholarship*, pp. 149–66, at p. 159.

28. Conybeare, *Illustrations*, pp. xxxvi–xxxvii.

29. J. Conybeare himself only marks alliteration with bolded capitals when he cites verse to illustrate his arguments about meter. His subsequent "illustrations of Anglo-Saxon poetry" are printed in hemistichs and adopt the following typographic peculiarities: the leveling of thorn and eth to eth (capital and lower cases), use of capital and lowercase ash, but the use of an insular "g" in lowercase only.

30. Benjamin Thorpe, *Cædmon's Metrical Paraphrase of Parts of the Holy Scriptures in Anglo-Saxon* (London, 1832), p. vii.

31. Thorpe, *Cædmon's Metrical Paraphrase*: "In the accentuation . . . I have followed the authority of manuscripts, and, except in a very few instances, that of the manuscript of Cædmon itself" (p. xiv). Such a typeface was traditional in the printing of Old English text. On Jefferson's recommendation to abandon "English black letter" see Hauer, "Thomas Jefferson," at 884 and 886.

32. "I am sorry to say that the English booksellers will have nothing to do with Salomon and Marcolf; they are afraid of it." See Raymond A. Wiley, ed., *John Mitchell Kemble and Jakob Grimm, A Correspondence 1832–1852* (Leiden: E. J. Brill, 1971), p. 111. The Aelfric Society published his Vercelli Codex in 1842 as the first number in the series.

33. John M. Kemble, *The Dialogue of Salomon and Saturn* (London: Aelfric Society, 1848). Kemble dismisses B in one sentence: "As the only interest of this second

codex is derived from the lines which it furnishes to the first, and the various readings, it requires no further remark," p. 133.

34. "An author's work possesses autonomy only when it remains an unheard melody. As soon as it begins its passage to publication it undergoes a series of interventions which some textual critics see as a process of contamination, but which may equally well be seen as a process of training the poem for its appearances in the world" (Jerome J. McGann, *A Critique of Modern Textual Criticism* [Chicago and London: University of Chicago Press, 1983]), p. 51. McGann argues for distinguishing among "text," "poem," and "poetical work," using the first in a purely bibliographical context and the last in the context of historical study (*The Beauty of Inflections: Literary Investigations in Historical Method and Theory* [Oxford: Oxford University Press, 1985], pp. 114–15, n. 3). The present essay uses "text" to refer to an idealized version of the poem and "work" to refer to the poem as it appears in an individual manuscript. The "work" is a realized "text."

35. Lee Patterson, "The Logic of Textual Criticism and the Way of Genius: The Kane-Donaldson *Piers Plowman* in Historical Perspective," in his *Negotiating the Past*, pp. 77–113.

36. See, for example, Julius Zupitza's diplomatic transcription in *Beowulf Reproduced in Facsimile from the Unique Manuscript British Museum MS. Cotton Vitellius A. XV*, 2d ed. Early English Text Society o.s. 245 (London: Oxford University Press, 1959 [for 1958]), p. 9. Zupitza's literate concept of "word" leads him to insert a hyphen wherever the scribe has spaced between free morphemes in "words" or has broken a "word" at line's end and insert a stroke between "words" which the scribe has joined.

37. George Kane, "Conjectural Emendation," in *Medieval Manuscripts and Textual Criticism*, ed. Christopher Kleinhenz (Chapel Hill, N.C.: University of North Carolina Department of Modern Languages, 1974), 211–25, at 223 (repr. London, 1969).

38. George Philip Krapp, *The Vercelli Book* ASPR II (New York and London, 1932), p. vi. In *Beowulf and Judith* (ASPR IV, p. vi), Elliott Van Kirk Dobbie regrets not including conjectural emendations for lacunae in vols. 3 and 6. Compare Kenneth Sisam, *Studies in the History of Old English Literature* (Oxford: Clarendon Press, 1953), p. 39: "But when, as is usual for Old English poetry, only one *late* witness is available, there is no safety in following its testimony. The difference between a better reading and a worse is, after all, a matter of judgement; and however fallible that faculty may be, the judge must not surrender it to the witness" (emphasis added). See also p. 43 where he argues for standardized spelling.

39. See Bruce Mitchell, "The Dangers of Disguise: Old English Texts in Modern Punctuation," *RES* 31 (1980): 385–413.

40. See F. Masai, "Principes et Conventions de l'Édition Diplomatique," *Scriptorium* 4 (1950): 177–93.

CHAPTER THREE

Making Identities in Fifteenth-Century England: Henry V and John Lydgate

LEE PATTERSON

COURTING THE SIGNIFICANT OTHER

The courtship to which the title of this section alludes was recently entered, not for the first time, as a metaphor for academic collaboration by Brian Stock, who rather lamented its pertinence.* "There are," he said, "fewer areas of agreement than there might be between empirical historians and students of literature. [We have achieved] neither marriage nor divorce but rather, after the fashion of medieval romance, endless extensions of an increasingly frustrating courtship."[1] Over a hundred years ago Gaston Paris, one of the founders of medieval literary criticism, confidently announced that now "we regard the poetic works of the Middle Ages as above all documents of history."[2] Yet after all this time we have apparently made little progress in brokering a permanent and emotionally satisfying relationship, or even a working partnership, between literature and history. Moreover, this extended courtship has recently been made more difficult by the arrival of a mysterious suitor, also from France, who has whispered a seductive message to literary critics quite different from that of Gaston Paris, a suitor who has promised an erotic isolation filled only with words, eliminating the need for contractual relations with the world outside. Historians, for their part, while observing this development with polite curiosity, have continued to believe that Isidore of Seville's definition of history as "narratio rei gestae" [the story of things done] is more helpful than Derrida's dictum that "il n'y a pas de hors-texte" [there is nothing outside the text].[3] While acknowledging that history is constructed rather than found, they have largely set aside metaphysical doubt in favor of practical tasks. Contemporary historiography, and especially that of the Middle Ages, operates for the most part within what Dominick LaCapra has called "a 'documentary' or 'objectivist' model of knowledge": it relies upon an archive of "informational documents" whose value is taken to be primarily factual or referential, it practices an objectivist method that sees subjectivity not as the necessary condition of understanding but as a dangerous contaminant, and it operates within a system of periodization that seems often to predetermine what a text can and cannot mean.[4] Since the texts of interest to literary critics are typically constructed within an intricate rhetorical system that makes them unproductive of hard data, and since their interpretation manifestly precludes verifiability, they rarely figure in historical accounts of the period. Indeed, historians of late medieval England seem rarely to use the work of literary critics.[5]

It must also be said that literary critics have done little to persuade their historian colleagues that their analyses can provide fresh access to the realities of the medieval past. Not that there are not many literary critics who are concerned with historical contextualization.[6] But for the most part this kind of work proceeds with little attention to recent poststructuralist thought, as if the linguistic turn taken by cultural studies had obviously led up a blind alley. On the other hand, critics who do apply contemporary theory to medieval texts tend to operate under the sign of Ezra Pound's modernist dictum to "make it new." Concerned to claim for medieval literary studies a currency usually denied it, they deploy the esoteric—and often counterintuitive—discourse of advanced literary criticism. Moreover, and more important, the programs that drive these studies tend to preclude specifically historical insights. For the very medievalness of the text under scrutiny—in effect, its historicity—is the embarrassment these theoretical readings seek to redeem; and since this historicity is a function of the social realities of the medieval world, they tend to disappear as well.[7]

Hence what we almost entirely lack is work that can show that historical understanding can actually be enabled rather than avoided by poststructuralist thought, that the enterprise currently known as poststructuralism, and particularly the deconstruction that is its fundamental element, can be more than a local fashion, more than a seductive exaggeration of procedural caveats and natural skepticism we have always already employed. In sum, I will argue that this exotic French import can reveal for us not just what makes the medieval past like the modern present but what makes it different as well; that it can elucidate social practice as well as literary form; and that it can be an agency not to divide but to bring together historians and literary critics.

To claim for deconstruction a capacity for *historical* analysis may seem quixotic. It has become customary to describe deconstruction as, in Terry Eagleton's words, "a hedonist withdrawal from history, a cult of ambiguity or irresponsible anarchism."[8] Since the deconstructionist is thought to wallow in a timeless aporia of pure textuality, any access to either history or historiography must be foreclosed.[9] Yet in fact deconstruction is, at least in conception if too rarely in enactment, nothing if not a historicism. Its central insight is that Western philosophic thought, and the social practices it credentials, bases itself upon an order of meaning conceived as primary, transcendental, and beyond history—an origin from which all other, merely historical instances are derived. As Derrida says, logocentrism is the belief in priority that is seen as "simple, intact, normal, pure, standard, self-identical, in order *then* to think in terms of derivation, complication, deterioration, accident, etc."[10] But the process actually works the other way around: the logos is not given but derived, "a determination and effect within a system that is no longer that of presence but of differ*a*nce."[11] However the deconstructive program may be enacted in individual instances, its fundamental insight is a challenge to idealism, essentialism, and transcendentalism—to all those metaphysical gestures by which Western thought has sought to avoid the historical, the material, and the social.

In this sense, then, in its relentless unmasking of transcendental value as historically contingent and historically constructed, deconstruction should be considered part of the Enlightenment project of modernity rather than either an offshoot of Nietzschean irrationalism or a cynical, fin de siècle postmodernism.[12] And many of the critical practices to which it has given rise have in fact proven to be genuinely liberatory. In demystifying the theology of the origin, deconstruction has shown that identity is relational rather than essential: just as for Saussure language is a system of differences without positive terms, so for deconstruction metaphysical thinking and social practice are not founded upon an essential being but organized according to a set of binary oppositions—thought and language, God and history, essence and existence, the individual and society, ego and id, male and female, white and black, straight and gay, and so on. What deconstruction seeks to unmask are the suppressions and elisions—the ideological constraints—that make possible these polarities. Its characteristic strategy is to show that each element, far from being either coherent in itself or independent of its designated other, harbors within itself an unacknowledged affinity with its opposite. Identity includes difference, difference masks identity: just as nothing is ever fully identical with itself, neither is it wholly different from the binary opposite in relation to which identity is established.

Thus deconstruction, far from either denying the reality of history or its availability to knowledge, is a critical practice that seeks to understand how "reality" is put into place by discursive means. When Derrida notoriously says that "there is nothing outside the text," he is restating the position, held by many sociocultural historians, that reality is culturally or discursively produced, that—in Jonathan Culler's words—"the realities with which politics is concerned, and the forms in which they are manipulated, are inseparable from discursive structures and systems of signification."[13] While of course such a program *could* lead to the neglect of the social, economic, and political institutions by which power is enforced, it need not; and while of course it *could* lead us to submerge agency into structure, nothing requires that it do so. Indeed, if we locate deconstruction within historiographical practice rather than in opposition to it, then it can be seen as a style of analysis directed toward understanding the production of cultural meanings.

The particular object of analysis in this essay is the making of identities in late medieval England, specifically the monarchical identity of Henry V and the poetic identity of John Lydgate. The oddly equivocal term "identity" refers in the first instance to social identity, to those distinctive characteristics that allowed Henry V and Lydgate to meet the definition of monarch and poet, a process that involved as well larger contemporary identities, especially the English national identity so much in the process of formation at this time. A second object of attention is the way in which disparate elements, personal as well as political, were consolidated to form a unity or identity of character and of interest. In this sense identity is the result of a process of making identical—by imposing direction and overcoming division, correcting waywardness and suppressing dissent. Finally, this essay proceeds on the assumption that this kind of analysis, far from being anachronistic, accords with (although it can hardly replicate) medieval habits of thought. Or, more precisely, and less modestly, I mean to suggest that bringing deconstruction so explicitly into the arena of medieval studies can benefit both parties. Deconstruction, and the poststructuralist formations that have followed from it, may become more conscious of their own historical origins, and medieval studies, as a working practice, more alert to its affiliations with other contemporary ways of thinking. If medieval culture did not invent the binarism of identity and difference, it reinvented it in spades, so much so that the Middle Ages is often defined by nonmedievalists in terms that imply identity and deny difference. Conformity, fixity, orthodoxy, and obedience are assumed to be everywhere; diversity, mobility, heresy, and skepticism are scarcely to be found. Indeed, part of my argument is that in early fifteenth-century England the language of identity and difference provided both Henry V and John Lydgate with sanctioned symbolic meanings that could be used in the service of political and literary stabilization. Yet I wish also to suggest that the intensity with which this language was deployed was a symptom of anxiety rather than certainty, both a reflexive dependence on old modes of persuasion and a doubt about their effectiveness. I wish to suggest, in other words, that the awareness that binarism is constructed rather than simply given is not unique to modern much less postmodern thought, that even a so-called premodern or traditional culture like the Middle Ages could recognize—albeit hesitantly and reluctantly—its own self-constructions for what they were.

I have chosen to discuss these two men in order to bring within the same interpretive practice a historical figure whose career epitomizes everything history has privileged—*res gestae* not only done in the public arena but done with consummate success—and a writer who all his life remained an observer. But the two men nonetheless had extensive dealings with each other: Henry seems to have known Lydgate throughout most of his adult life, and Lydgate produced a number of important poems at the king's request, especially the massive *Troy Book*, begun in 1412 but not completed until 1420. The object of my attention here is the *Siege of Thebes*, an ambitious poem written in 1421–1422, and although not the product of an actual commission nonetheless attentive to the king's success in France. Finally, Henry and Lydgate have always been considered typically, even reassuringly, medieval. Certainly Henry was acutely conscious of traditional values and practices, and modern historians have seen him as a man who made the medieval monarchy work.[14] The subtitle of the first twentieth-century biography of Henry—Charles Lethbridge Kingsford's *Henry V: The Typical Mediaeval Hero* (1901)—accurately sums up, in its admiration as in its assertion of representativeness—the modern consensus.[15] So too, some rather irresolute efforts to define Lydgate as an early humanist and as therefore protomodern have been subsequently, and persuasively, rejected, especially by the authoritative book by Derek Pearsall, whose Lydgate is a thoroughly conventional poet who "medievalizes" every progressive bit of material that comes his way, and especially the poetry of his great predecessor Chaucer.[16] These opinions are, I believe, essentially correct. But what might be questioned is their unspoken assumption that both Henry and Lydgate were somehow *unproblematically* medieval, that they lived their medievalness naturally and without self-consciousness. For if identity is never given but instead made through a double process of inclusion and exclusion, then we should be alert to the discursive materials and political and poetic strategies by which Henry V and Lydgate constructed themselves. And in this investigation we can perhaps also understand the larger cultural imperatives that encouraged these two men to adopt identities that were not simply traditional but *traditionalistic*, identities that were conspicuously, perhaps even deliberately "typically medieval."[17]

THE SIEGE OF THEBES: IDENTIFYING THE MONK OF BURY

Born about 1370, Lydgate began writing poetry in the first decade of the fifteenth century, and for fifteen years or so his career followed a double path. On the one hand, he produced an extensive body of court poetry whose primary effect was to affirm the supremacy and stability of the noble class, poetry such as "The Complaint of the Black Knight" (1402–1403?), "The Temple of Glass" (1404?), and "At the Departyng of Thomas Chaucyer on Ambassade into France" (1414, 1417, or 1420). A poetry of private amorousness set in an ideal landscape protected from the winds of history, the elegant figuration and extravagant emotions of this writing endorse the social superiority of its protagonists. And the *maker* responsible for its production presents himself as simply a transparent vehicle, a loyal subordinate whose craftsmanship allows him to deploy the cultic language of courtliness without taking part in its practices—an exclusion all the more pronounced when the poet is, as here, a monk.

On the other hand, and at the same time, Lydgate was commissioned by Henry to produce the massive *Troy Book* (1412–1420) and, in all likelihood, the similarly monumental *Life of Our Lady* (1409–1411?). Here he functions not as courtly *maker* but as a writer of weighty texts whose very existence witness to the monarch's historical legitimacy and spiritual seriousness. Moreover, in writing the *Troy Book* Lydgate provided Henry not just with a history—the genre most fully associated with monastic literary production—but with an authoritative version of the Trojan history that had, at least since the time of Henry II, served to support the legitimacy of insecure English kings.[18] In representing Henry as the patron of what was taken to be the founding moment of English history, Lydgate was both affirming Henry's proprietorship over the national culture and, in invoking the concept of *translatio imperii*, asserting the principle of genealogical transmission that underwrote medieval political legitimation. In these texts, then, Lydgate functioned not as the dutiful purveyor of the discourse of a class from which he was by definition excluded but as a monk providing his sovereign with the monastically-generated materials needed to sustain royal authority—a function also performed by other Benedictines such as Thomas Elmham and Thomas Walsingham.[19]

In the uncommissioned *Siege of Thebes*, a poem begun in the spring of 1421 and completed before Henry's death on August 31, 1422, Lydgate took it upon himself both to exemplify and to promote his role as the monastic supporter of Lancastrian rule, as worthy of becoming, as he did, "poet-propagandist to the Lancastrian dynasty."[20] The *Siege* promotes this poetic vocation in a number of ways. For one thing, as commentators have long noted, the text serves as a rudimentary *mirour de prince*: not only is each of the male characters carefully located on a scale of chivalric and regal virtue, but Lydgate provides explicit directions on virtuous governance.[21] His twofold message is that peace is preferable to war and, a topic relentlessly repeated, *trouthe* is preferable to duplicity or *doublenesse*. In part this topic is political: the sorry history of Polynices and Ethiocles teaches us to treasure unity and avoid the "Cokkyl of envye and debat" sown by "the olde Serpent" (4663, 4668–69).[22] And in part it is ethical: the cause of the war is the "doublenesse of Ethiocles" (1778), who—having "lefte trouthe" (1783) and become "false and double of entent" (2068)—refused to honor the agreement with Polynices that they should rule Thebes in alternate years. Consequently a ruler should be "pleyn and hool as a Centre stable" (1724), should avoid "eny doublenesse, / Variaunce or vnsicrenesse, / Chaunge of word or mutabilite" (1747–49). These oft-repeated injunctions are then drawn together at the end, and given a contemporary spin, through a citation from the Treaty of Troyes (4698–703), the accord signed in May 1420 by Henry and Charles VI that designated Henry as Charles's heir and "reunited" the crowns of France and England. While Lydgate's point at its simplest is that war can be avoided only if solemn agreements are honored, it draws on the larger metaphysical assumption that the opposition of "trouthe and resoun" to "falshed and tresoun" (2639–40) is built into the structure of reality. On the one hand, argues the poem, is integrity, simplicity, consistency, and self-identity; on the other is duplicity, complexity, variability, and self-contradiction.

The *Siege of Thebes* presents itself, moreover, not just as articulating but as itself exemplifying this absolutist opposition. Claiming that its promotion of *trouthe* over *doublenesse* is its "sentence hool, withoute variance" (54), the poem presents itself as an instance of perfect self-identity. As Lois Ebin has shown, throughout his career Lydgate promoted a remarkably crude semiotics.[23] For him the poet is a verbal craftsman whose "rethorik" "adournes" or "enlumynes" or "enbelissches" or "aureates" received truths in order to illuminate in turn the mind of the reader. According to this model, the form-content dilemma that rhetoric had always posed itself is no dilemma at all, and neither is the transmission of truth over time. The poet reads the truth out of one text, incorporates it into another, and passes it on to an audience that receives it clearly and completely—the "sentence hool, withoute variance." Although drawn from the unexamined clichés of medieval literary theorizing, this simplistically didactic poetics ignored all those complexities of interpretation and figuration that medieval hermeneutics and rhetorical theory in fact treated with great sophistication.

In the *Siege* Lydgate provides two demonstrations of his kind of "elloquence." One is in the narrative itself, where he presents examples of the poet as civic authority, first in his account of the founding of the city by the harpist Amphion, then in the representation of the prophet Amphiaraus (or Amphiorax, as Lydgate calls him).[24] Lydgate mentions only to set aside the darker version of the Theban founding by Cadmus and his dragon warriors—a founding myth that his sources use to establish the pattern of fratricidal violence and fatal recursion that will come to control Theban history—in favor of a model of Ciceronian eloquence. Amphion's raising of the walls by his music and his subsequent exile of Cadmus becomes for Lydgate a figure for the power of Mercury over Mars, and demonstrates the importance of eloquence in the provision of good governance.[25] Similarly, the prophet and priest Amphiorax functions in his narrative as the voice of prudent restraint, and we are clearly meant to see the disaster as caused, at least in part, by the Argives' refusal to attend: "For al his elloquence / He had in soth but lytyl audience" (3811–12).

Lydgate's other demonstration of his poetics, of far greater complexity, resides in his appropriation of Chaucer's *Canterbury Tales*. By presenting the *Siege* as a tale told by Lydgate the pilgrim as the first tale on the *return*

journey from Canterbury, Lydgate the poet deals with the anxiety of influence by literally joining the Chaucerian bandwagon. But in fact, while representing himself as a Chaucerian, Lydgate misrepresents Chaucer's poem.
By positing a return trip Lydgate ignores Chaucer's final understanding of
his pilgrimage as unidirectional and presided over by the Parson, Lydgate
instead reinstates the Host's discredited festive model of a circular movement centered upon the Tabard Inn. Not only is the displacement of the
Host by the Parson that Chaucer had engineered in the *Parson's Prologue*
here undone, but this Host is a petty tyrant—"ful of wynde and bost" (80)—
interested only in mirth. "Thow shalt be mery who so þat sey nay," he threatens Lydgate and demands that he

> leyn a-side they professioun.
> Thow shalt not chese nor þi-self withdrawe,
> ȝif eny myrth be founden in thy mawe,
> Lyk the custom of this Compenye;
> For non so proude that dar me denye,
> Knyght nor knaue, Chanon, prest, ne nonne,
> To telle a tale pleynly as thei konne,
> Whan I assigne and se tyme opportune. (132–39)

Unlike Chaucer's Host, whose treatment of the pilgrims varied from jocular
familiarity to gallantry and even obsequiousness, Lydgate's is simply overbearing; and whereas Chaucer's Host admired sententiousness as well as
jollity, and bowed at the end to the Parson's authority, Lydgate's demands
a universal mirth: "Telle vs some thyng that draweþ to effecte / Only of
Ioye!" (170–71).[26]

This reduction of an original complexity to uniformity is perhaps what we
should expect when Lydgate "medievalizes" a pre-text. But in fact this transformation is not a reflexive conservatism but part of a strategy of self-representation and identity formation. For Lydgate simplifies the *Canterbury
Tales* in order to provide a context in which his own monastic integrity—his
seriousness as the noble rhetor poet—will be most visible. Chaucer's multivalent *Tales* are reduced to a uniform frivolity in order to provide a foil for
Lydgate's seriousness: it is his difference from Chaucer that establishes
Lydgate's identity. This process of self-definition through difference is implicit as well in the tale he now tells. For whereas Chaucer began his outward journey with the *Knight's Tale*, a thematically complex and skeptical
rewriting of the Theban legend, Lydgate begins the return journey with a
historiographically traditional and thematically unambiguous version of the
same material. He will, moreover, tell this story of origins from its beginning,
providing a prequel to the *Knight's Tale*.[27] Chaucer's Knight had merely
gestured toward the full Theban story, while Chaucer's own versions—in
Anelida and Arcite and the "Complaint of Mars"—hopelessly entangled

Theban history with erotic supplements. Now Lydgate, fulfilling his monastic responsibility by carefully following "myn Autour" (3972) throughout, will restore the history to both narrative wholeness and thematic clarity.[28]

An analysis of the *Siege of Thebes* in terms of identity and difference thus reveals a clear pattern. For one thing, Lydgate here constructs his own identity as pious monk and advisor to the sovereign, in part through his self-representation within the *Siege* itself, in part by claiming a traditional monastic integrity in historiographical matters, in part by asserting his literary difference from Chaucer.[29] For another, he relies upon what can aptly be termed a poetics of identity: we are assured that his representation of the literal and moral truth of Theban history coincides at every level with its "real" or original meaning, a meaning whose self-evidence his carefully crafted language enforces rather than complicates. Meanwhile, the lesson Theban history teaches is itself about identity versus difference, about integrity and unity (*trouthe*) versus duplicity and division (*doublenesse*). And finally, as the citation of the Treaty of Troyes implies, the poem affirms an identity of interest between poet and sovereign: working together, they can achieve the "Pees and quyet, concord and vnyte" (4703) that is the goal of good government. This is, at any rate, the straightforward program that the poem proposes, although, as we shall see at the end of this essay, its enactment reveals a complexity of motive, and a resistance to power, that is interestingly unLydgatean.

THE MAKING OF A MONARCH

When Henry V became king of England on March 21, 1413, Lancastrian sovereignty faced fundamental problems. For one thing, the constitutionality of Henry's position was far from certain. Not only was he the son of a usurper, but for about eighteen months, during 1410–1412, he had himself been in implicit and at times virtually open rebellion against his father. There was also grave concern about the capacity of the Lancastrian regime to govern, for it seemed to have done little to solve the problems that had brought Richard's monarchy into disrepute. Law and order were inadequately enforced, the king's household was hardly less bloated and overbearing than under Richard, and Henry IV himself had been preoccupied with physical illness and spiritual apprehension.[30] Not surprisingly, then, Henry V was threatened within less than a year of his accession with the serious rebellion led by his old companion in arms, Sir John Oldcastle, and then, on the eve of what would become the Agincourt campaign, with the Southampton plot hatched from within his own court. Clearly the legitimacy of his authority was far from universally or even widely acknowledged, and when his ambassadors laid claim to the crown of France, it is hardly to be wondered at that the French should reply that he had no right even to the crown of England.

In seven years Henry had succeeded brilliantly in overcoming these and other disabilities, establishing himself not just as the legitimate king of both England and France but as the embodiment of the English nation as a whole. The narrative of this triumph is well-known, and historians have explicated in important detail its administrative, political, diplomatic, and military aspects. But what has been less fully described is Henry's own self-construction as a monarch within the discursive field of early fifteenth-century England. Both in image and practice Henry's kingship defined itself in terms of the contemporary language of public virtue, the same language that Lydgate deployed so skillfully in the *Siege of Thebes*.

The major theme of contemporary writings concerned with the public or communal interest—and few texts do not express such an interest—is the advocacy of unity or concord against the fear of division or disunity. The poet of MS Digby 102—so well-informed about public opinion that he may even have been a member of parliament—welcomed Henry's accession in 1413 by praying that "Among oure-self, god send vs pes" since "ʒif fiʒt be raysed, / Pan stroye we oure awen nest."[31] For him the royal crown symbolized national unity: "What doþ a kynges crownes signyfye, / Whan stones & floures on sercles is bent? / Lordis, comouns, & clergye / To ben all at on assent" (lines 9–12). And when in 1414 he urged Henry to make "pes wiþ-ynne," to bring together "All ʒoure reme in vnyte," he was actually echoing the speech given by the Chancellor, Archbishop Henry Beaufort, at the opening of the Leicester Parliament.[32] Similarly, a macaronic sermon delivered after the death of Oldcastle in 1417 stresses above all the need to reunify the kingdom: "Nostrum regnum quod est unum corpus" is the preacher's theme, and he celebrates the reign of Edward III when "clerus and þe laife huius terre wer knet to gedur in uno fagot and brenden super istum ignem"—with, that is, the fire of perfect charity.[33] In his poem commemorating Henry's reinterment of the body of Richard II in Westminster Abbey in 1413—itself a significant affirmation of continuity and hereditary legitimacy—Hoccleve recalled that "this land wont was for to be / Of sad byleeue & constant vnion" and begged Henry to return it to its former integrity.[34]

Not surprisingly, the king's enemies were seen as both agents of division and as themselves self-divided. Lord Scrope, a member of the Southampton conspiracy, was described by the loyal monk John Capgrave as a typical double-dealer: "Sobir was the man in word and chere; and undir that ypocrisie had he a ful venemous hert."[35] And for the *Brut* all the Southampton plotters were motivated by duplicity, by "fals couetyse and treson."[36] Oldcastle and the Lollards were the most obvious targets for invective since, as Hoccleve (among many others) put it, they were attacking "the vnitee / Of Holy Chirch."[37] God is "feith right, trouthe, & al bountee" (184), he says, a source of integrity who, as he put it in another poem, will both keep Henry "in feithful vnitee" and smite the Lollards who have introduced difference where there should be identity: "Dampnable fro feith were variance!"³⁸ In the *Brut* the word "false" rings like a chime throughout the description of Oldcastle and Lollardy: they are "fals heritikis" who pursue "fals treson, to haue slayn þe King," a "fals purpos," a "fals ordinaunce & worchyng," a "fals purpos & ordinaunce."³⁹ The Lollards were understood as false or duplicitous because they were incomprehensible as people who were sincere, who truly believed different articles of faith: since doctrinal difference was a denial of the God who is, in Hoccleve's words in the *Regement of Princes* (written for Henry in 1412–1414), both "þe auctour of trouthe" and "trouthe itself" (2393, 2411), it was a perversity possible only to the self-divided or self-deluded. Hence the contemporary chronicler John Strecche described Oldcastle as a "fictus hereticus" since a "true heretic" was a contradiction in terms; and a brief alliterative poem of 1415 presents the Lollards—despite a ferocious sincerity all too evident in their texts—as "gylers" who "Momelyn with here mouthes moche and malys in hert, / And of a mys menyng maketh a faire tale, / Vnder flateryng and fair speche falsehede foloweth."⁴⁰ Indeed Lydgate himself, in a poem written in 1413–1414 and addressed to Henry, warned that the religiously heterodox are politically unreliable: "He may dissymule with a feynyd hewe, / But take good heede."⁴¹

We can see from these examples how the complexities of contemporary politics were cast into the moral and metaphysical language of unity and division, identity and difference. What is perhaps surprising, however, is that this same language was applied to the central event of Henry's reign—the war with France—and applied across an extraordinary range of detail. The war was typically described not as the conquest of a foreign nation but as the recovery of the king's inheritance, not as a confrontation with the other but as reunion with part of oneself. When Henry invaded Normandy in 1415, according to the *Gesta Henrici Quinti*, a contemporary panegyric probably commissioned by Henry himself, he was simply seeking to recover that "which belongs to him entirely by right dating from the time of William the first, the Conqueror, even though now, as for a long time past, it is thus withheld, against God and all justice, by the violence of the French (*violentia Gallorum*)."⁴² And when he conquered Normandy, he emphasized the legitimacy of his sovereignty both by presenting himself as King John's rightful successor as Duke of Normandy—he wore the ducal robes in Rouen in 1419—and by returning the duchy "aux Usages et Coustumes qui estoyent en nostre dit Paiis au temps de noz Predecesseurs" [the usages and customs that existed in our country in the time of our predecessors], usages and customs that predated the French seizure.⁴³ Nor was Henry's sense of recovering that which was already his restricted to Normandy: the major theme of royal propaganda—which includes not just the *Gesta* but parliamentary and other pronouncements—was that justice required Henry to reclaim the dynastic rights that had belonged to the English royal line (with which Henry was thus firmly associating himself) since at least the reign of Edward I.[44] And Henry took care to compile and circulate dossiers of historical documents that supported his case, an example of what one historian has called his "romantic legalism."[45]

Since Henry already possessed France de jure if not de facto, the war was therefore to be understood not as a struggle between two separate nations but as the rebellion of a disloyal people against its rightful sovereign. It was, in short, a civil war: the *Gesta* called it an internal battle (*prelium intestinum*) in which fraternal blood (*fraternus sanguis*) was being shed. The goal of Henry's invasion was to be understood as the restoration of England and France to an original unity: "Would that the French nation might soon attain to peace and unity [*ad pacem et unitatem*] with the English," disingenuously lamented the *Gesta*.[46] Nor was it simply official texts like the *Gesta* that purveyed this view: according to the chronicler John Hardyng, the purpose of Henry's wars was to "make an vnyon / Betwyx Englonde and Fraunce," while in the *Troy Book* Lydgate said that the war was undertaken so that "Yngeland and Fraunce / May be al oon, withoute variaunce."[47] Indeed, as early as 1411, in the *Regement of Princes*, Hoccleve had claimed that since God deplores "þe hateful discorde" (5315) between France and England, Henry should "Purcheseth pees by wey of mariage" (5403): "By matrimoigne pees and vnite / Ben had" (5394–95).[48]

Contemporaries well knew that what made France vulnerable to English schemes was its own internal division, strife lamented by French writers from Christine de Pisan to Alain Chartier.[49] Far from gloating over the fratricidal self-destruction of the enemy, however, an English poet like Hoccleve saw it as an unnatural condition—an "vnkyndly disseueraunce" (5310)—that bespoke a suicidal lack of integrity: "Thi self manaseth þi self for to dye," he says to the French nation, "Thi self destroye, and feble is þi victorye! / Thow hast in þi self stryven oft" (5292–94). Consequently, the Treaty of Troyes was seen as an act of unification. Undertaken "for the peaceful reintegration of the kingdoms of France and England" (*pro Franciae & Angliae Regnorum reintegranda pace*), it made the crowns of France and England—if not the nations themselves—one. According to the English version of the Treaty,

> both the Crounes, that is to sey of France and of England, [shall] perpetuelly be togedyr, and be in Oone and in the same Persone, . . . and . . . both Roialme[s] shull be Governed from that tyme, that We [i.e., Charles VI] or ony of oure Heires [i.e., Henry V and his descendants] come to the same, not severally, under divers Kynges in oone tyme, but undir oone and the same Persone, the whiche for the tyme shall be Kyng of either Roialme and Soverayn Lord.[50]

As a definitive sign that this unity was not forced but natural, not a novelty but a reclamation, the language of the Treaty referred to the principals in familial terms: Henry was for Charles "nostre cher fils" and he and Queen Isabelle loved him "comme pere & mere" (896). As for Charles's legitimate son, the Dauphin who had murdered John of Burgundy at Montereau the previous fall, he was mentioned in the Treaty only to be excluded from the family unit as a treacherous and deceitful interloper.[51] With the replacement of the Dauphin by Henry, then, the French royal family, and by implication the French nation, had been restored to moral integrity and domestic unity.

Yet if we are to grasp how fully the discourse of difference and identity structured contemporary thinking, we must attend to the language by which national identities were being constructed during the Hundred Years War.[52] Beginning in earnest with Henry's 1415 invasion, the governing classes of both England and France, concerned to transform a dynastic quarrel into a national campaign, took pains to generate a sense of national feeling by reigniting the fear and dislike of the opponent that had been aroused in the previous century.[53] On the English side, French difference—the difference, that is, that set the French apart from both the English and from themselves—was understood as duplicity and double-dealing. The overriding theme of English war propaganda was what the *Gesta* called *Gallicana duplicitas*, what another text called *duplicitas Francorum* and *fraude Francorum*.[54] As early as the 1340s the English had contrasted "their own reasonableness, innocence, and even naiveté [to] the 'foxy cunning' and 'treachery' of the French," who pretended one thing only to do another (*unum agens et aliud simulans*).[55] For the vernacular chroniclers of Henry's reign the French were "dobil," full of "fraude and sotilte," practiced in "ymaginacionys, congettis and sleythis."[56] English writers often complained about the deceit even of their Burgundian allies: the "fals flemynges . . . loved vs neuer ʒit, by the roode, / ffor alle here fals flateryng fare," complains one poet bitterly, and another blamed John of Burgundy's murder on his own foolish manipulations as much as on the treachery of the Dauphin.[57] So when Philip of Burgundy abandoned the English at the Congress of Arras in 1435, Lydgate berated him in a language of French duplicity versus English integrity that was by now highly traditional: the English ambassadors had sought "of hool affeccioun . . . to haue concluded a parfyt vnyoun" but were thwarted by (of course) Philip's "doblynesse."[58]

This distinction between the frank, wholehearted English and the devious, guileful French—a distinction still to be found in English national self-identification—extends even to contemporary characterizations of the two languages. This linguistic issue is especially telling, for it shows how profoundly politicized the discourse of identity became, and provides an analogue at the level of national policy for Lydgate's reductive poetics. In his *Treatise of the Astrolabe*, written "in my lihte Englissh" about 1392, Chaucer had rather hopefully said that "the King [is] lord . . . of this langage," although Richard II may have preferred French; but it was the Lancastrians, and especially Henry V, who adopted "a policy," in John Fisher's words, "of encouraging the development of English as a national language."[59] Beginning perhaps as early as 1415 but certainly by the time of his second invasion of France in 1417, Henry worked to make English "an official language of central administration"—and with such personal direction that the bureaucratic vernacular promoted by his Chancery was actually modeled on the king's personal style (the King's English indeed!).[60] Lydgate was naturally hypersensitive to this royal policy, and in dedicating the *Troy Book* to Henry he says it was written "For to obeie with-oute variaunce / My lordes byddyng" (73–74), including the command that it be written "in englysche" (106):

> By-cause he wolde that to hyȝe and lowe
> The noble story openly wer knowe
> In oure tonge, aboute in euery age,
> And y-writen as wel in oure langage
> As in latyn and in frensche it is;
> That of the story þe trouthe we nat mys
> No more than doth eche other nacioun. (111–17)

The *Troy Book* is thus conceived as a work of national history (a "noble story") whose "trouthe" would submerge class differences ("hyȝe and lowe") within an overarching sense of a national identity equivalent to those of "eche other nacioun."

What accompanied this state-generated linguistic nationalism was a distinction between the French and English languages on the same moral and metaphysical grounds that were used to distinguish the nations as a whole. When the Brewers decided to keep their guild records in English, they explained (in Latin!) that they had done so because

> our mother-tongue, to wit the English tongue, hath in modern days begun to be honourably enlarged and adorned, for that our most excellent lord, King Henry V, hath in his letters missive and divers touching his own person [*personam suam propriam*], more willingly chosen to declare the secrets of his will [*secreta sue voluntatis*], and for the better understanding of his people, hath with a diligent mind procured the common idiom (setting aside others) to be commended by the exercise of writing.[61]

There the *materna lingua* becomes the natural medium for speaking about oneself and revealing the secrets of the will—for expressing, that is, one's essential selfhood or identity. Correspondingly, French was thought to be both foreign and capricious, both different from English and meretricious in itself.[62] This distinction was at no time more visible to the English than when they negotiated with their enemy—since, as one of Henry's captains said, "Certes all the ambassadors that we deal with be incongue, is to say in old

manner of speech in English, 'they be double and false.' "[63] A striking example are the negotiations of John of Gaunt and Richard, duke of York with
Philip of Burgundy and Jean, duc de Berry in 1394. According to Froissart,
the Englishmen had a difficult time of it, "car en parlure françoise a mots
soubtils et couvers et sur double entendement" while they "ne le veulent
entendre que plainement"; in Lord Berners's early sixteenth-century translation, "the Frenchemen . . . were full of subtyle wordes, and cloked perswa-
cions and double of understandynge," a verbal subtlety "which Englysshe-
men use nat in their langage, for their speche and entent is playne."[64] In
order to protect themselves from the smooth-talking French these plain-
spoken Englishmen submitted "aucune parlure obscure et dure ou pesant"
to the scrutiny of their learned clerks who would make sure that it was
"examinée et visitée et mise au cler." Froissart goes on to say that the English excused their scrupulousness by saying that since they had not learned
French in childhood they were not of the same "nature et condition" as the
Frenchmen. What might they have meant by this eliptical phrase is suggested by Lord Berners's significantly expanded translation of these three
words: "And the Englysshmen to excuse themselfe, wolde say, that Frenchemen lernynge suche subtlties in their youth, muste nedes be more subtyle
than they"—a passage that shows Lord Berners preserving his self-image as
a plain-speaker by employing the verbal manipulations he is censuring in his
Gallic opponents.

Linguistic self-images again became a matter of diplomatic policy in December 1418, when, with the help of the papal legate Cardinal Orsini,
Henry V sought to establish the terms of negotiation with the French. Henry
complained to Orsini that although the French wanted to conduct business
in French, he preferred Latin, which is *indifferens omni Natione*.[65] When
the French demurred, Henry continued to insist that all business be conducted "in a language which I can speak, understand, and write, that is,
English or Latin"—certainly a disingenuous requirement from a man who
for the first decade of his public life had conducted almost all his correspondence and official business in French. The impasse was resolved by Orsini's
proposal that all documents should be kept in French and Latin, and that in
cases of disagreement the Latin version should be authoritative. That more
than diplomatic jockeying was at issue here is suggested both by Henry's
insistence—which implies a real anxiety—and by Orsini's explanation that
Latin is required as an interpretive standard "because of the equivocations
and interchangeability of French words" (*propter AEquivicationes & Sino-
nima Verborum Gallicorum*). Apparently Italians also thought that French
was a language of dangerous complexity.

If the terms in which English identity was established were integrity and
truthfulness versus duplicity and guile, it is all the more interesting that
Henry's royal identity was constructed in essentially the same terms. To a

degree unusual even for a medieval monarch, Henry was taken to represent, even to embody, the nation as a whole, and he became a figure of fascination and awe for his contemporaries. His glories were commemorated in no less than five fifteenth-century Latin biographies, and although only one English biography survives, there is evidence that at least three others were written.[66] Given the fact that most medieval kings received no biographical treatment at all, this abundance witnesses to the remarkable degree to which Henry was able to identify the nation with himself.[67] And he accomplished this not only by his military and political talents (which should not be underestimated) but also by a careful strategy of self-construction that accorded with the values he was determined should prevail.[68]

The most evident means by which Henry defined himself as embodying the integrity or *trouthe* of the nation was his lifelong self-representation as a *vas electionis*, an agent of the God who has "þe auctour of trouthe." As early as the Welsh wars of his youth, he asserted that "la victoire n'est pas en la multitude de poeple . . . mais en la puissance de Dieu," a theme that reached its height with Agincourt.[69] Although most contemporary chroniclers knew full well that the stunning English victory was due at least in part to the lack of discipline of the French, there was none that did not also see in it the hand of God.[70] The theme of providential guidance was expressed with particular insistence in the magnificent pageant that greeted Henry on his entry into London in November 1415. The *Gesta* described how Henry first met a tower with a statue of St. George and a scroll reading *Soli deo honor et gloria*, and then passed by another tower where was "enthroned a figure of majesty in the form of a sun and emitting dazzling rays," and with the motto *Deo gracias*, "the tributes of praise to the honour and glory not of men but of God." The king, dressed in purple (the color of Christ's passion), walked in the midst of the procession with a small retinue: "Indeed, from his quiet demeanor, gentle pace, and sober progress," said the *Gesta*, "it might have been gathered that the king, silently pondering the matter in his heart, was rendering thanks and glory to God alone, not to man."[71]

Was this ostentatious humility? Or self-effacing arrogance? Only oxymorons can capture the manipulated and manipulating complexity of Henry's self-presentation. In other respects Henry's promotion of the almost theocratic grandeur of Lancastrian royalty was more straightforward, as in the changes in the coronation ceremony that stressed providential presence.[72] Nor was it only on festive occasions that Henry stressed the divine aura that encompassed his royal person. He was famously alert to the royal prerogative, demanding not just that ambassadors stand in his presence but that they avoid looking him in the face; and he would often sit under a canopy—as, for instance, when he received the surrendering citizens of Harfleur in 1415—that signified an authority derived from above.[73] And Henry's personal piety was famous: woe to the man who would interrupt the king while he communed with his Lord in prayer!

The *Gesta's* description of Henry's "sober progress" in the victory procession in London—the *Brut* refers to him as "sad," which in Middle English means "solemn"—is an early instance of a widespread attention to Henry's gravity, a seriousness of demeanor that bespeaks not merely resolution but a sense of higher purpose. John Page's poem on the *Siege of Rouen* describes Henry hearing mass "solemp with semeland so sad" and only then receiving the citizens of Rouen:

> Alle stylle he stode that whyle,
> Nothyr dyd he laughe nor smyle,
> But with a countenaunce fulle clere,
> And with a fulle lordely chere,
> Nor to mylde, nor to straunge,
> But in a mene withowtyn change,
> His countenans dyd he not a bate,
> But stylle he stode and in astate,
> Or hym lyste to geve an answere.[74]

It is this quiet uniformity of manner—what the version of Page's poem included in the *Brut* describes as being "ay in oon withoute chaunge"—that characterizes Henry throughout these writings.[75] Even his early wildness as Prince of Wales (in Frulovisi's oft-quoted phrase, he "exercised equally the feats of Venus and Mars") was turned to this purpose by providing the occasion for his almost religious conversion into Henry V: "And aftir his coronacion," says Capgrave, "he was everne turned onto anothir man, and alle his mociones inclined to vertu."[76]

The foil most persistently used to set off Henry's mature sincerity was not his own youthful excess but the frivolity of the French in general and the Dauphin in particular. The almost certainly apocryphal story of the gift of the tennis balls was designed to set Henry's seriousness of purpose against the Dauphin's trifling.[77] On the eve of Agincourt the French frolic—they "made mony grete fires, and moche revell with hontynge, and played our King and his lordeȝ at þe dys" (378), says the *Brut*—while Henry prayed; and his one-sentence speech to his troops before battle bespeaks a depth of seriousness, and a piety, that more flamboyant rhetoric would have betrayed: " 'Thanne,' said our King, 'nowe is gode tyme, for alle Engelond prayeth for vs; and þerfore be of gode chere, lette vs go to our iorney.' "[78] Pious, dutiful, letting his actions speak louder than his words, and bearing a very stiff upper lip indeed, Henry was presented by the contemporary sources as the prototype of a now familiar British national and imperial stereotype—the leader who eschews flamboyant gestures and bombastic words, whose depth of feeling is expressed by a terse matter-of-factness, who does his duty under difficult circumstances while modestly ascribing his triumphs to a force greater than himself.[79] And that this gravity was consistent with conquest rather than disaster—that it was equanimity in triumph rather than, as the heroic ethic had traditionally prescribed, resolution in defeat—made his economy of gesture all the more persuasive.

It would be wrong to think, however, that the construction of Henry's identity as an ideal type of the national character was an effect simply of image-making. For Henry's energetically pursued royal policy sought to place himself at the center of the nation's life, to provide his compatriots with not just a cynosure but the executive will that would bring them to coherence and direction. One of his first tasks was to reunite the governing classes of the country by imposing royal authority upon an increasingly law-less gentry. This he accomplished by deftly manipulating a system of royal rewards and punishment and, above all, by directing noble belligerence away from civil disorder and toward foreign conquest. Crucial to this disciplinary process was both the king's ability to behave with resolute and principled consistency—one of his epithets was *Justicia*—and the skillful deployment of his own prestige.[80] When he sought to reinvigorate a negligent judicial system, he relied on the court of king's bench, a court so "closely identified with the person and interests of the king [that] its proceedings were invested with peculiar authority."[81] And again, he was less interested in punishment than in reconciliation, a process accomplished largely by offering malefactors the opportunity to regain their monarch's grace by participating in the war in France: as Edward Powell says, "We may suspect that the courtrooms of 1414 had an aura of the recruiting-office about them."[82] Once these men entered into Henry's host they were again subject to a discipline rare in medieval warfare: Henry not only punished his soldiers for unauthorized depredations upon the populace but instituted such military practices as muster and review.[83]

There was, indeed, hardly an area of public life where Henry did not place himself at the center. Even while in France he insisted on maintaining close supervision over English affairs, and he took a personal interest in the details of administration throughout his ever-expanding French possessions, especially Normandy.[84] McFarlane characterized him as "the king who kept personal control of every branch of government," a control directed not just toward structuring and disciplining national practices but also toward placing the king always at the center of the national life.[85] His monastic foundations, for example, the most ambitious of any English monarch, were designed to produce, in Jeremy Catto's phrase, "a 'gigantic power-house of prayer' for the Lancastrian dynasty."[86] He also instituted liturgical changes that solicited spiritual support from his subjects, and in the spring of 1421 initiated a thoroughgoing reform of the Benedictine order—an event that had, as I shall shortly propose, a direct effect on the writing of the *Siege of Thebes* by the Benedictine Lydgate. His opposition to Lollard deviancy was of course unremitting—the Lollards called him "the prince of prestis and our uttir enmy"—and during his reign the Sarum Rite, refined at his monastery of Syon by Clement Maydeston, was promoted as the single authorized liturgy for the church in England.[87] In sum, in a striking prefiguration of the Tudor Reformation, Henry firmly and decisively brought religious life under state control. Nor was it only religious practice that Henry sought to supervise: in 1419 he had his brother Thomas, duke of Clarence, codify and register coats of arms, beginning the process by which the previously unregulated diffusion of armorial bearings was centralized, with the monarchy as the fount of honor.[88] Finally, even his choice of royal servants witnessed to what has been called the "personal dominance" of the king, a centralization that brought the business of governing "to new levels of professionalism and skill."[89]

In summation, then, Henry practiced what we can appropriately call the politics of identity, in the several senses in which that term has been used. His own monarchical identity stressed not just ethical integrity but psychological coherence, an unconflicted, forthright, and even artless selfhood confident in its values and resolute in pursuing its interests, a selfhood in which difference was subordinated to identity, *doublenesse* (as both ethical duplicity and psychological complexity) to *trouthe*. Furthermore, Henry was assiduous both in identifying the nation's interests with his own and in seeking to bring the various elements of fifteenth-century English society into identity with each other and with himself. This public policy was underwritten by an absolutism that was perhaps instinctive, perhaps deliberately fostered. But it succeeded not only because of Henry's extraordinary energy and skill, but also because it could draw upon a preexisting discursive field that named coherence and identity as proper while stigmatizing fragmentation and difference—and that endowed this opposition with the nationalist values of a country at war. In many ways Henry was a deeply conservative, even reactionary monarch, and we can see deep within his actions the great universalist dream of the Middle Ages. He was deeply committed to overcoming the scandal of the Great Schism—"ffor to make vnyon in hooly chirche," as a contemporary put it—and he always maintained that the reunification of France and England was only a prelude to the larger reunification of Christendom that he would accomplish with a Crusade to the Holy Land.[90] Yet he is also a preview of things to come, the age of absolutism that Europe was about to enter.[91]

CRACKS IN THE PEDESTAL

While Henry's making of himself and his world was immensely successful, even at the moment of his greatest triumph—his marriage to Catherine and designation as heir to the throne of France in May 1420—troubling complications were visible. The form these difficulties took are of interest to us because they show that the discursive field within which Henry operated so effectively also imposed restrictions that limited his largest ambitions. To be sure, Henry's problems were material as well as ideological. By 1419 the recruitment of soldiers and especially captains for service in France became difficult, so much so that the crown seems to have resorted to rather desperate means for finding "volunteers": in a letter of March 1420 one agent tells Henry that he will be recruiting at the sessions of the court of king's bench at York "opon the Deliverance of the Gaole there, and a Cession of the Pees also."[92] So too, parliament was becoming increasingly reluctant to approve taxes for the war: in December 1420 and May 1421 no money was granted, and in December 1421 only a small grant of one-fifteenth was approved.[93] Nor was it only men and money that were becoming more difficult to secure: "In 1418," we learn, "both archbishop Chichele and bishop Repingdon complained of the negligence, torpor and inaction with which their mandates to make patriotic prayers had been treated."[94] Apparently even spiritual support was becoming hard to come by.

There were no doubt many reasons for this waning of enthusiasm: the inevitable disillusionment when the brilliant victories of Harfleur, Agincourt, and Rouen gave way to the dispiriting prospect of a long, hard conquest, especially given the defeat and death of Clarence at Baugé in March 1421; the sense that since the king had now recovered his kingdom in France, its rebelliousness was a French not an English problem that should be paid for with French revenues; and a general lack of interest in foreign adventures when local concerns were so much more visibly pressing. But Henry's problems were ideological as well as practical. In the parliament of December 1420 the commons petitioned for the reenactment of a statute of 1351 that declared that the crown of England should never be subject to the crown of France.[95] Indeed, the Treaty of Troyes that had been signed six months earlier had acknowledged England's anxiety over its identity as an independent nation. After asserting, in a passage that has already been quoted, that the crowns of France and England shall "perpetuelly be togedyr . . . in Oone and in the same Persone" and that both realms shall also be governed "undir oone and the same Persone," the Treaty then adds:

> Kepyng ne the les, in all maner other thynges, to ayther of the same Roialmes here Ryghtees, or Custumes, Usages, and Lawes; not makyng subget in ony manere of wise oone of the same Roialmes to th'oder, nor puttyng under, or submittyng the Ryghtes, Lawes, Custumes, or Usages of that oone of the sayd Roialmes, to the Ryghtes, Lawes, Custumes, or Usages of that other of the same.[96]

The crowns are one but the nations are separate; the governing authorities are the same but the systems of government are different. This is a condition that is perhaps constitutionally conceivable, perhaps even practically possible. But it is also one that sets up within the discourse of identity and difference an intolerable contradiction.

The commons' petition expressed a concern for English separateness—for preserving the national identity that Henry himself had so assiduously developed.[97] And this concern allows us to see that the war had used the language of identity and difference in two, mutually exclusive ways. On the one hand, it had insisted on English integrity versus French duplicity, presenting England as politically unified and ethically coherent while France was riven by internal divisions and corrupted by duplicity. Yet on the other hand, it had also claimed that the war was undertaken to heal the rift between the fraternal nations England and France, to bring back to unity—to oneness and integrity—two crowns that were in truth parts of a single whole. In a sense, Henry was simultaneously prosecuting two different wars: a national war that required his compatriots to conceive of themselves as citizens of a state threatened by a foreign power, and a dynastic war that defined them as vassals loyal to their feudal lord and committed to regaining his rights. These conflicting identities then began to emerge as Henry moved closer to achieving the goal that perhaps not even he had fully believed within his grasp, and in the clauses of the Treaty of Troyes, as in the parliamentary statute six months later, it began to disturb his inexorable progress toward synthesis.

The best evidence of this disturbance can be found in the efforts that Henry's heirs made, beginning immediately upon his death and continuing for most of the next two decades, to generate support for what came increasingly to be felt as a *damnosa hereditas*.[98] Their impossible task was to demonstrate that the dual monarchy was not a constitutional and conceptual monstrosity but a desirable, even natural political arrangement. But given the privileging of singularity and unity, is it imaginable, as Lydgate put it, "To wer too crownys"?[99] A particularly interesting attempt to answer this question was produced in the year after Henry's death, when the duke of Bedford commissioned a genealogical poem from Laurence Calot, a French clerk, and had it illustrated by an accompanying manuscript picture. The painting—a later copy of which survives—traces out with elaborate care the descent of the royal lines of England and France and their ultimate unification in the young Henry VI, only two at the time.[100] (See Figures 1 and 2.) The picture is rigorously symmetrical: a central lozenge, which includes portraits of the Capetians from St. Louis on and is labeled the "Directe ligne de France," is framed by a band on the left, labeled the "ligne collateralle de France" and containing portraits of the Valois kings, and by an identical band on the right, which contains portraits of the "ligne d'Angleterre" from Edward I to Henry V. At the bottom of the page the bands curve together to join in a portrait of the infant Henry VI, over whose head hover two angels. These angels bear the crowns of France and England: here two become one.

1. Manuscript illustration. British Library MS Royal 15 E. vi.

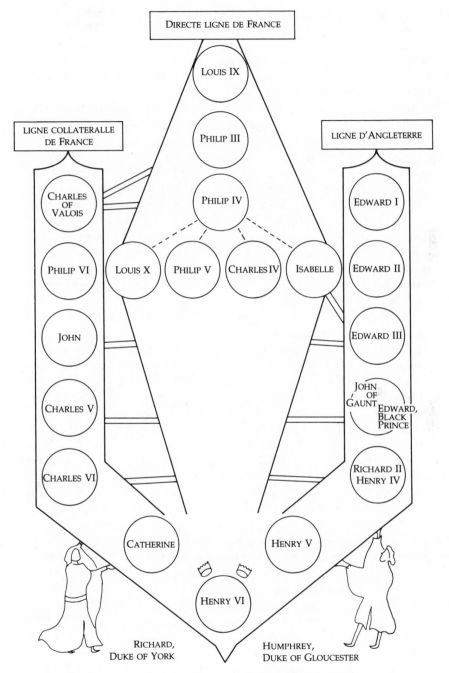

DIRECTE LIGNE DE FRANCE

LOUIS IX

PHILIP III

LIGNE COLLATERALLE DE FRANCE

LIGNE D'ANGLETERRE

CHARLES OF VALOIS

PHILIP IV

EDWARD I

PHILIP VI

LOUIS X   PHILIP V   CHARLES IV   ISABELLE

EDWARD II

JOHN

EDWARD III

CHARLES V

JOHN OF GAUNT   EDWARD, BLACK PRINCE

CHARLES VI

RICHARD II HENRY IV

CATHERINE

HENRY V

HENRY VI

RICHARD, DUKE OF YORK

HUMPHREY, DUKE OF GLOUCESTER

2. Schematic representation of Figure 1. Prepared by Christopher L. Brest.

Or do they? The purpose of the design is to present the random walk of the royal politics of England and France—a politics deformed by the accidents of reproduction, the hazards of the marriage market, the uncertainties of battle, and by insanity, incompetence, and betrayal—as a process of unbroken rectilinearity, a development so orderly as to be both inevitable and, in its visual representation, self-evident. Yet those hovering angels, forever holding two crowns over a single infant head form an image whose instability denies ideological closure. The angels must hover forever while Henry must remain forever *infans*, incompetent, heir to a split legacy whose contradictions he could hardly be expected to resolve. A king with two kingdoms and two crowns is by no means unfamiliar to the Middle Ages—indeed, the Pope wore *three*—and Kantorowicz has taught us that because kings, like other ruling figures, were both mortal persons and immortal offices they were subject to "innumerable germinations."[101] So it is not doubleness per se that causes the problem, but the practical reality of uniting France and England. In using this ungainly form of representation—which angel is going to get the crown on first, and then where will the second one go?—the picture is curiously at odds with itself: it makes visible the very difference it was meant to deny.

That there was a credibility gap among the French, for whom Calot's poem and its accompanying picture were initially intended, was only natural. But there was also a problem in England, and the propaganda campaign mounted there included a translation of Calot's poem by none other than John Lydgate. Commissioned by the earl of Warwick in 1427, in Lydgate's "The Title and Pedigree of Henry VI" the discourse of identity and difference—called here "trouthe" and "variaunce"—is deployed with an insistence, even an obsessiveness that pushes it to the breaking point.[102] The premise of the poem is that Christ, "Prince and souerain Lord / Of vnyte, of peas, and of accorde" (75–76), "hath for vs so graciously provided, / To make al oon that first was devided" (142–43), a "vnyte" (156) that the poem will make visible and self-evident: "We may *se* with euery circumstaunce / Direct the lyne of Englond of Fraunce" (136–37). This political submergence of difference into identity has an analogue in the poem's own method. Its sequential structure lays out the genealogical line "in order ceriously" (40), a structure identical with the putative rectilinearity of Henry's descent "from þe stok riall / Of Seint Lowis" (225–26); and its own meaning, we are assured, "woll nat vary" from the "truth[e]" (107). Moreover, Lydgate insists that he is both a faithful translator of Calot's original—"In substaunce filowyng the substaunce / Of his writyng and compilacioun" (62–63)—and a loyal servant of the earl of Warwick, whose "precept first and commaundement" (12) he here fully enacts. Finally, the poem is designed to bring about in its reader/viewer the uniformity and self-identity it everywhere displays,

"To put awey all maner [of] variaunce, / Holy the doute and þe ambyguyte" (6–7). Asserting identity and rejecting difference in every dimension, "The Title and Pedigree of Henry VI" bespeaks by the very ardor of its commitment the tenacity of the doubts it means to remove.

Henry V's enterprise was projected and justified in terms of identity and reunion—two would become one—but it concluded in difference and division: one was encumbered with two. No symbolic discourse, whether painting or poetry, could resolve this dilemma, and in Lydgate's "Title and Pedigree"—as in his many other poems supporting the dual monarchy—we witness the collision between language and fact, between rhetoric and truth, that Lydgate's poetics of identity refused to contemplate.[103] We witness universalism—both Henry's and Lydgate's—pushed to its discursive limits and beyond by the realities that rendered its ambitions unattainable. After his death, the absolutist politics of identity that had guided Henry in the construction of both himself and his world confronted differences that neither military nor linguistic *force majeure* could subdue: differences between French and English culture, between dynastic rights and national interests, between the imperial ambitions of the chivalric class and the local concerns of the nation at large, and between a heroic father and his saintly son.

As for Lydgate, it is not only in his translation of Calot, that we can recognize anxiety and even the intuition of failure. If we now, at the end of this essay, turn back to 1421–1422, and to the *Siege of Thebes*, there becomes retroactively visible Lydgate's own skepticism toward his identity as a spokesman for Lancastrian interests, and perhaps even an acknowledgment that poetry and power can never be brought to a perfect identity of purpose.

IDENTIFYING THE WRITER

Although I have described the general historical setting within which the *Siege of Thebes* was produced, there is as well a more specific context that needs to be mentioned. As mentioned earlier, in the spring of 1421 Henry undertook a campaign to reform Benedictine monasticism in England. In March he wrote to the Abbot of St. Edmunds (Lydgate's monastery) asking him to summon a meeting of the order. The meeting, presided over by the Abbot and attended by the foremost monks in England, convened in Westminster on 7 May. It was opened by an address by the king directing the order to dispense with recent innovations and return to Benedict's original foundation, what Henry called the *pristina religio monachorum*: we recognize here both Henry's desire to exercise royal control over the nation's spiritual institutions and his abiding belief in the power and purity of historical origins.[104] Naturally the monastic community politely de-

murred, explaining its deviations from Benedict's rule by reference to the
dispensing power of the abbot and the precedent of later canonistic authority. At any rate, by June the king had returned to France, never to return
to England alive, and when the monastic commission set up to consider
the king's suggestions reported in 1423, the question was good and truly
moot.

While the records of the May meeting maintain a blandly official tone, we
do have access to a more vivid monastic reaction. This is a contemporary
sermon, probably preached by a monk of St. Peter's, Gloucester named John
Pauntley, and probably preached before the king just before his return to
France on June 10, 1421.[105] Written in a mixture of Latin and English, and
witnessing to an equally mixed attitude toward the king, this sermon can
serve as an analogue to the *Siege of Thebes*, which was being written by
another Benedictine at exactly the same time. On its face the sermon is a
paean to Henry's leadership: although the ship of the kingdom is sailing
across what Pauntley calls (in bad Latin) a *duplici mari*—a double sea that
symbolizes both "welth and prosperite" and "woo and adversite" (88)—it is
under the sure hand of this "wise mariner and most worþi werriour" (91).
Henry's success, however, is interpreted not as a tribute to his own virtues
but as a reward for his protection and renovation of God's church: "Just as *he
hath qwyt* God, so God has rewarded him; just as his love has advanced God
and the church, so *his wele and honour* have been advanced" (92). Having
thus established the priority of religious values, Pauntley then launches into
a gloomily monkish warning about the dangers of chivalric achievement, an
admonition he illustrates with a somewhat tactless reference to the death of
Henry's brother Clarence only three months earlier.

> There is neither faith nor stability in worldly glory; worldly honor is *a sliper
> þinge and elvich*; now it is, now it is not; today a man, tomorrow not; today a
> lord, tomorrow *a lost man*; today *a dowti werrour*, tomorrow dead in the
> field. . . . So, *be þou never so worþi a werrioure, never so wise a governour*, even
> if you attain the highest point of honor, even if you sail over high seas *of welth
> and prosperite, be þou ones passid þi path schal wex fulle pleyn, þi worþi dedes*
> will be forgotten *and passe out of mynde*. (92–93)

Finally, turning to Henry's intervention in Benedictine affairs, he agrees
that the religious life has declined from its original integrity:

> Neither regulars nor seculars live as they ought. Our conversation and way of
> life is not as it once was. Our coat is of another color. Our life is not like the lives
> of our old fathers. *Many brekkes* are in every part of our ship. . . . But we will be
> saved by *oure sovereyn lord*. (95)

This passage would certainly seem to justify the editor's opinion that our
author "betrays no uneasiness about the king's concurrent attempt to reform

the Benedictines" (87). And yet the examples he gives of the high standards from which current monks have fallen away are instances of neither spiritual fortitude nor meditative transcendence but of political resistance to presumptuous monarchs.

> Once the lords temporal and spiritual were touched and moved by the spirit of God. . . . Behold this spirit moved the holy doctor Saint Ambrose to excommunicate the mighty emperor Theodosius because his ministers recklessly killed many innocent people in a particular city. This spirit moved saint Thomas of Canterbury to resist king Henry II and to spill his own blood for the liberty of the Church. The life of these men was such that they did not fear to reprehend sin, they dared to speak the truth, they placed the fear of God before themselves. (94)

Here, then, is a Benedictine performing the traditional role of advisor to the prince in a way that is, if not ironic, at least highly complex. The monarch is saluted for his achievements, but reminded that they are an effect of his devotion to Holy Church; celebrated for his leadership, but warned that pride goeth before a fall; praised for restoring the monastic order to its former integrity, yet told that this integrity is defined by the admonishment of abusive monarchs. Whatever Henry may have thought of this performance, it masterfully deploys traditional *topoi* to express both submission and independence, to identify its speaker with the royal program and yet to insist that the different interests of monk and king be respected. And it provides a telling analogue to Lydgate's similarly ambivalent text.

We should hardly be surprised that the *Siege of Thebes* cannot live up to its disingenuous assertions of transparency and self-identity. As literary critics never tire of pointing out, literary texts are always complex and self-conflicted, and it takes no great interpretive subtlety to deconstruct the *Siege*, a poem that virtually undoes itself through narrative digressions and thematic indecision. But rather than explain this irresolution globally, by reference to properties inherent in literature or even language, a procedure that itself universalizes and dehistoricizes, I prefer to invoke the specificities of Lydgate's situation. For one thing, Henry's proposed reformation of the Benedictine order helps to account for Lydgate's self-presentation in the *Siege* as a monk who is conscientious in performing his penitential and civic duties and yet alert to administrative challenges to his sense of monastic integrity. Put simply, the Prologue to the *Siege* argues that the king's program to reform the Benedictines is both unwanted and unnecessary: just as the pilgrim Lydgate resists the Host's overbearing directives, so the monastic establishment as a whole needs no political direction in order to perform its traditional functions. Thus Lydgate asserts both compliance with and independence from unreasonable commands, a double response not unlike that of John Pauntley's uncompromisingly ambiguous sermon.

Rereading the poem in the light of this more complex relationship, we can see that while at one level it is an admiring commentary on Henry's French war, telling the story of the recovery of a kingdom by its rightful ruler through the enforcement of "Couenauntys and conuencioun / Imad of olde" (3774–75), it also tells of fratricidal struggle that ends in bleak devastation. Indeed, its deepest message is that using war to right wrongs is a brutal and uncertain strategy. Even the moral differences between Polynices and Ethiocles, and between the Argives and Thebans—differences, after all, upon which the efficacy of the entire narrative depends—are not consistently maintained. Both Polynices and his Argive allies often behave in ways that impeach their moral superiority, and even the supremely virtuous Tydeus—who serves the poem as its premier mirror of princehood—ends his life gnawing in rage on the head of his enemy.[106] To be sure, none of the details that upset the clarity of the poem's moral structure is added by Lydgate to his source; and Statius's *Thebaid*, to which every medieval version of the Theban legend must finally be referred, is unremitting in its insistence that all that war can ever accomplish is the moral degradation of its participants. But in the spring of 1421, as the implications of Henry's triumph were beginning to come clear, it was this narrative that Lydgate chose to rewrite, a choice that entitles us to recognize that its darker meanings have contemporary relevance.

Nor is the poem's antiwar message the only or even the most telling way in which it challenges Henry's successes. For to invoke the Theban legend as a commentary on contemporary events was to summon up a dangerously subversive historiography. In medieval as in classical writing, Thebes was the site of endlessly repeated acts of hubric impiety and internecine slaughter. Most important, the grim history of Thebes was one of blind repetition: from its foundation by Cadmus's fratricidal dragon warriors through to its final extinction in the internecine combat of Ethiocles and Polynices, Thebes was a site where the inexpiable bloodletting of family violence was endlessly repeated. Even a bare list of Theban victims tells the story: Cadmus's wife Harmonia (the daughter of Mars and Venus and recipient of the famous and fatal Theban necklace, made by Vulcan as a bitter wedding gift), Semele (whose son Dionysius became immortal at the price of his mother's death), Agave (mother and murderer of Pentheus), Niobe (wife of Amphion, and responsible for the deaths of her children), and even Amphiaraus, not a Theban at all but a victim of its curse: his wife Euriphyle betrayed him to his death on the campaign against Thebes because she was bribed by Harmonia's necklace. The exemplary figure of Theban history, as the Middle Ages well knew, was above all Oedipus, whose parricide and incest trace the central pattern of violence and repetition, of family slaughter and of blind recursion to the source.[107]

Given this significance, the Theban story inevitably called into question both the commitment to purposive action and the rectilinear transmission of value from the past that underwrote medieval monarchy. This underwriting was articulated in medieval historiography by another classical legend, that of Troy. Troy served the Western monarchies as their founding myth of origins because it maintained that fall is followed by rise, that heroic achievement can be reachieved, that empire can be translated both geographically and temporally, and—most important—that a historical origin can provide a secure foundation upon which the future can be built. But Theban history challenged all these assertions by revealing a profound corruption at the very source of historical action: in the *Siege of Thebes* Lydgate names it "ynfecciouin called Orygynal" (2565), a phrasing that correlates the biblical concept of original sin with the antique sense of a fatal impurity, an irredeemable pollution.

Both psychologically and historiographically, then, Theban history questions the myth of origins promoted by Trojan history. For this "tale of woes," as Statius called it (2, 267), there is in effect no history, no linearity, no transmission, just the futile reenactment of a fatal desire. This is why we can say that Theban history deconstructs medieval historiography, that it articulates an anxious skepticism that medieval culture for the most part held at bay. But there had been an earlier occasion in the English historiographical tradition when the toxic Theban story was allowed to contaminate the Trojan foundation myth. This was Chaucer's *Troilus and Criseyde*, a Trojan poem that harbored an insistent and finally fatal Theban subtext.[108] In his own Trojan poem Lydgate assiduously avoided such dangerous material, a perfect example of his simplification of Chaucerian complexity. But in the *Siege of Thebes*, begun immediately after the completion of his own *Troy Book*, he allowed it voice. And if, in correlating this Theban material with Henry's triumph, he issued a monitory warning, he also offered a shrewdly ironic self-assessment. In the Prologue to the *Siege* he had in effect defined himself as an anti-Chaucer, as the serious historian who avoided Chaucerian frivolity and irresolution. Yet in the final analysis he wrote a poem that incorporated its own opposite, the same strategy that Chaucer had so brilliantly used in *Troilus and Criseyde*. Perhaps despite himself, then, Lydgate discovered that he was Chaucerian after all.

NOTES

* I wish to thank the members of the Medieval Seminar at the Institute for Advanced Study in the fall term, 1991, and especially Profs. Paul Hyams and Richard Tarrant, for the attentive and helpful reading they gave this essay.

1. Brian Stock, *Listening for the Text: On the Uses of the Past* (Baltimore: Johns Hopkins University Press, 1990), p. 78.

2. *La Poésie du moyen âge* (Paris: Hachette, 1887), p. 220.

3. Isidore, *Etymologiae* 1, 41; Jacques Derrida, *Of Grammatology*, trans. G. C. Spivak (Baltimore: Johns Hopkins University Press, 1976 [1967]), p. 158.

4. Dominick LaCapra, "Rhetoric and History," in *History and Criticism* (Ithaca: Cornell University Press, 1985), p. 17.

5. An example of such disregard, striking because of the very high level of the work, is Chris Given-Wilson's *The Royal Household and the King's Affinity: Service, Politics and Finance in England 1360–1413* (New Haven: Yale University Press, 1986), which discusses the Ricardian court while making no reference to Richard Firth Green's important *Poets and Princepleasers: Literature and the Court in the Late Middle Ages* (Toronto: University of Toronto Press, 1980); indeed, his book refers only once to the court's most prominent literary figure, Geoffrey Chaucer, and then his name is misprinted (61). Of course there are exceptions: David Aers's *Community, Gender, and Individual Identity: English Writing 1360–1430* (London: Routledge, 1988) has already been put to good use by P. R. Coss in his important essay "Bastard Feudalism Revised," *Past and Present* 125 (1989): 27–64. After this essay was completed, there appeared *Chaucer's England: Literature in Historical Context*, ed. Barbara A. Hanawalt (Minneapolis: University of Minnesota Press, 1992). Including splendid essays by both historians and literary critics, this collection represents one of the most promising developments in the study of late medieval English culture in many years.

6. For example, Stephen Knight, *Geoffrey Chaucer* (Oxford: Blackwell, 1985); Paul Olson, *The Canterbury Tales and the Good Society* (Princeton: Princeton University Press, 1986); Susan Crane, *Insular Romance* (Berkeley: University of California Press, 1987); David Aers, *Community, Gender, and Individual Identity* (see above, n. 5); Paul Strohm, *Social Chaucer* (Cambridge, Mass.: Harvard University Press, 1989); Peggy Knapp, *Chaucer and the Social Contest* (London: Routledge, 1988); Peter Brown and Andrew Butcher, *The Age of Saturn: Literature and History in the Canterbury Tales* (Oxford: Basil Blackwell, 1991).

7. Two examples—chosen not because they are egregious but because of the excellence of their literary analyses—are provided by H. Marshall Leicester, *The Disenchanted Self: Representing the Subject in the Canterbury Tales* (Berkeley: University of California Press, 1990) and Carolyn Dinshaw, *Chaucer's Sexual Poetics* (Madison: University of Wisconsin Press, 1989). Leicester's well-taken point is that most self-designated historicist criticism reduces both Chaucer and, more important, his tale-tellers, to agents of a supervening cultural practice they enact but are unable to conceptualize. But while he shows that the poet and his fictive surrogates have an ironic or "disenchanted" relation to their culture, he locates this disenchantment within the Weberian dynamic of modernization in only the briefest of ways (27–28). As he says, "I regard the kind of work I do here as a preliminary contribution to a more properly historical account of the late Middle Ages" (28). While Dinshaw includes a wider range of medieval literary references in her analyses, at important points she too substitutes modern theory for medieval meanings. For instance, her discussion of the Pardoner interprets his relics in terms of Freud's theory of the fetish as partial object, but ignores both medieval attitudes and practice (176–77).

8. Terry Eagleton, *Literary Theory* (Minneapolis: University of Minnesota Press, 1983), p. 150.

9. According to Frank Lentricchia, *After the New Criticism* (Chicago: University of Chicago Press, 1980), "On the matter of history, the deconstructionist position . . . appears equivalent to the position of the literary know-nothing, newly reinforced with a theory of discourse that reassures him that history-writing is bunk" (182).

10. Jacques Derrida, "Limited Inc., abc . . ." in *Glyph* 2 (1977): 236. As Derrida goes on to say, "All metaphysicians, from Plato to Rousseau, Descartes to Husserl, have proceeded in this way, conceiving good to be before evil, the positive before the negative, the pure before the impure, the simple before the complex, the essential before the accidental, the imitated before the imitation, etc. And this is not just *one* metaphysical gesture among others, it is *the* metaphysical exigency, that which has been the most constant, most profound, and most potent" (ibid.).

11. Derrida, "Differance," in *Speech and Phenomena* (Evanston: Northwestern University Press, 1973), p. 147.

12. See Christopher Norris, *What's Wrong with Postmodernism: Critical Theory and the Ends of Philosophy* (Baltimore: Johns Hopkins University Press, 1990).

13. Jonathan Culler, *On Deconstruction: Theory and Criticism after Structuralism* (Ithaca: Cornell University Press, 1982), p. 157.

14. As K. B. McFarlane said, "In his capable hands at least the medieval kingship betrayed no sign that age had brought fragility" ("Henry V, Bishop Beaufort and the Red Hat, 1417–21" [1945], reprinted in *England in the Fifteenth Century* [London: Hambledon, 1981], p. 79).

15. (New York: Putnam's, 1901). There have been negative accounts, including the fundamental work by J. T. Wylie and (for volume 3) William T. Waugh, *The Reign of Henry V*, 3 vols. (Cambridge: Cambridge University Press, 1914–1929) and, more recently, Desmond Seward, *Henry V: The Scourge of God* (New York: Viking, 1988), but these are very much minority opinions.

16. Derek Pearsall, *John Lydgate* (London: Routledge and Kegan Paul, 1970); see also Pearsall's fine essay, "Chaucer and Lydgate," in *Chaucer Traditions: Studies in Honour of Derek Brewer*, ed. Ruth Morse and Barry Windeatt (Cambridge: Cambridge University Press, 1990), pp. 39–53. The earlier attempts to present Lydgate as protohumanist were by Walter F. Schirmer, *John Lydgate: A Study of the Culture of the XVth Century*, trans. Ann E. Keep (London: Methuen, 1961 [1952]), and Alain Renoir, *John Lydgate: Poet of the Transition* (London: Routledge and Kegan Paul, 1967). An expert survey of Lydgate criticism is provided by A. S. G. Edwards, "Lydgate Scholarship: Progress and Prospects," in Robert F. Yeager, ed., *Fifteenth-Century Studies: Recent Essays* (New Haven: Archon Books, 1984), pp. 29–47.

17. I take the term "traditionalistic" from Stock, *Listening to the Text*, p. 165.

18. I have discussed the monarchical value of the Trojan myth to Henry II in *Negotiating the Past: The Historical Understanding of Medieval Literature* (Madison: University of Wisconsin Press, 1987), pp. 201–4, and to Richard II in *Chaucer and the Subject of History* (Madison: University of Wisconsin Press, 1991), pp. 161–62. That Henry understood this value is also suggested by his possession of a deluxe copy of Chaucer's *Troilus and Criseyde*, a manuscript adorned with his coat of arms as Prince of Wales. Henry commissioned the *Troy Book* from Lydgate in the spring of 1412, after his reconciliation with his father and his apparent acceptance of the fact that he would accede to the throne only by the natural process of inheritance: see McFarlane, *Lancastrian Kings and Lollard Knights* (Oxford: Clarendon, 1972), p. 110.

19. Elmham produced a *Liber Metricus de Henrico Quinto* in 1418 and Walsingham wrote a defense of Henry's conquest of Normandy, the *Ypodigma Neustriae*, in 1419.

20. Pearsall, *John Lydgate*, p. 169. Johnstone Parr, "Astronomical Dating for Some of Lydgate's Poems," *PMLA* 67 (1952): 251–58, dated the chronographia with which the *Siege* opens to April 27, 1421.

21. Robert W. Ayers, "Medieval History, Moral Purpose and the Structure of Lydgate's *Siege of Thebes*," *PMLA* 73 (1958): 463–74.

22. All citations from the *Siege of Thebes* are from the edition by Alex Erdmann and (for volume 2) Eilert Ekwall, 2 vols., EETS ES, 108, 125 (London: Oxford University Press, 1911–1930). I have omitted scribal slashes and editorial diacritical marks and have on occasion altered the punctuation. Immediately after Henry's death, and while the governing circle was trying to sort out the responsibilities of his brothers the dukes of Bedford and Gloucester in the governance of England and France, Lydgate wrote a prose treatise warning against disunity that took both its title—the *Serpent of Division*—and its inspiration from this passage in the *Siege*. His historical instance was in this case not the Theban legend but the Roman civil wars. See H. N. MacCracken, ed., *The Serpent of Division* (London: Oxford University Press, 1911). In the *Fall of Princes*, written between 1437 and 1450 for Duke Humphrey of Gloucester, the lesson of Thebes is that "kyngdamys deuyded may no while endure": Henry Bergen, ed., *Lydgate's Fall of Princes*, 4 vols. (Washington: Carnegie Institution, 1923–1927), 1.105 (Book 1, line 3822).

23. Lois Ebin, *Illuminator, Makar, Vates: Visions of Poetry in the Fifteenth Century* (Lincoln: University of Nebraska Press, 1988), pp. 19–48, and the earlier studies cited there.

24. This account of Amphion is Lydgate's addition to his source: see *Siege*, 2:100–101.

25. The role of Amphion in the *Siege* and the privileging of the "word" over the "sword" is discussed by Ebin in *John Lydgate* (Boston: Twayne, 1985), pp. 53–55.

26. In "Chaucer, Lydgate, and the 'Myrie Tale,' " *Chaucer Review* 13 (1978–1979): 316–36, Ebin provides a more benign assessment of Lydgate's revisions of Chaucerian values in the *Siege*. A different but not incompatible account to that presented here is provided by A. C. Spearing, "Lydgate's Canterbury Tales: *The Siege of Thebes* and Fifteenth-Century Chaucerianism," in Yeager, *Fifteenth-Century Studies*, pp. 333–64; see also Spearing's *Medieval to Renaissance in English Poetry* (Cambridge: Cambridge University Press, 1985), pp. 66–88.

27. John Bowers, "The *Tale of Beryn* and the *Siege of Thebes*: Alternative Ideas of the *Canterbury Tales*," *SAC* 7 (1985): 45.

28. In the *Troy Book*—Lydgate's version of the *historia* that Chaucer had so romantically retold in *Troilus and Criseyde*—he is even more insistent upon his *trouthefulnesse* as a historian: see the excellent discussion in C. David Benson, *The History of Troy in Middle English Literature* (Woodbridge: Brewer, 1980), pp. 97–129.

29. It should also be noted that in the Prologue Lydgate corrects what he would have seen as the Chaucerian misrepresentation of monasticism in the *Canterbury Tales*: Lydgate's Host suggests that Lydgate's name might be "Dan Piers" (82), the name of Chaucer's corrupt Monk, but is firmly corrected: "My name was Lydgate, / Monk of Bery" (92–93). The Host quickly responds: "Daun Iohn, . . . wel broke ȝe ȝoure name!" (96).

30. For law and order, see Edward Powell, *Kingship, Law, and Society: Criminal Justice in the Reign of Henry V* (Oxford: Oxford University Press, 1989), and E. F.

Jacob, *The Fifteenth Century 1399–1485* (Oxford: Clarendon Press, 1961): "In Henry V's first parliament (15 May 1413), . . . the commons spoke emphatically about the weakness of the last reign, of disobedience to the laws, and the lack of public order" (133). For Henry IV's household, see Given-Wilson, *Royal Household*, pp. 140–41.

31. J. Kail, ed., *Twenty-Six Political and Other Poems*, EETS, OS 124 (London: Kegan Paul, Trench, Trübner, 1904), pp. 50, 54 (lines 5 and 129–30). The poem is also printed by Rossell Hope Robbins, ed., *Historical Poems of the XIVth and XVth Centuries* (New York: Columbia University Press, 1959), no. 15.

32. Kail, *Political Poems*, p. 58 (lines 105–6); for Beaufort's speech, see Kail's Introduction, pp. xix–xx, and V. J. Scattergood, *Politics and Poetry in the Fifteenth Century* (London: Blandford, 1971), pp. 49–50. According to the speech, the purpose of the Leicester Parliament was to root out Lollardy, enforce maritime peace, and restore public order; see Edward Powell, "The Restoration of Law and Order," in G.L. Harriss, ed., *Henry V: The Practice of Kingship* (Oxford: Oxford University Press, 1985), p. 63.

33. Cited from MS Bodley 649 by R. M. Haines, "Church, Society and Politics in the Early Fifteenth Century, as viewed from an English Pulpit," *Church, Society and Politics*, ed. Derek Baker, *Studies in Church History*, 12 (Oxford: Blackwell, 1975), p. 156 n. 94.

34. Thomas Hoccleve, "On Richard II's Burial at Westminster," in *Minor Poems*, ed. F. J. Furnivall, EETS, ES 61 (London: Kegan Paul, Trench, Trübner, 1892), lines 1–2.

35. John Capgrave, *The Chronicle of England (from the creation to 1417)*, ed. F. C. Hingeston (London: Longman, Brown, Green, Longmans, and Roberts, 1858), p. 309.

36. Friedrich W. D. Brie, ed., *The Brut, or the Chronicles of England*, pt. 2, EETS, OS 136 (London: Kegan Paul, Trench, Trübner, 1908), p. 376.

37. "Address to Sir John Oldcastle," in Furnivall, *Minor Poems*, lines 37–38.

38. Hoccleve, "Balade au Tres Noble Roy Henry Le Quint," in Furnivall, *Minor Poems*, lines 60, 64.

39. Brie, *Brut*, pp. 373–74.

40. Frank Taylor, ed., "The Chronicle of John Strecche for the Reign of Henry V (1414–1422)," *BJRL* 16 (1932): 149; Rossell Hope Robbins, ed., *Historical Poems of the XIVth and XVth Centuries* (New York: Columbia University Press, 1959), no. 95, lines 86–90; see also no. 64, lines 57–64.

41. "A Defence of Holy Church," in MacCracken, ed., *Minor Poems*, p. 34 (lines 96–97).

42. F. Taylor and J. S. Roskell, eds., *Gesta Henrici Quinti* (Oxford: Clarendon Press, 1975), p. 17.

43. Cited from Rymer's *Foedera* by C. T. Allmand, *Lancastrian Normandy 1415–1450: The History of a Medieval Occupation* (Oxford: Clarendon Press, 1983), p. 123 n. 5. Henry's policy of repopulating the duchy with English men and women could also be justified in these terms: see Robert Massey, "The Land Settlement in Lancastrian Normandy," in A. J. Pollard, ed., *Property and Politics: Essays in Later Medieval English History* (Gloucester: Alan Sutton, 1984), p. 78.

44. This Henrician theme is discussed by virtually all modern historians; see, for example, Jacob, *Fifteenth Century*, p. 123. G. L. Harriss points out that "Henry V presented himself not as the conqueror but as the heir and saviour of France, the

very terms in which his father had claimed the crown of England" ("The Exemplar of Kingship," in Harriss, ed., *Henry V*, 1).

45. E. F. Jacob, *Henry V and the Invasion of France* (London: Hodder and Stoughton, 1947), p. 76.

46. Taylor and Roskell, *Gesta*, 2/3, 58/59, 94/95.

47. C. L. Kingsford, ed., "Extracts from the First Version of Hardyng's Chronicle," *EHR* 27 (1912): 744; John Lydgate, *Troy Book*, ed. Henry Bergen, part 3, p. 870. Schirmer argues that the central theme of the *Troy Book* is that "strife and discord are poison, the root of all trouble and disorder in every land. It is a motto for the times, as well as a timeless one, when Lydgate says, in connexion with the quarrel between the Greek commanders: 'Lo what meschef lyth in variaunce / Amonge lordis, whan þei nat accorde' " (*John Lydgate*, 49).

48. Similar to this argument is the oft-repeated claim that Henry was interested only in peace but that he could attain that goal only by war. On October 25, 1416, the anniversary of Agincourt, Bishop Beaufort preached to parliament on the theme, "Bella faciamus, ut pacem habeamus, quia finis belli, pax" (Allmand, *Lancastrian Normandy*, 7). See also Henry's letter to the citizens of London of 5 August 1419: "And forasmoch as our aduerse partie wol noo pees nor accord haue wiþ vs, but finally haue refused al meenes of pees, We be compelled ayein to werre thorough þair default, as he wot þat al knoweþ" (R. W. Chambers and Marjorie Daunt, eds., *A Book of London English* [Oxford: Clarendon Press, 1931], 78).

49. These laments were translated into English later in the century when England began to suffer its own civil war: see Diane Bornstein, ed., *The Middle English Translation of Christine de Pisan's 'Livre de corps de policie'* (Heidelberg: Winter, 1977), and Margaret S. Blayney, ed., *Fifteenth-Century English Translations of Alain Chartier's "Le Traité de l'Esperance" and "Le Quadrilogue Invectif,"* 2 vols., EETS, OS 270, 281 (London: Oxford University Press, 1974–1980).

50. The French and Latin versions of the Treaty are printed in Thomas Rymer, ed., *Foedera, Conventiones et Litterae*, 2d ed. 20 vols. (London, 1727–1735), 9.895–904; the English version is in 9.916–20.

51. Henry himself used this familial language of inclusion and exclusion: in a letter of 12 July 1421 to the citizens of London, he contrasted "oure fader of Fraunce," and "oure . . . trusty, louyng, and faithful brother," the Duke of Burgundy, to "the saide pretense Daulphin" (Chambers and Daunt, *Book of London English*, 84).

52. For an illuminating commentary on this often remarked process, see Rodney Hilton, "Were the English English?" in *Patriotism: The Making and Unmaking of the British National Identity*, ed. Raphael Samuel, vol. 1: History and Politics (London: Routledge, 1989), pp. 39–43.

58. That both English and French nationalism were state-sponsored rather than spontaneously generated by the conditions of the war has been argued by Bernard Guenée, "Etat et nation en France au moyen âge." *Revue historique* 237 (1967): 17–30, and especially by P. S. Lewis, "War Propaganda and Historiography in Fifteenth-Century France and England," *TRHS*, 5th ser., 15 (1965): 1–21. Lewis shows that the authors of the nationalist propaganda generated in France during the fifteenth century were speaking for very specific political and class interests: "No amount of patriotic special pleading can obscure the fact that the majority of Frenchmen were, as far as action went, at least apathetic about the identity of their ultimate

ruler and even about his nationality" (7). For a specific instance of the state enforcing national identity upon resistant individuals, see André Bossuat, "L'Idée de nation et la jurisprudence du Parlement de Paris au XVe siècle," *Revue historique* 204 (1950): 54–61.

54. *Gesta*, 16/17; *Versus rhythmici de Henrico Quinto*, in Charles A. Cole, ed., *Memorials of Henry Fifth, King of England* (London: Longman, Brown, Green, Longmans, and Roberts, 1858), lines 851, 1019 (137, 146).

55. W. R. Jones, "The English Church and Royal Propaganda during the Hundred Years War," *Journal of British Studies* 19 (1979): 28, citing the *Foedera* and the *Register of John de Grandisson*.

56. Capgrave, *Chronicle*, pp. 314–15; *Brut*, p. 395; for another example, see B.J.H. Rowe, "A Contemporary Account of the Hundred Years' War from 1415 to 1429," *EHR* 41 (1926): 504–13.

57. Robbins, *Historical Poems*, nos. 27 and 15.

58. "A Ballade, in Despyte of the Flemynges," in *The Minor Poems of John Lydgate*, part 2: The Secular Poems, ed. H. N. MacCracken and Merriam Sherwood, EETS, OS 192 (London: Oxford University Press, 1934), pp. 600–601.

59. John H. Fisher, "A Language Policy for Lancastrian England," *PMLA* 107 (1992): 1178.

60. John H. Fisher, "Chancery and the Emergence of Standard Written English in the Fifteenth Century," *Speculum* 52 (1977): 870–99 (the citation is from 877); Malcolm Richardson, "Henry V, the English Chancery, and Chancery English," *Speculum* 55 (1980): 726–50; still useful is V. H. Galbraith, "Nationality and Language in Medieval England," *TRHS*, 4th ser. 23 (1941): 113–28.

61. Chambers and Daunt, *Book of London English*, p. 139; the Latin original is printed on page 16.

62. That French *was* a truly foreign language to the English in the late fourteenth and early fifteenth centuries is clear from the fact that French had by then become an entirely official language, the only exception being the possibility of its occasional use for social intercourse in the court of Richard II. An expert account that corrects previous misconceptions is Rolf Berndt, "The Period of the Final Decline of French in Medieval England (Fourteenth and Early Fifteenth Centuries)," *Zeitschrift für Anglistik und Amerikanistik* 20 (1972): 341–69.

63. Cited by Kingsford, *Henry V*, p. 281.

64. Froissart, *Oeuvres*, ed. Kervyn de Lettenhove, t. 15 (Brussels: Devaux, 1871), pp. 114–15; Sir John Bourchier, Lord Berners, trans., *The Chronicle of Froissart*, vol. 6 (London: David Nutt, 1903), pp. 113–14.

65. The documents in this case are printed in *Foedera*, 9.655–56.

66. The five Latin biographies are the *Gesta Henrici Quinti* (1416–1417); Thomas Elmham, *Liber Metricus de Henrico Quinto* (to 1418: written shortly after the *Gesta*); Titus Livius Frulovisi, *Vita Henrici Quinti* (1437–1438), commissioned by Humphrey of Gloucester; John Capgrave, *Liber de illustribus Henricis* (1444); and the Pseudo-Elmham, *Vita et Gesta Henrici Quinti* (1446–1451). As for the English lives, the section on Henry V found in the Common Version of the *Brut* was excerpted as a separate biography in BL MS Cotton Claudius A.viii and entitled "The chronicle of King Henrie ye fifte." While this is the only surviving life written in English there were probably others. The text edited by Charles Kingsford as *The First English Life*

of King Henry V (Oxford: Clarendon Press, 1911) was based in part on Titus Livius but also upon a lost book by someone in the service of James Butler, the fourth earl of Ormond (d. 1452). Kingsford also thought that the abridgment of the Pseudo-Elmham life in Harley 530 was based on a fifteenth-century work written in English. There is also the English biography thought by Benedicta Rowe to have been written by Peter Basset: B. J. H. Rowe, "A Contemporary Account of the Hundred Years' War from 1415 to 1429," *EHR* 41 (1926): 504–13. For bibliography on most of these texts, see Edward Donald Kennedy, "XII: Chronicles and Other Historical Writing," in *A Manual of the Writings in Middle English 1050–1500*, gen. ed. Albert Hartung (New Haven: The Connecticut Academy of Arts and Sciences, 1989), item 10, pp. 2629–37, 2818–33, and 2826–27.

67. See Antonia Gransden, *Historical Writing in England*, vol. 2: *c. 1307 to the Early Sixteenth Century* (London: Routledge and Kegan Paul, 1982): "No other medieval king of England was honoured with such an abundance of literature" (196). See also Jacob, *Henry V*, pp. 185–86. Kingsford's judgment in his *Henry V, The Typical Mediaeval Hero*—that Henry was "the most English of our Plantagenet kings, heart and soul in sympathy with his subjects, marked out by nature to be the leader of a united nation" (93)—is a theme taken up by almost all later biographers; see, for example, G. L. Harriss's 1985 account of Henry as responsible for the "liberation of the national spirit" ("Introduction," 28).

68. Henry's memory exerted a powerful nostalgic influence on the later fifteenth century, a period bereft of royal leadership. When in the 1440s an anonymous author was arguing for a shift in English maritime policy he harked back to Henry V: "To speke of hym I stony in my witte," he says, an astonishment evidently shared by many: George Warner, ed., *The Libelle of Englyshe Polycye* (Oxford: Clarendon Press, 1926), line 1047. This power is also visible in Malory's account of Arthur's continental campaign against the Emperor Lucius, which in significant respects recalls Henry's Agincourt campaign: see Eugene Vinaver, ed., *The Works of Sir Thomas Malory*, 2d ed., 3 vols. (Oxford: Clarendon Press, 1967), 3.1368, 1396–98. Henry's "personal magnetism" is one of the persistent themes of modern historians, affecting even the hard-to-impress K. B. McFarlane: "Take him all round and he was, I think, the greatest man that ever ruled England" (*Lancastrian Kings*, 133).

69. Jacob, *Fifteenth Century*, p. 123.

70. For the disorder of the French, with citations from contemporaries, see Wylie, *Reign of Henry the Fifth*, 2.199–200.

71. *Gesta*, pp. 110–13.

72. For the Lancastrian changes in the coronation ceremony, and especially the introduction of the holy oil of Canterbury, see J. R. Lander, *The Limitations of English Monarchy in the Later Middle Ages* (Toronto: University of Toronto Press, 1989), pp. 42–45, and C. T. Wood, "Queens, Queans and Kingship: An Inquiry into Theories of Royal Legitimacy in Late Medieval England and France," in *Order and Innovation in the Middle Ages*, ed. W. C. Jordan, B. McNab, and T. F. Ruiz (Princeton: Princeton University Press, 1976), pp. 387–400.

73. For this interpretation of the canopy, see Dorothy Styles and C. T. Allmand, "The Coronations of Henry VI," *History Today* 32 (May 1982): 32.

74. James Gairdner, ed., *Historical Collections of a Citizen of London in the Fifteenth Century*, Camden Society, 2d ser., 107 (London: Camden Society, 1876), pp. 29–30.

75. *Brut*, p. 410.

76. For Frulovisi, see McFarlane, *Lancastrian Kings*, p. 123; Capgrave, *Chronicle*, p. 303.

77. Jacob, *Henry V*, provides a judicious account (72–73). John Strecche, who is one of the primary sources for the story, contrasts the *verba fellis eructantes* of the French messengers with Henry's *verbis brevibus, discretis et honestis circumstantibus* (Taylor, "Chronicle of John Strecche," 150).

78. *Brut*, p. 378.

79. Distrust of loquaciousness and a belief that silence befits the strong is an English characteristic as early as the Anglo-Saxons. As the speaker of the *Wanderer* says, "I know for a fact / In an earl it is always a noble habit / To seal fast the soul's chest." These lines are translated and discussed by James W. Earl, "*Beowulf* and the Origins of Civilization," in *Speaking Two Languages: Traditional Disciplines and Contemporary Theory in Medieval Studies*, ed. Allen J. Frantzen (Albany: State University of New York Press, 1991), p. 76.

80. For this process, see G. L. Harriss, "The King and His Magnates," in Harriss, *Henry V*, pp. 31–51.

81. Powell, "Restoration of Law and Order," 64.

82. Ibid., 71.

83. That Henry possessed a disinterested sense of justice was recognized even by the French, although the war he waged in France was probably not less brutal than those of his predecessors. Accounts of Henry's campaigns that give due weight to the French experience are provided by Seward, *Henry V*, and especially by Wylie and Waugh, *The Reign of Henry V*. For Henry's military discipline, see Richard A. Newhall, *Muster and Review: A Problem of English Military Administration 1420–1440* (Cambridge, Mass.: Harvard University Press, 1940).

84. Jacob, *Henry V*, pp. 162–63.

85. McFarlane, *Lancastrian Kings*, p. 117.

86. Jeremy Catto, "Religious Change under Henry V," in Harriss, ed., *Henry V*, p. 111.

87. Capgrave, *Chronicle*, p. 309.

88. Jacob, *Henry V*, p. 135; and see Mervyn James, *English Politics and the Concept of Honour, 1485–1642, Past and Present*, supplement No. 3 (Cambridge: Cambridge University Press, 1978).

89. Jeremy Catto, "The King's Servants," in Harriss, *Henry V*, pp. 31–51.

90. Charles L. Kingsford, ed., *Chronicles of London* (Oxford: Oxford University Press, 1905), p. 69.

91. As McFarlane says, with oddly undisguised enthusiasm, "The age of the Crusade was over and that of world empires not begun. But it is possible to believe that Henry V might have bridged the gap that divides Napoleon from Godfrey de Bouillon, and have succeeded where Richard I and St. Louis had failed" (*Lancastrian Kings*, p. 125).

92. *Foedera*, 9.883. See also the letter from the bishop of Norwich, Sir Thomas Erpingham, and John Wodehouse, Esq., to the Chancellor on 22 March 1419 explaining that despite all their efforts among the local gentry they "can nat gete on þat wol wiþ his gode will go" (N. H. Nicolas, ed., *Proceedings and Ordinances of the Privy Council of England* [London: HMSO, 1834], 2.246). See also Kingsford, *Henry V*, p. 341; Lander, *Limitations*, pp. 15–17; and C. T. Allmand, *Henry V*, Historical

Association Pamphlet, 68 (London: The Historical Association, 1968), p. 21. A concern was also expressed in the counties that the war was draining the country of the men required to fill county offices: Simon Payling, *Political Society in Lancashire England: The Greater Gentry in Nottinghamshire* (Oxford: Clarendon Press, 1991), p. 139.

93. J. L. Kirby, "Henry V and the City of London," *History Today* 26 (1976): 231.

94. A. K. McHardy, "Liturgy and Propaganda in the Diocese of Lincoln during the Hundred Years War," *Studies in Church History*, 18 (1982): 224.

95. Jacob, *Henry V*, p. 162.

96. *Foedera*, 9.919.

97. That the commons had reason to be anxious is suggested by a contemporaneous letter written by Henry that "we ben advised for to have oon Chauncellor, bothe for our matiers that we have adoo in this land [France], and also for England" (cited by J. W. McKenna, "Henry VI of England and the Dual Monarchy: Aspects of Royal Political Propaganda, 1422–1432," *JWCI* 28 [1965], 153 n. 26).

98. A survey of this material is provided by McKenna, "Henry VI of England and the Dual Monarchy" (see n. 113).

99. "The Kings of England," in MacCracken, *Minor Poems*, p. 716. For an important discussion of the textual history of this poem, and of its officially-sponsored dissemination, see Linne R. Mooney, "Lydgate's 'Kings of England' and Another Verse Chronicle of the Kings," *Viator* 20 (1989): 255–89.

100. The picture survives in BL MS Royal 15 E. vi, a book of poems and romances presented to Margaret of Anjou on her marriage to Henry VI by John Talbot, earl of Shrewsbury, and is reproduced here by permission of the British Library.

101. Ernst H. Kantorowicz, *The King's Two Bodies: A Study in Mediaeval Political Theology* (Princeton: Princeton University Press, 1957), p. 57.

102. MacCracken and Sherwood, *Minor Poems*, part 2, pp. 613–22; line numbers are included in the text. This poem has also been well discussed in a recent dissertation by Richard Fehrenbacher, Duke University, 1992.

103. In a "Roundel for the Coronation of Henry VI," (MacCracken and Sherwood, 622), Henry VI is advised to be like his father, "Stable in vertue, withoute variaunce" (11); in a "Ballade to King Henry VI Upon His Coronation" (ibid., 624–30), Edward and Louis, Arthur and Charlemagne are brought together in the figure of Henry VI, a unification that is analogized to the "soþefast vnytee / Of three persones in þe Trynyte" (28–29), Henry makes it possible for the royal lines to be "Grounded in feyth, with-outen varyaunce" (31–32); and in "King Henry VI's Triumphal Entry in London, 21 Feb., 1432," (ibid., 630–48), the citizens wear white "To showe the trouthe that they dyd[e] mene / Toward the Kyng" (40–41), the king's French and English subjects are now at peace, "theyre hertes made both oon" (98), and Henry's genealogical descent is represented by the natural metaphor of the tree (398–404). See also in MacCracken, *Minor Poems*, part 1: Religious Poems, a "Prayer to St. Edmund" (124–27) and "A Prayer for Henry VI, Queen, and People, 1429" (212–16).

104. The documentary evidence is available in William Abel Pantin, ed., *Documents Illustrating the Activities of the General and Provincial Chapters of the English Black Monks 1215–1540*, vol. 2, Camden Third Series, 47 (London: Camden Society, 1933), pp. 98–134.

105. Roy M. Haines, " 'Our Master Mariner, Our Sovereign Lord': A Contemporary View of Henry V," *MS* 38 (1976): 85–96. Subsequent references are included in

the text; the modern English in the citations are my translations from the Latin. I have accepted Haines's proposals on authorship and occasion. This sermon is also discussed and in part translated by G. R. Owst, *Literature and Pulpit in Medieval England* (Oxford: Basil Blackwell, 1961), pp. 70–75. For another sermon by Pauntley, see Patrick J. Horner, F. S. C., "John Pauntley's Sermon at the Funeral of Walter Froucaster, Abbot of Gloucester," *American Benedictine Review* 28 (1977): 147–66.

106. For examples of bad behavior by Polynices, see Lydgate's description of the "pompous Surquedye" (1076) that motivated both brothers at the outset of their dispute, and then the "hegh pride" (1323) that led Polynices to battle Tydeus in the porch of Adrastus's palace. As for the Argives, their refusal to negotiate with the Thebans, their killing of the tame tiger—the event that sparks the war—and their refusal to listen to the warnings of Amphiorax (3811–12) indicate their culpability.

107. Useful guides to the Theban materials available to the Middle Ages are Leopold Constans, *La Légende d'Oedipe étudiée dans l'antiquité, au moyen âge et dans les temps modernes* (Paris: Maisonneuve, 1881) and Lowell Edmunds, *Oedipus: The Ancient Legend and Its Later Analogues* (Baltimore: Johns Hopkins University Press, 1985).

108. I have offered a full reading of the poem in these terms, and a discussion of the medieval understanding of Thebes, in *Chaucer and the Subject of History* (Madison: University of Wisconsin Press, 1991), pp. 47–164.

CHAPTER FOUR

Shakespeare Bewitched

STEPHEN GREENBLATT

FOR THE GREAT WITCHMONGERS of the late Middle Ages and early Renaissance, those who wrote that there should be more fear, more denunciations of women, more confessions extorted under torture, and above all more executions, the initial task was to reverse a dangerous current of literate disbelief. They saw themselves as beginning, that is, less with a confused mass of folk practices that they had to sift through and organize into a coherent demonology, than with well-established and socially acceptable doubt. Indeed the doubt was not only socially acceptable but had for centuries been theologically sanctioned, for in a series of important medieval texts church authorities had attacked those people—for the most part, as the church conceived it, women—who had been seduced by what Reginone of Prüm in the tenth century called "the phantasms and illusions of demons" (*daemonum illusionibus et phantasmatibus seductae*).[1]

Reginone's phrase leaves unclear the exact status of the seductive fantasies: they could refer to a mistaken belief in the existence of certain demons who do not exist or to illusions caused by demons who do in fact exist or to a belief in nonexistent demons caused by Satan. His work, *De Ecclesiasticis Disciplinis*, is not, it needs hardly be said, a thoroughgoing skeptical critique of supernatural agency, but it vigorously encourages skepticism about a whole series of claims associated with the witch cult:

> Wicked women who have given themselves back to Satan and been seduced by the phantasms and illusions of demons believe and declare that they can ride with Diana the pagan goddess and a huge throng of women on chosen beasts in the hours of night. They say that in the silence of the night they can traverse great stretches of territory, that they obey Diana as though she were their mistress and that on certain nights she calls them to her special service.[2]

For Reginone, the world of the ancient gods is not a solid, undeniable reality that must be proven demonic rather than divine but a mirage, a set of vain, seductive dreams behind which lurks the Father of Lies. Reality is leached out, as it were, from the old beliefs and concentrated in the figure of Satan.[3]

This project was furthered in the early eleventh century by Burchard, bishop of Worms. In his influential penitential canon, known as the *Canon episcopi*, Burchard wrote that belief in witchcraft was itself a sin, a heretical relapse into paganism. He is, like Reginone, particularly contemptuous of dreams of night-flying with Diana, Hecate, or the German Holde, and his skepticism extends to tales of horrific acts:

> Do you believe this, in common with many women who are followers of Satan? Namely that, in the silence of the night, when you are stretched out upon your bed with your husband's head upon your breast you have the power, flesh as you are, to go out of the closed door and traverse great stretches of space with other women in a similar state of self-deception? And do you believe that you can kill, though without visible arms, people baptized and redeemed by the blood of Christ, and can cook and eat their flesh, after putting some straw or a piece of wood or something in the place of the heart? And then that you can resuscitate them after you have eaten them and make them live again? If yes, then you must do forty days of penance, that is, a Lent, on bread and water for seven consecutive years.[4]

It is important to note the relative leniency of the penalties Burchard assigns here and elsewhere. These penalties, ranging from forty days to two years,[5] reflect a conviction that witches have no real malevolent powers but rather have succumbed to illusions of diabolic agency, vain dreams of night-flying and animal metamorphosis, and impotent fantasies of murderous potency. The fact that such fantasies are widespread does not, for Burchard, testify to their reality but rather suggests that they are the stuff of nightmare: "Who is there who has not been taken out of himself in dreams and night-mares and seen in his sleep things he would never see when awake? Who is imbecile enough to imagine that such things, seen only in the mind, have a bodily reality?"[6]

By the later fourteenth century, in the wake of the Black Death, intellectual convictions and institutional alignments had shifted, skepticism was no longer officially encouraged, and nightmares began to assume once again a bodily reality. But the *Canon episcopi* remained on the books and there must have been a considerable reservoir of doubt, for in the famous *Malleus maleficarum* of 1484, the Dominican inquisitors, Heinrich Kramer and James Sprenger evidently believe that they can swing their hammer at witches only by swinging it simultaneously at skeptics. The *Canon episcopi*, they argue, has been completely misunderstood; it condemned a narrow range of heretical beliefs but was never intended to deny the actual existence of witchcraft practices attested to in the Holy Scriptures and credited by a wide range of unimpeachable authorities. Indeed, write Kramer and Sprenger, it would be heretical to deny the real menace of witchcraft (4); hence "all Bishops and Rulers who do not essay their utmost to suppress crimes of this sort . . . are themselves to be judged as evident abettors of the crime, and are manifestly to be punished."[7]

The *Malleus maleficarum* then sets as its task the transfer of a set of concepts, images, and fears from the zone of the imaginary to the zone of the real. What is the zone of the imaginary? In the late sixteenth century Spenser imagined it as a chamber of the mind filled with "leasings, tales, and lies," a jumble of images that sober reason or common sense or those in positions of power deem misshapen, confused, forged, incredible, or simply false.[8] Churchmen like Reginone and Burchard had painstakingly crated up and moved into such a chamber the whole vast furniture of pagan belief, and with it the nightmare images of witch cults. Now Kramer and Sprenger take it upon themselves to unpack those images and officially confer upon them once again the unfeigned solidity of embodied reality. But the task is not uncomplicated.

Dogmatic assertion is, of course, the inquisitor's stock-in-trade—as Empson put it, "heads I win, tails I burn you at the stake"—but to confer the air of truth on practices that had been earlier condemned by the church itself as pernicious fantasies called for a supplement to threats of "terrible penalties, censures, and punishment . . . without any right to appeal" (xlv). Such threats by themselves were more likely to bully people into grudging, silent compliance than to inspire them to robust belief. Hence Kramer and Sprenger are drawn to supplement their affirmations with something like evidence, the evidence of narrative. "There was in the diocese of Basel," a typical passage begins, "in a town called Oberweiler situated on the Rhine, an honest parish priest, who fondly held the opinion, or rather error, that there was no witchcraft in the world, but that it existed in the imagination of men who attributed such things to witches." This sentence characteristically introduces not simply a theory (in this case, the rationalizing theory of imaginative projection that Kramer and Sprenger oppose) but an anecdote, an instructive tale in which the misguided doubter is brought to a correct view of the matter: "And God wished so to purge him of this error that . . ." (103).

We don't need to rehearse the nasty little story that follows, but the point is that they did. They evidently felt that scholastic arguments and belligerent appeals to authority were not enough to establish witchcraft doctrines on a stable footing; Kramer and Sprenger needed to confer on what their own church had labeled fantasies the solidity of palpable truth, to give invisible agents, secret compacts, obscene rites, spectacular transformations both a compelling general theory and a convincing local habitation. After all, they wanted men and women not merely to assent formally to a set of abstract theoretical propositions about the operation of evil but to denounce and kill their neighbors. Faced with the necessity of producing the effect of the real out of the materials of fantasy, the inquisitors turned to narrative. The *Malleus maleficarum* rehearses dozens of tales crafted to redraw the boundary between the imaginary and the real, or rather to siphon off the darkest contents of the imagination and pour them, like a poison, into the ear of the world.

Why shouldn't we say the same thing about Shakespeare's *Macbeth*? Why shouldn't we say that the play, with immeasurably greater literary force, undertakes to reenchant the world, to shape misogyny to political ends, to counteract the corrosive skepticism that had called into question both the existence of witches and the sacredness of royal authority? Recent criticism has come close to saying this: *Macbeth*, writes Peter Stallybrass, "mobilizes the patriarchal fear of unsubordinated woman, the unstable element to which Kramer and Sprenger attributed the overthrow of 'nearly all the kingdoms of the world.' "[9] And in a compelling analysis of the play's fantasies of masculine vulnerability to women, Janet Adelman has suggested that "the final solution, both for Macbeth and for the play itself, though in differing ways, is . . . [a] radical excision of the female." "The play that begins by unleashing the terrible threat of maternal power and demonstrates the helplessness of its central male figure before that power," Adelman argues, "ends by consolidating male power, in effect solving the problem of masculinity by eliminiating the female."[10] Why shouldn't we say then that *Macbeth*, with its staging of witches and its final solution, probably contributed, in an indirect but powerful way, to the popular fear of demonic agency and the official persecution and killing of women? Why shouldn't we say that this play about evil is evil?[11]

There are important and cogent reasons why we should not say anything like this. First, though it gestures toward history, *Macbeth* is a self-conscious work of theatrical fiction, an entertainment in which nothing need be taken as real, in which everything can be understood, as Shakespeare suggested elsewhere, to be "shadow" or "dream." Second, no one in the period, least of all the players themselves, understood the designation "King's Men" to imply an official, prescriptive function, the equivalent of the papal bull that was printed with the *Malleus maleficarum*. Neither Shakespeare nor his company was speaking dogmatically or even indirectly on behalf of any institution except the marginal, somewhat disreputable institution of the theater, disreputable precisely because it was the acknowledged house of fantasies. Third, there is no attempt in the play to give counsel to anyone about how to behave toward the witches and no apparent sanctioning—as in Dekker's *Witch of Edmonton*, for example, or in Shakespeare's own *I Henry VI*—of legal prosecution or execution. It would have been simple enough to have the victorious Malcolm declare his determination to rid his kingdom of witches, but he does no such thing. Instead, with none of the questions their existence poses answered, they simply disappear: "The Witches Dance, and vanish." Fourth, within *Macbeth*'s representation of the witches, there is profound ambiguity about the actual significance and power of their malevolent intervention. If the strange prophecies of the Weird Sisters had been ignored, the play seems to imply, the same set of events might have occurred anyway, impelled entirely by the pressure of Macbeth's violent ambition and his wife's psychological manipulation. (Macbeth, Hecate complains to her followers, is a "wayward son" who "loves for his own ends, not for you" [3.5.13]).[12] And fifth, even if we could demonstrate that witch prosecutions in England were somehow prolonged or intensified by *Macbeth*—and, of course, the actual proof of such horrible consequences is almost impossible to establish—in the absence of evidence of malign authorial intention, we would not, I think, deem Shakespeare's play evil, any more than we have held Salmon Rushdie's *Satanic Verses* to be evil because of the deaths that occurred in the riots caused by its publication.[13]

It is possible to identify evil texts—the *Malleus maleficarum* is one, I believe—and these in principle may include works of art. Such a judgment would involve, at a minimum, the demonstration of a calculated attempt to produce by means of discourse effects that are morally reprehensible—for example, to incite racial hatred and murder.[14] But it is notoriously hazardous to submit works of art to political or moral judgment or to calculate their practical consequences. If it is perilous to try to gauge the political valence of works of art written in our own time, how much more implausible is it to apply a test of progressive politics to works written almost four hundred years ago? I should add that I think it important, in the interest of preserving the small breathing space of the imagination, to resist the recent tendency to conflate, or even to collapse into one another, aesthetics, ethics, and politics.

And yet, and yet. What is the point of speaking at all about the historical situation of works of art if ideological entailments and practical consequences are somehow off-limits, and if they are not off-limits, how can we avoid moral judgments? What is the point of interrogating the status of literature—of challenging the cult of autonomy, undermining the illusion of aesthetic aloofness, questioning the very existence in the Renaissance of an independent aesthetic sphere—if we are not to insist that the power of a work like *Macbeth* must be a power *in* the world, a power *for* something? We may tell ourselves that its power is to produce a specific form of pleasure and that a distinction between the production of pleasure and other purposes such as exchange or functional utility is quite important.[15] But a radical distinction between pleasure and use is difficult to maintain, especially for a Renaissance text. The period's defenses of the stage routinely include accounts of the social power of drama, accounts echoed in Hamlet's deployment of *The Murder of Gonzago*, and if the claims seem extravagant to the point of absurdity, there is ample evidence of a significant, if less spectacular, cultural and political power. More important, perhaps, the specific pleasure produced by *Macbeth* is bound up with the representation of witches, and that representation was only possible in and through a particularly fraught cultural negotiation with theological and political discourses that had a direct effect on the lives of men and women. The play may not be reducible to its political and ethical consequences, but it cannot escape having consequences, even if those consequences are difficult to trace and to evaluate.

In the early seventeenth century, it was impossible to contain a depiction of witches strictly within the boundaries of art, for the status of witches—the efficacy of their charms, their ability to harm, the reality of their claims or of the charges brought against them, their very existence—was not a fixed feature in the cultural landscape but a subject of contestation.[16] The contestation was not, of course, due to any censoring power possessed by those who were called or who called themselves witches—one of the central paradoxes of the discourse of witchcraft, widely recognized in the period, is that the women identified as wielding immense metaphysical power were for the most part socially marginal.[17] In their own local communities some of them may well have exercised power both to harm and to heal, but they had no control over their representations (let alone access to the means of self-representation in print), so that a playwright, for example, could figure them as he wished without calculating any conceivable objections from them. It was principally among the educated elite, among those who had it in their power to punish, to pardon, and to represent, that there was serious disagreement about how witches should be conceived or even whether they should be said to exist at all.[18] To represent witches on the public stage was inevitably to participate in some way or other in the contestation.

Let us recall the anonymous parish priest who claimed that "there was no witchcraft in the world, but that it existed in the imagination of men who attributed such things to witches." The skeptics against whom Kramer and Sprenger write had withdrawn witchcraft from the real world and relocated it in the "imagination," the place haunted by what Reginone and others had called demonic illusions and phantasms. "It is useless," the *Malleus maleficarum* replies, "to argue that any result of witchcraft may be a phantasy and unreal, because such a phantasy cannot be procured without resort to the power of the devil, and it is necessary that there should be made a contract with the devil, by which contract the witch truly and actually binds herself to be the servant of the devil and devotes herself to the devil, and this is not done in any dream or under any illusion, but she herself bodily and truly cooperates with, and conjoins herself to, the devil" (7). The reality of witchcraft here is secured by the reality of the demonic contract—a contract insisted upon dogmatically, we may suggest, precisely because it is the one thing (unlike withered arms, dead cattle, or male impotence) that is *never* actually witnessed. That founding reality, theoretically necessary and secured by inquisitorial authority, then licenses a sophisticated blurring of the boundaries between reality and illusion: Kramer and Sprenger concede that allegedly demonic harms may at times be fantasies, because they claim that such fantasies are themselves consequences (and hence evidence) of the demonic contract.[19]

According to the scholastic psychology of the *Malleus maleficarum*, devils provoke and shape fantasies by direct corporeal intervention in the mind: demonic spirits can incite what Kramer and Sprenger call a "local motion" in the minds of those awake as well as asleep, stirring up and exciting the inner perceptions, "so that ideas retained in the repositories of their minds are drawn out and made apparent to the faculties of fancy and imagination, so that such men imagine these things to be true." This process of making a stir in the mind and moving images from one part of the brain to another is, they write, called "interior temptation" (50).[20] It can lead men to see objects before their eyes—daggers, for example—that are not in fact there; conversely, it can lead men *not* to see other objects—their own penises, for example—that are still there, though concealed from view by what Kramer and Sprenger call a "glamour" (58). Hence, they write, "a certain man tells that, when he had lost his member, he approached a known witch to ask her to restore it to him. She told the afflicted man to climb a certain tree, and that he might take which he liked out of a nest in which there were several members. And when he tried to take a big one, the witch said: You must not take that one; adding because it belonged to a parish priest." "All these things," they soberly add, attaching the ribald anticlerical folktale to their humorless explanatory apparatus, "are caused by devils through an illusion or glamour . . . by confusing the organ of vision by transmuting the mental images in the imaginative faculty" (121).[21]

One hundred years after the publication of the *Malleus maleficarum*, an English country gentleman, Reginald Scot, was tempted to regard much of the work as a "bawdie discourse," a kind of obscene joke book. But he checked the impulse: "These are no jestes," he writes, "for they be written by them that were and are judges upon the lives and deaths of those persons" (45). Scot's response to Kramer and Sprenger and Bodin and the whole persecutorial apparatus is *The Discoverie of Witchcraft*, the greatest English contribution to the skeptical critique of witchcraft. The *Discoverie* attacks witchcraft beliefs across a broad front, but at its center is an attempt to locate those beliefs not *in* but *as* the imagination. That is, Scot's principal concern is with the boundary between the imaginary and the real, and where Kramer and Sprenger had viewed that boundary as porous, Scot views it as properly closed. The sickness of his own times is precisely its inability to distinguish the projections of troubled fantasy from the solid truths of the material world. The principal cause of this sickness—spiritual weakness—turns out to be one of its principal consequences as well: "The fables of Witchcraft have taken so fast hold and deepe root in the heart of man," the book begins, "that fewe or none can (nowadaies) with patience indure the hand and correction of God."

It is, Scot's language suggests here, fables rather than devils that have taken possession, invading the body and fixing themselves in the heart: the world, he writes, is "bewitched and over-run with this fond error" (3). This shift from demonic agency to the vicious power of human fictions is the crucial perception of the *Discoverie*.[22] Hence Scot's obsession with the exact operation of sleights of hand, his tireless description of what from this distance seem to us jejune parlor tricks, his careful exposition of the hidden mechanisms by means of which certain theatrical illusions, such as decapitation, are achieved. For these tricks, in Scot's view, have fueled the spiritual impatience and shaped the anxious fantasies of men, until maddened crowds, deluded by fraudulent spectacles, call for the death of witches, and magistrates hang unloved, vulnerable, and innocent old women.

Scot's project is disenchantment in the interest of restorating proper religious faith: he must take away from the witches themselves and from the culture that has credited (and, as Scot perfectly understands, largely created) their claims and confessions their air of wonder. Accordingly, his witches are blear-eyed, toothless village misfits or contemptible swindlers. Scot would have dismissed as pernicious nonsense the notion, recently revived by certain anthropologists and historians, that the "wise women" and "cunning men" of this period represented half-suppressed currents of ancient ecstatic religion or articulated a deep popular protest against the social order or exercised significant power to threaten and to cure.[23] Women accused of witchcraft, he strenuously argues, are for the most part harmless melancholiacs and hysterics incapable of distinguishing between reality and fantasy.[24] Scot is willing to concede a small measure of initiative to a few self-described witches, but only the initiative of unscrupulous "jugglers," itinerant tricksters willing to profit from the gullibility and foolishness of country folk. Even a juggler of modest talent can convince people that they have seen with their own eyes what does not in fact exist; hence the eyewitness testimony so often advanced to prove the existence of witchcraft only proves the unreliability of the sense and what Marx called the idiocy of rural life.

To succeed in his project it is not enough to challenge the authority of the eyewitness. Scot must not only demystify vision, but also expose the extent to which the experience of wonder—the thrilled recognition of the presence of supernatural power in the material world—depends upon language. "Naturall magic," Scot remarks, "consisteth as well in the deceit of words, as in the sleight of hand" (250). Hence he writes portentously of two "most miraculous matters." Of one of these, he says, he has himself been "*Testis oculatus*," of the other he has been "crediblie and certeinelie informed"; that is, one comes to him via sight, the other via words. The extended descriptions of the exotic objects—a "peece of earth" from Russia that shrinks from heated steel but pursues gold and silver; an Indian stone that contains within it a substance of "marvellous brightnes, puritie, and shining"—are an anthology of the verbal cues for wonder, but the wonder lasts only as long as the reader fails to realize that Scot is describing man and fire. Once the reader understands what is going on, admiration vanishes, leaving a sense of irony that borders on contempt: these are, after all, deliberately bad jokes. In both of them, it is the language of description that confers upon the objects their supernatural strangeness,[25] and, Scot observes, the "deceipt of words" here need not involve any outright falsehood: "Lieng is avoided with a figurative speech, in the which either the words themselves, or their interpretation have a double or doubtfull meaning" (176).

It is figurative speech then, supported by visual illusion, that for Scot lies at the heart not only of the discourse of witchcraft but of the practices and persecutions that are linked with this discourse. Men cannot stand the experience of certain powerful emotions—uncertainty, for example, or fear—that are not attached to *figures*, and they are consequently vulnerable to anyone who offers them the satisfaction of figuration: "Men in all ages have beene so desirous to know the effect of their purposes, the sequele of things to come, and to see the end of their feare and hope; that a seelie witch, which had learned anie thing in the art of cousenage, may make a great manie jollie fooles" (197). And what makes men vulnerable also makes them murderous. In their impatience or their terror or their desire, men compulsively cross what we may call the threshold of figuration; they have fashioned metaphors and then killed the crazed women who have been unprotected or foolish enough to incarnate their appalling fantasies. Hence the force of the word-play, ironically reenchanting what he most wishes to disenchant, to which Scot is repeatedly drawn: "The world is now so bewitched . . . with this fond error" (3) or again, the whore's "eie infecteth, entiseth, and (if I maie so saie) bewitcheth" (172) or again, "illusions are right inchantments" (9). For it is this figurative capacity of language that has led men to take witchcraft literally and even to find support for their fatal mistake by misreading the Scriptures.

The Scriptures are driven by the grossness of human understanding to express spiritual truths in figurative expressions that men characteristically misinterpret; many men are "so carnallie minded," observes Scot, "that a spirit is no sooner spoken of, but immediatlie they thinke of a black man with cloven feet, a paire of hornes, a taile, clawes, and eies as broad as a bason" (507). To be "carnally minded" is to have a mind that is flesh, a mind inextricably linked to the material world, a mind that resists the saving, bodiless abstractions of the spirit. Such a mind cannot pass, as it properly should, from the Bible's figures to immaterial, other-worldly truths but moves instead in the opposite direction: from imaginary figures to literal bodies. And the key to this fatal error is the dangerous power of human language, its capacity to figure what is not there, its ability to be worked into "double or doubtfull meaning," its proneness to deceit and illusion. Witches are the immaterial figures of the mind made flesh; behind the twisted belief and fear and killing lurks a misplaced faith in metaphor.

The problem then, to adapt a phrase of Wittgenstein's, is "the bewitchment of our intelligence by means of language."[26] And, predictably, it is the masters of language, the poets, who have been the principal sources of the false figures. "*Ovid* affirmeth," writes Scot, that witches

can raise and suppresse lightening and thunder, raine and haile, clouds and winds, tempests and earthquakes. Others do write, that they can pull downe the moone and the starres. Some write that with wishing they can send needles into the livers of their enimies. Some that they can transferre corne in the blade from one place to another. Some, that they can cure diseases supernaturallie, flie in the aire, and dance with divels. . . . They can raise spirits (as others af-firme) drie up springs, turne the course of running waters, inhibit the sunne, and staie both day and night, changing the one into the other. They can go in and out at awger holes, & saile in an egge shell, a cockle or muscle shell, through and under the tempestuous seas. They can go invisible, and deprive men of their privities, and otherwise of the act and use of venerie. They can bring soules out of the graves. . . . But in this case a man may saie, that *Miranda canunt/sed non credenda Poetae.* (1.4.8)

The poet's wonders must not be believed. "All this stuffe," Scot writes, "is vaine and fabulous" (260). Human language, as opposed to the word of God, does not possess authentic creative power, only the ability to counterfeit that power; "for by the sound of the words nothing commeth, nothing goeth, otherwise than God in nature hath ordeined to be doone by ordinary speech" (124). Against bewitching metaphors the *Discoverie* marshals the skeptical, aphoristic wisdom—empirical, political, and aesthetic—of the everyday:

If all the divels in hell were dead, and all the witches in *England* burnt or hanged, I warrant you we should not faile to have raine, haile, and tempests. (3)

They can also bring to passe, that chearne as long as you list, your butter will not come; especially . . . if the maids have eaten up the cream. (6)

The pope maketh rich witches, saints; and burneth the poore witches. (179)

I for my part have read a number of their conjurations, but never could see anie divels of theirs, except it were in a plaie. (258)

"Except it were in a plaie." I do not know what plays Scot who published the *Discoverie* in 1584 had in mind. (He had been a student at Oxford and may have seen or acted in plays there.) The great English Renaissance drama—including, of course, *Doctor Faustus* and *Macbeth*—lies ahead. What, if anything, does it mean for this drama to come after Scot? Scot's book had no official or semiofficial standing. We are not dealing with a situation comparable to exorcism in the 1590s, where the state and the church decided to stop a controversial charismatic practice, a practice consequently branded by institutional spokesmen as a kind of illicit theater. In that case, as I have argued elsewhere, Shakespeare could appropriate for the stage the intense social energies that were under attack as theatrical; he could at once confirm the theatricality of exorcism and recreate its suspect power, now dutifully marked out as fraudulent, for his own purposes. But this model of mutually profitable circulation does not apply to witchcraft. We are dealing instead with a contestation in which a straightforward appropriation or exchange is not possible. For while the Elizabethan ruling elite shared very little of the Continental enthusiasm for witchcraft prosecutions, they were in general unwilling to adopt Scot's wholly skeptical position and had no ideological interest in handing over the representation of witches to the theater.

Even before James (whose *Demonologie* includes an attack on Scot) brought his own complex interest in witchcraft to the throne, English intellectuals were struggling to work out ways of answering Scot—often by adopting certain aspects of his skepticism and at the same time containing them within a continued persecutorial structure. Hence George Gifford's spokesman, Daniel, in *A Dialogue Concerning Witches and Witchcraftes* (1593), grants that witches can harm no one through supernatural intervention—they are only miserable and deluded old women—but argues that they should be "rooted out and destroyed" (H1v) because of their evil intentions and their threat to the faith. The threat is a serious one because if the witches' compact with the devil gives them no power beyond nature, it does give them access to extraordinarily acute knowledge of nature. The devil has, after all, been around for millennia; he has become a brilliant pathologist and can see long before any human observer when a child or a valuable animal is about to become ill through entirely natural causes. He then hurries to his follower the witch and incites her to claim credit for the incipient illness, whereupon a natural cause is read by everyone as a supernatural cause and a tribute to the devil's power. Similarly, King James (who had Scot's book burned) concedes that much of what passes for manifestation of the demonic is mere trickery, but then he reminds his reader that the devil is notoriously agile. Hence it stands to reason that Satan will teach his followers "many juglarie trickes at Cardes, dice, & such like, to deceiue mennes senses thereby" (*Daemonologie*, 22)—and hence too what is for Scot a sign of the fraudulence and emptiness of the discourse of witchcraft becomes for James a further proof of the demonic compact.

There is textual evidence—especially in *Midsummer Night's Dream* and *Macbeth*—that Shakespeare had read the *Discoverie*, but even if he had not, he could not have escaped an awareness of the contestation. And his own early plays suggest that he was well aware of the alternative positions. Thus in *The Comedy of Errors* Antipholus of Syracuse recalls that Ephesus is said to be "full of cozenage":

> As, nimble jugglers that deceive the eye,
> Dark-working sorcerers that change the mind,
> Soul-killing witches that deform the body,
> Disguised cheaters, prating mountebanks,
> And many such-like liberties of sin. (1.2.97–102)

Antipholus does not distinguish between the histrionic and the satanic: confidence tricks, feats of prestidigitation, and soul-killing witchcraft are jumbled together in a vision of dangerous, sinful urban liberties.[27] By the fourth act, mystified by the familiarity of perfect strangers, the poor fellow is convinced that it's true what they say about Ephesus: "Lapland sorcerers inhabit here" (4.3.11). When the courtezan approaches him and asks for her gold chain, Antipholus quotes Jesus' words from Matthew, "Satan, avoid, I charge thee tempt me not," and makes his escape, "Avaunt, thou witch! Come, Dromio, let us go" (4.3.48ff). Three distinct models in the discourse of witchcraft—classical, Christian, and shamanistic—are blended together here. But the audience's pleasure is its knowledge that none of these models is appropriate, its understanding that it is witnessing a misrecognition arising from the play's zany coincidences and the psychological and social disorientation of the characters. In place of "soul-killing witches that deform the body" there is only the amorous fat kitchen wench from whom Dromio runs "as a witch." Demonic possession is represented only to be scoffed at, and the exorcist—the conjurer or "doting wizard" Pinch—is a hopeless fraud. There are no sorcerers or devils in Ephesus, no witches save those projected by male sexual anxiety, no magic save the natural magic of twinship and the linguistic magic of the shared proper name.

If *Comedy of Errors* suggests that Shakespeare is very close to the views of Scot and that he has contrived a brilliant comic device for staging the emptiness of the hypothesis of witchcraft, two other plays from the early 1590s, the first and second parts of *Henry VI*, convey exactly the opposite impression. Joan of Arc is not only likened by her enemies to an "ugly witch," she actually *is* a witch who by "charming spells and periapts" calls her "familiar spirits" to aid her. The play then can give a gratifying visual "proof" of the charges brought against her in a trial that Shakespeare does not need to represent, for the demonic spirits themselves appear unambiguously for all the spectators to witness. When these spirits refuse to speak, Joan offers to intensify her customary offerings:

> Where I was wont to feed you with my blood,
> I'll lop a member off and give it you
> In earnest of a further benefit. (5.3.14–16)

Hence the audience can see as theatrical representation what the witchmongers could only deduce or extract through torture as confession: the compact, based on the exchange of fluids, upon which the entire edifice of imaginary and real malice was said to rest. To the offer of blood, Joan adds the offer of her body and finally of her soul, but the spirits refuse to assist her: there would always come a point, the witchmongers observed, when the demons would abandon their human servants. And this was the moment of justice: in the words of York, "Bring forth that sorceress condemn'd to burn" (5.4.1).

What can we make of the close temporal conjunction in Shakespeare's work of two radically opposed representations of witchcraft? We can take it as a sign of deep ambivalence—a mind divided between sunlit, disenchanted rationality and the night-birds of ancient metaphysical fear—but there is no necessary logical contradiction between the two representations, since the dramatist could have believed (as King James did) that in some instances accusations of witchcraft were delusional, in others perfectly accurate. Moreover, a search for consistency (or, for that matter, ambivalence) is quite probably misguided. There is evidence throughout Shakespeare's works of a peculiarly intense interest in witchcraft; though witches themselves make infrequent appearances on his stage, the subject is invoked constantly. Sebastian's beauty is a "witchcraft" that draws Antonio into danger; the princess of France has "witchcraft in her lips"; Brabantio thinks that Othello must have used witchcraft to seduce his daughter, just as Egeus thinks that Lysander has "bewitch'd the bosom" of his child; the language of conjuring, charm, possession, and fascination is everywhere. And at the close of Shakespeare's career, as at the beginning, skeptical and credulous representations of witches are temporally conjoined in Paulina of *The Winter's Tale*—a "mankind witch" only in the eyes of the paranoid Leontes—and the "damn'd witch" Sycorax of *The Tempest*.

Witches then—imagined as real or imagined as imaginary—are a recurrent, even obsessive feature in Shakespeare's cultural universe. It seems that he could not get them out of his mind or rather out of his art, as if he identified the power of theater itself with the ontological liminality of witchcraft and with his own status as someone who conjured spirits, created storms, and wielded the power of life and death. But how he represented witchcraft in any given play—as metaphorical projection or metaphysical reality—depended on his specific and local theatrical needs. Hence there is a strong sense in both *The Comedy of Errors* and *I Henry VI* of an undisguised theatrical opportunism, an opportunism that would in effect pull against any decisive choice between the position of inquisitor and skeptic. The appearance of fiends in *Comedy of Errors* would quite simply destroy the play: the comedy's decorum rests upon the strict absence of supernatural agency. Conversely, the slightly brittle, disillusioned wit of the comedy would decisively deflate the strained attempt in *I Henry VI* to discover metaphysical causes underlying the otherwise inexplicable charismatic power of the base-born Joan.

But what does theatrical opportunism in these cases mean? It means that the dramatist follows out the inner imperatives of the genres in which he is working; it means that his choices are governed by the overriding will to achieve certain histrionic effects; it means that he takes what he wants from the world and gives no sign of concern for the fate, either exculpation or execution, of the miserable old women actually or potentially facing trial on charges of sorcery. According to Scot, witchcraft is an illicit crossing of the threshold of figuration, a confused tangle of anxieties improperly given a local habitation and a name. Shakespeare's concern—his business as a dram-atist and the business of the joint-stock company in which he was a share-holder—is precisely to cross that threshold.

Scot had argued that any credible representation of a witch was an illegit-imate attempt to give form to an inchoate emotion; to discredit witchcraft beliefs was to return the individual to a proper acceptance of God's judg-ments. But giving visible form to inchoate emotions is exactly the task of the dramatist. His whole project is the imaginative manipulation of the verbal and visual illusions that Scot tirelessly sought to expose as empty. What is at stake here is a divergence between the ethical and theatrical conditions of figurability.[28] For Scot the passage from inchoate emotion to figuration—from fear or impatience or desire to an identifiable, luminously visible figure—is the source of evil; for Shakespeare it is the source of the drama-tist's art.

Witchcraft provided Shakespeare with a rich source of imaginative en-ergy, a collective disturbance upon which he could draw to achieve powerful theatrical effects. But a dramatist could only achieve these effects, as both classical and Renaissance literary theorists argued, if this energy were conjoined with what Aristotle called *enargeia*, the liveliness that comes when metaphors are set in action, when things are put vividly before the mind's eye, when language achieves visibility.[29] The most important classi-cal account of *enargeia* is by the great first-century rhetorician Quintilian for whom it is an essential technique in arguing cases before a court of law. How do you make your legal arguments persuasive? That is, how do you impress your account of what really happened, your version of the truth, upon your auditors and, for that matter, upon yourself? By drawing on the power of fantasies or visions, "images by which the representations of absent objects are so distinctly represented to the mind, that we seem to see them with our eyes, and to have them before us" (*Institutes* 6.2.29). The person who best conceives such images, who can "vividly represent to himself things, voices, actions, with the exactness of reality [*verum optime finget*]," will have the greatest power in moving the feelings. We all produce such images readily, Quintilian observes, whenever we idly indulge in chimerical dreams, disposing of wealth or power that is not our own; and shall we not, he asks, "turn this lawless power of our minds to our advantage?"

For Quintilian then the orator's task is to make something out of the imagination's capacity to fashion illusions—specifically, to bring forth the strong emotions that accompany the conviction of reality. "I make a complaint that a man has been murdered; shall I not bring before my eyes everything that is likely to have happened when the murder occurred? Shall not the assassin suddenly sally forth? Shall not the other tremble, cry out, supplicate, or flee? Shall I not behold the one striking, the other falling? Shall not the blood, and paleness, and last gasp of the expiring victim, present itself fully to my mental view? Hence will result that *enargeia* which is called by Cicero *illustratio* and *evidentness*, which seems not so much to narrate as to exhibit; and our feelings will be moved not less strongly than if we were actually present at the affairs of which we are speaking."

It is this imaginative capacity to make what is absent present, to give invisible things the emotional force of embodied realities, that Reginald Scot fears and despises, for it has led in his view to a massive collective delusion and to the persecution of thousands of innocent victims. And Quintilian's account enables us to see why Scot is so deeply critical of poets: poets are particularly dangerous because they are the masters of *enargeia*. Scot seeks in effect to block the fusion of emotional disturbance and illusory embodiment in the discourse of witchcraft, for if inward anxieties are given no visible outlet, if they fail to achieve credible representation, if they are not enacted, witches will no longer be either believed or persecuted. We have no way of knowing if Shakespeare took Scot's position seriously, though *The Comedy of Errors* may suggest that on at least one occasion he did;[30] we do know from *Henry VI* and from *Macbeth* that Shakespeare was willing to present witchcraft as a visible, credible practice.

But there is a crucial difference—beyond the quantum leap in theatrical power—between the representation of witchcraft in *I Henry VI* and *Macbeth*. The demonic in Shakespeare's early history play makes history happen: it accounts for the uncanny success of the French peasant girl, for her power to fascinate and to inspire, and it accounts too for her failure. The witches in *Macbeth* by contrast account for nothing. They are given many of the conventional attributes of both Continental and English witch lore, the signs and wonders that Scot traces back to the poets: they are associated with tempests, and particularly with thunder and lightning; they are shown calling to their familiars and conjuring spirits; they recount killing livestock, raising winds, sailing in a sieve; their hideous broth links them to birth-strangled babes and blaspheming Jews; above all, they traffic in prognostication and prophecy.[31] And yet though the witches are given a vital theatrical *enargeia*, though their malevolent energy is apparently put in act—"I'll do, I'll do, and I'll do"—it is in fact extremely difficult to specify what, if anything, they do or even what, if anything, they are.[32]

"What are these," Banquo asks when he and Macbeth first encounter them,

> So wither'd and so wild in their attire,
> That look not like th'inhabitants o'th'earth,
> And yet are on't? (1.3.39–42)

Macbeth echoes the question, "Speak, if you can:—what are you?" to which he receives in reply his own name: "All hail, Macbeth!" Macbeth is evidently too startled to respond, and Banquo resumes the interrogation:

> I'th' name of truth,
> Are ye fantastical, or that indeed
> Which outwardly ye show? (1.3.52–54)

The question is slightly odd, since Banquo has already marveled at an outward show that would itself seem entirely fantastical: "You should be women, / And yet your beards forbid me to interpret / That you are so." But "fantastical" here refers not to the witches' equivocal appearance but to a deeper doubt, a doubt not about their gender but about their existence. They had at first seemed to be the ultimate figures of the alien—Banquo initially remarked that they did not look like earthlings—but now their very "outwardness," their existence outside the mind and its fantasies, is called into question.[33]

What is happening here is that Shakespeare is staging the epistemological and ontological dilemmas that in the deeply contradictory ideological situation of his time haunted virtually all attempts to determine the status of witchcraft beliefs and practices.[34] And he is at the same time and by the same means staging the insistent, unresolved questions that haunt the practice of the theater. For *Macbeth* manifests a deep, intuitive recognition that the theater and witchcraft are both constructed on the boundary between fantasy and reality, the border or membrane where the imagination and the corporeal world, figure and actuality, psychic disturbance and objective truth meet. The means normally used to secure that border are speech and sight, but it is exactly these that are uncertain; the witches, as Macbeth exclaims, are "imperfect speakers," and at the moment he insists that they account for themselves, they vanish.

The startled Banquo proposes a theory that would keep the apparition within the compass of nature: "The earth hath bubbles, as the water has, /And these are of them." The theory, whose seriousness is difficult to gauge, has the virtue of at once acknowledging the witches' material existence—

they are "of the earth"—and accounting for the possibility of their natural disappearance. If witches are earth bubbles, they would consist of air around which the earth takes form; hence they could, as Macbeth observes, vanish "into the air." But Banquo's theory cannot dispel the sense of a loss of moorings, for the hags' disappearance intensifies the sense of the blurring of boundaries that the entire scene has generated: "What seem'd corporal," Macbeth observes, "Melted as breath into the wind" (1.3.81–82).[35]

Virtually everything that follows in the play transpires on the border between fantasy and reality, a sickening betwixt-and-between where a mental "image" has the uncanny power to produce bodily effects "against the use of nature," where Macbeth's "thought, whose murther yet is but fantastical" can so shake his being that "function is smother'd in surmise, / And nothing is, but what is not" (1.3.141–42), where one mind is present to the innermost fantasies of another, where manhood threatens to vanish and murdered men walk, and blood cannot be washed off.[36] If these effects could be securely attributed to the agency of the witches, we would at least have the security of a defined and focused fear. Alternatively, if the witches could be definitively dismissed as fantasy or fraud, we would at least have the clear-eyed certainty of grappling with human causes in an altogether secular world. But instead Shakespeare achieves the remarkable effect of a nebulous infection, a bleeding of the demonic into the secular and the secular into the demonic.

The most famous instance of this effect is Lady Macbeth's great invocation of the "spirits / That tend on mortal thoughts" to unsex her, fill her with cruelty, make thick her blood, and exchange her milk with gall. The speech appears to be a conjuration of demonic powers, an act of witchcraft in which the "murdering ministers" are directed to bring about a set of changes in her body. She calls these ministers "sightless substances": though invisible, they are—as she conceives them—not figures of speech or projections of her mind, but objective, substantial beings.[37] But the fact that the spirits she invokes are "sightless" already moves this passage away from the earth-bubble corporeality of the Weird Sisters and toward the metaphorical use of "spirits" in Lady's Macbeth's words, a few moments earlier, "Hie thee hither, / That I may pour my spirits in thine ear" (1.5.24–25). The "spirits" she speaks of here are manifestly figurative—they refer to the bold words, the undaunted mettle, and the sexual taunts with which she intends to incite Macbeth to murder Duncan—but, like all of her expressions of will and passion, they strain toward bodily realization, even as they convey a psychic and hence invisible inwardness. That is, there is something uncannily literal about Lady Macbeth's influence on her husband, as if she had contrived to inhabit his mind—as if, in other words, she had literally poured her spirits in his ear. Conversely, there is something uncannily figurative about the "sightless substances" she invokes, as if the spirit world, the realm of "Fate and metaphysical aid," were only a metaphor for her blind and murderous desires, as if the Weird Sisters were condensations of her own breath.[38]

We can glimpse the means by which Shakespeare achieves what I have called "bleeding"—the mutual contamination of the secular and the demonic—if we recall the long passage from Scot about the fraudulent wonders that Ovid and the other poets attribute to witches: raising thunder and lightning, causing unnatural darkness, going in and out at auger holes, and so forth. We happen to know that Shakespeare read this passage: his eye was caught by the phrase "auger hole." But he did not use it to characterize his witches; instead it surfaces after the murder of Duncan when the justifiably terrified Donalbain whispers to Malcolm that they should flee:

> What should be spoken here,
> Where our fate, hid in an auger hole,
> May rush and seize us? (2.3.117–19)

The auger hole has ceased to be an actual passageway, uncannily small and hence virtually invisible, for witches to pass through and has become a figure for the fear that lurks everywhere in Macbeth's castle. And the Weird Sisters, of whose existence Malcolm and Donalbain are entirely unaware, have been translated into the abstraction to which their name is etymologically linked—fate. The phantasmagorical horror of witchcraft, ridiculed by Scot, is redistributed by Shakespeare across the field of the play, shaping the representation of the state, of marriage, and, above all, of the psyche. When Lady Macbeth calls upon the "spirits / That tend on mortal thoughts" to unsex her, when she directs the "murdering ministers" to take her milk for gall, the terrifying intensity of her psychological malignity depends upon Shakespeare's deployment or—to borrow a term from Puttenham's *Arte of English Poesie* (1589)—his "translacing" of the ragged, filthy materials of inquisitorial credulity.[39]

Translacing is a mode of rhetorical redistribution in which the initial verbal elements remain partially visible even as they are woven into something new. Hence Lady Macbeth is not revealed to be a witch, yet the witches subsist as a tenebrous filament to which Lady Macbeth is obscurely but palpably linked.[40] This redistribution does not, let us note, enable the playwright to transcend what we have identified as the ethical problem inherent in staging witches in early seventeeth-century England. If I were a woman on trial for witchcraft, I would call upon Reginald Scot, misogynistic, narrow-minded, suspicious of the imagination, to testify on my behalf, not upon Shakespeare. *Macbeth* leaves the Weird Sisters unpunished, but manages to implicate them in a monstrous threat to the fabric of civilized life. The genius of the play is bound up with this power of implication by means of which we can never be done with them, for they are most suggestively present when we cannot see them, when they are absorbed in the putatively ordinary relations of everyday life. That is what translacing means: if you are worried about losing your manhood, it is not enough to look to the bearded hags on the heath, look to your wife. "When you durst do it, then you were a man" (1.7.49). If you are worried about "interior temptation," fear your own dreams: "Merciful powers, / Restrain in me the cursèd thoughts that nature / Gives way to in repose" (2.1.7–9). If you are anxious about your future, scrutinize your best friends: "He was a gentleman on whom I built / An absolute trust" (1.4.14–15). And if you fear spiritual desolation, turn your eyes on the contents not only of the hideous cauldron but of your skull: "O, full of scorpions is my mind, dear wife" (3.2.39).

The whole point of the discourse of witchcraft was to achieve clarity, to make distinctions, to escape from the terror of the inexplicable, the unfore-seen, the aimlessly malignant. Whatever other satisfactions it gave the mag-istrates, the torture to which accused witches were subjected was intended to secure this clarity by extracting full confessions, gratifying confirmations of the theoretical truths. The fact that these confirmations were produced by torture did not compromise their usefulness; indeed for King James, *volun-tary* confessions were suspect, since they suggested an unhinged mind neu-rotically bent on self-incrimination: "Experience daylie proues how loath they are to confesse without torture, which witnesseth their guiltines, where by the contrary, the Melancholicques neuer spare to bewray them-selues. . . ."[41] In *Macbeth* the audience is given something better than con-fession, for it can see visible proof of the demonic in action, but this visibil-ity, this powerful *enargeia*, turns out to be maddeningly equivocal. The "wayward" witches appear and disappear, and the language of the play sub-verts the illusory certainties of sight. The ambiguities of demonic agency are never resolved, and its horror spreads like a mist through a murky land-scape.[42] "What is't you do?" Macbeth asks the Weird Sisters; "A deed with-out a name" (4.1.49–50).[43]

For Reginald Scot, to relocate witchcraft as theatrical illusion was to move it decisively into the zone of the imaginary and to end the equivocation: "I for my part have read a number of their conjurations, but never could see anie divels of theirs, except it were in a plaie" (258). Scot does not rail against the theater; it is imposture he hates, fictions pretending to be realities. He confidently expects that anything self-consciously marked out as fiction, any play recognized as a play, will have no force. The playhouse, for Scot, is the house of unbelief. Show people how the juggling tricks are done; show them how their desire to know "the sequele of things to come, and to see the end of their feare and hope" is manipulated; show them how they are deceived by the "double or doubtfull" sense of language, and they will henceforth be free—free, that is, to submit themselves to the Almighty. *Macbeth* rehearses many of the same disillusioning revelations, including even a demonstration of the bad jokes by which, as Scot puts it, "plaine lieng is avoided with a figurative speech." Birnam Wood come to Dunsinan and the man "of no woman born" are close relations to the piece of earth from Russia and the marvelous substance in the Indian stone with which Scot sought to work his disenchantment. And when Macbeth understands the equivocations by which he has been deceived, he takes a step toward unbelief:

> And be these juggling fiends no more believed
> That palter with us in a double sense,
> That keep the word of promise to our ear
> And break it to our hope. (5.7.49–52)

Not believing the juggling fiends, of course, is different from not believing in their existence, but that skeptical doubt too, as we have seen, has been articulated in the course of the play. Moreover, Shakespeare's play does not attempt to conceal the theatricality of witchcraft;[44] on the contrary, a self-conscious theatricality tinges all of the witches' appearances, becoming explicit in the scene, possibly part of Middleton's contribution to the play, in which Hecate complains that she was "never called to bear my part / Or show the glory of our art."[45] But in *Macbeth* the acknowledgment of theatrical artifice is a sign not of polemical skepticism but of the tragedy's appropriative power, an effect not of ethical redemption but of irresistible histrionic life.

In the last analysis—if there ever is a last analysis—Shakespeare's theater, like most of the art we value, is on the side of a liberating, tolerant doubt, but on the way to that doubt there is the pleasure and the profit of mystification, collusion, imaginary enchantment. Shakespeare was part of a profession that made its money manipulating images and playing with the double and doubtful senses of words. If the life of the player comes to seem an empty illusion, it does so in the light not of Scot's faith but of Macbeth's despair:

> Life's but a walking shadow, a poor player
> That struts and frets his hour upon the stage,
> And then is heard no more. It is a tale
> Told by an idiot, full of sound and fury
> Signifying nothing. (5.5.24–28)

The closing moments of the play invite us to recoil from this black hole just as they invite us to recoil from too confident and simple a celebration of the triumph of grace. For Shakespeare the presence of the theatrical in the demonic, as in every other realm of life, only intensifies the sense of an equivocal betwixt-and-between, for his theater is the space where the fantastic and the bodily, *energia* and *enargeia* touch.[46] To conjure up such a theater places Shakespeare in the position neither of the witchmonger nor the skeptic. It places him in the position of the witch.

NOTES

1. Quoted in Carlo Ginzburg, *Storia natturna: Una decifrazione del sabba* (Torino: Einaudi, 1989), p. 65.

2. Quoted in Valerie I. J. Flint, *The Rise of Magic in Early Medieval Europe* (Princeton: Princeton University Press, 1991), p. 122. I have changed "phantasms" to a plural, in keeping with the Latin.

3. Reginone's project is not, like that of Eusebius in the fourth century, to persuade his readers that the ancient gods and goddesses were actually demons. Eusebius begins with the assumption that the apparitions of the pagan deities were real enough; that is, they did not simply occur in the minds of the credulous believers. Demons, he suggests, cunningly play the parts of pagan deities in order to shore up superstitious beliefs. See Eusebius, *Evangelicae praeparationis* (*The Preparation for the Gospel*), ed. and trans. E. H. Gifford (Oxford: Oxford University Press, 1903): "The ministrants of the oracles we must in plain truth declare to be evil daemons, playing both parts to deceive mankind, and at once time agreeing with the more fabulous suppositions concerning themselves, to deceive the common people, and at another time confirming the statements of the philosophers' jugglery in order to instigate them also and puff them up: so that in every way it is proved that they speak no truth at all" (p. 139).

Eusebius argues that the fact that spirits can be compelled to appear by magical charms is proof in itself that they are not good spirits. (He cites Porphyry on the fact of the compulsion.) "For if the deity is not subject to force or to compulsion, but is in nature superior to all things, being free and incapable of suffering, how can they be gods who are beguiled by juggling tricks managed by means of such dresses, and lines, and images?—beguiled, I say, by wreaths also and flowers of the earth, and withal by certain unintelligible and barbarous cries and voices, and subdued by ordinary men, and, as it were, enslaved by bonds so that they cannot even keep safe in their own control the power of independence and free will" (p. 214). Presumably, then, the fact that Christian angels will not necessarily come when they are called is a sign of their reality.

4. Quoted in Flint, p. 123.

5. See Julio Carlo Baroja, *The World of Witches*, trans. Nigel Glendinning (Chicago: University of Chicago Press, 1968). Burchard argued that those who believed in witchcraft were participating in a revival of paganism and were crediting what were only satanic delusions.

6. Quoted in Flint, p. 123.

7. P. 155. A similar hard-line toward authorities unwilling to prosecute witches is taken by Bodin. Here, as elsewhere, the issue of witchcraft is linked to an intensification of the claims of sovereignty. Such a link would seem to be present—though only in an oblique way—in *Macbeth*, where the "existence" of the witches is part of a strategy whereby Macbeth is not simply a ruthless political opportunist but a metaphysical nightmare and Duncan, Malcolm, Banquo (and Fleance), and ultimately James VI/I are not simply admired rulers but agents of the divine will.

8. Edmund Spenser, *The Faerie Queene*, ed. Thomas P. Roche, Jr. (Middlesex:

Penguin, 1978), book 2, canto 9, stanza 51. The chamber of *Phantastes* swarming with such things "as in idle fantasies do flit," includes "Infernall Hags."

9. Peter Stallybrass, "*Macbeth* and Witchcraft," *Focus on 'Macbeth'*, ed. J. K. Brain (London: Routledge and Kegan Paul, 1982), p. 205.

10. Janet Adelman, " 'Born of Woman': Fantasies of Maternal Power in *Macbeth*," in *Cannibals, Witches, and Divorce: Estranging the Renaissance* (English Institute Essays), ed. Marjorie Garber (Baltimore: Johns Hopkins University Press, 1987), pp. 103, 111. I should make it quite clear that Janet Adelman is not concerned to condemn the play as evil. Indeed it is one of the strengths of psychoanalytic criticism that it can accept, even celebrate, the expression of dangerous fantasies.

11. The question of the play's evil would involve at least three distinct or distinguishable questions: (1) was it morally responsible for Shakespeare to represent women as witches? (2) did the representation have bad consequences in its own time? (3) does the representation have bad consequences in our own time?

12. The sense that the witches are marginal is explicitly thematized in Hecate's complaint to the hags that she was "never called to bear my part / Or show the glory of our art." Though these words seem initially to refer only to the fact that the "saucy and overbold" hags had trafficked with Macbeth without involving Hecate, they imply that the art of witchcraft has somehow been displaced on the stage by something else. Within the psychological and moral world of the play, the displacement seems to be focused on Macbeth's motivation. He is not a worshipper of the dark powers whom the witches serve; hence Hecate's complaint that he is a "wayward son." In the metatheatrical sense that I am pursuing in this paper, the "glory" of the witches' art is displaced by the glory of Shakespeare's.

13. That is, our belief system requires evidence of a more direct and premeditated malice in a text we would judge to be evil. By "our belief system" I refer to the secular humanism—the heritage of what Pocock calls "the Machiavellian moment"—that has largely dominated Western conceptions of culture, and particularly of literary culture, since the eighteenth century. I am well aware that this belief system is neither timeless nor universal—a bitter controversy about belief is, after all, the historical situation addressed in this paper—and I understand, of course, that the little word "our" is contestable.

14. Of course, what one culture or generation or ideological faction regards as repellent or criminal, another may regard as an exalted necessity, but this possibility of conflicting evaluation is the condition of all moral judgments and does not place art beyond good and evil. Nor can art be exempted from judgment on the principle that it is a kind of dream—and hence, as even Plato said of dreams, outside the canons of morality. For even if we all agree that art functions as a kind of culturally-sanctioned dream work, art is *intended* dreaming and hence morally accountable.

We might, however, want to separate an aesthetic judgment of art works from a moral judgment: that is, it would be possible to find a work evil and at the same time to acknowledge its aesthetic power. Moreover, it is possible to imagine a response that would find the intention behind a particular work of art to be evil, while at the same time finding a moral value in that very work of art on the grounds that it allows a kind of imaginative freedom or that the revulsion it inspires awakens a moral response. (One could, conversely, find that a particular work was moral in intention but immoral in action.)

15. Cf. Thomas Greene, "Magic and Festivity at the Renaissance Court," in *Renaissance Quarterly* 40 (1987): 641.

16. The possibility of prosecuting anyone for witchcraft depended on the prior public recognition that witchcraft "actually" existed—that it was not a brainsick fantasy or a fraud but a malevolent reality—and this recognition is precisely what is in question in this period. As Christina Larner writes, "If the relatively simple crimes of adultry and murder were ambiguous without social indentification, witchcraft was non-existent. Witchcraft is the labelling theorist's dream" (*Witchcraft and Religion: The Politics of Popular Belief* [Oxford: Blackwell, 1984], p. 29).

17. In disputing the claim the witches are melancholiacs, James VI's spokesman in the *Daemonologie*, Epistemon, claims that they are "rich and worldly-wise, some of them fatte or corpulent in their bodies, and most part of them altogether given over to the pleasure of the flesh, continual haunting of companie, and all kind of merrines." (*Daemonology*, pp. 28–30, quoted in Stuart Clark, "King James's *Daemonologie*: Witchcraft and Kingship," in Sydney Anglo, *The Damned Art* [Boston: Routledge & K. Paul, 1977], p. 171.) This view, which is apparently linked to James's response to the principal North Berwick defendants, is wildly at variance with the marginality, poverty, and hence vulnerability of witches amply documented elsewhere, and not only by those who were challenging the persecution. The most powerful theatrical acknowledgment of the vulnerability of witches is in Dekker's *Witch of Edmonton*, a play that nonetheless stages without protest the witch's execution.

18. It will not do to exaggerate the extent of this contestation; in England, unlike Germany, France, or Scotland, witchcraft prosecutions were relatively infrequent, and while there is a substantial discourse, there is no sign of a cultural obsession. But even before James came to the English throne and greatly intensified the official interest in witchcraft, its ramifications were broad, and there is a constant recourse to witchcraft (as metaphor or image, for example) in a wide range of discourses.

19. The contract also licenses the violent persecution (rather than medical treatment or exorcism) of witches, for it is the sign of their "absolute liberty" (16) and hence their full responsibility for their actions.

20. "Again, although to enter the soul is possible only to God Who created it, yet devils can, with God's permission, enter our bodies; and they can then make impressions on the inner faculties corresponding to the bodily organs. And by those impressions the organs are affected in proportion as the inner perceptions are affected in the way which has been shown: that the devil can draw out some image retained in a faculty corresponding to one of the senses; as he draws from the memory, which is in the back part of the head, an image of a horse, and locally moves that phantasm to the middle part of the head, where are the cells of imaginative power; and finally to the sense of reason, which is in the front of the head. And he causes such a sudden change and confusion, that such objects are necessarily thought to be actual things seen with the eyes" (125).

21. What is going on here? Kramer and Sprenger may tell this tale less to address a particular hysterical symptom that they claim is widespread than to represent the sense that the penis is independent of one's control. Hence they remark that witches

"sometimes collect male organs in great numbers, as many as twenty or thirty members together, and put them in a bird's nest, or shut them up in a box, where they move themselves like living members, and eat oats and corn, as has been seen by many and is a matter of common report" (121). In its grotesque way, the story registers an Augustinian anxiety that the stirrings and appetites of sexuality are not under the control of the rational will.

22. It is also the source of its originality in relation to the Continental sources on whom Scot greatly depends. For, as Michel de Certeau has observed, in the Continental debates over witchcraft, the issue is the relation between the supernatural and the natural: Wier and Bodin grant the same facts and then disagree bitterly about the cause of those facts. But there is another response to phenomena that apparently escape the ordinary and observable norms of the natural, a response that consists in suspecting the presence of illusion. And, as de Certeau remarks, while this perspective seems less theoretical, it is in fact the more radical, for it challenges perception itself: visual testimony which was the principle of verification ("I would have doubted it, if I hadn't seen it for myself") is now called into question. See Michel de Certeau, L'Absent de l'histoire (Paris: Maison Mame, 1973), p. 30. Similarly, Michel Foucault points out that neither Molitor at the end of the fifteenth century nor Wier or Erastus in the sixteenth century actually abandons the idea of the demonic. Their argument against Sprenger, Bodin and others, Foucault remarks, does not contest the existence of the devil or his presence among men but centers on his mode of manifesting himself, on the way he conceals himself beneath appearances. See Michel Foucault, "Les déviations religieuses et le savoir médical," in Heresies et sociétés dans l'Europe pre-industrielle 11e-18e siècles, Communications et debats du Colloque de Royaumont, ed. Jacques Le Goff (Paris: Mouton, 1968).

23. See, above all, Jules Michelet's visionary Satanism and Witchcraft: A Study in Medieval Superstition [La sorcière], trans. A. R. Allinson (Secaucus, N.J.: Citadel Press, n.d.). Michelet's views, long dismissed as romantic claptrap, were revived for feminism by Hélène Cixous and Catherine Clément, The Newly Born Woman, trans. Betsy Wing (Minneapolis: University of Minnesota Press, 1975). It would be possible too to see a connection between Michelet's attempt to reconstruct a secret history of ecstatic experience among medieval peasants and Carlo Ginzburg's remarkable Ecstasies: Deciphering the Witches' Sabbath, trans. Raymond Rosenthal (London: Hutchinson, 1989). The crucial point, for our purposes, is that Scot cannot concede any authentic heterodox religious experience to witches, any more than he can concede to them the possession of any actual power. To do so would be both to compromise his own religious convictions and to endorse the arguments of the witchmongers. One peculiar consequence is that Clément and Ginzburg seem far closer in their views to the inquisitors than to those who, like Scot, worked to stop the persecution.

24. Scot participates then in the process described by Juliana Schiesari in The Gendering of Melancholia: Feminism, Psychoanalysis, and the Symbolics of Loss in Renaissance Literature (Ithaca: Cornell University Press, 1992). The melancholy that functions as a sign of genius in the elite male Hamlet is in these village women a mark of impotence and confusion. But it is important to recognize that the misogynistic diagnosis, like the insanity defense, plays a role at this time in mitigating judicial punishment.

Scot's position is very close to that articulated, again in a juridical context, by his contemporary Montaigne:

A few years ago I passed through the territory of a sovereign prince, who, as a favor to me and to beat down my incredulity, did me the kindness of letting me see, in his own presence and in a private place, ten or twelve prisoners of this nature, and among others one old woman, indeed a real witch in ugliness or deformity, long very famous in that profession. I saw both proofs and free confessions, and some barely perceptible mark or other on this wretched old woman, and I talked and asked questions all I wanted, bringing to the matter the soundest attention I could; and I am not the man to let my judgment be throttled much by preconceptions. In the end, and in all conscience, I would have prescribed rather hellebore than hemlock. *It seemed to me a matter rather of madness than of crime* [Livy] ["Of Cripples," in *The Complete Essays of Montaigne*, trans. Donald M. Frame (Stanford: Stanford University Press, 1948), p. 790].

25. Alternatively, it is our banalization of the marvelous aspects of the familiar world that has made these authentic wonders seem ordinary and has led to the invention of false miracles.

26. Ludwig Wittgenstein, *Philosophical Investigations*, 3d ed., trans. G. E. M. Anscombe (London: Blackwell, 1958), p. 47 (#109).

27. In the term "liberties" we can perhaps hear an ironic allusion to the very zone in which the public theaters of Shakespeare's time were located, the Liberties of London. Cf. Steven Mullaney, *The Place of the Stage* (Chicago: University of Chicago Press, 1988).

28. In "The Index of the Absent Wound (Monograph on a Stain)," *October* 29 (1984), Georges Didi-Huberman speaks of "a sense of *figurability*, understood as a *means of staging*—a translation suggested by Lacan for what is generally called the consideration of representability, which Freud refers to as *Rücksicht auf Darstellbarkeit*. This is where the field I referred to as *figurative Aufhebung* has its fantasmatic extension, in thoughts expressed as images or, as Freud says, as pseudothoughts; in substituting for logic pure relationships of formal contiguity; in the play of displacements of plastic intensity, in their ability to focus and fascinate" (73).

29. Aristotle counseled the dramatist to "put the actual scenes as far as possible before his eyes. In this way, seeing everything with the vividness of an eyewitness as it were, he will devise what is appropriate" (*Poetics* 455ª in *The Complete Works of Aristotle*, ed. Jonathan Barnes, 2 vols. [Princeton: Princeton University Press, 1984], 2:2328–29). Florio translates *energia* as "efficacie, or effectuall operation"; *enargeia* as "evidence, perspicuitie, evident representing of a thing," *A Worlde of Wordes, Or a Most copious, and exact Dictionarie in Italian and English*, collected by John Florio (London, 1598).

30. In *The Comedy of Errors* the ethical and theatrical conditions of figurability converge, as they do whenever Shakespeare uses the discourse of witchcraft solely to designate the confusion and projection of a troubled consciousness.

31. Their prognostications, to be sure, turn out to depend upon equivocations, the "double or doubtful words" that Scot saw as sources of credulity. But the bitter disillusionment that follows—"And be these juggling fiends no more believed / That palter with us in a double sense" (5.7.48–49)—is not at all what Scot had in mind, for it does not signal a recognition that witchcraft is itself fraud and delusion.

32. On the insistent thematizing of vision in *Macbeth*, see Huston Diehl, "Horrid Image, Sorry Sight, Fatal Vision: The Visual Rhetoric of *Macbeth*," in *Shakespeare Studies* 16 (1983): 191–203. "The play itself," Diehl argues, "is centrally concerned with the problematics of vision. It examines the act of seeing and interpreting an uncertain visible world" (191). Diehl suggests that the audience is led to realize what Macbeth, Lady Macbeth, and Duncan all fail to grasp: "that sight is both objective and ethical" (191). But I have tried to show throughout this paper that, in the context of the witchcraft contestation, there is something ethically problematical in sight.

33. "What matters here is not hunting down an answer to the question 'What are the witches?' All the critical and theatrical efforts to answer that question demonstrate that the question cannot be answered. What those frantic answers also demonstrate—and what matters—is the fact of the question." Stephen Booth, *"King Lear," "Macbeth," Indefinition, and Tragedy* (New Haven and London: Yale University Press, 1983), p. 102.

34. The questions were almost impossible to resolve, even for Scot, because virtually everyone who had access to print (and presumably most of the population as well) was committed to maintaining traditional Christian beliefs in the supernatural. Those beliefs were so closely bound up with fantasies of the demonic that it was extremely difficult to dismantle the latter without irreparably damaging the former. In a fuller account of the play, we would have to explore not only the problematic character of these traditional Christian beliefs but the extent to which sovereignty too is bound up with the queasy and ambiguous status of the witches.

35. "Were such things here, as we do speak about," Banquo asks, "Or have we eaten on the insane root, / That takes the reason prisoner?" (1.3.83–85).

36. Paul Alpers has pointed out to me that the English repeatedly psychologized enargeia, by confusing it with energia.

37. From this Walter Curry concluded that Lady Macbeth must actually have been possessed: "Without doubt these ministers of evil do actually take possession of her body even in accordance with her desire" (in *Shakespeare's Philosophical Patterns* [Baton Rouge: Louisiana State University Press, 1937], p. 87).

38. Lady Macbeth's two invocations of spirits are conjoined by a brief scene in which a nameless messenger brings her the startling news, "The King comes here tonight." When she expresses her incredulity that Macbeth himself has not brought word in person, the messsenger answers,

> One of my fellows had the speed of him,
> Who almost dead for breath, had scarcely more
> Than would make up his message. (1.5.33–35)

The lines have the odd effect of insisting on the literal meaning of a phrase like "breathless haste," and in doing so they provide a clue to the connection between the literal and figurative uses of the term spirit: both rest on the breath.

The relation between breath, spirit, and inspiration was well-known in the early seventeenth century. Hobbes remarks,

> On the signification of the word *Spirit* dependeth that of the word INSPIRA-TION; which must either be taken properly; and then it is nothing but the blowing into a man some thin and subtile aire, or wind in such manner as a man filleth a bladder wilth his breath; or if Spirits be not corporeall, but have their

existence only in the fancy, it is nothing but the blowing in of a Phantasme; which is improper to say, and impossible; for Phantasmes are not, but only seem to be somewhat. (*Leviathan*, 440)

39. Puttenham introduces the term in an account of the rhetorical figure of "*Traductio*, or the Translacer," "which is when ye turne and tranlace [sic] a word into many sundry shapes as the Tailor doth his garment, & after that sort do play with him in your dittie," *Arte of English Poesie* (Menston: Scolar Press Facsimile, 1968), p. 170.

40. As Jonathan Crewe has observed (in a response to this paper), Lady Macbeth in consequence comes to seem evil in excess of anything that she actually *does*; the history of *Macbeth* criticism is a history of incrimination, a long bill of indictment brought less against the murderous hero than against his wife. For example, there are children murdered in the play, but their murder is ordered by Macbeth who does so without consulting his "dearest chuck." And yet critics return compulsively to the horrible inward intensity of Lady Macbeth's fantasy of infanticide:

> I would, while it was smiling in my face,
> Have plucked my nipple from his boneless gums
> And dashed the brains out, had I so sworn
> As you have done to this. (1.7.56–59)

Lady Macbeth's evil has been so obsessivley discussed by criticism, Crewe suggests, because she has made an effort to repossess her body, to empower herself (by identifying with what she perceives as masculine strength, even as she intuitively understands that she herself has created masculine strength), to be something other than the figure of reproduction in the nuclear family. In fact her power comes from a literacy—her ability to read Macbeth's letter, to read his character—virtually uncanny in a woman. She is, Crewe suggests, the place of greatest ideological resistance in a play that implies that the proper role of a woman should be that of a sleepwalker.

41. *Daemonologie*, p. 30.

42. For an alternative view, see Ninian Mellamphy, "Macbeth's Visionary Dagger: Hallucination or Revelation?" in *English Studies in Canada* 4 (1978): 379–92. Mellamphy argues that the play's ambiguities are sorted out if one keeps in mind "the Renaissance distinction between distorting fantasy (the fantastic imagination) and good fantasy (the icastic imagination)" (385). But it is just this distinction that continually breaks down in *Macbeth*.

43. The witches, Dennis Biggins observes, "occupy a kind of twilight territory between human and supernatural evildoing," "Sexuality, Witchcraft, and Violence in *Macbeth*," in *Shakespeare Studies* 8 (1968): 256.

44. Shakespeare in effect endorsed Scot's association of witchcraft with illusion-mongering, but of course Scot's fury is at those who do not admit that they are the purveyors of illusion, who allow people to believe that their powers are supernatural. Shakespeare, however, seems less persuaded than Scot that a frank acknowledgment of theatricality substantially reduces the power of the representation.

45. In an astonishing moment, Hecate and the witches actually sing a song from another play, Middleton's *The Witch*. The scene has been much lamented by scholars: "It is to be hoped that this song was altered for *Macbeth*, as some lines are

relevant only to the plot of Middleton's play. But the 1673 edition of *Macbeth* prints them without alteration. No exit is marked for Hecate and the spurious witches; but the sooner they depart the better" (Kenneth Muir, Arden *Macbeth* [New York: Random House, 1962], note to 4.1.43). But the moment seems to me not a regrettable "non-Shakespearean interpolation" but rather a deliberate quotation, a marking of the demonic as the theatrical.

46. Touch but not fuse: their relation remains itself equivocal. "Equivocation is not so much a major theme in the play, as a number of critics have observed, but the very condition of the play," in Lucy Gent, "The Self-Cozening Eye," *Review of English Studies* 34 (1983): 419. Gent argues that "the work of art's equivocation is innocuous; that of the world of Macbeth is mortal" (424). I'm not sure that this consoling distinction can hold up; for Reginald Scot, the equivocation of the work of art is a key to the whole sickness.

For Shakespeare to identify the theatrical with witchcraft was to invent the fantasmatic as the site of the psychological—that is, to invent the staged discourse of interiority—and to do so out of the odds and ends of Continental witchcraft. (Adelman thinks that that Continental beliefs are "transferred away from the witches and recur as the psychological"—but I would argue that these beliefs are the materials out of which the psychological is constructed.)

CHAPTER FIVE

Re-visioning the Restoration: Or, How to Stop Obscuring Early Women Writers

MARGARET J. M. EZELL

"Re-vision—the act of looking back, of seeing with
fresh eyes, of entering an old text from a new critical
direction—is for women more than a chapter in
cultural history: it is an act of survival."
(Adrienne Rich, "When We Dead Awaken:
Writing as Re-Vision")

"There are no limits to the irony of history."
(Frederick Engels, The Origin of the Family, Private
Property and the State)

AT FIRST SIGHT, my title probably is rather puzzling. Why should the Restoration, of all periods, need "re-visioning" by those of us interested in early
women's writing? After the so-called "golden age" of women novelists in the
nineteenth century, few periods have been given so much attention in
women's studies as the years after Charles II's return to the English throne.
Following Virginia Woolf's injunction, we have flung flowers on the grave of
Aphra Behn as the first professional female writer, a writer, as her recent
biographer informs us, who "would signal a turning in feminine history,
[and] augur a whole new spectrum of possibility for her sex."[1] To celebrate
Behn's appearance in the commercial world of letters and a little later the
publication of Mary Astell, labeled "the first English Feminist" by her biographer, women's literary history has traditionally begun its narrative with
Restoration women authors.[2]

Furthermore, this period has recently been well-served by feminist
bibliographers, biographers, and anthologists. Texts such as Janet Todd's
Dictionary of Women Writers, Fidelis Morgan's *The Female Wits*, and Germaine Greer et al.'s *Kissing the Rod* have made available—in paperback—
the lives and writings of literally dozens of "lost" women writers from the

period. So how can I justly invoke Adrienne Rich's "re-vision" which demands that we lift the obscuring veil of preconceptions about gender and authorship in connection with this well-studied period? I do so, because I believe that significant writers and works of the seventeenth century and in particular the Restoration are still waiting to be seen and read.[3] In spite of the groundbreaking work of the feminist literary critics cited, on whose work my own is based, I believe that we still have not yet seen the extent of women's literary activities in the period. The question then becomes why has the feminist re-visioning of the past not brought to light certain types of writers lost in a traditional literary history?

In *Jane Eyre*, the heroine often escapes her confining duties as a governess by climbing up to the roof and gazing out over the distant landscape. She looks "afar over sequestered field and hill, along dim skyline. . . . Then I longed for a power of vision which might overpass that limit; which might reach the busy world, towns, regions full of life I had heard of but never seen" (chap. 12). Jane Eyre's vision is restricted in two senses: first, by the boundaries of physical sense or the strength of her sight, and second, by what her society has decided is appropriate for a female of her circumstances to see or experience. Those of us studying early women's writings share similar frustrations. Until very recently we have been circumscribed by the physical difficulty of seeing women's texts, locked away in the rare book rooms of distant libraries or captured on fuzzy microfilms, a circumstance which projects such as the NEH-supported Women Writers Project, which is creating a full text data base of pre-Victorian women's writings, will go some distance in changing. But we have also had our sight of the past restricted by preconceived notions of what we will see there and, even more important, what we should be looking for in the first place.

In 1983, Joanna Russ published a witty polemic entitled *How to Suppress Women's Writing* which explored the agencies through which women's writings have historically been trivialized or erased in a patriarchal academic literary criticism. "Once the informal prohibitions [against women writing] have failed to work," she asks, what has the institution done, "to bury the art, to explain it away, ignore it, downgrade it, in short make it vanish?"[4] Her categories of critical response which erase women's writings and discourage new efforts include prohibition (women cannot write), "Bad Faith" (the denial of the status quo), denial of agency (she didn't write it, her husband/brother did), pollution of agency (she wrote it, but she must be mad/eccentric), double standard (she wrote it, but it is ignorantly unconventional, not innovative), false categorizing (she wrote it, but it is not "high" or important literature), and isolation and anomalousness (she wrote it, but she only wrote one thing; she wrote it, but no other woman has).

In setting up her categories, Russ is concerned with revealing the institutional practices and preconceptions found in male accounts of women's writ-

ing which stifle female creativity. Her observations, however, can also illuminate for us problems existing in women's literary historiography when it
carries over traditional perceptions of literary hierarchy and categorization.
Ironically, the very texts and institutions created by women's studies, which
initially *enabled* the serious study of women's writing in the university and
the retrieval of authors lost to women readers, now may act to obscure a
significant portion of female authorship. In the process of celebrating certain
types of women writers, we have exiled many others writing before 1700; in
some instances this has happened unwittingly, but in other instances because the writers and their works do not fit our received notions of authorship and of literary production.

To supplement Russ's observations, I see three types of critical response
to the past which have influenced the presentation of early women writers.
While on one hand, these practices have successfully encouraged the study
of women's literature in a scholarly context, on the other, these very same
interpretive strategies have obscured certain types of women and women's
writings from study. When one examines the underlying structures of current accounts of Restoration women's literary history, three characteristic
features emerge: the drive to conceptualize, the search for sameness, and
the interpretation of the distant past in terms of the more recent, or "backward projection."

I

One assumption behind the decision to begin the "tradition" of women's
writing in the Restoration is that women did not write in significant numbers
before then. Virginia Woolf in *A Room of One's Own* is the most eloquent
exponent of this position. "It is a perennial puzzle why no woman wrote a
word of that extraordinary literature," she mused, considering the Renaissance, "when every other man, it seemed, was capable of song or sonnet";[5]
the rest of her text and the efforts of her followers are devoted to explaining
the social forces which silence women's creative expression. This configuration of women's literary past also underlies the previously noted emphasis in
feminist literary histories on Restoration and early eighteenth-century
women writers being "first": to add another example, the eighteenth century, we are told, was "the first period, in England, when [women] found a
voice in literature."[6]

This perception of the Restoration as the turning point in women's literary history not only shapes our sense of literary activity in that period, but,
of course, it also strongly affects the presentation of earlier periods. Indeed,
the criticism written about later stages of women's literary history has often
been founded on an implicit negation of earlier periods' activities. When one
asserts that the eighteenth century was the *first* period in which women

writers had a voice or one discusses the "rise" of the woman novelist, one is implying that previous generations had been kept silent and "low." This negation of earlier periods, for example, underlies discussions of Restoration women dramatists which assert that the formation of a female tradition was of "crucial importance" to those women "who sought a role as writers in a world hitherto closed to them."[7] Likewise, the presentation of Aphra Behn offers a clear and graphic example of how in the process of celebrating one woman and one period, others are denied: she is offered to us as "the first English woman to make her living by writing," who says "things so far unheard from women's pens."[8] In the chronicle of women's literary history, Behn is presented as the possessor of a "voice [which] had not been heard in English literature before. . . . It invented itself without precedent out of the life of the woman who owned it."[9]

In short, to hear the voices of those women writing in the eighteenth century or the "golden age" of nineteenth-century fiction, we have unwittingly condemned to silence those who spoke earlier. When they persist in being heard, we have tended to dismiss them to the margins of women's literary history by defining them as isolated cases, or eccentric individuals crippled by their struggles with oppressive structures. In Woolf's *A Room of One's Own*, women writing before Aphra Behn are depicted as "harebrained, fantastical," "a bogey to frighten clever girls with," women "disfigured and deformed" by their creative drives; "any woman born with a great gift in the sixteenth century," Woolf summarizes, "would certainly have gone crazed, shot herself. . . . Tortured and pulled asunder by her own contrary instincts . . . she must have lost her health and sanity to a certainty" (64–65, 51). In this literary history, the names of early women writers have not been erased—only their accomplishments. Continuing this line, one important anthology, which presents the whole span of women's writing in English, describes Renaissance women writers as being "spiritually or socially exceptional." Individual writers are presented with labels which emphasize their anomalous situation: "a solitary visionary," a woman "impelled by inner voices," "extraordinarily well educated," and in general "atypical in both education and intellectual authority."[10]

Even when early women writers are the primary object of the study, they are commonly discussed in terms of silence and repression. Gilbert and Gubar's introduction to *Shakespeare's Sisters* (whose title itself creates the context for our perception of the early woman writer as Woolf's Judith Shakespeare, the isolated, tormented dramatist who destroys herself) prefaces one's reading of three essays about pre-1800 women writers by remarking that these pieces "remind us of those ages of silence when women did not publish poetry at all."[11] Although this may seem like a small point, such an introduction directs the reader's attention away from the activity and the achievement to focus on the oppression which resulted in these "eccentric" figures.

The assumption that early women writers were silent or anomalousness was based in many instances simply on the inaccessibility of early texts. The problem for women's historiography is that the drive to conceptualize has led to the formation of a pattern for women's literary history before all, or even a significant representation, of the data was available to consider. The danger is that the pattern perceived in this limited range of early women's writing will blind us to materials which do not conform to it. Obviously, there are many compelling reasons why this drive to conceptualize so early in the life of the discipline occurred—the most central was the need to create a context for the serious study of women's works. Historically, too, the formation of women's studies coincided with an explosion of controversial activity in the study of literary theory in general, in which archival work took a secondary and distinctly less glamorous role.

This approach has served women's studies well. However, must this be the final vision of women's literary past? Shortly before Russ's work appeared, Germaine Greer published an article, "The Tulsa Center for the Study of Women's Literature: What We Are Doing and Why We Are Doing It," in which she declared, "We have not reached the moment when we may generalize about women's work, because no generalization which is not based upon correct understanding of individual cases can be valid."[12] To a large extent, the theorization of women's literary history took place before the preliminary bibliographical work on Renaissance and Restoration women writers had collected and documented those individual cases. As Jane Marcus has noted,

> It is an ironic turn of events when one declares that a socialist feminist criticism should defend its old enemies, the very bibliographers, editors, textual scholars, biographers, and literary historians who wrote women out of history to begin with. But without the survival of these skills and the appropriation of them, women will again lose the history of their own culture.[13]

One sees the force of this warning when surveying accounts of early women's literature. Too many of the existing literary histories of women's writing have been based on a small group of texts, where the drive to conceptualize has us galloping ahead of archival work; in such literary histories, Anne Finch's "Introduction," Katherine Philips's lament over her pirated verse, and Dorothy Osborne's letter criticizing Margaret Cavendish's literary activities are cited repeatedly as the only specimens of pre-1700 women's texts. Premature generalizations about literary practices by women in the past are derived too often from examples marked more by their availability than their representativeness in terms of literary production.

This drive to conceptualize and to present the theory before the descriptive and illustrative particulars in women's literary history also has a strong ideological base. To challenge the theory of early women's silence may be read as an attack on feminism itself, an apparent denial of the repression experienced. As Linda Gordon has observed of developments in writing women's social history, "In the history of women's history, the greatest of our contradictions has been that between domination and resistance":

> Sometimes we feel impelled to document oppression, diagram the structures of domination, specify the agents and authors of domination, and mourn the damages. Sometimes we feel impelled to defend our honor and raise our spirits by documenting our struggles and identifying successes in mitigating the tyranny.[14]

In Gordon's view, women's social history has not yet become comfortable with interpretations of women's lives in the past that include both repression and resistance. To some historians, attention to women's authority in the domestic sphere seemed like "a romanticization of oppression"; on the other hand, Gordon asserts, "I still read too many histories of female experience as powerless, which is false and impossible. To be less powerful is not to be power-less, or even to lose all the time" (24).

One senses this contradiction in feminist literary history as well. There seems to be a belief that if one questions assertions about women's silence in early periods, one is challenging the fact that women were socially restricted. An attempt to dismantle the construction of the Restoration as the monumental starting point of feminine literary accomplishment may be read as an attempt to diminish or dismiss the achievements of writers such as Behn or Astell; but it is, in fact, an attempt to free Behn's and Astell's precursors and contemporaries from the negation of their literary activities done to highlight other particular modes of literary production. To say that Aphra Behn was not the first professional woman writer or that Katherine Philips was quite happy to have her translations in print, if not pirated copies of her verse, should not take away from Behn's literary successes or imply that Katherine Philips experienced the same authorial situation as her male contemporaries. But it is difficult to make such comments and not to feel the need to defend oneself against charges of being co-opted by a patriarchal ideology attempting to deny social repression; this difficulty arises in part because of the second feature of women's literary historiography, the search for sameness.

II

As I have discussed elsewhere, one of the primary functions of current women's literary history is to provide a literary family for contemporary women readers and writers.[15] The drive behind women's literary history has been to recover lost texts, lost voices, in order to provide models. Agreeing with Ellen Moers, Russ, for example, believes that while role models are important to all artists, "to aspiring women artists they are doubly valuable" (87). One of the goals of groundbreaking classics of feminist literary history such as Elaine Showalter's *A Literature of Their Own* was to stop the cycle whereby "each generation of women writers has found itself, in a sense, without a history, forced to rediscover the past anew, forging again and again the consciousness of their sex."[16] The cry from the heart of *A Room of One's Own* is that women writers have "no tradition behind them, or one so short and partial that it was of little help. For we think back through our mothers if we are women" (79). Jane Marcus refers to Woolf's ability to "think back through her mothers" as freeing her from "the loneliness of individual anxiety" and giving her "her first collective identity," and permitting the "collective sublime" to replace the " 'egotistical sublime' of the patriarchy."[17] This belief that the function of writing literary history is to provide a genealogy, based on a notion of the continuity of female experience, is a common one in existing literary histories; it has been an invaluable agent in the integration of women's texts in a modern university curriculum and in the support of the growing body of women writing in the current literary world—no longer do we demand that every female writer re-discover or re-invent for herself her literary mothers.

It is also the search for sameness, of finding women in the past with whom we can identify. Because of the emphasis on continuity, there has been a marked tendency to see women's writings as transhistorical.

> There is a connection from woman to woman, present to past, artist to artist, that is never spoken of. That connection is based on identification; the direct communication of inner experience that comes from women poets of the past is a heritage for poets in the present time.[18]

This belief in transhistoricism is presented as separating feminist literary history from the standard patriarchal one. It has the valuable function of restoring significance to works traditionally dismissed and devalued as secondary to "great" literature; it also re-visions women's writings by doing away with the traditional practice of always discussing a woman writer in relation to a man, whether it be her father, husband, or mentor.

This historiography places the emphasis on discovering what women of different generations have in common with one another rather than what early women writers had in common with their male contemporaries. From this approach also arises the desire to read their writings as autobiographical statements of female experience (to celebrate the voice which "invented itself without precedent out of the life of the woman who owned it") rather than in the context of contemporary literary conventions, or, as I will discuss, even as part of an older female tradition using an unfamiliar form. The principle of this historiography is to search for sameness, to find ourselves in the past. It is part of what Linda Gordon describes as a "feminist retelling of the past," a way of challenging existing structures by redefining past ones and an invaluable agent for changing the traditional academic ordering of the past.

On the other hand, the deliberate close identification with earlier women writers which this practice encourages can make difficult any reassessment of women writers and their position in women's literary history. When writing literary history is defined and depicted as establishing a literary family, a challenge to a canonical woman writer—Aphra Behn was not a unique female voice in Restoration literature, Virginia Woolf was wrong about her assessment of Margaret Cavendish—it can be read as a treacherous attack not only on one's intellectual mother but also on her contemporary daughters.

The emotional impact of material which is perceived as transhistorical and autobiographical is very strong. The success of this drive to rediscover and to celebrate "mothers" to free us from alienation with the present by forming a collective identity hinges on the establishment of "sameness" and continuity. The goal of women's literary history has been to establish and delineate the difference between male and female—not, however, between women. Such differences between women make us uneasy. This has been the complaint by many, that women's studies has homogenized the "female" and ended up with a primary focus on an Anglo-American, middle-class experience. We see some of the unease with female difference in discussions of women's literary history in the explanations of early women writers' "conservatism" or, as noted earlier, in a tendency to dismiss some women writers as not part of our tradition.

There is a further element in this perception of female writings as transhistorical which has strongly affected our vision of pre-1700 women's writings. Germaine Greer set down as one of the goals of the Tulsa Center the recovery of lost texts for this purpose: "It is only by correct interpretation of individual cases that we can grasp what we have in common with the women who have gone our chosen way before us" (14). I find myself parting company with this statement as the agenda of women's literary history: while I applaud the conscious attention to the particular as part of the drive to establish a "tradition" to support the continuing creative work of women writers, I still lament the way in which we are directed to order our findings. All scholarship may indeed be ideological, but this sounds very much as though the goal of feminist historicism is to recreate the past in its own present image; such an attitude toward historical scholarship, ironically, functions in the same fashion that traditional patriarchal tellings of history do to reaffirm existing power structures.

Is this focus on commonality—the searching for sameness as I call it—the assertion that what we seek are women who "have gone *our chosen* way" (emphasis mine), really the only effective perspective from which to view or to generalize about the literary landscape of women writers in the past? What of those early women writers who went quite another way—their own ways—ways which we may not understand or perhaps with which we may not identify or sympathize? Do we ban them from our literary tradition—as they have been banned from the traditional one? Does this model of women's literary historiography, which makes its key texts in effect transhistorical documents in a continuous line of feminist thought, extend the limits of our vision?

III

The final critical response which obscures the study of pre-1700 women's literature I call "backward projection." Essentially, this is the practice of making assumptions about literary practices of earlier periods based on the activities of later ones. It involves, first, a hierarchical ranking of history into different periods or phases which is manifest in the crowning of the Restoration as the starting point of the female tradition and the nineteenth century as the norm. Second, it is characterized by the application of literary terms and categories derived from one period to the literary activities in an earlier one; this practice of projecting definitions and motivations backward in time reaffirms the formation of a literary hierarchy by suggesting that periods be evaluated comparatively—on grounds which are applicable only to later eras.

The backward projection of literary values and assumptions about literary practices from the nineteenth century on to the Renaissance and Restoration underlies the evolutionary pattern found in most feminist literary histories. In this scheme, the historian views the past through the discovery of the "progress" of women's literature. The classic statement of female literature as evolutionary in nature after Woolf's *A Room of One's Own* is found in Showalter's *A Literature of Their Own*. Working strictly within the context of nineteenth-century novels, she identifies three "phases" in the formation of a female tradition: the feminine, a "prolonged phase of *imitation* of the prevailing modes of the dominant tradition, and *internalization* of its standards of art and its views on social roles"; the feminist, marked by protest and advocacy of minority rights; and finally, the female, a phase of "self-discovery" and a search for identity not dependent on opposition (13). Showalter's study discusses a specific genre in the nineteenth century, but the same framework of the evolution from imitation and internalization to self-discovery can be clearly seen in later representations of pre-1700 women's writings.

The celebration of the "firstness" of the protests of Astell and other early eighteenth-century women writers and of Behn's commercial success in the

Restoration is one indication of a evolutionary sense of the past, where the primitive evolves into the stronger, the more sophisticated, the better—that is, the more familiar. As we have seen, it leads in part to the relegating of earlier women to the earliest phase of the female tradition, not very high up on the evolutionary ladder. Renaissance women, in this hierarchical scheme, display a "protected quality, as well as their apparently greater docility"; they were "economically dependent . . . [and] they seem for the most part to articulate conventional pieties, as if to prove their loyalty to the system that supported them."[19] Women writers before the eighteenth century, another source assures us, were moved to write only to express religious experiences or were protected by their husbands' social rank which enabled them to produce "academic plays and translations."[20] In short, they are presented as fitting neatly within that phase of evolution characterized by imitation and internalization of patriarchal literary and social values. The transition to the next phase, the feminist one, is in this evolutionary scheme marked by the appearance of commercial literature by women writers in the Restoration, the "emergence of productive, publishing literary women, who began to form a unique tradition of their own" and who began to "subvert the literary traditions they inherited from an overwhelmingly male-dominated literary history" (NALW, 41, 57).

To question this evolutionary scheme of women's literary history is not the same as denying that Restoration women writers confronted their society's assumptions about gender and genre in the literary marketplace. It is not to suggest that the difficulties faced by women such as Behn, Mary Pix, and Susanna Centlivre entering the commercial battleground of Restoration and early eighteenth-century drama were not acute, or that their struggle is not a central issue in the study of women's writings. It is to suggest that we need to re-vision that earlier period and attempt to see it not as a primitive stage, not always in comparison with another, and not inferior for being other than our ideal. For, ironically, the very attention to one area of women's literary life in the past, the commercial "feminist" phase in an evolutionary pattern which has led to the recovery of writers such as Behn, has led to a large and significant portion of women's literature being obscured.

Backward projection also affects our view of the past on a finer level because it gives us the very structures and organizing labels we use to create the overall evolutionary scheme. These terms focus attention on the act of publication; preconceptions concerning the mode of literary production and genre lead in turn to the highlighting or privileging of certain types of writing and certain types of authors in our critical studies and anthologies. The majority of terms used to order and discuss Renaissance and Restoration literary practices are derived from nineteenth- and twentieth-century commercial literature. This is a literary environment centering around texts printed for profit, which was not the dominant literary scene even by the end of the Restoration.

The assumptions found in current feminist literary histories about literary activity and concepts of authorship in the Renaissance and Restoration are derived in part from generalizations about authorial intentions and audience for early women's writings which have been based solely on the means or mode of a text's circulation. Coterie writers, for example, who circulated their works in manuscript, are characteristically portrayed as not daring to print their works. Their use of pseudonyms is characteristically interpreted in terms of nineteenth-century women writers' use, as an attempt to hide their sex. "Women knew quite well if one woman signed her work with her own name, she opened herself to moral and social abuse," generalizes one such account; another refers to a seventeenth-century woman writer being unprotected "even when she was hidden behind a coterie name."[21] Such use of pseudonyms, in turn, is offered as a further indication of early women being "intimidated" into what is labeled "closet" literature. We assume, furthermore, that works not printed during the author's lifetime were intended for "the fireplace" or at very best an uncritical "family" audience. Publication, in our present view of the past, seems to be the identifying feature of the emergence of a real "female tradition."

Such emphasis on commercial publication has thus removed from our sight or cast an obscuring haze on the most common and perhaps the most important forms of literary activity for both sexes, I would argue, well into the eighteenth century. In our enthusiasm for celebrating the victories of Behn, we have to an extent marginalized the activities of women working in different literary genres and modes through the implication that their writings were covert, ignored in the larger literary world. Our attention has focused on women's texts as "private enterprise." To put it crudely, we are presented with two options for early women's writings—either women created commercial productions and are celebrated for their "success" or they wrote in "private" and are pitied for their failure to achieve a public voice. In setting up such choices about Restoration and earlier women's writings, ironically, women's literary history has preserved the primary patternings of traditional history, the bourgeois or Whig myth of progress and the Marxist evolutionary "rise" of a class. These models privilege the "bourgeois" or commercial phase of literary production beginning in the early eighteenth century and continuing to dominate today. Such perceptions of the past devalue significant modes of Restoration women's literary production which are aristocratic in origin, such as the coterie tradition, as well as working class ones, such as the prophetic and polemic texts printed by the Quaker presses.

In this way, we have dismissed to the periphery successful coterie writers such as Damaris Masham, Anne Killigrew, Mary Monck, and Anne Wharton, whose various pseudonyms—Chloris, Sappho, Clio, Marinda, Urania—made no attempt to hide the writer's sex, but instead created and cemented a literary community. Their chosen form of literary production—circulated manuscript copy and print through the miscellanies and journals—had its strengths as well as what we perceive as weaknesses, strengths waiting to be seen and to be recognized as belonging to a past which is marked by its difference from us.

For example, I believe one of the most important strengths of so-called coterie writing, which has been hitherto obscured by our concentration on the commercial success of the individual, was the creation and continuance of a thriving female literary network. Because of the backward projection about the practice of the use of pseudonyms and the nature of coterie litera-ture, the existing scheme of literary history has always seen early women writers as isolated and excluded from literary networks. Renaissance women did not belong to "literary communities comparable to the loosely organized groups of male writers who supported and encouraged the works of artists like Marlowe," declares one introduction; women "had almost nothing to do with such congregating, except perhaps to serve tea or sit in a back room copying over manuscripts," states another.[22] The existence of such commu-nities, however, is convincingly demonstrated in the so-called "low" genres of verse epistles and dialogue poems exchanged between women writers, so frequently found in early women's writings; the titles of the individual poems, for example, frequently reveal the context of composition, such as Mary Barber's "To a Lady, who commanded me to send her an Account in Verse, how I succeeded in my Subscription" or Ephelia's "To the Honoured Eugenia, commanding me to Write to Her." At this point, too little attention has been paid to the networks implied in the titles and contents of women's poems, much less to the actual mechanisms by which women circulated their writings.

In addition to our difficulty in seeing coterie writers clearly, our eye has also failed to see or failed to linger on the activities of those women writers during the Restoration who did publish their works—but not for worldly profit. The Quaker women hardly appear in our perception of the literary past, although they were the largest group of women publishing during the period. They, too, fall outside the inherited labels with which we have been trained to categorize literature and organize history—they did not write dramas or pastoral. They were not part of the aristocratic world of letters, but were mostly lower- and middle-class women. Frequently, their writings were collaborative, a characteristic of early modern literary life which cur-rent histories have yet to explore. They wrote satires, autobiographies, "cap-tivity narratives," and prophetic visions, to mention a few of their forms. In their prophetic discourse they tried to recreate the speech of Eve before the Fall.

They wrote poetry, too, but we have rested with the received notion that they did not. If one looks more closely, however, one finds that in fact, it was the decision of a controlling board of ten men appointed in 1672 to rule on what would be published and reprinted by Quaker presses who determined the later fate of the Restoration Quaker muse of poetry; for example, they returned Abigail Fisher's manuscript with the recommendation that "as to what's in verse, they rather advise to have it in prose."[23] When we look back at the past today, however, their preferences need not still direct our gaze.

Together, the two examples alone of the coterie writers and the early Quakers offer a substantial body of women's writings which have been marginalized in the overall scheme of Restoration women's literary history. They also suggest that part of what obscures their study are the very terms and categories we use when discussing and presenting them. Restrictive definitions and misleading literary labels can and have silenced or obscured these women's writings as effectively as any contemporary group of censors. In our current scheme of women's literary history, the concept of authorship is a nineteenth-century one, as are the categories and the hierarchies assigned to the texts. One uses such labels, of course, in the admirable desire to organize material into a coherent scheme, to bring the unruly mass of the past into a sharper focus for our study. This, I would argue with Greer, can only be done through careful attention to particular authors and individual cases—but we must include in this view of the past those who participated using methods and modes which do not fit our traditional terms.

IV

Finally, let us consider the metaphor which has guided our study of the past—vision. Ironically, our concept of writing history as "seeing" the past also may be blocking our sight. Women's literary history has been written with the unstated assumption that if we climbed to a high enough tower and got a pair of binoculars, we could see all that there is to see—the perceived difficulty is overcoming physical boundaries, far away horizons. Such a notion obscures the fact that neither the human eye nor the human brain is all-encompassing when confronted with the vast reality of the historical past. There are many things now in our field of vision which bibliographical and textual studies have unearthed; but there are also many which we simply have overlooked which were in no way hidden except by our assumptions about what we would see and should be looking for.

A closer look at the limits of historiography, how literary histories can suppress and obscure in addition to preserving and celebrating, will result, I believe, in feminist literary historians dropping or modifying the notion implied in the search for a "tradition" that can organize the past into a comprehensive and tidy package. If we are to have a "tradition of our own," we must recognize that for women's literary history, there can be no single great evolutionary track such has served the patriarchal canon. Instead, I believe we should create a flexible scheme, one more conscious of its interests, and a history not based on the negation of activities but the celebration of diverse, multiple ones. It would be a history which expresses a consciousness of other possibilities; in short, it would be a history which does not does not present a part of the picture as being the whole in a desire to answer all the questions here and now, a history not directed by the desire to control and organize the unruly past.

Jane Eyre explains her desire to see more as a product of her "restless nature." There are many of us working in earlier periods largely left out of current feminist historiography who seem to share this spirit. Placing unfamiliar texts and unfamiliar types of literary materials side by side with the ones we have already begun to study will not diminish our appreciation of Behn and her followers, but will add a diversity and complexity to our sense of the literary past of which their works form a part. The inclusion of other means of literary production in our evaluation of different periods' activities, the consideration of other concepts of authorship, will certainly reveal a much more confusing literary landscape than we have now—but, like the world Jane Eyre knew to exist and longed to see, it is a vibrant, energetic region, one "full of life."

NOTES

1. Angeline Goreau, *Reconstructing Aphra: A Social Biography of Aphra Behn* (Oxford: Oxford University Press, 1980), p. 8.

2. See Ruth Perry, *The Celebrated Mary Astell: An Early English Feminist* (Chicago: University of Chicago Press, 1986) and Bridget Hill, ed., *The First English Feminist: "Reflections on Marriage" and Other Writings by Mary Astell* (London: St. Martin's Press, 1986).

3. Recently several fine studies on individual women writers in the Renaissance have drawn our attention to the valuable discoveries waiting to be uncovered in earlier periods and reinforce the need to re-vision our general scheme of the literary past in order to incorporate these new materials. See, for example, collections edited by Betty Travitsky, *The Paradise of Women: Writings by Englishwomen of the Renaissance* (1989), Mary Beth Rose, *Women in the Middle Ages and Renaissance* (1986), and Katherina M. Wilson, *Women Writers of the Renaissance and Reformation* (1987); see also the book-length studies by Elaine V. Beilin, *Redeeming Eve: Women Writers of the English Renaissance* (1987), Elaine Hobby, *Virtue of Necessity: English Women's Writing 1649–88* (1989), and studies of Lady Mary Wroth by Josephine Roberts.

4. Joanna Russ, *How to Suppress Women's Writing* (Austin: University of Texas Press, 1983), p. 17.

5. Virginia Woolf, *A Room of One's Own* (New York: Harcourt Brace Jovanovich, 1929), p. 43.

6. Katharine M. Rogers, ed., *Before Their Time: Six Women Writers of the Eighteenth Century* (New York: Frederick Ungar, 1979), p. 14.

7. Jacqueline Pearson, *The Prostituted Muse: Images of Women Dramatists 1642–1737* (London: St. Martin's Press, 1988), p. 22.

8. Louise Bernikow, ed., *The World Split Open: Four Centuries of Women Poets in England and America, 1552–1950* (London: The Women's Press, 1974), p. 68.

9. Bernikow, *The World Split Open*, p. 24.

10. Sandra M. Gilbert and Susan Gubar, eds., *The Norton Anthology of Literature by Women: The Tradition in English* (New York: Norton, 1985), p. 2.

11. Sandra M. Gilbert and Susan Gubar, eds., *Shakespeare's Sisters: Feminist Essays on Women Poets* (Bloomington: Indiana University Press, 1979), p. xxiv.

12. Germaine Greer, "The Tulsa Center for the Study of Women's Literature: What We Are Doing and Why We Are Doing It," *Tulsa Studies in Women's Literature* 1 (1982): 5–26 (p. 14).

13. Jane Marcus, "Still Practice, A/Wrested Alphabet: Toward a Feminist Aesthetic" in *Art and Anger: Reading Like a Woman* (Columbus: Ohio State University Press, 1988), pp. 215–50 (pp. 225–26).

14. Linda Gordon, "What's New In Women's History," in *Feminist Studies/Critical Studies*, ed. Teresa de Lauretis (Bloomington: Indiana University Press, 1986), pp. 20–30 (p. 23).

15. Margaret J. M. Ezell, "The Myth of Judith Shakespeare: Creating the Canon of Women's Literature," *New Literary History* 21 (1989–1990): 579–92.

16. Elaine Showalter, *A Literature of Their Own: British Women Novelists from Brontë to Lessing* (Princeton: Princeton University Press, 1977), pp. 11–12.

17. Marcus, "Thinking Back Through Our Mothers," in *Art and Anger*, pp. 73–100 (pp. 82–83).

18. Bernikow, *The World Split Open*, p. 10.

19. *NALW*, p. 14.

20. Rogers, *Before Their Time*, p. vii.

21. Bernikow, *The World Split Open*, p. 20; Germaine Greer et al., eds., *Kissing the Rod: An Anthology of 17th-Century Women's Verse* (London: Virago Press, 1988), p. 20.

22. *NALW*, p. 3; Bernikow, *The World Split Open*, p. 16.

23. The minutes of the Morning Meeting II (ii.vii.1693), quoted in Arnold Lloyd, *Quaker Social History, 1669–1738* (London: Longmans, 1950), p. 151.

CHAPTER SIX

Re-presenting the Body in *Pamela II*

JANET E. AIKINS

NEAR THE BEGINNING of *Pamela II*,[1] Samuel Richardson's continuation of his highly successful first novel, the enraged Sir Simon Darnford throws a book at the head of his favorite daughter Polly. Her crime, as she writes to Pamela, was a mere two hour's absence from reading and telling stories to her father as a diversion from his gout. Sir Simon then writes to Pamela's husband of having been stung, himself, by Pamela's words:

> This fine Lady of yours, this Paragon of Meekness and Humility, in so many Words, bids me, or tells my own Daughter, which is worse, to bid me, never to take a Book into my Hands again, if I won't make a better Use of it: And yet, what better Use can an offended Father make of the best Books, than to correct a rebellious Child with them?[2]

My comments on the re-presentation of the body in *Pamela II* begin with this graphic joke on the materiality of the reading experience and on perverse parental authority. Polly has been, quite literally, struck by a book within an epistolary text whose visualized scenes are meant to strike or even "Slap" an attentive reader, as Pamela's sister-in-law, Lady Davers, suggests (III, 97; 57). Although this incident of family violence passes virtually unnoticed among the few commentators on the sequel to Richardson's first novel, it surely was significant for Richardson himself, for it is prominently featured in the series of twenty-nine illustrations which its printer/author commissioned for both parts of *Pamela* in 1741–1742. (See Figure 3.)[3]

In the engraving, as with each such illustration, the picture and the text to which it refers mutually reinforce each other. Here, for example, within the verbal narrative, the book throwing scene gives rise to Sir Simon's remarkable claim that an almost maternal physical unity binds all fathers to their daughters. He tells his male friend, Mr. B., that daughters "have neither Souls nor Senses, but what they have borrowed from *us* [my emphasis]," and he adds that daughters' "very Bones, and the Skin that covers them, so much their Pride and their Ornament, are so many Parts of *our own* [my emphasis] undervalued Skin and Bones" (III, 128; 71).

Not only does Sir Simon claim a bodily identity with the child whom he has engendered and now physically harms, as is graphically displayed in the

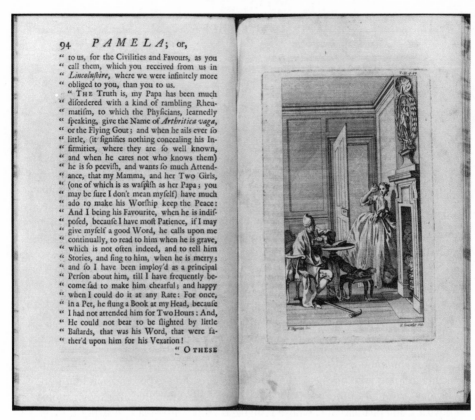

94   *PAMELA*; or,

" to us, for the Civilities and Favours, as you
" call them, which you received from us in
" *Lincolnshire*, where we were infinitely more
" obliged to you, than you to us.
     " THE Truth is, my Papa has been much
" disordered with a kind of rambling Rheu-
" matism, to which the Physicians, learnedly
" speaking, give the Name of *Arthritica vaga*,
" or the Flying Gout; and when he ails ever so
" little, (it signifies nothing concealing his In-
" firmities, where they are so well known,
" and when he cares not who knows them)
" he is so peevish, and wants so much Attend-
" ance, that my Mamma, and her Two Girls,
" (one of which is as waspish as her Papa; you
" may be sure I don't mean myself) have much
" ado to make his Worship keep the Peace:
" And I being his Favourite, when he is indif-
" posed, because I have most Patience, if I may
" give myself a good Word, he calls upon me
" continually, to read to him when he is grave,
" which is not often indeed, and to tell him
" Stories, and sing to him, when he is merry;
" and so I have been imploy'd as a principal
" Person about him, till I have frequently be-
" come sad to make him chearful; and happy
" when I could do it at any Rate: For once,
" in a Pet, he flung a Book at my Head, because
" I had not attended him for Two Hours: And,
" He could not bear to be slighted by little
" Bastards, that was his Word, that were fa-
" ther'd upon him for his Vexation!
                                    " O THESE

3. Illustration from *Pamela II* by Samuel Richardson, 6th corrected ed. (London, 1742),
Vol. III, p. 94. Designed by F. Hayman and engraved by H. Gravelot.

illustration that we as readers see, but he fears that Polly's visit to Mr. B and
his pregnant wife, Pamela, will bring about an alternative physical awaken-
ing in her; he anticipates that Mr. B. will use his own wife's body to show
Polly "all the Game of a Lying-in" and "set the Girl a longing to make one in
the Dance, before I [Sir Simon] have found out the proper Man for her
Partner!" (III, 139; 77). Sir Simon here wishes not merely to intervene in the
choice of his daughter's husband but to control her desire or "longing" for a
sexual partner and prevent B. from such intimate manipulations of his child.
Both in word and image, the depiction of Sir Simon hurling a book at his
daughter's face thus posits a complex equation between the consumption of
books and human procreation. Moreover, its implications would not have
been lost on Richardson, for by the time he embarked on his project as a
writer of narrative, he was deeply experienced as a father, husband, and
professional printer.

In this essay I will explore what might be called the ontology of *Pamela II* both as Richardson's creation and as its readers' experience. This text is less a sequel than a Richardsonian "reading" of his own earlier work. Moreover, it evokes a powerful "image" of the heroine's body which becomes the obsessive substance that replaces "story" in any conventional sense. Indeed, readers of *Pamela* must learn to see the body of the woman within her text if they are to discern the true distinctions between the tragedy of a Clarissa and "joys" of the married Pamela, for *Pamela* is not, as Terry Eagleton calls it, merely "a kind of fairy-tale pre-run of *Clarissa*, a fantasy wish fulfilment in which abduction and imprisonment turn out miraculously well."

The few recent commentators on *Pamela II* including Eagleton have complained of its lack of "story," in an uneasy echo of Samuel Johnson's often quoted remark that "if you were to read Richardson for the story, your impatience would be so much fretted that you would hang yourself." Typically, such critics have also affirmed the judgment of Sir Walter Scott, who in 1824 wrote that *Pamela II* has "met with the fate of other continuations, and has been always justly accounted an unnatural and unnecessary appendage to a tale so complete within itself as the first part of *Pamela*."[4] Scott's dismissal is telling, however, for its use of the term "unnatural . . . appendage" implicitly conjures an image of the human body as metaphor for the unity of Richardson's text.

In addition to condemning, as does Scott, the sheer irrelevance of *Pamela II* or its lack of story, critics from the eighteenth century onward have eagerly debated the effect of *Pamela I*'s "inflaming Descriptions"[5] and have read the sequel as a correction of the earlier work. For example, in April of 1741, the author of *Pamela Censured* complained of the original text's tendency to "*excite Lasciviousness* in the Minds of the Youth of both *Sexes*," and in the following November, Charles Povey wrote that Pamela's letters are "proved to be immodest Romances painted in Images of Virtue: Masquerades in Disguise, that receiv'd Birth now Vice reigns in Triumph, and swells in Streams even to a Deluge."[6] With an awareness of such remarks, whose metaphors of "birth" and natural "swelling" posit the visceral affect of Pamela's own literary texts, modern commentators have then read *Pamela II* as Richardson's attempt to cancel out the sexually suggestive nature of his own earlier work.

In her study of actual eighteenth-century masquerades, for example, Terry Castle unfavorably compares the sequel to its original and calls "the body of the married Pamela . . . a kind of rigid, unchanging bastion, hardly a body at all." She enlists Bakhtin's formulation of the "carnivalesque" in *Rabelais and His World* to argue that *Pamela II* is a "decarnivalization" of *Pamela I*, or an effort to remove from Pamela's story its subversive element.[7] As my essay will argue, this explanation of the genesis of the second *Pamela* simply dissolves in the face of the Gravelot and Hayman illustrations which, through their self-reflective powers, give us a fresh understanding of Richardson's beliefs about the substance of both bodies and books.

Indeed, *Pamela* was not the first book Richardson decided to illustrate. In 1739 he published an edition of *Aesop's Fables* which he substantially revised from two earlier editions, and he accompanied each of the two hundred and fifty fables he chose to include with an engraved illustration because of what he described in the preface as the "alluring Force which Cuts or Pictures, suited to the respective Subjects, have on the Minds of Children." Richardson eliminated many of the fables in Sir Roger L'Estrange's edition, one of which was #454, about a boy who "would not learn his Book." As we shall see, that text found its way into *Pamela*, both in word and image, a year later.

Quite apart from the fact that Richardson illustrated *Aesop's Fables* and *Pamela*, all of his novels reveal a fascination with the visual arts and attempt, in narrative, to approximate visual effects. In an earlier essay, I have explored some of the mechanisms by which his works stimulate "secondary illusions,"[8] or imagined impressions of tangible substance, along with a curious temporal simultaneity that contradicts our usual expectations for narrative sequence. Richardson's contemporaries in the art world proposed a corollary, the idea that the skilled face-painter must incorporate temporal change and "multistable" visual images within the static medium of painting.[9] One attempt to put this corollary into practice was Jonathan Richardson's picture of Alexander Pope in which the artist conflates Pope's features with known representations of Milton, thereby creating a "composite portrait" of the "*idea* of the poet."[10] In this period, both painters and writers sought to overcome the apparent limits of their chosen media, and the pictorialism of *Pamela II* carries the experiment to such an extreme that the status of the "book" as a physical artifact becomes the narrative action.

The first readers of Richardson often recognized his novels' effects as pictorial although nonstatic. Charles Povey's attack on *Pamela* begins with the typical remark that "Authors may be compar'd to Painters, who draw Representations according to their Fancy." An even more intriguing example is Sarah Fielding's *Remarks on "Clarissa,"* in which one of the speakers calls that work a "Picture of human Life, where the Story can move but slowly, where the Characters must open by degrees, and the Reader's own Judgment form them from different Parts, as they display themselves according to the Incidents that arise." Implicit in this remark is a concept of human identity as a gradual process of visual self-display which, as we shall see, Pamela undergoes in the course of her tale.

In writing the *Remarks on "Clarissa,"* Fielding established a model for collective reading of which Richardson would have approved and which itself evokes an impression of the physical presence of its participants. Her brief work is not an essay but a sequence of debates about the effects of the novel's volumes as they are read by a company of friends who together contemplate the fluctuating stasis of what they "see" in the text. One comments, for example, "there is an inimitable Beauty in *Belford* differing from himself." Diderot also admired Richardson's ability, along with the greatest poets and painters, to show how to make multiple "physiognomies succeed each other upon a face, without its ceasing to be the same."[11] We cannot know how deliberate Richardson was in the use or study of visual aesthetics; however, the amateur art theorist Joseph Spence may have influenced his thinking about such matters, for there are suggestive links between their writing and publishing careers.

In *An Essay on Mr. Pope's Odyssey*, the second edition of which Richardson printed for his friend in 1737, Spence defines the curious visual conflation that early readers of Richardson often noticed in their reactions to his narratives. Within Pope's translation of Homer, Spence identifies the representation of "*Double Passions*" as an attribute of both poetry and painting, and he marvels at "What seems a Paradox of Art in either, . . . their Power of expressing two *opposite Passions* in the same face." In particular, the *Essay* praises Pope's use of metaphor as a device "to cloath Words . . . with Substance; and to make Language visible." In his criticism of Pope's weaker lines, however, Spence briefly warns against taking the "*Figurative*" for the "*Proper*" or "mixing *Fable* and *Reality*." He insists, "It sounds but oddly to talk of a Person, and of his Picture, without any manner of distinction."[12] Spence's caution here nevertheless implies that there is something irresistible about regarding either a painting or a visual image as an incarnation of the person it re-presents, or, as a corollary, that it is natural to assess the attributes of physical "person" according to the principles of visual art, as happens frequently in Richardson's fiction. Spence, too, was concerned with the nature of re-presentation in his own essay, for he makes a special point of writing it as a dialogue, giving full names rather than mere initials to his speakers as a means of instilling more "Action and Reality" in his "talk . . . with Pen and Ink," lines that anticipate Richardson's famous description of his epistolary craft as "writing to the moment."

The conviction that unites Richardson with some of his contemporaries is thus the belief that all forms of speaking, writing, and aesthetic production are acts of re-presenting an otherwise unseeable reality, a making incarnate, rather than mere imitation. For them, art is an ontological and not a mimetic enterprise. The violence of Sir Simon Darnford reminds us that books are physical artifacts of controversial social import because of their curious ability to exert power over readers through imaginative illusion. Richardson keeps the power of artifice before us in *Pamela II* by depicting the physical impact on the hearers of Pamela's letters read aloud, and the palpable effect on all viewers of the sight of Pamela's body. Both her body and her book are fundamentally scenic and affect us through their visual power.

Twentieth-century neglect of the actual illustrations of this curious text may in part be explained by the fact that they did not appear in the first five editions of *Pamela I*, nor in the first edition of *Pamela II*. Richardson commissioned them for the first joint octavo edition of *Pamela I* and *II* that was published on May 10, 1742. What is striking about the history of this work's production is that at the very time that Richardson was printing the first edition of *Pamela II* in duodecimo, he was revising the text substantially for publication in the illustrated octavo form. None of the commentators who document the events of these days explores the tantalizing possibility that the illustrations themselves were at the center of Richardson's attention or that his revisions, perhaps even the very genesis of *Pamela II*, were results of his collaborative labors with Hubert François Gravelot and Francis Hayman whom he commissioned for the pictures perhaps as early as February of 1741.[13] To acknowledge these possibilities is to suggest that *Pamela I and II* were parts of a single narrative project that we have misunderstood.

The decision to illustrate *Pamela* preceded Richardson's plan for a sequel, for on February 14, 1741, he published the second edition of *Pamela I* in which the preface mentions two frontispieces which had been planned for the edition but had been rejected, both for lack of time and for "*having fallen very short of the Spirit of the Passages they were intended to represent.*" We know that he had enlisted the prominent artist, William Hogarth, for these engravings, but the reason for Hogarth's disappearance from the project remains obscure. Richardson's decision to write a sequel is thought to have been made two months later, when he learned of a plan for John Kelly, a minor playwright, to publish a spurious continuation of the work. On May 7, 1741, Richardson denied Kelly's claims to authority and announced in print that he, himself, was at work on a continuation using genuine "Materials" that he would not otherwise have published.[14] Meanwhile, he had published a third edition of *Pamela I* in March, and a fourth in May. The fifth edition came out in the following September and for the first time hinted at the imminent appearance of the true sequel which by then he had nearly finished writing. For reasons that are not known, the first edition of *Pamela II* in duodecimo was not in fact published until a full three months later, on December 7, 1741, at the very time when Richardson was at work printing the illustrated octavo version of both *Pamela I* and *II* with substantial revisions in Part II, as well as an unillustrated duodecimo edition of Part II alone which would contain all of the textual revisions he included in the octavo.

A plausible reason for his publishing the first edition of the sequel while simultaneously working on two different revised editions of the text was his desire to publish it as swiftly as possible in a duodecimo format which would match the two volumes of *Pamela I* that his readers already owned, even though the verbal text was undergoing changes inspired by his work with the illustrators. The artists could not reasonably have completed their designs for *Pamela II* until October, when the manuscript itself was finished, yet Richardson felt considerable pressure to make his sequel public. Oddly, the revised and illustrated octavo version of *Pamela II* was actually its third edition, for although Richardson printed an unillustrated duodecimo version of its revised text which he called the "second edition," he did not actually publish the second edition until a year later, in January of 1743, in response to public demand. Thus, the revised and illustrated third edition, which he produced at considerable expense, appears to be the text in its most complete form. It must have been particularly irritating to Richardson that in the fall of 1741, before he was able to bring out his own illustrated version, yet another spurious sequel appeared. It was a single volume called *"Pamela" in High Life: or, Virtue Rewarded* that was apparently designed to accompany an illustrated, one-volume piracy of Richardson's own first two volumes.[15] Its five comparatively crude engravings depict scenes from *Pamela I*, and strangely, four of them feature scenes or situations similar to those which Richardson's own illustrators would depict, perhaps suggesting that the creators of the piracy had information about Richardson's project.

Even without the Gravelot and Hayman illustrations, which are not reprinted in modern editions, *Pamela II* invites us to read by a process of "visualization." Lady Davers, after all, calls Pamela's letters "Conversation-pieces" (III, 98; 58), borrowing the term for one of the most popular genres of early eighteenth-century painting, and Pamela uses the term herself for her descriptive letters to friends. Nevertheless, readers have failed to apprehend what might be called the "visual power" of Richardson's second *Pamela* because of their expectations about causality as fundamental to the nature of storytelling. A desire for plot seems to intrude with particular force in *Pamela II* which is often described as a series of dull incidents meant to illustrate Pamela's pious principles about such matters as household management and child rearing. Terry Castle argues, for example, that to understand what she sees as the appeal of the masquerade episode—the one incident with " 'faint hints' of a story in a text otherwise devoid of such enjoyments"—"we must consider first," she says, "our displeasure with all those scenes of 'humdrum Virtue' preceding it."[16]

The scenes of "humdrum Virtue" tend to recede into the background, however, when the illustrations are taken as the organizing principle for the text, for they urge us to engage in a process that the text itself calls "Observation." At the end of the narrative Pamela tells an allegorical nursery story to her adopted daughter about the "amiable Prudentia" who improved her already virtuous life "By Reading, by Observation, and by Attention" (IV, 450–51; 470). She names this special genre of nursery tale a "*Woman's* story" (IV, 442; 464), and reminds us that like Prudentia, grown-up readers must also be practiced "observers" of the scenes and persons that a text re-presents either in words or actual pictures.

290   *PAMELA*; or,

spairing of the Mercies of a protecting God, has blemish'd, in this *last Act*, a *whole* Life, which they had hitherto approv'd and delighted in?

WHAT then, presumptuous *Pamela*, dost thou *here*? thought I: Quit with Speed these perilous Banks, and fly from these curling Waters, that seem in their meaning Murmurs, this still Night, to reproach thy Rashness! Tempt not God's Goodness on the mossy Banks, that have been Witnesses of thy guilty Purpose; and while thou hast Power left thee, avoid the tempting Evil, lest thy grand Enemy, now repuls'd by Divine Grace, and due Reflection, return to the Assault with a Force that thy Weakness may not be able to resist! And lest one rash Moment destroy all the Convictions, which now have aw'd thy rebellious Mind into Duty and Resignation to the Divine Will!

AND so saying, I arose; but was so stiff with my Hurts, so cold with the moist Dew of the Night, and the wet Grass on which I had sat, as also with the Damps arising from so large a Piece of Water, that with great Pain I got from this Pond, which now I think of with Terror; and bending my limping Steps towards the House, took Refuge in the Corner of an Out-house, where Wood and Coals are laid up for Family Use, till I should be found by my cruel Keepers, and consign'd to a more wretched Confinement, and worse Usage, than I had hitherto experienc'd; and there behind a Pile of Fire-wood I crept, and lay down, as you may

4. Illustration from *Pamela II* by Samuel Richardson, 6th corrected ed. (London, 1742), Vol. I, p. 290. Designed by F. Hayman and engraved by H. Gravelot.

Pamela II exemplifies this process of reduplicative or reproductive observation; *Pamela II* is a "reading" of *Pamela I* in that Richardson organizes its verbal narrative, its illustrations, and the sights of the "persons" it represents by a principle of repetition. Both fictional characters and actual readers view and re-view the same scenes, read and reread the letters that depict them, and tell and retell the incidents of *Pamela I*. For example, the newly repentant Mrs. Jewkes of *Pamela II* writes to Mrs. B. that she "put Pen to Paper, in that very Closet, and on that very Desk, which once were so much used by your dear Self, when I was acting a Part, that now cuts me to the Heart, to think of" (III, 80; 46). She lists the many places in "this melancholy fine House, that call one thing or other to my Remembrance, that gives me Remorse!" She includes in her list the pond and woodhouse which appear in two illustrations from *Pamela I*. The first (Figure 4) depicts Pamela's near

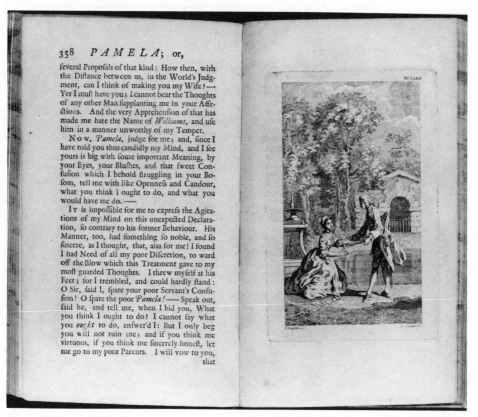

Vol.I,p.358.

358 *PAMELA*; or,

feveral Propofals of that kind : How then, with
the Diftance between us, in the World's Judgment, can I think of making you my Wife?——
Yet I muft have you; I cannot bear the Thoughts
of any other Man fupplanting me in your Affections. And the very Apprehenfion of that has
made me hate the Name of *Williams*, and ufe
him in a manner unworthy of my Temper.

N o w, *Pamela*, judge for me; and, fince I
have told you thus candidly my Mind, and I fee
yours is big with fome important Meaning, by
your Eyes, your Blufhes, and that fweet Con-
fufion which I behold ftruggling in your Bo-
fom, tell me with like Opennefs and Candour,
what you think I ought to do, and what you
would have me do.——

I T is impoffible for me to exprefs the Agitations of my Mind on this unexpected Declaration, fo contrary to his former Behaviour. His
Manner, too, had fomething fo noble, and fo
fincere, as I thought, that, alas for me! I found
I had Need of all my poor Difcretion, to ward
off the Blow which this Treatment gave to my
moft guarded Thoughts. I threw myfelf at his
Feet ; for I trembled, and could hardly ftand :
O Sir, faid I, fpare your poor Servant's Confu-
fion ! O fpare the poor *Pamela* !—— Speak out,
faid he, and tell me, when I bid you, What
you think I ought to do? I cannot fay what
you *ought* to do, anfwer'd I: But I only beg
you will not ruin me; and if you think me
virtuous, if you think me fincerely honeft, let
me go to my poor Parents. I will vow to you,
that

F. Hayman inv.   *H. Gravelot ofc.*

5. Illustration from *Pamela II* by Samuel Richardson, 6th corrected ed. (London, 1742),
Vol. I, p. 358. Designed by F. Hayman and engraved by H. Gravelot.

suicide, the second (Figure 5), Mr. B.'s suspicious proposal to her. The
second scene is set in what might be called a "close-up" of the same, now
ominous setting in which the near suicide occurred, showing both the rec-
tangular pond and the Palladian gateway in the background. The illustrations thus establish connections between these scenes, and Mrs. Jewkes
then prompts us to recall and conflate a whole series of remembered moments, thereby creating the effect of temporal simultaneity I mentioned
earlier.

A second kind of multiple viewing occurs in the illustration of Sir Jacob
Swynford's unexpected visit to the B.'s. If Mr. B. remains childless, Sir
Jacob's son will be heir to the "maternal Estate," and Lady Davers specu-
lates to Mr. B. that his purpose in visiting is to see if the B.'s are "in a way
to cut out his own Cubs" (III, 268; 146–47). In the picture (Figure 6), Sir
Jacob views Pamela without knowing that he is doing so. In his anger, he has

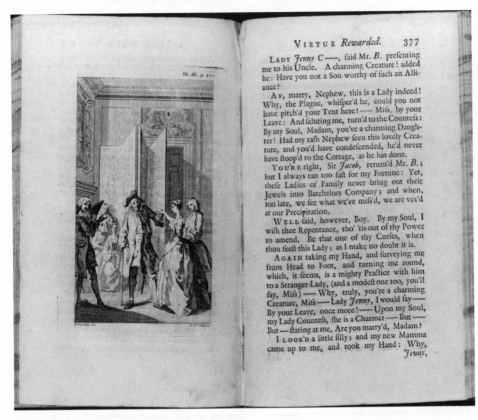

Vol. III. p. 377

VIRTUE *Rewarded.* 377

LADY *Jenny* C——, faid Mr. *B.* prefenting me to his Uncle. A charming Creature! added he: Have you not a Son worthy of fuch an Alli-ance?

AY, marry, Nephew, this is a Lady indeed! Why, the Plague, whifper'd he, could you not have pitch'd your Tent here?—— Mifs, by your Leave: And faluting me, turn'd to the Countefs: By my Soul, Madam, you've a charming Daugh-ter! Had my rafh Nephew feen this lovely Crea-ture, and you'd have condefcended, he'd never have ftoop'd to the Cottage, as he has done.

YOU'RE right, Sir *Jacob,* return'd Mr. *B.*; but I always ran too faft for my Fortune: Yet, thefe Ladies of Family never bring out their Jewels into Batchelors Company; and when, too late, we fee what we've mifs'd, we are vex'd at our Precipitation.

WELL faid, however, Boy. By my Soul, I wifh thee Repentance, tho' 'tis out of thy Power to amend. Be that one of thy Curfes, when thou feeft this Lady; as I make no doubt it is.

AGAIN taking my Hand, and furveying me from Head to Foot, and turning me round, which, it feems, is a mighty Practice with him to a Stranger-Lady, (and a modeft one too, you'll fay, Mifs) —— Why, truly, you're a charming Creature, Mifs——Lady *Jenny,* I would fay—— By your Leave, once more!——Upon my Soul, my Lady Countefs, fhe is a Charmer—— But—— But——ftaring at me, Are you marry'd, Madam?

I LOOK'D a little filly; and my new Mamma came up to me, and took my Hand: Why, *Jenny,*

6. Illustration from *Pamela II* by Samuel Richardson, 6th corrected ed. (London, 1742), Vol. III, p. 377. Designed by F. Hayman and engraved by H. Gravelot.

refused to meet Mr. B.'s low-born wife, so she has been introduced to him instead as Lady Jenny, the daughter of the Countess of C. In the midst of this ruse, Sir Jacob's interested reaction to the sight of Pamela confirms Sir Simon Darnford's earlier suspicions about the visually potent affect of her pregnant body on his daughter. As we view the illustration, we not only contemplate these various kinds of seeing but are invited into the two-di-mensional surface by one of the figures in the scene who looks us straight in the eye.

Within the image, the screen in the background signals the ambivalent visual deception taking place. Sir Jacob, whom Pamela had earlier described as having a "shrewd penetrating Look" (III, 305; 157), here stares at Pamela's form and asks, "Are you marry'd, Madam?" (III, 312; 161). Her pregnant body is thus seen despite her disguise as Lady Jenny. On the left, we see Mr. H., the wild nephew of Lady Davers, peeping out at us, thereby fracturing the illusion of the illustration by calling attention to the artifice of the engraving itself. The wild "Jackey," as Mr. H. is called, will figure importantly in an incident following Sir Jacob's visit where Pamela looks through a keyhole to see Jackey seducing one of her maids, an event which further re-presents the incidents of *Pamela I*. In both of these scenes within the sequel, Richardson seems almost determined to elicit a second attack from the author of *Pamela Censured* who had specifically objected to the keyhole incident in *Pamela I*. "The Idea of peeping thro' a Keyhole," he wrote, "to see a fine Woman extended on a Floor in a Posture that must naturally excite Passions of Desire, may indeed be read by one in his *grand Climacteric* without ever wishing to see one in the same Situation, but the Editor of *Pamela* directs himself to the *Youth* of both Sexes."[17] As if it were a direct challenge to such criticism, the Jacob Swynford illustration disproves the claim that only young people are susceptible to visual stimulation and explicitly engages us, as readers and observers of the illustration, in a suggestive act of multiple viewing.

Jackey's function in this illustration is especially appropriate because of what he says about himself in his eventual letter of apology to Pamela for attempting to steal the affections of her maid who, like Miss Darnford, is named Polly.[18] He depicts himself as a poorly educated young man who has made the mistake of paying attention to pictures in books in isolation from their texts: "I knowe I write a *clumsy* Hand, and *spelle moste lamentabelly*. . . . I was readier by halfe to admire the *Orcherd-robbing Picture* in *Lillie's* Grammer, then any other Parte of the Book." As a child, Jackey had wilfully misread the image which appears at the end of the well-known grammar text by William Lily and which is intended as a warning against boyish misbehavior and neglect of the books which lie strewn on the ground, another version of the fable of the boy who would not learn his book (Figure 7). "Excuse my Nonsense, Madam," he writes, "Butt many a time have I help'd to fill a *Sachil* [with stolen fruit]; and always supposed thatt Picture was putt there on purpose to tell Boyes whatt Diversions are *alowed* them, and *propper* for them." He adds that he and his "Schoole-fellows . . . coulde never reconsile itt to oure Reason, why wee shoulde bee punished for *practissing* a Lesson *taughte* us by our Grammers" (III, 393–94; 204). What Jackey has failed to grasp is that pictures and the words of a text must not be seen as separate discourses, but apprehended by an active reader as two interrelated parts of a whole textual "image." Indeed, when we view Jackey himself in the illustration with Sir Jacob, Jackey's glance breaks out of the two-dimensional surface and invites us, as implicated "viewers" of the epistolary text, into the visual discourse. Just as pictures without words mislead people like Jackey, the words of *Pamela II*, when published without the pictures, have caused readers to misinterpret the married Pamela as a woman of pious complacency.

7. Illustration from *A Short Introduction of Grammar* by Lily (London, 1699).
STC# L2304A.

Readers have failed to realize that the visual discourse of *Pamela II* is of a radically different order from that of *Pamela I*, however similar their epistolary style may seem, for in the sequel the heroine struggles with a new problem of physical identity. Now that she is married to such a noble and generous man, Pamela's parents say they hardly know "how to look upon [her], but as an Angel indeed," while Pamela herself urges Lady Davers to "keep in View the poor *Pamela Andrews* in all I write," rather than keeping "Mrs. *B.* in your Eye" (III, 6 and 48–49; 4 and 30). Pamela Andrews was of course transformed from maidservant to aristocratic wife in the first novel, but the new Mrs. B. is now unable to see herself in terms of that change. This fact is surprising, too, for Sir Simon Darnford says to Pamela's husband, your "What-shall-I-call-her of a Wife, with all the Insolence of Youth and Beauty on her side, follows me with a Glass, and would make me look in it, whether I will or not" (III, 139–40; 78). Pamela's words thus have the power to make other people see themselves, yet she herself is strangely ill at ease with the changes in her own body that her mirror reveals, for what *we* "see" reflected in Pamela's letters is her advancing pregnancy.

From the very first page, *Pamela II* builds toward the birth of the B.'s first child, however subtle the references may be. In the opening letter to her father and mother, Pamela describes the house that Mr. B. is redecorating as her parents' new home, and she quotes his description of it as a place fitting for the time when "we shall have *still added* Blessings, in *two or three* charming Boys and Girls [my emphasis], to place there in their Infancy" (III, 3; 2). The implication here is that the newly married couple has already been blessed not just in the marriage itself but in the conception of a first child. Indeed, in the first paragraphs of this letter, Pamela recalls standing with Mr. B. at the "Bow-windows" of their "Bed-chamber," hearing the "responsive Songs of two warbling Nightengales," and being kissed by her husband who remarks on the now "innocent Pleasures" of married life. The first illustration of *Pamela II* shows the very house that she so suggestively describes (Figure 8).[19]

In the following pages, Pamela's pregnancy is not directly mentioned; her parents only delicately allude to her "Time" being "some Months off," since it is "a Matter so very irksome to [Pamela] to hear of" (III, 28; 17). There is no mistaking the fact that she is pregnant, however, when Lady Davers stares at her body in the midst of an assembled company and asks, "Why do you let her lace so tight, Mr. *B*?" (III, 167; 91). This close "observation" deeply embarrasses Pamela, and the fact of her tight lacing suggests her reluctance to reveal the change in her physical appearance. The implied distortion of her body also justifies the choice, in the illustration closest to this moment in the text (Figure 9), to depict Pamela with no discernible change in her shape. By his wording on the page facing the illustration, Richardson invites us to read her slender body as a distortion of the truth,

8. Illustration from *Pamela II* by Samuel Richardson, 6th corrected ed. (London, 1742), Vol. III, p. 11. Designed by F. Hayman and engraved by H. Gravelot.

while the decision to illustrate this particular scene draws attention to her advancing pregnancy as a dynamic of narrative action.

In the picture, we see Mr. B. reprimanding Pamela with Sir Simon Darnford's letter of complaint about her remarks on the book throwing incident. In the page of text facing the illustration, we read that the precarious state of her physical body is shielding Pamela herself from greater mental and potentially physical abuse. B. makes the ominous remark, " 'Tis *well*, your present Condition pleads for you! and I must not carry what I have to say too far, for Considerations less in your Favour, than for one unseen" (III, 132; 73). That is, he must not cause Pamela to miscarry by upsetting her too much. These disturbing words invite us to contemplate her pregnancy and even to picture the unseen child within her, or perhaps the unseen force of nature that makes pregnancy possible. Mr. B. then describes how Pamela turned her "half-affrighted Eyes, this way and that, on the Books, and Pic-

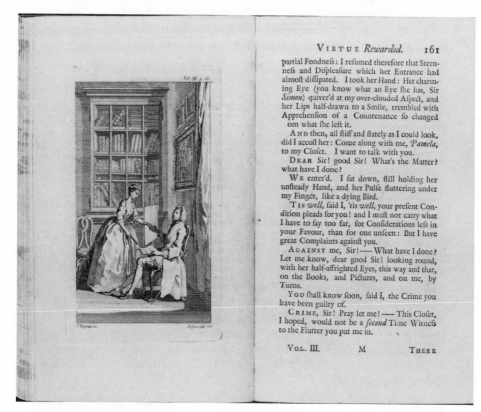

9. Illustration from *Pamela II* by Samuel Richardson, 6th corrected ed. (London, 1742), Vol. III, p. 161. Designed by F. Hayman and engraved by H. Gravelot.

tures, and on me, by Turns," words that hint once again at an affective equivalency among books, pictures, and the human body. It is important to realize that Richardson creates these effects by carefully juxtaposing word and image in a single opening of the text.

Richardson keeps the image of Pamela's pregnancy before us by ending the first volume of *Pamela II* with a series of somber letters depicting her terror of the birth itself, and in the revisions of *Pamela II*, he added a phrase stressing the necessity in such situations for tenderness "from one Woman to another" (III, 405; 210). This comment is actually made about the dying Mrs. Jewkes, but it prompts Pamela to plead with her mother to come to her when her labor begins. Here Pamela voices fears about the possibility of her own death in childbirth, and although she says she speaks foolishly, "just as if no-body was ever in my Case before," and calls herself an especially "sad weak, apprehensive Body," she begs compellingly for her mother's support.[20]

Pamela's justification for the request is, in part, the claim that "a Tenderness, a Sympathy" from one woman to another differs both physiologically and spiritually from the support any man can provide, for it

> mingles from one Woman to another with one's very Spirits, thins the animal Mass, and runs thro' one's Heart, in the same lify Current, (I can't cloathe my Thought suitably to express what I *would* express) giving Assurance as well as Pleasure in the most arduous Cases.

Pamela here finds that words are inadequate to express the special nature of the physiological "Pleasure" to be derived from a woman's sympathy in the midst of the most dire physical trauma. Pamela also uses the word "Pleasure" in her description of how her body is altered by the household prayer meetings in such a way that she becomes more sexually stimulating to Mr. B. She reports that when she returns to him after such meetings, "he is pleased to say sometimes, that I come to him with such a Radiance in my Countenance, as gives him double Pleasure to behold me; and often he tells me afterwards, that, but for appearing too fond before Company, he could meet me, as I enter, with Embraces as pure as my own Heart" (III, 252; 137–38). In this remarkable passage we learn that B.'s physical desire for his new wife is stimulated by her bodily response to the communal worship of God. He feels a "double Pleasure" in viewing her because her body, which is itself doubled by her pregnant state, offers a dual representation of sexuality and spirituality in her glowing face. In several senses, here, unseen realms are made visible.

One further part of this literature of pleasure and terror within the text is Pamela's "posthumous letter" to her husband—a letter she secretly writes to "my dearest, my best beloved Master, Friend, Husband, my *first*, my *last*, and *only* Love" for delivery in the event of her death (IV, 106; 265). In it, we encounter a text that anticipates Clarissa's posthumous letters which Richardson would write for the powerful end of his second novel. In the case of Pamela's farewell letter, the sentiments we are allowed to experience are not those of a woman whose death has resulted from sexual and spiritual violation, as in the case of Clarissa, but of one who has perished in the trauma of childbirth, and yet they share a somber affinity.

Strangely, even feminist readers have not recognized the centrality of Richardson's concern with pregnancy and sexual intimacy in this work. Nevertheless, the importance of this aspect of the married Pamela's life is affirmed by the particular specimen from John Kelly's spurious sequel which Richardson chose to publish in *The Daily Advertiser* of June 6, 1741, as evidence of the book's inauthenticity. The passage from Kelly's work which Richardson selected is one in which the pregnant Pamela's drinking gives rise to the speculation that a pregnant woman can drink "six times the Quantity of Wine," without being affected, "which at another Time would deprive her of Sense and Motion." Moreover, in letters written during the composition of *Pamela II*, Richardson makes a point of mentioning Pamela's "pregnant Circumstance" as one of the subjects he felt bound to treat.[21]

The most powerful evidence about pregnancy as an informing motive for this text comes in a letter he wrote but never sent to his physician, George Cheyne. Cheyne had written to him in August, 1741, urging him in the sequel to avoid depictions of "Fondling and Gallantry, tender Expressions not becoming the Character of Wisdom, Piety, and conjugal Chastity." He reminded Richardson that, as St. Paul says, " 'It is a Shame for you to speak of those Things that are done by you in secret;' and clasping, kissing, stroking, hugging are but Approaches to those others, and are really dangerous to be proposed to or read by young Persons of either Sex."[22] In the text of the first edition, Richardson somewhat wickedly reversed this sentiment and placed it in the mouth of the sly Lady Davers who identifies Pamela's physical state and says to her, "to talk to thee in thy own grave Way, thou has verify'd the Scripture, *What is done in Secret, shall be known on the House-top*," a remark Richardson softened in his revisions to "Works of this Nature [pregnancy] will not long be hidden" (III, 167–78; 91).

Cheyne's letter produced an impassioned reply from Richardson who defended his representation of physical affection or the "Fondness of ye Pair" as a justifiable "Grossness." He wrote, "In my Scheme I have generally taken Human Nature *as it is*; for it is to no purpose to suppose it Angelic, or to endeavour to make it so. There is a Time of Life, in which the Passions will predominate; and Ladies, any more than Men, will not be kept in Ignorance." In the midst of this defense Richardson quoted Mr. B.'s comment to his wife in the very first letter of *Pamela II* which I have already noted: "*How greatly do the innocent Pleasures I now hourly taste, exceed the guilty Tumults, that used formerly to agitate my unequal Mind!*"[23] The context of this remark within the letter to Dr. Cheyne confirms that the implicit subject of the first letter of *Pamela II* is sexuality within marriage, however discreetly Richardson may handle it. It is worth noting, too, that during the time that Richardson was writing *Pamela I*, his second wife was pregnant with the twelfth and last child he was to father, only four of whom would live to adulthood. Moreover, by 1740, seven of his infant children had already died, along with his first wife whose death may have been connected in some way with the birth of her sixth child (a boy called Samuel, after his father) but was certainly "accelerated" by grief over the death of her young son, William, for Richardson tells us as much in a letter.[24]

Richardson was clearly familiar with many issues respecting childbirth, and the first engraving in the second volume of his sequel (Figure 10) depicts yet another aspect of the heroine's uneasy adjustment to motherhood:

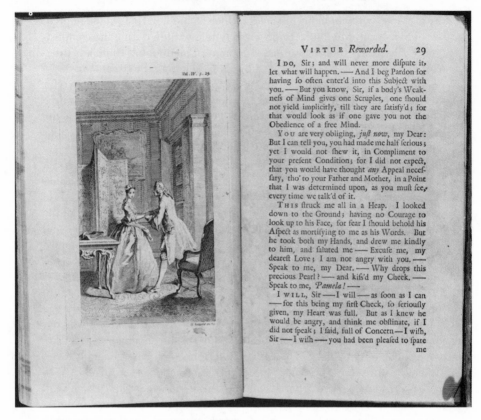

10. Illustration from *Pamela II* by Samuel Richardson, 6th corrected ed. (London, 1742), Vol. IV, p. 29. Designed and engraved by H. Gravelot.

the B.'s' dispute over her nursing the child when it is born. As if to signal the subject of their debate, within the engraving we dimly distinguish in the background, on the wall, a painting of a mother with a child before her breast. The picture is partially obscured by a screen that divides it within the visual space of the engraving from the arguing Mr. and Mrs. B. The screening of the maternal scene thus forecasts what will be the outcome of the argument.

Among other things, Mr. B. is afraid that nursing will ruin Pamela's figure and divert her attention from his body to that of the baby. Moreover, he feels that the activity is not suitable to her new rank in society, that the office of a nurse is "an Office beneath my *Pamela*." The quarrel has made Mr. B. angry, and yet he says, in words that face the illustration, "I would not shew it, in Compliment to your present Condition" (IV, 14 and 24; 229 and 233). Here, in the engraved edition, Richardson substituted the word "Condition" for "*Circumstance*" which he had used in the first edition and had italicized for emphasis. Both words signify Pamela's pregnancy, but while "*Circumstance*" tends to direct the attention to externals—meaning literally "that which surrounds"—the word "Condition" subtly shifts the meaning to the realm of the internal. When called a "condition," pregnancy is something that inheres within a woman.

Pamela's "Condition" thus refers to her state of physical being, as well as her rank in society with regard to wealth and position. A second subject of concern in the first letter of *Pamela II*, in addition to the heroine's pregnancy, had been the difference between the "Condition" of the privileged Mr. B. and the more lowly "Condition" of Pamela's humble, laboring parents. The variable use of the word "condition" in all of these contexts makes clear that the status of Pamela's body—as medical, maternal, sexual, social, and aesthetic text—lies at the center of her discomfort in the transformation from Pamela Andrews to Mrs. B. The crisis in Pamela's vision of herself then comes with her visit to the masquerade, which is the culmination of these eariler scenes rather than the sole incident of interest in a boring text, as Castle and others have argued.

The outing occurs shortly after Polly Darnford joins the B.'s in London, and in her eyes, they are, along with plays, operas, and masquerades, among the most interesting sights of the town. She even calls them "the greatest Curiosity in *England*," a husband and wife who have not once repented their marriage. When she first lays eyes on Pamela, Miss Darnford remarks the changes in Mrs. B's body; Pamela writes, "But the dear Lady put me into some little Confusion, when she saw me first; taking Notice of my Improvements, as she called them, before Mr. *B.*" "Improvements" was an eighteenth-century term for the fashionable alterations made by the wealthy to the architecture and landscape of their estates, and when both Miss Darnford and Mr. B. reprove Pamela for her "Maiden Airs," Pamela uses "Improvements" as a self-defensive metaphor. She says, "I have heard Mr. B. observe, with regard to Gentlemen who build fine Houses, and make fine Gardens, and open fine Prospects, that Art should never take the place of, but be subservient to Nature." As if her body were a stately home, Pamela says that she must endeavour "to make the best" of her "natural Defects" out of fear that "by assuming Airs and Dignities in Appearance, to which [she] was not born" she will "act neither Part tolerably." In Pamela's mind, being either a humble maiden or a noble wife is to "act a Part," a notion Lady Davers cuts through by saying quite simply, "People who see you at this time, will take it for granted, that You and Mr. *B.* have been very intimate together" (IV, 36–43; 240–44).

These moments in the text, which graphically depict Pamela's failing efforts to masquerade as the virginal "Pamela Andrews" and not the obviously pregnant "Mrs. B.," provide a context for the masquerade episode and the

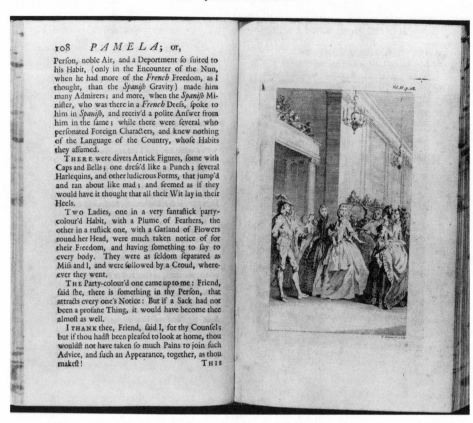

11. Illustration from *Pamela II* by Samuel Richardson, 6th corrected ed. (London, 1742), Vol. IV, p. 108. Designed and engraved by H. Gravelot.

next illustration (Figure 11). The words facing the picture describe what Pamela saw at the masquerade: "divers Antick Figures, . . . several Harlequins, and other ludicrous Forms," words which unwittingly recall Mr. B.'s earlier description of Pamela herself as his mother's "Harlequin" (IV, 97 and III, 187; 260 and 104). Here her pregnant condition makes her a "ludicrous Form," for her disguise as a Quaker, at the urging of Mr. B., is a paradoxical choice. Although she herself regards such clothing as "prim" and makes no objection to B.'s choice for her since she feels she can act "up to the Character" she has assumed, she is clearly unaware that Quakers were steadily ridiculed from the Restoration to the first decade of the eighteenth century for their reputed sexual license, a fact that both Richardson and his artists would have known.[25]

Through the choice of her dress, B. has turned his wife into a visual joke, for in the text facing the illustration, a masquerader approaches Pamela and says, "Friend, . . . there is something in thy Person, that attracts every one's

Notice." Readers who admire this scene are more typically interested in Mr. B.'s near affair with a countess who is here disguised as a nun;[26] however, the picture and the accompanying text when taken as a single image insist that we contemplate Pamela's own "ludicrous Form" which so graphically reveals her sexual intimacy with Mr. B. This is not the first such joke at Pamela's expense within this epistolary text, however. Pamela is initially unaware that what she calls the *"good* Book" (III, 127–28; 71) which Sir Simon hurled at his daughter's face was in fact Rabelais's *Pantagruel*, the beginning of which recounts the monstrous birth of Pantagruel to his giant father and to a mother who dies in the process of producing his massive form from her own body. Rabelais's grotesque image of childbirth—as one of physical smothering—thus lies at the imaginative center of this book both visually and verbally. Moreover, one of the remarks that Sir Simon most deeply resents is Pamela's criticism of his *"innocent* double Entendres" (III, 108; 62), and in the masquerade she, in effect, becomes one.

The birth of Pamela's child literalizes the change that Pamela is so reluctant to see in herself, and in doing so it resolves a question about the relative status of art and nature which is implicitly debated in the novel's many incidents. We view Pamela's experience of birth through the eyes of Polly Darnford who, in the course of her account of it, somewhat comically remarks, "Not one of these Men, that I have yet seen, . . . is worth running these Risques for!" The seriousness of the moment is conveyed, however, by Polly's eloquently brief description of what Pamela went through in labor: "Mrs. *B.* had a very sharp Time" (IV, 120; 270). The elliptical rendering of this moment of extreme physical trauma lies at the center of the novel and in its somber eloquence anticipates Richardson's handling of Lovelace's notorious rape of Clarissa, although it is hardly the "cartoon version of *Clarissa"* that Eagleton describes. When Lovelace finally conveys the news of the terrible violation around which the whole of Richardson's monumental second novel develops, he simply says, "And now, Belford, I can go no farther. The affair is over. Clarissa lives."[27] In both works, the brief words stand in inverse relation to the power of incident for character and reader. Lest we come away from *Pamela II* with an idealized image of motherhood, the Editor of its "Conclusion" tells us that Miss Darnford, "after a happy Marriage of several years, died in Childbed of her fourth Child." Richardson's image of motherhood thus incorporates the harsh physicality of the act of birth and a woman's terror of it. When Polly writes to her own "Papa and Mamma" after the birth of Pamela's first baby, she declares that "we have nothing but Joy and Festivity in this House"; for Pamela herself, however, the "Pleasure" has surely been what Bakhtin calls the ambivalent laughter which accompanies the spectacle of the Rabelaisian "double body"—an image of the body as a grotesque and "inexhaustible vessel of death and conception."[28]

The illustration accompanying the birth of Pamela's baby articulates the

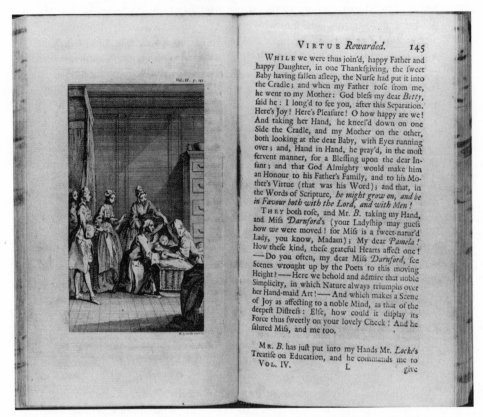

12. Illustration from *Pamela II* by Samuel Richardson, 6th corrected ed. (London, 1742), Vol. IV, p. 145. Designed and engraved by H. Gravelot.

central aesthetic of this odd text (Figure 12). It depicts a movement of eyes, both in and on the page. We see the reunited Mr. and Mrs. Andrews looking at each other and "at the dear Baby." Moreover, it is a scene within a scene, for Pamela, Miss Darnford, and Mr. B. survey the moving sight, and in the page of text facing the engraving, Mr. B. actually tells Pamela and her friend how to look at it:

> Do you often, my dear Miss *Darnford*, see Scenes wrought up by the Poets to this moving Height?—Here we behold and admire that noble Simplicity, in which Nature always triumphs over her Hand-maid Art!—And which makes a Scene of Joy as affecting to a noble Mind, as that of the deepest Distress: Else, how could it display its Force thus sweetly on your lovely Cheek! (IV, 132; 276)

In a paradoxical fusion of narrative text and image, Richardson uses an engraved illustration—a work of art—to make the point that, as B. says, "Nature always triumphs over her Hand-maid art!" His words on how to

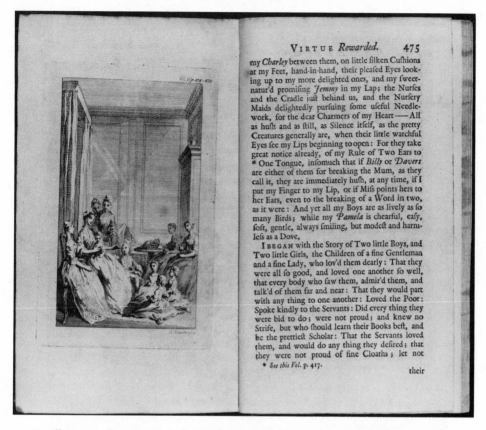

13. Illustration from *Pamela II* by Samuel Richardson, 6th corrected ed. (London, 1742), Vol. IV, pp. 474–75. Designed and engraved by H. Gravelot.

read this scene, however, depict the human body as the most noble work of art in nature, from the blush that paints the cheek, to the creative power of birth. Moreover, scenes of "Joy" and scenes of the "deepest Distress" are curiously united in their powerful capacity to "affect" the "noble Mind."

Unfortunately, we know little about Richardson's relations with the two artists who produced his illustrations.[29] In the absence of more detailed information, readers of *Pamela II* have privileged the word and discounted the pictures although they are central to both the structure and technique of Richardson's art. The materiality of Pamela's body, however, which is so graphically diplayed in its creation of new life, offers a new understanding of Richardson's art. In that sense the last illustration in the text (Figure 13) gives the fullest view of Pamela as creator. We see her telling the nursery tales to five of her seven children, her adopted daughter Miss Goodwin, and four maids. The words describe the children's "watchful Eyes" as they intensely observe Pamela's "Lips beginning to open" and their physical proximity to her body in the room (IV, 475; 462). Moreover, the children themselves are, quite literally, what Pamela has produced in the course of text that we are reading; they are the material substance or "image" of her married self.

Through language and picture we thus experience the married Pamela's growing awareness of her changing being, a process which constitutes the distinctive "epistolarity" of this text. While in *Pamela I*, letters serve as vehicles for social and sexual negotiations among the characters, here both the words and the illustrations realize an image of body and text in flux. Pamela's unseen child first inheres within her "Person" and then brings forth her new "self" through the traumatic act of birth. So, too, a series of visual and verbal texts inhere within the body of *Pamela II* and engender substantial images in the reader's imagination. Pamela's changing body stands as Richardson's incarnation of the complex power of books and opens fresh possibilities for assessing her creator's concern with the intimacies of women's lives.

NOTES

1. For convenience, I will refer to the original, two-volume *Pamela* (1740) as *Pamela I* and to Richardson's sequel to it as *Pamela II*.

2. *Pamela; or, Virtue Rewarded* (Oxford: Shakespeare Head Press, 1929), III, 128 and *Pamela*, vol. II (London and Melbourne: Everyman's Library, 1914), pp. 71–72. All further page references will be noted parenthetically in the text. I have taken all *Pamela* quotations from the four-volume Shakespeare Head edition because it reprints the sixth corrected edition of *Pamela* in four volumes which Richardson published in 1742. Volumes III and IV of what is known as the sixth corrected edition were, in fact, the third edition of *Pamela II*. For the reader's convenience, I will also list the page numbers of the Everyman edition which roughly correspond to the passages quoted, but it is important to keep in mind that the Everyman is based on a very much abridged version of the text from which many of the quotations on which my argument relies have been cut. See Peter Sabor, "The Cooke-Everyman Edition of *Pamela*," *The Library*, 5th ser., 32 (1977): 360–66 and Philip Gaskell, *From Writer to Reader: Studies in Editorial Method* (Oxford: Clarendon Press, 1978).

3. All of the illustrations from *Pamela* reproduced for this essay come from the four-volume, sixth corrected edition which Richardson himself printed and published in 1742. Volume and page numbers were engraved on each illustration to indicate the page across from which the image was to appear. The sole exception is Figure 13—the only illustration in the series of twenty-nine to designate two pages rather than a single one to which its image refers. The illustration in Figure 13 is bound facing page 475 in the copies of *Pamela* I have examined.

4. Scott's remark occurs in a memoir of Richardson's life which prefaces his edition of *The Novels of Samuel Richardson* in *Ballentyne's Novelist's Library* (London, 1824), VI, p. xxiv. Many of the major studies of Richardson share Scott's negative view of this text including Elizabeth Bergen Brophy, *Samuel Richardson: The Triumph of Craft* (Knoxville: University of Tennessee Press, 1974), p. 88; Margaret Anne

Doody, *A Natural Passion: A Study of the Novels of Samuel Richardson* (Oxford: Clarendon Press, 1974), pp. 76 and 90; T. C. Duncan Eaves and Ben D. Kimpel, *Samuel Richardson: A Biography* (Oxford: Clarendon Press, 1971), pp. 149–50; Carol Houlihan Flynn, *Samuel Richardson: A Man of Letters* (Princeton: Princeton University Press, 1982), pp. 166–67; and Mark Kinkead-Weekes, *Samuel Richardson: Dramatic Novelist* (Ithaca: Cornell University Press, 1973), pp. 84–85. For Eagleton's remarks, see *The Rape of Clarissa* (Minneapolis: University of Minnesota Press, 1982), pp. 36–39.

5. The phrase is used by Richardson himself in a letter to George Cheyne of 31 August 1741. See John Carroll, *Selected Letters of Samuel Richardson* (Oxford: Clarendon Press, 1964), p. 47.

6. *Pamela Censured: In a Letter to the Editor* (London, 1741), p. 63 and *The Virgin in Eden: or, The State of Innocencey. Deliver'd by way of Image and Description*. (London, 1741). For the publication dates of these works, see William Merritt Sale, *Samuel Richardson: A Bibliographical Record* (New Haven: Yale University Press, 1936), pp. 114 and 125.

7. *Masquerade and Civilization: The Carnivalesque in Eighteenth-Century English Culture and Fiction* (Stanford: Stanford University Press, 1986), pp. 151 and 137. See also Sylvia Kasey Marks, *Sir Charles Grandison: The Compleat Conduct Book* (London and Toronto: Associated University Presses, 1986), pp. 52–53. For an alternative argument that Richardson is highly successful in achieving the "felt presence of the body" in the last of his narratives, see Juliet McMaster, "*Sir Charles Grandison*: Richardson on Body and Character," *Eighteenth-Century Fiction* 1 (1989): 83–102.

8. "Richardson's 'speaking pictures,'" in *Samuel Richardson Tercentenary Essays*, ed. Margaret Anne Doody and Peter Sabor (Cambridge: Cambridge University Press, 1989), pp. 146–66. Works that have influenced my thinking in this essay include Steven Cohan, "Figures Beyond the Text: A Theory of Readable Character in the Novel," *Novel* 17 (1983): 5–27; Joseph Kestner, "Secondary Illusion: The Novel and the Spatial Arts," in Jeffrey R. Smitten and Ann Daghistany, *Spatial Form in Narrative* (Ithaca and London: Cornell University Press, 1981), pp. 100–128; Alan T. McKenzie, "The Countenance You Show Me: Reading the Passions in the Eighteenth Century," *Georgia Review* 32 (1978): 758–73; W. J. T. Mitchell, "Spatial Form in Literature: Toward a General Theory," *Critical Inquiry* 6 (1980): 539–67; Joel Snyder, "Picturing Vision," *Critical Inquiry* 6 (1980): 499–526; and Richard Wendorf, "'Visible Rhetorick': Izaak Walton and Iconic Biography," *Modern Philology* 82 (1984–1985): 269–91.

9. On the "multistable" visual image see Stephen C. Behrendt, "Art as Deceptive Intruder: Audience Entrapment in Eighteenth-Century Verbal and Visual Art," *Papers on Language and Literature* 19 (1983): 37–52. Richard Shiff explores the related concept of the "inherent intertextuality" of visual representation in "Representation, Copying, and the Technique of Originality," *New Literary History* 15 (1983–1984): 333–63.

10. Richard Wendorf, "Jonathan Richardson: The Painter as Biographer," *New Literary History* 15 (1983–1984): 551.

11. *The Virgin in Eden*, p. 68; *Remarks on "Clarissa"* (1749), ed. Peter Sabor, Augustan Reprint #231–32 (Los Angeles: William Andrews Clark Memorial Library, 1985), pp. 35 and 39; and Denis Diderot, "Éloge de Richardson," in *Oeuvres Esthétiques* (Paris: Éditions Garnier Frères, 1968), p. 35. The translation is mine.

12. *An Essay on Mr. Pope's "Odyssey." In Five Dialogues.* 2d ed. (London, 1737), pp. 74, 37, 30–31, and preface.

13. Sale, pp. 11–32. See also T. C. Duncan Eaves, "Graphic Illustrations of the Novels of Samuel Richardson, 1740–1810," *Huntington Library Quarterly* 14 (1950–1951): 349–57.

14. *Daily Gazeteer*, quoted in Eaves and Kimpel, p. 135.

15. *"Pamela" in High Life: or, Virtue Rewarded* (London, 1741). Sale's description of this work (pp. 120–21) does not mention the illustrationed piracy of volumes I and II which is now shelved with *"Pamela" in High Life* at the Houghton Library.

16. Castle, pp. 132–33. See also Eagleton, pp. 36–37, and Marks, p. 52.

17. *Pamela Censured*, p. 31.

18. The naming of both Miss Darnford and Pamela's maid "Polly" is one more example of the narrative's reduplicative structure. Late in the novel Polly Darnford rejects a proposed match with Jackey after he has extricated himself from the affair with Polly the maid.

19. Sale notes (p. 31) that although this illustration was clearly intended to face page eleven of the original text, it is "usually" bound to face page two, across from the passages I have been discussing. In the copies I have examined at Harvard and Cambridge University, however, it is correctly placed opposite page eleven on which Mr. Andrews tries to persuade Mr. Longman to allow him, secretly, to pay rent for the livelihood of the estate rather than receiving it as a gift from his son-in-law. Longman refuses to participate in the deception, saying, "Would not his Honour think, if I hid one thing from him, I might hide another?" By placing the fruit tree with its ladder in the background of the image, Hayman thus provides us with an alternative version of the orchard robbing picture to which Jackey alludes, and this time it establishes the honorable natures of both Pamela's humble father and the loyal Mr. Longman.

20. This is an especially clear example of the distortions in the Cooke-Everyman edition of *Pamela II*. In this instance, the editors omitted an entire section of the letter to Polly Darnford in which Pamela makes the direct appeal to her mother, and their decision to do so made the altered text especially misleading. Philip Gaskell claims that the editors' goals in such changes were "to refine and modernize the novel for early nineteenth-century readers" (p. 77), but my own preliminary study suggests that far more complicated motivations lay behind this curious episode in the interpretive history of one of the most often studied novels of the eighteenth century.

21. Letters to James Leake and Stephen Duck in Carroll, pp. 45 and 53.

22. Charles F. Mullett, ed., *The Letters of Doctor George Cheyne to Samuel Richardson* (1733–1743), *University of Missouri Studies*, 18 (1943): pp. 68–69.

23. Carroll, pp. 47–48.

24. Eaves and Kimpel, pp. 48–50.

25. Hugh Ormsby-Lennon, "Swift and the Quakers," *Swift Studies* 4 (1989): 34–62.

26. In 1785, a four-volume, newly illustrated edition of *Pamela* was published as part of *The Novelist's Magazine*, and this time the depiction of the masquerade scene prominently features Mr. B. seducing the countess who is disguised as a nun, unlike the Gravelot and Hayman illustration in which the nun is barely visible.

27. *Clarissa* (New York: Viking Penguin, 1985), p. 883.

28. Mikhail Bakhtin, *Rabelais and His World*, Helene Iswolsky, trans. (Bloomington: Indiana University Press, 1984), p. 318.

29. Francis Hayman must have cared about the project, however, since he later chose to rework one of the illustrations as a supper box painting for Vauxhall Gardens. See Brian Allen, *Francis Hayman* (New Haven and London: Yale University Press, 1987), p. 151.

CHAPTER SEVEN

Fictions and Freedom: Wordsworth and the Ideology of Romanticism

TERENCE ALLAN HOAGWOOD

IN CONTRAST TO AN EARLIER CONSENSUS which treated the works of Romanticism in either biographical and personalistic or abstract and thematic terms, one contemporary school of critical thought unfolds polemically the dimension of Romantic discourse which is powerfully political.[1] We are coming to learn how the Romantic discourse of ideality and mental forms persistently engages a theory of mentality and imagination with immediate material change in the organization of society.[2] Wordsworth and Shelley, for example, both argue that there is a connection between mental structures and social institutions.[3] The faculty of the human imagination, for early Romantics and late, reproduces and underlies concrete structures (including political formations) as well as their notional bases, including the concept of freedom. Fictionality—the structuration of reality—is essential, in this Romantic mode of thought, to the conditions of material life, including the concept of freedom. Fiction is a word that means construction: from Latin *fictus*, shaped, made, formed, constructed. The order of reality which constitutes its very perceptibility is itself a construction of the perceiving mind.

This tendency of Romantic thought and literature, to engage mental forms and mentalistic preoccupations with material and social change, has its roots in the development of ideological theory in the eighteenth and nineteenth centuries. Destutt de Tracy's materialist and revolutionary school of *ideologistes* in the eighteenth century, and the Marx-Engels arguments on ideology in *The German Ideology* and elsewhere, for example, formulate under the name *ideology* a critical theory that explains the reciprocal determinism of forms of thought and forms of social order and political power. These preoccupations, however, range far outside the nominal treatments of that word, "ideology": under the rubrics of "custom" and "prejudice," writers of social theory including Wordsworth, Shelley, Mary Wollstonecraft, William Godwin, Mary Hays, William Drummond, and many others make this linkage a cultural leitmotif.

This point about the mental structures of the human world is common to the skeptical epistemology of Drummond, to the French revolutionary philosophy of Diderot, Condorcet, Holbach, and Destutt de Tracy, to the philosophy of Kant and his followers Fichte, Schelling, and Hegel (whose *Science of Logic* opens with an original formulation of this problem), and to the poetry of the British Romantics. Poetry, as Shelley says in the *Defence of Poetry*, "is the root and blossom of all other systems of thought."[4] That periodic sentence begins with poetry but culminates at its point in *all other systems of thought.*[5]

In fact, Shelley was given to periodic sentences that work in similar ways, as when he says that "poets and philosophers are the unacknowledged legislators of the world."[6] Here he begins with poets and culminates at his point—legislators, and world. As Anthony John Harding once pointed out to me, Shelley is here following Wordsworth, who in his famous Preface of 1800 says that "poetry is the breath and finer spirit of all knowledge" (*Selected Prose*, 292). I emphasize that Wordsworth's sentence begins with poetry to arrive at a culmination in his point—all knowledge. Similarly, Wordsworth says that "the poet binds together by passion and knowledge the vast empire of human society" (292). As Shelley was to do, Wordsworth begins with poetry to culminate with a point in a larger purpose—"society." The cultural realities of which both Shelley and Wordsworth write include not merely poetry as a specialized act but rather and far more importantly *all other systems of thought*. This tendency opens the great works of Romanticism onto the question of legislators, of world, of all knowledge, and of the comprehensive and actual circumference of human endeavor—what Wordsworth calls society.

This mode of Romanticism, the ideological mode, opens often in poetry and poetics, often in explicitly political theory. Rousseau's argument that all right originates in social convention is germane,[7] and so is Rousseau's best-known contention about the power of ideological forms—that humankind lose everything in their chains, including the desire to escape from them. Like Rousseau, the British Romantic writers characteristically treat structures of thought and feeling which are prior to any particular thought or known fact. Romanticism is about these preexisting structures of perception and cognition. This set of theoretical preoccupations is also ascendant in modern and contemporary theory: for example, when Foucault writes of a collective and cultural "positive unconscious," a "set of categories that make it possible for us to name, speak, and think," he offers the term *episteme* for the historically relative frameworks that function thus, not personally but across a culture, to organize our perception and knowledge, before we perceive and know.[8] In a more precisely political context, the theory of ideological structuration as it is articulated by Anthony Giddens and analyzed by John B. Thompson, for example, presents an analogous notion.[9] I am arguing that the Romantic writers—Wordsworth among them—lift these shared structures of perception, thought, and feeling into the foreground of their discourse, in poetry and also in their prose that is given to political theory.

One of the ways—and perhaps the most powerful and enduring way—in which Wordsworth and his contemporaries reach across the alienating gap of historical distance is thus by exhibiting directly the structures that, beneath, above, beyond, and within the specificity of conjunctural events, organize our world. These structures—in Romantic formulations as in the framework of contemporary ideological theories—are mental but not private, and are human-made though not personal. As Wordsworth says in his "Reply to Mathetes" in 1809, the analysis of ideological frameworks concerns "not the power or worth of individual Minds, but the general moral or intellectual [structures] of an Age" (111). The Romantic writers work their way toward a practical engagement in a revolutionary moment in European history—in Wordsworth's case involving revolutionary action in France, where, prior to the September massacres of 1792, he was an activist member of the revolutionary Girondin, and where (as David V. Erdman has recently suggested) he seems to have been active in a group called the British Club, whose mission was to export the democratic revolution from France into England.[10] As Shelley was later to do, Wordsworth effects this practical action on the basis of an ideological analysis. For both writers, mental configurations are not personal things. Ideologies are social in scope.

The Romantic writers—Wordsworth, Coleridge, Hazlitt, Godwin, Byron, Shelley, and many another—do write voluminously about the topically political events of their historical moment, but they do more: they engage in a criticism of the underlying and collective mental acts that constitute the human world in which politics and economic change take their place. These mental acts are not our beliefs; they are those unconscious preconditions to which Hans Georg Gadamer points, for example, when he says that it is not so much our judgments as our prejudgments that constitute our being; human reality is constituted less by opinions or self-conscious thoughts than by those latent mental structures that constitute the possibility of opinions and self-conscious thoughts.[11] To analyze collective mental modes, including the unconscious epistemic features that underlie a culture, is a political act. It is commonplace among Romantic modes of thought that the act of mind and the life of freedom or slavery are mutually implicated, mutually constitutive modes of being. In their fusion arise human works, including political constructions.

Of course Wordsworth did not remain a revolutionary all his life; Chandler and Levinson have argued that Wordsworth did not remain revolutionary long enough for *Lyrical Ballads* to be, really, the poetic correlative to the French Revolution which Hazlitt had said it was. Shelley's prose extends relentlessly the imaginative arguments of Wordsworth's youth; in *A Philosophical View of Reform*, Shelley develops principles nascent in Wordsworth, to produce the most advanced work of political theory of his age.[12] I limit myself here to the shape that the Romantic ideology—the fusion of fictions and freedom—takes in the poetry and prose of Wordsworth, though

I hope to be noting as I go along how these principles in Wordsworth's works arise from and open back into his culture at large and into ours, including disciplines and spheres of life outside his own.

Imagination is seen—in the preface to the *Lyrical Ballads* as in Shelley's *Philosophical View of Reform* and *A Defence of Poetry*—as a mental faculty that precipitates or follows social renovation. Civil and domestic life are constituted in patterns created by the imagination: and that point is the central one in Wordsworth's letter, for example, to the Whig statesman, Charles James Fox; in 1802, Wordsworth sends Fox a copy of *Lyrical Ballads*, and an account of the poems' political implications and purposes. Structures of mind and feeling, he suggests, are social and not personal things. This is also the central point of Wordsworth's famous preface to the *Lyrical Ballads*: the linkage of thought-forms with the material forms of daily social living. In a disingenuous maneuver seventeen years later, Coleridge was to write influentially of this preface as though it concerned chiefly the narrowly poetic matter of versification and diction;[13] instead, though generations have been blinded by Coleridge's apparently depoliticized account in the *Biographia Literaria*, Wordsworth's preface in 1800 indicates explicitly that his poems employ "the language of conversation in the middle and lower classes" for no narrowly poetic aim: he aims rather to exhibit and to treat critically "our own pre-established codes of decision" (I quote Wordsworth's Advertisement to the *Lyrical Ballads* [1798], 275–76). Language is not an alienated aesthetic event but a medium and ground of ideological confrontation: Wordsworth's preface in 1800 points out how "language and the human mind act and re-act on each other," and he writes of "revolutions, not of literature alone, but likewise of society itself" (preface to the *Lyrical Ballads*, 280). Wordsworth's sending his volume to the Whig Fox was not therefore a surprising move: Fox had long been fighting for the enfranchisement of excluded population groups, and for the abolition of slavery. He exhibited his own ability to reimagine forms of political life when, in 1798, the year of the first edition of the *Lyrical Ballads*, he proposed a toast that inflamed those still given to the divine right of kings: he raised a glass and said, "To our Sovereign—the people." He was hereupon excluded from the privy council, the tightening conservatism of the administration intolerant of such redefinitions and the corresponding revolutions (as Wordsworth says) not of literature alone, but of society itself.[14] Wordsworth's preface of 1800 is of course largely devoted to an analysis of mental faculties; for him as for the other major Romantic writers, imagination is the prime agent of human perception, the exercise and formation of perceptual schemata as in the psychology of Piaget or the construction below consciousness of the categories of time and space, as in the philosophy of Kant.

The science of perceptual structures becomes a science of political structures. A short parable by William Blake illustrates the process. The ancients "animated all sensible objects with Gods"; an act of imagination assigned

power and value to natural forms. Objects are infused with human significance by means of a value-laden projection of the human will. "A system was
formed," Blake says, "which some took advantage of & enslaved the vulgar."
A specialized class of political and religious authorities seized power over
the population by seizing power over the imagination, in an attempt to "realize or abstract the mental deities from their objects."[15] The power of making
figments made people free; priests and kings, however, treat these delusions
as truths, and the ensuing power has made people slaves. Whether religious
or political projections, fictions formed by human makers are reified into
objects to be obeyed: this structure of argument, from Destutt de Tracy,
Holbach, Condorcet, and other French writers of the eighteenth century,
shows itself repeatedly in the prose and poems of the British Romantic
writers.

This theoretical orientation resembles in some ways Fredric Jameson's
notion of the political unconscious.[16] A populace lives in ideological chains,
which Blake calls "mind-forged manacles"; these are the chains in which, as
Rousseau points out, slaves lose everything, including the desire to resist.
John Stuart Mill points out that the most effective enslavement—the most
desirable, from the point of view of the oppressor—is that which enslaves
the subject from within.[17] Mental structures are made, not given; in what
feels like the privacy of subjectivity an enslaved mind puts on like clothing
the ideological (mental) fetters whose mental origin the slave soon forgets.[18]
To reacquaint the public with its own mental power is (to oversimplify) the
central project of Romanticism.

As Antonio Gramsci was to argue early in the twentieth century, hegemony is no longer a matter of force, but rather moral and intellectual bases
for maintenance of consent in a given social order.[19] The power of ruling
thought-structures can be illustrated in almost any range of human endeavor.
I will turn to Wordsworth's poems later for a major ground of argument;
Romanticism, including Wordsworth's, is characterized by a self-consciousness about the power and pervasiveness of such thought-structures. The
issue can be illustrated first, however, from a relevant issue in eighteenth-
century science.

Perhaps the greatest scientific mind of the eighteenth century was Joseph
Priestley. He was also a leading figure in the ideological enterprise of syn-
cretizing historically relative mind-sets and structures of belief: in *Doctrines
of Heathen Philosophy Compared with Those of Revelation* he compares the
mental frameworks exhibited in Jesus Christ, Socrates, Plato, Pythagoras,
Aristotle, and the Stoics including Epictetus and Marcus Aurelius.[20]

The importance of Priestley's conceptual work in the area of comparing
thought-structures is only now being explored by Romanticists, but his
scientific accomplishments have been well-known: Priestley can be credited
with first isolating and identifying nitric oxide and anhydrous hydrochloric

acid gases. Priestley discovered sulfur dioxide. He discovered ammonia. He contrived a laboratory process that enabled him to achieve his most famous breakthrough in chemistry: the discovery of oxygen. (He placed a piece of mercuric oxide into a vessel in turn placed within a pneumatic trough, and he heated it then with a burning lens of his own contrivance.)[21]

In the history of scientific thought, however, it is far more interesting to me that Priestley did not *know* that he had discovered oxygen. He hadn't been looking for it. He had been trying to make progress in the study of phlogiston.

Of course there is no such thing as phlogiston. The word names a mere fiction. But the fiction of phlogiston worked every bit as well in explaining the known facts of the composition of air, and so Priestley persisted to the day of his death in explaining what he had found according to phlogiston. When he actually held a bottle of oxygen in his hand, for the first time in human history, he thought he had a bottle of normal air from which all the phlogiston had been removed. Phlogiston was a unifying elemental substratum for material and organic reality—fire and life depended on its animating and vital properties. For a uniformitarian worldview, it was a very appealing figment. Priestley stuck to it with legendary tenacity.

My point is not that Priestley made a mistake. My point is that a ruling structure of conception shows itself in Priestley's syncretic historicist scholarship: he finds ideological and cognitive grounds of unity on which the diversity of creeds has historically been spread. His unitarian theology—an indefatigable writer, he produced a library full of it—argues similarly in theological terms for a unifying basis below the surface structures of apparent diversity. And phlogiston (which does not exist) had the advantage of appealing to this same structure of uniformitarian thought. And he adhered to it.

Priestley had better reason for believing in phlogiston than you or I have for believing in oxygen: he had personally applied the most accurate and reliable scientific techniques, whereas you and I simply take others' word on the question. The fact that there is no such thing as phlogiston has nothing to do with the concept's explanatory utility: there is no such thing as "up," or "down," or "permanent," either—these words name organizing tendencies in our own perception, not existing things at all. But the conditions of living test and reward the imaginative fertility whereby we build and rebuild our world in working conceptions.

The enslavement of which the Romantic writers write most often, and most critically, is what happens when somebody else's working conception is taken as permanent and given truth. To shift examples will transpose the same issue into political discourse, and simultaneously bring us directly to Wordsworth's most explicit arguments. Up to and including most of the seventeenth century, among monarchists the divine right of kings was a given reality with which the monarch's subjects simply had to live. It was not perceived as a working conception for utility; it was perceived as a truth. It was a law not of government but of God.[22] But then in 1688 there was suddenly no such thing as divine right of kings after all; there was social contract. Divine right was converted from truth to figment. It is the phlogiston story all over again. This time, the argument of fictionality involves directly the facts of freedom.

Wordsworth gives a similar shape to the issue of social contract when he first engages it in his writing in a sustained work—his *Letter to the Bishop of Llandaff*. Bishop Richard Watson had long been known as an effective liberal theorist, supporter of the American Revolution and forcible writer on behalf of enfranchisement and political freedom—as in his *Principles of the Revolution Vindicated* in 1776. In 1793, however, he republishes his 1784 *Sermon Preached Before the Lords Spiritual and Temporal* with a new appendix in which he renounces the republican form of liberation exhibited in France, where Louis XVI was executed in January of that year. Wordsworth—who had spent much of 1791–1792 working in France, within and for the revolutionary government—publishes his *Letter to the Bishop of Llandaff* as a response to this reactionary turnabout and as a theoretical defense of the French revolutionary ideology.[23] As Godwin was to say of a comparable turn of argument in Edmund Burke, he "had been warmly loved by the most liberal and enlightened friends of freedom, and they were proportionately inflamed and disgusted by the fury of his [subsequent] assault upon" the cause of freedom.[24]

The centrality of Llandaff's reactionary attack against the cause of democracy is also suggested by the fact that one copy of Sir William Drummond's book on the French revolutionary theory—his *Philosophical Sketches of the Principles of Society and Government*—is inscribed by Drummond to Richard Watson.[25] One large-scale issue that Wordsworth shares with Drummond he shares equally with Rousseau: this is a utilitarian and relativist root-conception, opposed to the absolutist and authoritarian forms of reasoning on which monarchy and state religion had been based. All right, according to Rousseau, Drummond, and Wordsworth in 1793, originates in social convention, in human constructive acts of mind and consent, and forms of social order are accordingly relative, conventional, and time- and place-specific. At this point the argument from illusion arises: given the human construction of the forms of social order, the absolutist (monarchical) claims for absolute and divine right must be deconstructed as fictions. The position—Wordsworth's, Rousseau's—predicated upon the fictionality of social orders can *employ* that notion of fictionality to obliterate the enslaving authority of any one form of order that claims the givenness of permanent truth. At the heart of Wordsworth's most solidly political argument is thus his theory of imagination.

He characterizes in these terms those public figures who, like Watson, oppose vehemently the democratizing French Revolution: "misled by the phantoms of avarice and ambition, they fall victims to their delusion" (*A Letter to the Bishop of Llandaff*, 140). This delusion is the divine right of king and of state church, the absolute and eternal authority of the status quo; it is the political point of an apparently epistemological passage like this one from Drummond's *Academical Questions*:

> Deluded by his own mind, man continues to wander in the mazes of the labyrinth, which lies before him, unsuspicious of his deviations from the truth. Like some knight of romance in an enchanted palace, he mistakes the fictitious for the real, and the false for the true. . . . [How many among us] grasp at shadows, and follow phantoms . . . the dupe and often the victim of the illusions which [we ourselves] have created?[26]

As the French Encyclopedists had done, and as Godwin and then Blake had done, Wordsworth argues for the reciprocal relationship of mental structures and political institutions: "It is the province of education to rectify the erroneous notions which a habit of oppression . . . may have created." The point is a dual one: apart from knowledge at the level of information, "facts," Wordsworth refers to the more powerful sets of notions, the mental habits, the total ideological structures that (in a phrase of Shelley's from the manuscript of *A Philosophical View of Reform*) "cement oppression."[27]

The political theory of fictionality or fictional theory of politics appears in brief simplicity. Wordsworth says outright: "The King's name is confessedly a mere fiction" (*A Letter to the Bishop of Llandaff*, 149). As in Blake's parable, fictionality freezes into oppression: the people "confound the person with the power," the figment with the given, the fictional with the real. Democracy, Wordsworth argues in the Llandaff letter, will mitigate this delusion.

Even apart from monarchy and aristocracy, however, "another distinction will arise amongst mankind" and this is "the distinction of wealth" (*A Letter to the Bishop of Llandaff*, 152). Wealth is not an indifferent or objective reality operating only in material terms: "Wealth," writes Wordsworth, "not only can secure itself, but includes even an oppressive *principle*" (my stress). "Extremes of poverty and riches have a necessary tendency to corrupt the human heart." What can be said of aristocrat and monarch thus applies in Wordsworth's argument to the distinctions of wealth: titles and marks of inequality are what he calls "badges of fictitious superiority." Fictions undergirding aristocracy of all kinds proliferate, he suggests, as dissimulation in public and private life. Fictions in the sense of falsehoods multiply in proportion as their fictional status is forgotten; their power to oppress inheres in our amnesia.

Accordingly, Wordsworth writes of Burke's and Watson's argument on the permanent (eternal) authority of the Constitution: "We and our posterity were bound to cherish a cor[p]se at the bosom." This argument about the authority of an unamended constitution is of course also important in Paine's *Rights of Man*. Wordsworth argues that "the consequence of such fatal delusion would be that they must entirely draw off their attention not only from the government but from their governors" (*A Letter to the Bishop of Llandaff*, 158).

I emphasize: For Wordsworth the political doctrine is a delusion, and delusions can be fatal. They also have, pointedly in this context, the power and tendency to deflect attention from what is actually going on.

The revolutionary rhetoric that Wordsworth uses in 1793 does not last long, as I have suggested. In 1796, he writes (in the form of a preface for his own play, *The Borderers*) an essay that is a counterattack on the critique founded in fictional theory. Wordsworth says of his play's central character—who is the villain of the piece—that "in his retirement he is impelled to examine the reasonableness of established opinions." In his *Letter to Lord Ellenborough*, Shelley says similarly that Thomas Paine and his publisher are on trial and under sentence because they "questioned established opinions."[28] Wordsworth says that Oswald, his central character, is "a moral sceptic"—and he produces this moral skepticism, this tendency to question established opinion, as an explanation of his criminal insanity (preface to *The Borderers*, 98).

By 1796, Wordsworth appears hostile about such skepticism, sensitive to its power and danger: "Power is much more easily manifested in destroying than in creating." That charge of destructiveness has often been made against deconstruction critics—what is charged negatively with skepticism is seen as dangerously inimical to the positive constructs and assumptions on which we have in the past relied. It makes us nervous (it makes Wordsworth nervous) to be shown so compellingly that those constructs and assumptions *are* constructs and assumptions. Fond of them now, dependent on them now, it would be a more comfortable repose if we could again take them for absolute truths. Such a delusion is however undermined by the skeptical critique, which is a critique of ideological formations. Paradoxically, it is undermined by the very critique that Wordsworth himself had written three years earlier. It is the villain Oswald now who (in Wordsworth's words) "is perpetually ch[u]sing [or chasing] a phantom" (preface to *The Borderers*, 99). The fictionality to be deplored is no longer (as in 1793) the fictions of royalism; now he criticizes the fictions of skeptical theory.

The theory of fictionality, which is a theory of the imagination, had been liberating in the revolutionary days of deconstructing the prerogative of kings and inherited right of aristocracy. Now, that skeptical act of exposing the fictional thought-forms upon which an ideology rests, unconsciously, is seen as a dangerous vice. Delusions were said to be fatal in 1793; in 1796, unmasking them is said to be the fatal deed. In 1793, skeptical relativity had been an empowering tool for freeing subjects from mind-forged fictions; in 1796, this weapon in the hands of skeptics is to be feared.

Wordsworth's arguments concerning the mind's activity in the construction of ideology have thus changed. Imaginative construction and deconstruction are in 1796 presented as a nihilistic pit into which the imaginative thinker has fallen; in 1793, such an imaginative deconstruction and reconstruction of the social world had set that thinker free. In 1796, Wordsworth is hostile to imagination.

Of course he works his way back to a fondness for it, theorizing it all over again in a wholly different way. What I will be showing in the remaining illustrations from Wordsworth's work is his reversal of value that happens yet once more: having learned to deplore the former concept of his devotion—imagination and skeptical relativity—he comes to embrace it again in the work of his maturity, but differently. Wordsworth refictionalizes his theory of fiction, and he re-forms his theory of ideological formations.

About a decade later, in 1805, Wordsworth writes to an abstraction called "Duty": "In the light of truth thy Bondman let me live."[29] But by this time he has reforged his theory of fictionality to make it consort with this language of bonds, as once it consorted with the language of liberty and even regicide. Language of bonds, of course, had long been recurrent among the British poets and polemicists sympathetic to the democratic revolutions of the late eighteenth century: for example,

the chains are the cunning of weak and tame minds which have power . . .

(Blake, *The Marriage of Heaven and Hell* [1790], plate 16)

And this place our forefathers made for man!
. . . at the clanking hour,
. . . the steams and vapour of his dungeon.

(Coleridge, "The Dungeon" [1798])[30]

. . . the mysterious veil formed by laws, by prejudice, and by precedent, shall be rent asunder . . . Justice herself shall appear . . . her fetters shall be unbound.

(Mary Hays, *Appeal to the Men of Britain on Behalf of Women* [1798])[31]

. . . thought is an essential link in the chain.

(Godwin, *Political Justice* [1793])[32]

Was not the world a vast prison, and women born slaves?

(Mary Wollstonecraft, *The Wrongs of Woman* [1798])[33]

Wordsworth uses frequently this imagery, which carries a political and specifically revolutionary content: in "Ode: Intimations of Immortality" [1802, 1804], "Shades of the prison-house begin to close"; that poem pictures "a

Master o'er a Slave"; and in "To Toussaint L'Ouverture" [1802], Wordsworth depicts the Haitian leader who resisted Napoleon's restoration of slavery: "Alone in some deep dungeon's earless den." Even here, however, in "To Toussaint L'Ouverture," Wordsworth transforms his rhetoric of bondage to accommodate a more cheerful tone: "Wear rather in thy bonds a chearful brow." I shall argue later that this change in tone is a rhetorical maneuver with historically specifiable importance; here, I want simply to show that the discourse of bondage, which had characterized Wordsworth's poetry no less than others' in the immediately post-Revolutionary years, persists, though transfigured, in his later and ostensibly more conservative poems.

The dual concerns of the preface to the *Lyrical Ballads*, however, involve more than the common topic of bondage or liberty; that concretely political frame of reference is, as I have said, characteristically joined with an explicit treatment of the mind's involvement in the construction of the social order. This rhetoric, too, undergoes substantial transformation in Wordsworth's work; in the 1799 *Prelude*, Wordsworth includes this new way of formulating the mind's involvement in the formation and order of the real world: he ascribes it to babies. In infants—now, not politicians, kings, priests, tyrants, but babies—there is

> A virtue which irradiates and exalts
> All objects through all intercourse of sense.
> No outcast he, bewildered and depressed;
> Along his infant veins are interfused
> The gravitation and the filial bond
> Of nature that connect him with the world.
> . . . .
> . . . his mind,
> Creates, creator and receiver both,
> Working but in alliance with the works
> Which it beholds. Such, verily, is the first
> Poetic spirit of our human life.
>
> (2:289–306)[34]

The power which had been treated in openly political terms (as in the *Letter to the Bishop of Llandaff*) is here presented in a frame of psychological relevance; what had organized the social world is now discussed in the language of privacy, of an individual and infant mind. The faculty of creating the shapes we call reality belongs to the apparently safe confinement of infancy, ideality, and privacy. This account elides what Shelley's includes—an *explicit* culmination and point in the reformation of social and political life.

The extent to which Wordsworth would transpose his theory of fictionality into the safe space of his private head is likewise exhibited in the following passage:[35]

> At the first hour of morning, when the vale
> Lay quiet in an utter solitude . . .
> Oft in those moments such a holy calm
> Did overspread my soul that I forgot
> The agency of sight, and what I saw
> Appeared like something in myself, a dream,
> A prospect in my mind.
>
> (2:393–401)

The fictionality of reality, the mind's participation in the composition of the world, is here presented in a way that permits internal evasion. In contrast to *The Borderers* preface of 1796, Wordsworth *does* in 1799 recover the theory of fictionality enough to articulate the mind's shaping power—

> An auxiliar light
> Came from my mind, which on the setting sun
> Bestowed new splendor.
>
> (2:417–19)

The power, or rather the *sign* of power, has been displaced from political struggle to personal sunsets. In Romantic discourse, of course, *sun* and its *setting* are not entirely personal or neutrally descriptive images; rather, they are icons in the discourse of liberty and enlightenment. For example, in *Salisbury Plain* Wordsworth narrates his return to England after the violent demise of the French revolutionary ideal; war, bloodshed, and economic inequality are his themes in the poem that scarcely veils its lament for the failed revolution: "The sun unheeded sunk."[36] This iconography of the sun is important for interpretation of the great "Ode: Intimations of Immortality" in its most political frame—for example,

> The sunshine is a glorious birth;
>   But yet I know, where'er I go,
> That there hath passed away a glory from the earth.
>
> (ll:16–18)

The 1799 *Prelude* engages this symbol of democratic revolution with its ideological framework ("Came from my mind"), almost exactly as Coleridge does, in *France: An Ode*:

> Thou rising Sun! thou blue rejoicing Sky!
>   Yea, every thing that is and will be free!
>   Bear witness for me, wheresoe'er ye be,
>   With what deep worship I have still adored
>   The spirit of divinest Liberty.
>
> (ll:17–21)

This ode's last stanza emphasizes the need for ideological transformation to redeem and undergird the merely physical one that had, by 1798, collapsed into tyranny.

At about the same time, and enduringly afterward, Wordsworth allows a language of domination, oppression, and authoritarian hierarchy to invade his treatments of fictionality and imagination. Wordsworth reintegrates his theory of fictionality with this more intellectualized and more openly ideological frame of reference (and I use the word, "ideology," in its theoretical sense). For example, in the 1805 *Prelude*:

> This love more intellectual cannot be
> Without imagination, which in truth
> Is but another name for absolute strength.
>
> (13:166–68)

Phrases like "absolute strength" have been transcoded out of the language of politics and physical conflict, and are placed into the language of conceptualization. As Antonio Gramsci points out, however, this movement from material force to intellectual levels of power and consent does not dissipate political power, but rather solidifies it; Gramsci's name for this displacement from physical force to the intellectual levels which are contrived to produce consent is *hegemony*.

The fact that a hierarchically organized system of political power rests on this kind of abstract idealization is treated by a famous passage, also from the 1805 version of the *Prelude*—the poet's moonlight climb of Mt. Snowdon:

> A meditation rose in me that night
> Upon the lonely mountain when the scene
> Had passed away . . .
> The perfect image of a mighty mind . . .
> Nature . . . and
> That domination which she oftentimes exerts . . .
> That even the grossest minds must see and hear . . .
> . . . the glorious faculty
> Which higher minds bear with them as their own.
>
> (13:66–90)

Not only does Wordsworth write here of "domination"—his language encoding, as it almost always does, the ideological preoccupations that were formative for him all his adult life—he also is prepared to praise a class of higher minds whom he distinguishes from the vulgar, the "grossest minds," in his phrase (cf. "The Sensual and the Dark" who, in Coleridge's famous phrase, "rebel in vain" [*France: An Ode*, l.85]).

There is a great ideological distance between this language about lifting "the grossest minds" and "the language of conversation of the middle and lower classes of society." In the 1790s (even, sometimes, in 1798) Wordsworth still wrote openly in the cause which had, by 1805, failed so totally— internally by its collapse into bloodshed and tyranny on the part of the Jacobins, as in their execution of the relatively peaceful Girondin, and externally by the notorious invasion of the peaceful Swiss republic in 1798. In England, too, forces abounded which drove the discourse of liberty out of the empire (as for Paine and Priestley), or underground; energies of revolution were concealed under the sign of the mental (rather than material) life. In 1797–1798, Paine was tried and convicted; his lawyer, Thomas Erskine, was then tried for sedition; Coleridge had testified at the trial for sedition of William Frend, and thus knew the power of the state and its reactionary tendencies personally, as a participant in the state's proceedings as well as, later, a journalist reporting on both the antirevolutionary war effort and the domestic poverty and bread riots which that war effort brought about. Coleridge and Wordsworth both knew of the spy who had been sent to watch them as they looked so suspiciously over the Bristol channel. Symbolically vested treatments of revolutionary ideology were at once intellectually richer for the Romantic writers of this generation, and also more safe, even more feasible, in the most narrowly practical terms.

Subsequently Wordsworth's poetry characteristically displaces his ideological frame; his poetry transcodes political issues to conceptual levels where *minds* are enslaved or liberated. My point is that this transposition to a manifest level of ideological preoccupation—that is, treatment of the structures of thought—need not be interpreted as a reactionary retreat into Wordsworth's private head. Rather than the turncoat politics of toryism, which Shelley and Byron certainly thought it was, this rhetorical transposition may represent a submergence of the discourse of freedom, aimed precisely at preserving and empowering that discourse, rather than effacing it. Perhaps the most conspicuous example from the *Prelude*, and the one with which I shall conclude, is an insertion in the last (1850) version of an incident that ostensibly occurred in 1790, when Wordsworth first went to revolutionary France. He describes, in 1850, his visit to the Convent of Chartreuse in these terms: he saw a

> soul-affecting solitude . . .
> . . . though our eyes had seen,
> As toward the sacred mansion we advanced,
> Arms flashing, and a military glare
> Of riotous men commissioned to expel
> The blameless inmates [of the monastery] . . .
> Stay, stay your sacrilegious hands!
> 　　　　　. . . spare

These courts of mystery . . .
[the priests] Leave far behind life's treacherous vanities . . .
. . . to equalise in God's pure sight
Monarch and peasant.

(6:421–56)

The revolutionists whom in fact he had *joined*, whose cause he had in fact *shared*, are here called "riotous men"; the church institution, equalitarian dispersal of whose lands and profits constituted a revolutionary goal, are rendered (half a century later) as "blameless men." And the French revolutionary dream of equality, for whose realization Wordsworth had been such an eloquent and committed proponent, is apparently denied. I would argue, however, that equality is displaced in the symbolic discourse rather than elided.[37] It is the violence and tyranny of the Reign of Terror which Wordsworth repudiates (Wordsworth was one of the few revolutionary Girondin to escape alive when the Jacobin party seized power, advocated force rather than democracy, and effected political purges). The ideology of democratic revolution remains even in the latest (1850) emendations: Wordsworth celebrates at a distance of sixty years the "dances of liberty" which he had seen in 1790 (6:71), and he reiterates the goal of the French Revolution—"to equalise . . . Monarch and peasant" (6:455–561). Such diction would hardly count as a symbolic *displacement* of the political theme, except that Wordsworth has, in the sixth book of *The Prelude*, dislocated this language from the Bastille to the convent. Britain's counterrevolutionary politics still flourished, of course, and the *Prelude* places the discourse of liberty and equality under the sign of orthodoxy; but the ideological content of that discourse has thus been permitted to survive.

Equality of monarch and peasant, the freedom and flourishing of all classes of society, are here transcoded as a figure of speech, exempted by the abstraction of the discourse from the "Shades of the prison-house" which had begun, in the 1790s, to close around supporters in England of the Revolution in France. The claims of political equality and amelioration of economic class conflict are, however, preserved, and even deepened, by this maneuver; Wordsworth's poetic act is semiotic in its medium, and its symbolic submergence is conditioned by *Realpolitik* as well as intellectual sophistication.

A Romanticism which is a conservative retreat into the privacy of one's own subjectivity has for too long been permitted to constitute our notion of *all* British Romanticism. These values and tendencies are *not* all of Romanticism; they are not even all of Wordsworth, as his own life and work demonstrate amply. Wordsworth's poems from 1799 onward constitute a politically and ideologically invested action on the world. Notions of Romanticism which identify the literature almost wholly as a conservative idealizing have of course flourished for more than a century. By this interpretation, Romanticism can threaten no one and can launch no critical change. But a "double interpretation" of the kind that Coleridge (another supposed apostate) calls for must be brought to the symbolic discourse of Romanticism. The apparent reversals of symbolic form transform evasion to engagement. As the supposed apostate Coleridge states explicitly,[38] the poets' aims included the referring of *action* to *opinion*, of *opinion* to *principle*; the teleological journey then transfers "absolute principles to politics."[39] This sequence, and not an idealist evasion, animates, drives, and ideologically warrants the apparently mentalistic symbols of the high Romantic poetry of Coleridge and no less the poetry of Wordsworth as well.

The passage from the 1850 *Prelude* in which Wordsworth displaces "equality" into merely spiritual realms warrants juxtaposition against a passage that he wrote much earlier, and which actually seems to interrogate the supposed conservative retreat: in 1800, in the fragment of his planned (but never completed) epic, *The Recluse*, Wordsworth had written:

> Paradise, and groves
> Elysian, Fortunate islands . . .
> . . . Wherefore should they be
> A History or but a dream . . .

> (ll.996–999)

Why, in Wordsworth's revised phrase, should they be a "mere fiction of what never was"? Wordsworth's writings, early and late, exhibit the engagement of fictional forms with political realities. Wordsworth's works enable us to ask, apart from the fiction of what never was: What about the fiction of what it *actually* was? And the fictions that are with us now, and the fictions that are to come.

NOTES

1. An earlier version of this paper was presented in September 1988 as a lecture in the series, *Wordsworth and the Age of English Romanticism*, at College Station, Texas, sponsored by The Texas Committee for the Humanities and the Interdisciplinary Group for Historical Literary Study. I wish to express my gratitude to the coordinators of that series, Jeffrey Cox and Mark Lussier, and to the attentive audience, and to the other speakers in the series, especially Jonathan Bate and Marjorie Levinson, whose learned and engaging lectures stimulated memorable dialogue.

2. Among the books I have in mind here, the following are specifically germane to the present essay's argument: Jerome J. McGann, *The Romantic Ideology* (Chicago: University of Chicago Press, 1983), and *Social Values and Poetic Acts* (Cambridge, Mass.: Harvard University Press, 1988); James K. Chandler, *Wordsworth's Second*

Nature: A Study of the Poetry and Politics (Chicago: University of Chicago Press, 1984); Marjorie Levinson, *Wordsworth's Great Period Poems: Four Essays* (Cambridge: Cambridge University Press, 1986); David Simpson, *Wordsworth's Historical Imagination: The Poetry of Displacement* (New York: Methuen, 1987); and Daniel P. Watkins, *Keats's Poetry and the Politics of the Imagination* (Rutherford, N.J.: Fairleigh Dickinson University Press, 1989). For a polemical account of the theoretical issues at stake here, in Romantic studies, see Terence Allan Hoagwood, "Keats and Social Context: *Lamia*," *Studies in English Literature* 29 (1989): 675–97. On the specifically political issues that surface most tenaciously in the period, see Chandler's account of Burke and Watson, and also Sir William Drummond, *Philosophical Sketches of the Principles of Society and Government* (London: W. Bulmer, 1795). This book has been issued in facsimile edition, with my critical essay on Drummond (Delmar, N.Y.: Scholars' Facsimiles and Reprints, 1986). A more extended and philosophical account of the political philosophy of the period is my *Skepticism and Ideology: Shelley's Political Prose and Its Philosophical Context from Bacon to Marx* (Iowa City: University of Iowa Press, 1988).

3. Wordsworth, preface to *Lyrical Ballads*, in *William Wordsworth: Selected Prose*, ed. John O. Hayden (Harmondsworth: Penguin, 1988), especially pp. 280, 292 (unless otherwise indicated, all quotations from Wordsworth's prose refer to this edition); Percy Bysshe Shelley, *A Philosophical View of Reform*, in *The Complete Works of Percy Bysshe Shelley*, ed. Roger Ingpen and Walter E. Peck (London: Ernest Benn, 1926–1930), 7:6; and Shelley, *A Defence of Poetry*, in *Complete Works*, e.g., 7:121, 130, 134.

4. Shelley, *A Defence of Poetry*, in *Complete Works*, 7:125.

5. For the relevant philosophical argumentation, see Sir William Drummond, *Academical Questions* and Hoagwood, *Skepticism and Ideology*.

6. Shelley, *A Philosophical View of Reform*, in *Complete Works*, 7:20.

7. Rousseau, *The Social Contract*, trans. G. D. H. Cole (New York: Dutton, 1950), pp. 4, 7.

8. Michel Foucault, *The Order of Things: An Archeology of the Human Sciences* (an anon. trans. of *Les mots et les choses* [1966]) (1970; repr. New York: Random House, 1973), pp. xi, xix.

9. Anthony Giddens, *New Rules of Sociological Method: A Positive Critique of Interpretative Sociologies* (London: Hutchinson, 1976); Giddens, *Studies in Social and Political Theory* (London: Hutchinson, 1977); Giddens, *The Constitution of Society: Outline of the Theory of Structuration* (Cambridge: Polity Press, 1984); John B. Thompson, "The Theory of Structuration," in Thompson's *Studies in the Theory of Ideology* (Berkeley: University of California Press, 1984), pp. 148–72.

10. David V. Erdman, "The Dawn of Universal Patriotism: William Wordsworth Among the British in Revolutionary France," in *The Age of William Wordsworth*, ed. Kenneth R. Johnston and Gene W. Ruoff (New Brunswick: Rutgers University Press, 1987), pp. 3–20; Nicholas Roe, *Wordsworth and Coleridge: The Radical Years* (Oxford: Oxford University Press, 1988).

11. Hans Georg Gadamer, *Truth and Method*, trans. Garrett Barden and John Cumming (New York: Seabury Press, 1975); and Gadamer, *Philosophical Hermeneutics*, ed. David E. Linge (1976; repr. Berkeley: University of California Press, 1977). See also Jurgen Habermas's critique of Gadamer's argument: "A Review of Gada-

mer's *Truth and Method*," in *The Hermeneutic Tradition*, ed. Gayle L. Ormiston and Alan D. Schrift (Albany: State University of New York Press, 1990), pp. 213–44; and Habermas's major study, *Knowledge and Human Interests* (Boston: Beacon Press, 1972).

12. I make that claim in *Skepticism and Ideology*, e.g., p. 20; I am there following Kenneth Neill Cameron's excellent account in his *Shelley: The Golden Years* (Cambridge, Mass.: Harvard University Press, 1974), p. 149.

13. Coleridge, *Biographia Literaria*, ed. James Engell and W. Jackson Bate (Princeton: Princeton University Press, 1983), 2: 5–106. I call Coleridge's description "disingenuous" because, I would argue, Coleridge too transposes his ideological critique into the latent forms of symbolism; but Coleridge's work is matter for another essay.

14. For information on Charles James Fox, see John W. Derry, "Charles James Fox, in *Biographical Dictionary of Modern British Radicals: Volume 1, 1770–1830*, ed. Joseph O. Baylen and Norbert J. Gossman (Sussex: Harvester Press, 1979), pp. 177–82.

15. Blake, *The Marriage of Heaven and Hell*, pl. 11, from *The Complete Poetry and Prose of William Blake*, ed. David V. Erdman (Berkeley: University of California Press, 1982).

16. See Fredric Jameson, *The Political Unconscious: Narrative as a Socially Symbolic Act* (1981; repr. Ithaca: Cornell University Press, 1986), especially pp. 28–31 on the ideological investments of literary interpretation.

17. John Stuart Mill, "The Subjection of Women," in *Essays on Sex Equality: John Stuart Mill and Harriet Taylor Mill*, ed. Alice S. Rossi (Chicago: University of Chicago Press, 1970), p. 141; and compare Harriet Taylor's arguments on the intellectuality of women, in "Enfranchisement of Women," 91–121.

18. The sort of critique which exposes the fictitiousness of custom and prejudice, as mental structures, is of course founded in arguments of Godwin's in *Political Justice*, and arguments of Wollstonecraft's from *A Vindication of the Rights of Woman*; see also Mary Hays, *Appeal to the Men of Great Britain on Behalf of Women* (London: Joseph Johnson, 1798).

19. Antonio Gramsci, *Selections from the Prison Notebooks of Antonio Gramsci*, ed. and trans. Quintin Hoare and Geoffrey Nowell Smith (New York: International Publishers, 1971), pp. 12–13 *et passim*.

20. Joseph Priestley, *Doctrines of Heathen Philosophy Compared with Those of Revelation* (Northumberland: John Binns, 1804). See also the facsimile edition of this work (Delmar, N.Y.: Scholars' Facsimiles, 1988), with my critical essay of introduction.

21. See Robert Schofield's commentary in *A Scientific Autobiography of Joseph Priestley* (Cambridge, Mass.: MIT Press, 1963); and Schofield, "Priestley," in *Dictionary of Scientific Biography*, ed. Charles Coulston Gillespie (New York: Charles Scribner's Sons, 1975).

22. Of course the regicide and the interregnum interrupt the virtual continuance of those institutions that expressed this implacable given, the divine right of kings; the *doctrine*, however, and its eternal truth, do not undergo a revolution in the minds of monarchists until at least 1688; accordingly, the Restoration is perceived *as* a restoration, not an innovation. To restore the divinely warranted order for the city of

man is to recognize no interruption in the divine authority of its warrant. Of course the doctrine had its critics, as the regicide makes grotesquely plain; Hobbes's formulations of the social contract are an important instance of critical conceptions prior to the Restoration, and so are the arguments in Milton's *The Tenure of Kings and Magistrates*. On these issues see Christopher Hill, *Intellectual Origins of the English Revolution* (Oxford: Clarendon Press, 1965). I am grateful to Donald Dickson and Margaret Ezell for conversations about the English Revolution, which led me to recognize the need for this note of qualification.

23. Here again, I am indebted to Chandler's *Wordsworth's Second Nature*, especially pp. 13ff. See also my introduction to Drummond's *Philosophical Sketches of the Principles of Society and Government*.

24. William Godwin, *Memoirs of the Author of a Vindication of the Rights of Woman* (London: Joseph Johnson, 1798), p. 76.

25. The copy of *Philosophical Sketches* which Drummond inscribed to Watson is in the Carl H. Pforzheimer Collection, New York Public Library. For my opportunity to examine it I wish to record my gratitude to Donald H. Reiman and to Mihai Handrea.

26. Drummond, *Academical Questions*, pp. 166–67.

27. See Donald H. Reiman's transcription of the manuscript of *A Philosophical View of Reform*, in *Shelley and His Circle* (Cambridge, Mass.: Harvard University Press, 1973), 6:963.

28. Shelley, *A Letter to Lord Ellenborough*, in *Complete Works*, 5:284.

29. Except for quotations from *The Prelude*, all of my references to Wordsworth's poetry refer to *William Wordsworth*, ed. Stephen Gill (Oxford: Oxford University Press, 1984). Gill's edition prints the earliest completed versions of poems (published or where necessary in manuscript), and this fact makes this edition especially useful for arguments founded on historically specific transformations. Compare the long-standard edition by Ernest de Selincourt and Helen Darbishire, *Poetical Works of William Wordsworth*, rev. ed., 5 vols. (Oxford: Clarendon Press, 1952–1959), which uses the latest authorized versions of the poems (1850).

30. Quotations from Coleridge's poetry refer to *Poetical Works*, ed. Ernest Hartley Coleridge (1912; repr. Oxford: Oxford University Press, 1986).

31. Mary Hays, *Appeal to the Men of Britain on Behalf of Women*, p. 100.

32. William Godwin, *Enquiry Concerning Political Justice and Its Influence on Morals and Happiness* [1793], ed. F. E. L. Priestley (Toronto: University of Toronto Press, 1946), 1:403.

33. Mary Wollstonecraft, *The Wrongs of Woman* [1798], ed. Gary Kelly (1976; repr. Oxford: Oxford University Press, 1988), p. 79.

34. Quotations from *The Prelude* refer to *The Prelude: 1799, 1805, 1850*, ed. Jonathan Wordsworth, M. H. Abrams, and Stephen Gill (New York: Norton, 1979).

35. I take this metaphor for the ideology of reductive individualism from Reed Whittemore: "Oh private head, I love your small size, / I love your shrinking thinking" ("Meditative Stomp on the State of Something," in *The Feel of Rock: Poems of Three Decades* [Washington, D.C.: Dryad Press, 1982], 105).

36. This phrase opens stanza nine of the poem; owing to this poem's long and complex history of revisions, an especially valuable resource is *The Salisbury Plain Poems*, ed. Stephen Gill (Ithaca: Cornell University Press, 1975).

37. In *Wordsworth: The Sense of History* (Stanford: Stanford University Press, 1989) Alan Liu argues differently, though treating the same issues with respect to the same passages that I discuss here. Liu writes that "the description of the 1790 tour in Book 6, read in its own context, is a sustained effort to deny history by asserting nature as the separating mark constitutive of the egotistical self" and "Book 6 creates a mirror denying history"; I have tried to suggest that submergence is not denial. I find useful Liu's observation that "by a conceit carried in diction—sovereign, seizing, charter—Wordsworth already allows history to infiltrate the very core of nature. Nature is the ground, but the figure—the Revolution—tends to usurp the status of the ground" (14).

38. Thomas McFarland's essay, "Coleridge and the Charge of Political Apostasy" (in *Coleridge's "Biographia Literaria": Text and Meaning*, ed. Frederick Burwick [Columbus: Ohio State University Press, 1989], pp. 191–232), also argues, on different grounds, against the commonplace assumption that Coleridge engaged in apostasy, turning from the radicalism of his youth to the conservatism of his age.

39. Coleridge, *The Friend*, in *Samuel Taylor Coleridge*, ed. H. J. Jackson (Oxford: Oxford University Press, 1985), pp. 624, 622. In Jackson's fine edition this essay is collected conveniently for juxtaposition with earlier and more openly political prose—especially the "Moral and Political Lecture," where the reversal of manifest content is most openly politicized.

CHAPTER EIGHT

Beyond the Valley of Production; or,
De factorum natura:
A Dialogue

JEROME J. MCGANN

> Not that I agree with everything that I said in this
> essay. There is much with which I entirely disagree.
> The essay simply represents an artistic standpoint,
> and in aesthetic criticism attitude is everything.
> . . . A Truth in Art is that whose contradictory is
> also true.
> *(Oscar Wilde, "The Truth of Masks")*

> But then the fact's a fact—and 'tis the part
> Of a true poet to escape from fiction.
> *(Byron,* Don Juan *Canto VIII)*

[INTERLOCUTORS: J. J. ROME, ANNE MACK, GEORG MANNEJC]

JJR: It was a fine lecture—at once learned, elegant, and imaginative.* He even sketched the late nineteenth-century revolution in decorated book production, and described the links—really, the unbroken continuity—between that history and the visual aspects of key works produced in the early modernist period between 1910 and 1930. He wanted to show that the first two book installments of Pound's *Cantos*—Cantos 1–16 were published in 1925 and Cantos 17–27 in 1928—are at once an apotheosis and final transcendence of the work done by William Morris and the Kelmscott Press, Charles Ricketts and the Vale Press, Lucien Pissarro and the Eragny Press—Doves Press, Cuala Press, Unicorn Press, Ovid Press, publishers like John Lane, Day and Son, William Mosher, and so many others that trace themselves, in the nineteenth century, back to Blake and the Chiswick Press. The intimate relation between book production and textual meaning—that is, the hermeneutic significance of book production economics, on one hand, and all the material aspects of "the text" on the other: these matters were brought forward until one could not evade the general conclusion he was trying to argue, that between the emergence of the Pre-Raphaelite movement and 1930, the literary text was consistently being imagined and executed as a *social* text in the most material way.[1]

And of course an even larger argument was always suggesting itself. The farthest thing from McGann's mind was the idea that this history of decorated texts was a special case. The lecture assumed the audience's knowledge of his sociohistorical interpretive approach to nondecorated textual production throughout the nineteenth century, as well as his more general work on "theory of texts"—for instance, the detailed arguments for a theory of texts as comprising a double helix of grammatological and bibliographical codes, or the more recent elaboration of the three forms of "reading" (linear, spatial, and radial). And all this in the still larger context of the parallel work being carried out by others—Robert Darnton, Donald McKenzie, and the large group of people now working the fields of cultural studies and literary pragmatics, or the smaller group of scholars (people like Michael Warren, Randall McLeod, Stephen Urkowitz) who have been exploding our imagination of the Shakespearean texts.

AM: What an enthusiast you are! McKenzie's work, to me, is "confused in argument," and I have no patience at all with his "politicizing of scholarship." As for McGann, I remain unpersuaded by his polemical schemes. "Up to now his effectiveness has been seriously undercut by a lack of rigorous thought, at least as reflected in his often careless prose."[2] The best part of the lecture was the part you left out entirely—that brief interlude when he engaged the specific example of *Hugh Selwyn Mauberley*.

———————

Pound was of course well aware of the semiotic potential which lay in the physical aspects of book and text production. One of his most famous poems—the imagist manifesto "In a Station of the Metro"—has been reprinted and commented upon many times, but because scholars have not gone back to the original printing of the poem, none have recognized the extreme performativity of this text as originally conceived.

The poem was first printed in Harriet Monroe's new magazine *Poetry* along with eleven other short poems by Pound. Of these eleven poems, ten appear in standard typographical form—but not "In a Station of the Metro." This, the last of the series printed, appears in the following unusual typographical format:[3]

IN A STATION OF THE METRO

The apparition   of these faces   in the crowd   :
Petals   on a wet, black   bough   .

The arrangement of the text's signs distinctly recalls Pound's typewriting habits—especially in the extended spacing before the final punctuation marks. Pound regularly left this kind of spacing before various marks of punctuation in his typescripts. The point to be emphasized, however, is that he did not *regularly* carry this habit over to the printed texts.

Pound himself (not Harriet Monroe) was almost certainly responsible for the performative typography of "In a Station of the Metro." In any case, we know he took an active part in the physical presentation of many of his later texts. The case of *Hugh Selwyn Mauberley* is especially interesting. This book was published by John Rodker's Ovid Press in 1920. Rodker was an important figure on the scene of modernism as both a writer and a producer of some key modernist books, including Eliot's *Ara Vos Prec* (also published in 1920) as well as the first two book installments of Pound's *Cantos*.

An extant set of corrected proof sheets of *Hugh Selwyn Mauberley* displays Pound's recurrent directions to the printer about minor details of the text's physical presentation. Next to the half title Pound writes "? higher in page," and the motto page has two of his notes: "T[op] of margin shd always be narrower than bottom. even excessively so." and next to the motto: "Set higher in page." On page 10 (the opening page of section "II. The Age Demanded") Pound circles the printer's handwritten number 10 at the top and pulls it to the bottom with the note: "numerals at bottom of page." Once again Pound adds a note for the placement of the page's block of type: "Set Higher."[4]

Perhaps the most startling typographical intervention was made in Pound's manipulation of the book's decorated capitals. *Hugh Selwyn Mauberley* was designed to have these ornamental initials (made by the artist Edward Wadsworth) at the beginning of each new section of the work. In the published book, however, there is one deviation from the pattern: the initial letter on page 16 (the "Brennbaum" section) is an italic capital, not a decorated capital. The letter is the letter "T" (the "Brennbaum" section opens with the line, "The skylike limpid eyes").

Let me begin by stating in simple declarative terms the significance of that italic cap, so far as Pound was concerned. It constituted a bibliographical allusion to what Pound called the practices of "old printers" who, when they ran out of decorated initials, would use "plain caps or italics" instead. The italic cap was a deliberate moment of modernist constructivism in the text—a moment which, by breaking from the pattern of the decorated capitals, called attention to the book's self-conscious imitation of decorated book production. A good part of the satire in the poem operates through the bibliographical code consciously deployed at the typographical level of the work. The physique of *Hugh Selwyn Mauberley* raises an image of an artistic practice that would triumph over all that "The Age Demanded." The fact that this work, this book, is itself a part of what "the age demanded" only underscores the extremity of Pound's satiric idealism.

How shall I persuade you that this "reading" of the italic capital on page

16 is not simply my personal interpretive fantasia? The answer is, by laying out the scholarly evidence. The extant proofs of the book are now in the Rodker collection of the Humanities Research Center (HRC) at the University of Texas. They are a composite set, with two pages from an earlier proof (i.e., received pages 21 and 22 containing the sections "Envoi [1919]" and "1920 [Mauberley]").

Collation of the HRC composite proof with the first edition shows that at least one more proof of the text must have been made. This fact is apparent not least of all from the decorated capitals in the proof. In a number of cases these do not correspond to the letter called for by the text, and in each of these instances Pound crosses out the wrong capital and indicates the proper letter (i.e., on pages 12 and 13, where the printer had put decorated capitals "F" and "L," respectively).

In order to print *Hugh Selwyn Mauberley* according to the design program evidently decided upon, the printer needed five decorated Ts. He needed one for the first letter of each of the following sections of the poem: sections III, IV, V, "Brennbaum," and "1920 (Mauberley)," corresponding to pages 11, 12, 13, 16, and 22, respectively. However, during his initial course of typesetting the printer seems to have had access only to two decorated Ts. He used one to set the type on the separate earlier proof of pages 21 and 22, while on the other set of coherent proofs—the main body of the extant material, which includes pages 11, 12, 13, and 16—he only puts a decorated T on page 11.

In correcting the proofs Pound noted the three instances where the printer put the wrong decorated capital (i.e., on pages 12, 13, and 16). So, for example, the decorated initial on page 12, which is wrongly an F, is corrected by Pound, and at this point he adds the significant note in the margin: "Use plain caps or italics as in H. S. Mauberley [i.e., as in the italic half-title]. The old printers did this when fancy caps ran out."[5] Similarly, the decorated initials in the HRC proof for pages 13 and 16 are not Ts; Pound indicates the proper letter in each case, and on page 13 has this note: "Supply of Ts ran out."

But if Rodker's printer did not have his five decorated Ts when he was actually setting the type at the first two proof stages, he must have had access to the five at the final stage of printing. When the book appeared, four of the five Ts were decorated capitals, the fifth being the italic capital which is the central subject of this discussion. It is important that the italic capital in this case should appear on page 16, because in that position one becomes aware of the character's arbitrary placement. That is to say, in the final printed text the single undecorated T does not come as the last in the sequence of initial Ts (the last is on page 22), but as the next to last, on page 16.

One might conclude, from this bibliographical anomaly, that Rodker's printer finally and in *fact* had only four decorated T initials, and that the undecorated T appears on page 16 because *in the final printing sequence* page 16 was the last to be corrected. Page 22, that is to say, already had its decorated T, as we can tell from the extant (early) proof of pages 21 and 22. This theory of the text might be supported from Pound's marginal note next to his page 13 correction of the decorated T: "Supply of Ts ran out."

When Pound wrote that note, however, the proofs he was correcting suggested that the "supply of Ts" had run out with the setting of page 11, not the setting of page 13. However, the note probably does not mean to indicate that Pound thought the "supply of Ts" had run out after page 13. Rather, it must be a general note, indicating his belief—after having had to correct two successive decorated capitals (on pages 12 and 13)—that Rodker's printer had only two decorated Ts.

But we know from the final printed text of *Hugh Selwyn Mauberley* that the printer had—in the end at any rate—access to at least four decorated Ts. Furthermore, we know from other evidence that the printer could have put decorated Ts for all five of the initials on pages 11, 12, 13, 16, and 22. We know this because the Ovid Press edition of Eliot's *Ara Vos Prec* prints each poem with the same set of decorated initials designed by Edward Wadsworth, and in this book six ornamental Ts are needed. All are present in the printed text.

This narrative has involved a thorny mass of detail, so let me summarize its significance from my immediate point of view. Evidently Pound assumed, when he was correcting the HRC proofs, that there were only two decorated Ts in the printer's shop, and on that assumption he imagined a way to make the deficiency a "meaningful" element in the text of the work. In the end, although *Hugh Selwyn Mauberley* could have been printed with five ornamental Ts, a decision was made to leave one of those Ts undecorated, thereby introducing into the typography a symbolic moment it would have otherwise lacked. Tiny as it is, that moment—by the differential it represents—does more to call attention to the work's general bibliographical codes than perhaps any other feature of the text.

More than that, however, the bibliographical moment only functions because of the general historical allusion it entails. *Hugh Selwyn Mauberley* is a satire on the tawdry world of cultured London immediately after the Great War. The 1920 Ovid Press edition, by the symbology of its carefully crafted printing, means to comment on the debasement of art and imagination in the contemporary and commercial world of England; and it means to develop its commentary by aligning itself with what it sees as other, less debased cultures. Pound's poetic sequence is well aware of the limits and ineffectualities of the Pre-Raphaelite inheritance—including the inheritance of the decorated book which the Pre-Raphaelites passed on. Nevertheless, his work is also aware of the faith which the Pre-Raphaelite tradition had kept with those earlier European cultural traditions that Pound saw as less debased and less commercially driven. The italic T on page 16 is not merely Pound's allusion to certain "old printers," it is the index of a massive act of reverential recollection which is being executed in *Hugh Selwyn Mauberley*.

AM: A nice piece of scholarly detective work, that.

JJR: And nicer still, to my mind, because its scholarship is carried out in a consciously invoked hermeneutical horizon. The archival materials and bibliographical analysis fund a larger interpretive and critical program.

AM: True enough—or maybe what you say is *too true*. I mean, McGann's contemporary polemic is so insistent, even messianic, as if he had a mission to rescue the study of poetry from the suffocated enclosures of his various theoretical antagonists: from the New Critics, the structuralists, the intertextualists, the deconstructivists. And yet what has this kind of "historical" criticism done except bring certain new kinds of materials—archival and historical materials—within that same suffocating hermeneutic circle? Memory itself is now being consumed by the aesthetic imagination.

JJR: In this respect, surely, the criticism replicates Pound's own work. Like the *Cantos*, *Hugh Selwyn Mauberley* is a "poem including history," a poem which gives an aesthetic habitation to both past and contemporary historical materials. The criticism operates in the same spirit that the author writ.

AM: Not exactly in the same spirit. It is true, of course, that Pound and McGann both assume the textual foundation of historical understanding: that we can only "know" history through (and as) the texts which deliver it into our hands. It is also true that both are textual materialists, as it were— readers (and writers) whose "texts" are always social, institutional, and *materialized* in specific ways by particular people under specific conditions. But the similarities end there. Pound's work "remembers" certain facts about book production, for example, as part of a general memorializing act in which the present is analyzed and critiqued by the past. Like Blake's illuminated work done a hundred years or more earlier, *Hugh Selwyn Mauberley* is initially imagined and produced as an act of social resistance against an evolving age of mechanical reproduction and its one-dimensional men.

The resistance is raised at the textual level because, in Pound's mind, the immediate world is conditioned by how we receive the past: by *the way* the past is read, as well as *what* from the past is read. The Ovid Press edition of Pound's work—like the first twenty-seven cantos in their original boards— thickens and materializes the text's immediate moment of self-representation. In that very act the work sketches a critical history for the text as it appears before us. It exposes the historical deficiencies imaged (and imagined) in the mass-produced book. Pound's ornamented book is a commentary on the mass-produced book; and book production itself—whether mechanical or handcrafted—becomes, through the poem, the chief emblem and focus of a debased or a healthy social imagination.

JJR: But all that could just as well be said of McGann's criticism—indeed, it seems to me that McGann himself has said (more or less) exactly the same thing, somewhere or other.

AM: But the horizon within which McGann says these things is different. His work is scholarly and descriptive, not critical. What he does may be called literary criticism but it is really nothing more than literary interpretation: that is to say, it is the consumption and reproduction of our institutionalized literary codes (of their materials, means, and modes of production). As I said earlier, it simply offers a new way to pay old debts—a new way to expand the range of institutionalized hermeneutics. It is new historicism with a materialist face.

JJR: But what is it that you want from literary studies—that they become the locus of general social change, if not revolution? So far as the recent "turn to history" is concerned, surely it is enough, as Catherine Gallagher and others have said, that these new literary interests have made deep inroads into the schools and their curricula: "introducing non-canonical texts into the classroom . . . making students more aware of the history and significance of . . . imperialism, slavery, and gender differentiation in Western culture."[6] These are localized social changes, it is true, but because they are taking place within the state's chief ideological apparatus, their effects may be deep and far-reaching.

AM: It comes back to Marx's eleventh thesis on Feuerbach once again, does it not: "The philosophers have only *interpreted* the world in various ways; the point, however, is to *change* it." And at the moment I do not even ask for evidence of significant social change in society at large. Suppose we consider only the academy; or, even more particularly, those special academic regions where cultural literacy is defined and reproduced.

Literary interpretation is one dominant function of education in the human sciences, but the turn to sociohistorical studies has not really altered that function in any significant way. New historicism, materialist or otherwise, is a new set of interpretive procedures. They are being executed, however, entirely within the established social conventions and protocols of "literary studies." It is Stanley Fish's awareness of this situation—his clear view of the ways in which our established "interpretive communities" operate—which leads him to his avuncular remarks on what he has recently called "the young and the restless" left-liberal historical scholars. His soap opera epithet is an excellent index of his general argument: that literary studies today is a professional career whose truth-function is (and is to be) measured by personal success (or, in the jargon of the schools, the ability to persuade the interpretive community of one's peers that one is doing work that is professionally interesting and rewarding).[7]

To interpret the world in various ways, *within the horizon of a community of professional interpreters*, is to carry out the expected and well-established social functions of the group. It is to reinvest the credentials of the group. Furthermore, since this group functions to (re)produce the ideological needs of the state and society at large, its interpretations serve to *conserve* those larger social formations.

GM: But surely—may I enter this conversation for a moment?—everyone now is aware of those limitations. Or do you think that educators and professors are doomed to exhaust themselves and their interpretive acts in careerism or even professionalism? To imagine these things dominating personal or social action is to submit to what Roberto Unger calls "false necessity."[8] And if hermeneutic activity is socially conservative, do you believe that there are *no* aspects of "those larger social formations" which we might do well to conserve? Is the "larger social formation"—are our institutions of letters themselves—wholly and hopelessly debased, in every aspect, root and branch?

Besides, such an absolute distinction between "interpreting" and "changing" something reifies an illusion which a materialist theory of texts is specially armed to expose, as if "interpretation" did not involve specific acts carried out under particular circumstances, and executed *as* certain determinate material forms. Roland Barthes, for some good reasons and to great effect, urged readers in 1971 to move "from work to text."[9] He did so because he wanted to alter our imagination of the literary "work" as a finished and self-defined "thing." His move ushered in what some now think of as the final phase of that idealist program in hermeneutics stretching from Kant and Coleridge on one end, to Gadamer and Derrida on the other.

But for about ten years now we observe readers and writers turning against the Barthesian current and urging us to move "from text to work."[10] Implicit here is an argument to reimagine the term "work" in "textual" terms, and the term "text" in material terms. We do not have to follow Barthes in defining a literary "work" as a closed or finished system. The work named *Hugh Selwyn Mauberley*, for example, comprises a determinate and ongoing series of specific textual productions. Pound has a hand in some but by no means all of these productions. Besides, even for the texts of this poem that he was directly involved with—these include texts printed in 1920 (two texts here), 1921, 1926, 1949, and 1955—the poem's character, even its simple typographical character, changes and shifts.[11]

In the same way, we may think of a "text" as something else—something more determinate—than the fluid medium for free interpretive play which Barthes had imagined. The "text" one *works with* is particular and material, even in the case where one's attention is focused on a certain set of texts: for example, the set of the texts of *Hugh Selwyn Mauberley* which Pound was directly, and more or less deeply, involved with.

But all this may and must be said of literary work in general, which necessarily appears as a series of particular texts produced and reproduced in
different times and places for different uses and ends.

JJR:　And the consequence of what you are saying, for interpretation, is
twofold: first, present "meaning" is shown to emerge from an immediate
dialogue with certain concrete social acts carried out in (and handed down
from) the past; and second, those acts are multiple, so that determinate
choices must be made about how and where to engage with this multiple
past. As such, then, scholarship and literary studies would have to be judged
neutral with respect to the issue of whether they are reactionary, conservative, liberal, or radical. The event is determined by particular choices that
are made, roads taken and not taken.

AM:　How agreeable and sanguine you both sound in your Heideggerian
conversation. Yet it seems to me that you forget—I shall use one of your own
favorite code words—the "particular" character of *literary* work (by which *I*
mean—as I take it that you also mean—imaginative works and their secondary critical treatments).

No doubt [speaking to GM], Coleridge *was* the romantic ideologue you
have suggested, but he understood, at any rate, that works of imagination
deal with opposite and discordant qualities. The instance of *Hugh Selwyn
Mauberley*, which you bring forward, will do as well as any. I mean, if that
poem works to satirize contemporary culture by raising up an alternative
model of imaginative production, it equally dismantles its own ideological
representations. That italic T in the "Brennbaum" section, which you and
McGann find so elegant and intelligent, could as well be made the locus for
an alternative, and antithetical, critical meditation.

I recall your attention to those multiple printings of the work you mentioned—one in 1920 preceding the Ovid Press edition, and at least four later
printings. None of them display the decorative symbology of the Ovid Press
edition. All are, in fact, dominated by the conventions of mechanical book
production. Neither Pound nor his poem have any difficulty being translated
into that (presumably) foreign and evil tongue. In the case of Pound's poem,
this event seems all the more shocking because *Hugh Selwyn Mauberley*, as
"initially" produced (forgive the irresistible pun), had—as you say—made
such a symbolic parade of its typographic materials. In the end Pound's
poem does not merely succumb to what "the age demanded," it emerges,
like *The Waste Land*, as the very epitome of that age and the demands it
made.

JJR:　This argument is a far cry from your original presentation of *Hugh
Selwyn Mauberley* as a satire of cultural resistance.

AM:　I do not recant that view; I am merely saying that other views of the
work become possible—become necessary—when the scale of one's attention is changed. If we look at the poem strictly in terms of the Ovid Press

edition, we will be inclined to see it in a certain way. But if we read it in the horizon of all its authoritative printings, the poem becomes a very different work.

Much more could be said on these topics. For instance, Pound's entire involvement with the decorated book was, as you yourselves have noted, part of a large historical argument he was making about the history of Western culture. He was, in this respect, continuing the work of certain Victorians, but especially Browning, Ruskin, and Morris. The first twenty-seven cantos are simply *Hugh Selwyn Mauberley* in a fully elaborated form—in the same way that *Prometheus Unbound* is the "Ode to the West Wind" in its complete version, as it were. Cantos 1–27 are also produced through John Rodker, in two books even more lavishly printed and decorated than the original *Hugh Selwyn Mauberley*. Furthermore, Cantos 1–27 make book production an explicit subject and theme at the semantic level, and they connect it back to the early history of book production in the West, and in Italy especially, between the fourteenth and the sixteenth centuries.

That connection, however, only further destabilizes the *Cantos* project. Like *Hugh Selwyn Mauberley*, the first twenty-seven cantos moved east of their initial decorative and ideographical Eden. This fall into the quotidian world took place between 1925, when Three Mountains Press brought out *A Draft of XVI. Cantos* in Paris, and 1933, when Farrar & Rinehart published its trade edition of *A Draft of XXX Cantos*. As with *Hugh Selwyn Mauberley*, these bibliographical transformations trace the work's descent from craft to commerce. But in the case of the *Cantos*, the symbolic-cultural distinction between decorative and commercial book production is undermined by the historical lines which the *Cantos* draw between Renaissance book-making and Renaissance capitalism. The *Cantos'* historical materials do not permit the clear distinction, which the work itself offers, between late fourteenth-century Italian commerce and early twentieth-century European commerce. Indeed, the *Cantos'* own commitment to a historical imagination works to connect rather more than to disconnect the two.

Works of imagination like Pound's traffic in opposition because poetry—unlike any other form of discourse—is committed to the presentation of "opposite and discordant qualities." The integrity of that commitment can be measured by the way such works bring their own most cherished ideological visions into contradiction.

Furthermore—and this is for me the crucial point—by opening themselves to such radical self-alienation, imaginative work escapes the happy valley of production and consumption. The latter, which is technically called a restricted economy, is the dynamic underlying hermeneutics and the basis of the hermeneutical imagination of literature. In this context, one has to grant contemporary materialist historicisms like McGann's a certain usefulness. They help to expose the presence of this production/consumption dynamic operating at the superstructural level. Baudrillard, of course, has analyzed the same dynamic in his theoretical studies of "the mirror of production."[12]

Hermeneutics operates a restricted economy by producing "meaning" for general social consumption. It does this by conceiving the object of its studies, the poem, as a producer of meanings which can be consumed (because the meanings are determinate) and reproduced. The cycle is imagined to be endless and self-replicating. The ceaseless reproductions carried out under deconstructive signs, as Baudrillard has shown, merely reinstall the original productive model of the text.

I would oppose this hermeneutic imagination of imaginative work to a properly textual imagination. The latter corresponds to what has been called a "general economy," which is an economy of luxury and waste, of gift and loss. In this economy, acts of writing are not mirrored by (or in) acts of reading. "Meaning," the goal of interpretation, is alienated from writing in the realization that all texts are alienated from themselves. They are carnivals, masquerades, superfluities. From a purely productive vantage, they are useless. In that very uselessness, however, lies the ground of their (radical) critique of the quotidian orders of getting and spending.[13]

So far as Ezra Pound is concerned, we will come to see his poetry as itself part of the waste(d) world his work was conceived to oppose. Pound very definitely committed his writing to the service of restricted economies—to use functions and (American) pragmatistic ends. But in choosing poetry as his principal medium of exchange, he doomed his work to self-contradiction. His commitments to power, will, and control would reveal themselves as an astonishing luxury of waste, fragmentariness, and incoherence.

JJR: What is "useless" about that—or about carnivals and masquerades? Your distinction between restricted and general economies seems to me far too restrictive. Ceremonies of luxury and waste are "useless" only in the narrow perspective of (say) Plato's *Republic* and *Laws*. Indeed, when utilitarian and pragmatic imaginations dominate, poetry's "use functions" emerge more clearly than ever—as Shelley, for one, has shown (in the *Defence of Poetry*).

And I also object to your sharp distinction between "poetry" and "interpretation": as if the two were not completely interinvolved. You yourself have been talking about the ideological purposes invested in *Hugh Selwyn Mauberley*. But the interpretive voice of literary criticism is an echo of the sense of the poetry it reads. As such, interpretation—whether it is hermeneutically charged (like De Man's studies), or empirically oriented (like McGann's)—reimagines the works which come into its hands.

Of course one could think of hermeneutics as the "science" of poetry's "nature," the vehicle by which the hidden secrets of an originary existence are translated into knowable and usable forms. Nor would I even object to *this* model, misleading as it can be, so long as one does not employ it to equate the terms "science" and "truth." One of the great (historical) virtues of the hermeneutic appropriation of the "science model" of experience and understanding lies exactly in the way it undermines the positivist inertia of the scientific imagination of the world. In this sense, hermeneutics can be imagined as the science of the *un*knowing of scientistic illusions of truth. In vulgar terms: because meaning and truth are imaginations of those things, every science (including hermeneutics) is a way of knowing that subsists on the edge of its own falsifiability. The knowledge of both "nature" and "poetry"—that is to say, the activities of "science" and "hermeneutics"— ought to replicate their originary heterocosms at the level of mind and self-consciousness.

GM: I see you are not one who goes in fear of abstractions. Come on— what we want to know is *how* precisely this dynamic of unknowing operates—and, even more to the point, how it could possibly be called a form of knowledge.

Two broad lines of explanation have recommended themselves. The first, brilliantly pursued and elaborated during the last twenty years of his life by Paul De Man, reads literature as a mechanism of disillusionment. The self-alienation of imaginative texts becomes the means by which readers find their interpretive moves weighed in the balance and found wanting. This immediate and positive deconstruction of the reader, consistently executed, reveals the ontological and "quasi-objective" truth of personal knowledge and subjective experience. In Byron's summary and paradoxical words: "All that we know is, nothing can be known" (*Childe Harold's Pilgrimage* II. 56). Byron's statement is useful, in this context, just because of its deceptive poetic simplicity. Both grammar and rhetoric carry a clear performative illustration of how general and even assured knowledge can be made, literally, out of "nothing." De Man arrives at similar views by more abstract and circuitous methods. According to him, the failures and *aporias* of knowledge become the ground for a positive metaphysics by which the mind is able "to give rational integrity to a process [i.e, the blindness/insight dynamic] that exists independently of the self."[14]

According to this line of explanation, however, that self-independent "process" is the insight (and construct) of what Wordsworth once called "Reason in her most exalted mood" (*Prelude* XIV: 192). The process is revealed from the individual mind's specific acts of critical self-reflection—in De Man's terms, from its reflective engagements with particular literary texts. For this "science" of criticism, however, the question arises: What is the "nature" being pursued, what is the "object" of the knowing process? Or, to put the problem in Blakean terms: What prevents such self-reflective activity from collapsing into a Urizenic self-absorption? I take it that this is more or less the same question you [addressing AM] raised earlier.

Blake's answer, reduced to its simplest terms, appeared in that set of activities to which he gave the magical name, Los. This power is Blake's constructive genius, the figure who creates, along with his "sons," the historical world. The maker of this world is named Los because such a world comprises what Blake calls "the perishing . . . Memory" (*Milton* 26:46). The function of Los, in his world of continuous losses, is to carry on a perpetual process of (re)constructions. Los's function is to ensure that not one moment of time or space should fall into "Nonentity." Though he is often called "Imagination," therefore, he is equally the agent of inspired and salvific acts of memory.

I recall Blake's views here because his work helps to clarify the relation between "fact" and imagination.[15] As etymology suggests, a "fact" is something that is made, an artificial construct. From any immediate point of view a fact is the consequence of some particular deed, a locus of agents and their interactions. Reflexively, "the facts" are those bodies of knowledge which we choose to construct and record in various ways. In Blake's view, therefore, the "facts" of any case are as various as the agents involved in the events, either immediately or belatedly. An extreme factive multiplicity prevails in the immediate moment of human action as well as in the secondary moment of human reflection. This multiplicity, in the context (for example) of contemporary literary studies, is exactly what licenses every move to revise and reimagine the canon. Such revisions become possible when memory is opened to re-membering.

In contrast to De Man, Blake's work throws the burden of authority on energy rather than on reason, on the prolific rather than the devouring, on all those "Minute Particulars" which make up processes of generation and regeneration. The ultimate point of Blake's minute particulars is not so much to create or to "decreate" meaning—although this is most certainly part of what they do—but to establish the grounds on which ideological activity of every kind occurs. More clearly than most, Blake's work foregrounds its own critical and imaginative limits.

From this perspective, hermeneutics is not a science of the "meanings of things"—the blindness/insight dialectic—but a science of the aspects of things, a science not of the way things *are* but of the way they are perceived to be. An anthropological rather than an ontological science—rooted in case studies, "fieldwork," facticities. The historical reconstruction of the text(s) and editions of *Hugh Selwyn Mauberley* should therefore be seen as a model of what hermeneutics entails: the factive revelation of several different frameworks and scales within which that work has been and continues to be constituted.

Nothing illustrates these matters so well as the italic T on page 16 of Pound's work. That T is a "fact" in the sense that it had to be *executed* as what it is, had to be made (*factum*). For the *fact* is that the text could have had a decorated T on this page, that the "supply of Ts" had not in *fact* run out. The italic T is thereby made into an allusion to another (historical) fact about the practice of "old printers"; and that allusion serves as a factive synecdoche for the larger memorial acts which *Hugh Selwyn Mauberley* carries out. In the end, the italic T may well come to stand as an index of the way Pound's work, and poetry in general, *makes* its escape from fiction.

Hermeneutics may of course defend and maintain a work's dominant interpretive inheritances, thereby relegating indomitable and unwarranted claims to obscurity. But if one's interest is in having "the scale of one's attention . . . changed," as you said [speaking to AM], then a materialist and historical literary criticism seems one of the more reliable methods to pursue. After all, the antithetical reading of *Hugh Selwyn Mauberley* which you yourself deployed was only managed because a critical scholarship was able to restore certain aspects of the poem to memory. Critical reflection is nothing but your "mirror of production" without an archive of facts—"facts" understood in the sense I have been discussing. Innocent readers of *Hugh Selwyn Mauberley* confront a transparency when they confront what has been variously called "a text" or "the poem itself." One has to move "from text to work" in order to break free into the particular (dis)orders which works of imagination solicit.

There is a moment in every poem, in every reading of every poem, which Satan's watchfiends cannot find. It is a moment of freedom when the work discovers a door through which it may escape from its own rational inertias. The decorated Ts in Pound's poem are one such moment we may call back to mind. Pound once opened their door, and when scholarship later remembers to reopen it, the act can reimagine the whole work in an entirely new way.

JJR: And let me add that it is the "thickness" of the facticities, the extravagance and even the irrelevance of the detail, which grounds the differential play you speak of. The more a work is materially and historically particularized, the greater the secondary particularity (interpretive and ideological translation) it draws to itself. The many differentials that swirl within *Hugh Selwyn Mauberley*'s fundamental self-contradictions replicate themselves at the interpretive level of the text. Literature is the single house of life which stands only when it *is* divided against itself.

AM: Such a pretty piece of paganism, that last remark. In our day, I suspect even Christians would find it charming. Because it isn't *serious* about its call for literature's self-division. It speaks an ingratiating irony, the wit of accommodation. It might even raise smiles in the halls of academe.

Besides, you both should beware giving lectures on the evils of rationalizing criticism, especially when you have such orderly and authoritative concepts of imaginative fact and memory.

You approve McGann's bibliographical demonstration of one of the hidden histories in *Hugh Selwyn Mauberley*, and you want to accommodate my "antithetical reading" of that hidden history and its relevant facts into your defense of hermeneutics. Well then, tell me what to do with the following (not so hidden) history of the text of Pound's work.

The first poem in the *Hugh Selwyn Mauberley* sequence begins, "For three years, out of key with his time." It appears on page 9 in the Ovid Press edition, where it goes under the title "E. P. ODE POUR L'ELECTION DE SON SEPULCHRE." In the table of contents of that edition, however, the title is *Ode pour l'election de son sepulchre*. I leave aside the typographical difference between these two titles (small capitals as opposed to italics) even though it is just the sort of apparently irrelevant differential detail which poetry is so apt to exploit. For the titles are skewed in two other, even more dramatic, particulars: first, the table of contents does not begin the title with the initials "E. P."; and second, the roman numeral I is placed *after* the title on page 9.

The work was next printed in Boni and Liveright's American edition of Pound's *Poems 1918–21*, where "E. P." does not appear either on the poem's page title or in the table of contents, and where the roman numeral again appears after the poem's title. Everything changes once again in the work's next printing, the 1926 edition of *Personae* (again, Boni and Liveright). Here the roman numeral from page 9 appears before the poem's title, not after it, and the "E. P." is printed as part of the title in both table of contents and text. All subsequent printings follow this text.

John Espey was the first to notice the textual problem here, and he argued (persuasively, I think) that the physical texts of 1920 and 1921 urged the reader to see a close "identification of Pound and Mauberley."[16] Espey wants to read the sequence so that the two figures are clearly distinguished, and in the case of the first poem to see it as "Ezra Pound's ode" for or about Mauberley (Espey, 18). He therefore argues that the final and now dominant text is the correct text in the sense that it is the text which most strongly intimates a clear distinction between Pound and Mauberley.

In fact, the first printing of the "Ode," in *The Dial* of September 1920, also did not print "E. P." as part of the title.[17] Espey regards all the texts of 1920 and 1921 as clear evidence of a "misleading . . . confusion" (Espey, 19) in the work which only becomes gradually cleared up in subsequent editions. But one could, of course, equally argue from this textual evidence that Pound might have changed his mind about his own work as he began to see it in print—that he only gradually came to desire "a complete divorce between Pound and Mauberley" (Espey, 16).

More than that, one could also argue that the received text still does not by any means make the clear distinction Espey wants. One could read the placement of the initials "E. P." in the title of the "Ode" not as an indication that "E. P." is the author of the ode, but the referent of the pronoun "son." The introduction of the "E. P.," far from separating Pound from Mauberley, suggests that both are part of the same debased cultural milieu—that "E. P.," in short, is as much a character in Ezra Pound's poetic sequence *Hugh Selwyn Mauberley* as the figure named in the title of the sequence. "E. P." does not simply mean the historical author Ezra Pound.

The texts as we receive them cannot finally decide between these interpretive options. Espey wants to persuade us that the texts of 1920–21 have come about through oversights and "confusion" on the author's part. But in fact the entire textual history—even if we assume that Pound eventually wanted to draw the clear distinction that Espey favors—shows that the work, as it were, randomly and on its own initiative, maintains its ambiguous and unstable features.

Poetry resists rational and clarified orders, whether these be authoritative or hermeneutic. In poems, something there is that cannot love those walls. I am reminded here of Saussure's strange discoveries of the (apparently random) paragrams and anagrams in late Latin verse—in Lucretius's *De rerum natura*, for example, where numerous anagrams of the name Aphrodite continually appear. To Steve McCaffery, these textual phenomena do not emerge "from an intentionality or conscious rhetoricity" but rather seem "an inevitable consequence of writing's alphabetic, combinatory nature":

> Seen in this way . . . meaning becomes partly the production of a general economy, a persistent excess, non-intentionality and expenditure without reserve through writing's component letters.[18]

I would only add that this kind of "persistent excess" arises not merely from the *letters* of scriptural forms, but from the entire physique of every (and whatever) communicative medium one works in. In all, excess reigns. The facts of a case will not be contained by the interpretations we try to put upon them. Indeed, the interpretations are only other facts disguising themselves as meanings. The word is always and everywhere made flesh.

NOTES

* This essay appears in a slightly different form in Jerome J. McGann, *The Textual Condition* (Princeton: Princeton University Press, 1991).

1. The date of 1862 is probably most significant, for it was then that Christina Rossetti's *Goblin Market* volume was published, with a title page ornament by her

brother, and decorated covers, also designed by D. G. Rossetti. From that point on Rossetti, Morris, and Burne-Jones became increasingly concerned about book production and design. For good introductory treatments of these subjects see Douglas McMurtrie, *The Book: The Story of Printing and Bookmaking* (Oxford: Oxford University Press, 1937), chaps. 32–36; Ruari McLean, *Victorian Book Design and Color Printing* (London: Faber and Faber, 1963).

2. See G. Thomas Tanselle, "Textual Criticism and Literary Sociology," *Studies in Bibliography* 44 (1991): 87, 90, 112.

3. See *Poetry* II (April, 1913): 12. All subsequent printings give the poem in its received (and conventional) typographical form.

4. Pound's directions to the printer show the clear influence of William Morris's ideas about page design, especially on the matter of the margins; see Morris's two papers "Printing" and "The Ideal Book," reprinted in *The Ideal Book. Essays and Lectures on the Arts of the Book by William Morris*, ed. William S. Peterson (Berkeley and Los Angeles: University of California Press, 1982), especially pp. 64–65, 70–71.

5. Once again the influence of Morris appears, this time in Pound's phrase "the old printers" (see ibid.).

6. Catherine Gallagher, "Marxism and the New Historicism," in *The New Historicism*, ed. H. Aram Veeser (New York: Routledge, 1989), p. 45.

7. See Stanley Fish's "Commentary: The Young and the Restless," which concludes and reflects upon the various essays in Veeser's collection *The New Historicism* (pp. 303–16).

8. See Roberto Unger's *False Necessity* (Cambridge: Cambridge University Press, 1987), the second volume of his three-part *Politics, a Work in Constructive Social Theory*.

9. See Roland Barthes's famous essay (first published in *Revue d'esthetique*), reprinted and translated in his *Image-Music-Text*, ed. and trans. Stephen Heath (London: Fontana, 1977).

10. The allusion here is to Jerome McGann's "The Text, the Poem, and the Problem of Historical Method," reprinted in *The Beauty of Inflections: Literary Essays in Historical Method and Theory* (Oxford: Oxford University Press, 1985), pp. 111–32.

11. The two 1920 texts are *The Dial*'s initial printing of the first six sections of the poem and the Ovid Press edition. In 1921 Boni and Liveright brought out the first American edition, in 1926 the first edition of *Personae* printed the poem again, with changes, and further changes were made in the 1949 printing of *Personae*. A few more changes were made, with Pound's authority, when John Espey printed a text of the work in his important study *Ezra Pound's Mauberley*. For further details see note 16.

12. See Jean Baudrillard, *The Mirror of Production*, trans. Mark Poster (St. Louis: Telos Press, 1975).

13. What Mack says here recalls the general argument in Baudrillard's *De la seduction* (Paris: Galilee, 1979), recently published in English as *Seduction*, trans. Brian Singer (New York: St. Martin's Press, 1990).

14. See Paul De Man, *Blindness and Insight: Essays in Rhetoric and Contemporary Criticism*, 2d rev. ed., introduction by Wlad Godzich (Minneapolis: University of Minnesota Press, 1983), p. 19.

15. It is commonly believed that Blake's commitment to "Imagination" entailed a

reciprocal hostility to fact. This view is quite wrong. What Blake wanted to free poetry from was what he called "morals," which is his term for what we would call "meanings" and "interpretations." See Jerome McGann's "William Blake Illuminates the Truth," in *Towards a Literature of Knowledge* (Oxford: Oxford University Press, 1989), chap. 1.

16. See John Espey, *Ezra Pound's Mauberley: A Study in Composition* (Berkeley and Los Angeles: University of California Press, 1955, 1974), p. 19.

17. *The Dial* text prints the first six poems from Part 1 of the sequence: see vol. 69, no. 3, pp. 283–87.

18. Steve McCaffery, "Writing as a General Economy," in *North of Intention: Critical Writings 1973–1986* (New York: Roof Books, 1986), p. 208.

CHAPTER NINE

Literary History as a Hybrid Genre

LAWRENCE BUELL

THIS ESSAY examines one of the most familiar genres of literary history for the light it sheds on the important question of how literary-historical discourse negotiates between a model of interpretative criticism and a model of empiricist historiography. I have fixed my attention on textbook codifications of American literary history, specifically on the three most important compendia to date, even though such works have generally been disregarded in recent theoretical discussions of literary historicism that have brought into focus the issue on which I shall concentrate.[1] In particular, I shall discuss the relationship between the critical reading of texts and the representation of historical context in light of the contrast between the older empiricist-historical notion that the latter is objectively retrievable and the "new historicist" position that history itself must be considered textualized. My own view is that the porousness of the older text/context distinction does not invalidate it, nor does it cease to be fundamental to the newer historical criticism. Thus we might look for more continuity in the practice of literary history than one might expect.[2]

I

Literary history's mission was once well understood. Its task was to conjoin intrinsic and extrinsic, literary texts and their historical settings, in narrative that represented history's actual course. Literary history was a hybrid but recognizable genre that coordinated literary criticism, biography, and intellectual/social background within a narrative of development. A half-century ago, therefore, René Wellek could construct his *The Rise of English Literary History* on the premise that he was writing about an established discipline that had begun to jell in the late eighteenth century.[3]

By contrast, today's literary historians, thanks partly to Wellek's own further thoughts, are agnostic if not downright atheistic about the viability of such a project, for reasons familiar enough to list brusquely. First, the thrust of intrinsic criticism from formalism through poststructuralism blurs the old text/context distinction so as to collapse the latter into the former. Picturing ourselves as inhabitants of textuality leads us to image the object-world beyond text as an alien, maybe nonexistent realm separated from us by an abyss. Wellek himself helped usher in this perception by calling for a kind of literary history that would concentrate more squarely on literature's development according to its own inherent laws.[4] Second, the plurality of available historicisms increases skepticism about each, not to mention the prospect of bringing them together. Consider this dyad: genetic study of the composition of texts, and Marxian study of text production—each of which has its own subdivisions. Practitioners of the first tend to ignore the second as speculative dogmatics, practitioners of the second to ignore the first as naively positivistic. Yet both can be reckoned avatars of historicism. Both pride themselves on being more accountable to history than, say, most new critics or most poststructuralists. Third, whatever our doctrines, the increasing division of labor within academe imprisons us more and more within subdisciplinary enclaves.

The anxiety provoked by such factors may weigh harder on Americanists than on British literature specialists because of certain complications endemic to the former field, which for one thing relies for its self-definition more heavily on extratextual claims about the distinctiveness of the nation's social structure, physical environment, and so forth. Therefore Americanists may be destined to make a particularly conflicted contribution to the debate over how to do literary history in a time of undoing. We may be exceptionally resistant to specific formulations of American literary history while remaining exceptionally anxious to see it formulated; we may be expected to show sturdy resistance yet at the same time unusual vulnerability to the proposition that history can never be more authoritative than story. It may be symptomatic that major presses have recently produced a number of one-volume narrative histories of English literature by individual scholars as against one on the American side.[5]

Yet Americanists have struggled no less hard to define their literary tradition; and I want to focus here on the three most conspicuous monuments of that preoccupation to date: the *Cambridge History of American Literature* (*CHAL*) (1917–1921), the *Literary History of the United States* (*LHUS*) (1948), and the *Columbia Literary History of the United States* (*CLHUS*) (1988).[6] These monuments have both the disadvantages and the advantages of being collaborative collages, rather conservative in method: codifications, rather than state-of-the-art displays. The *LHUS*, for instance, reflected only fitfully the analytical power of the new criticism, and was criticized as such; the *CLHUS* shows only an intermittent consciousness of being conceived in the age of theory. These ostensible disadvantages, however, are actually merits for my present purposes.

To begin with, large-scale codification projects are arguably what we're really driving at when we question whether literary history can achieve a formulation of a literary heritage sufficient to command wide assent if not consensus. A successful history of a nation's literature would seem the realization of such a desire.

That's a tall order, never to be fulfilled according to our utopian dream, yet we press on—and understandably so. Big books on American literature, like American literature survey courses, are a practical reality that has been with us for a century. Professors will continue to write them, as they labor to transmit the current revised version of American literature to the less initiated, for many of whom their compendia provide useful training. Literary history of the codifying sort is thus sure to endure, despite our epistemological finickiness, as a pragmatic test of our ability to explain ourselves to those outside specialists' clubs. As such, it constitutes a kind of intellectual bottom line: what we have to say for ourselves when forced to stand and deliver. These codifications speak more strongly for us than we like to think. Though we desubtilize when we contribute to these projects, the result ought in principle to be taken as the quintessence of what we are prepared to be held accountable for believing about our province.

By the same token, the collaborative nature of these compendia, however awkwardly structured, make them illuminating as institutional symptoms. Among the three I shall discuss, the degree of programmatic unity differs greatly but in no case is limited to the doctrines of a single school. The groups of fifty or more contributors apiece provide a decent cross section of current literary-historical practices.

To be sure, the heteroglossia produced by such juxtapositions raises all the more insistently the question of what, if anything, literary history is apart from criticism. The question is exacerbated by the degree to which codified or standard literary histories intersperse various kinds of summary: précis, biography, and recitation of public events. At worse, one experiences a collage of disparate strata, none of which seemingly gets at the reading experience itself, seemingly occluded by layers of schematic impressionism. Hybridization, that is, in the bad sense.

That this worst case is not inevitably the case I shall also argue. But first it will help to immerse ourselves a little further in the destructive element by way of three parallel passages from our respective chronicles, passages superficially very disparate, yet manifesting upon closer inspection some fundamental continuities of method: indeed, nothing less than the surprising emergence of the methodological core we seek. These three brief discussions, of Mark Twain's *A Connecticut Yankee in King Arthur's Court*, will be our central exempla from here on.

1. CHAL

A Connecticut Yankee in King Arthur's Court (1889) is a work of humorous invention set in motion by G. W. Cable, who first brought Malory's *Morte d'Arthur* to Mark Twain's attention. . . . The hero is, despite the title, no mere Yankee but Mark Twain's 'personal representative'—acquainted with the machine shops of New Haven but acquainted also with navigation on the Mississippi and with Western journalism and with the use of the lariat. The moment that he enters 'the holy gloom' of history he becomes, as Mark Twain became when he went to Europe, the representative of democratic America, preaching the gospel of commonsense and practical improvement and liberty and equality and free thought inherited from Franklin, Paine, Jefferson, and Ingersoll. Those to whom Malory's romance is a sacred book may fairly complain that the exhibition of the Arthurian realm is a brutal and libellous travesty, attributing to the legendary period of Arthur horrors which belong to medieval Spain and Italy. Mark Twain admits the charge. He takes his horrors where he finds them. His wide-sweeping satirical purpose requires a comprehensive display of human ignorance, folly, and iniquity. He must vent the flame of indignation which swept through him whenever he fixed his attention on human history—indignation against removable dirt, ignorance, injustice, and cruelty. As a radical American, he ascribed a great share of these evils to monarchy, aristocracy, and an established church, and he made his contemporary references pointed and painful to English sensibilities. *A Connecticut Yankee* is his *Don Quixote*, a sincere book, full of lifelong convictions earnestly held, a book charged with a rude iconoclastic humour, intended like the work of Cervantes to hasten the end of an obsolescent civilization. Whether it will finally be judged a great book will depend in considerable measure on factors outside itself, particularly on the prosperity of western democratic sentiment in the world at large. Since the War of the German Invasions there has been an increase of Quixoticism in his sense, and what used to be considered his unnecessary rage at windmills now looks like prophetic tilting at giants.[7]

2. LHUS

A Connecticut Yankee . . . shows just such an ingenious mechanic as Clemens must often have met on visits to the Hartford shops of Pratt & Whitney, a Yankee who is swept back in time to Camelot. With one hand he transforms Arthurian England into a going concern of steam and electricity; with the other, seeks to plant the seeds of equalitarianism. He remarks that in feudal society six men out of a thousand crack the whip over their fellows' backs: 'It seemed to me that what the nine hundred and ninety-four dupes needed was a new deal.' This passage, as the late President Roosevelt testified, furnished the most memorable phrase in modern American government. The Connecticut Yankee asserts that the mass of a nation can always produce 'the material in abundance whereby to govern itself.' Yet the medieval mob is shown collectively to be gullible, vicious, invincibly ignorant, like the populace of Hannibal or Hartford, so that the Yankee sets up not a true democracy but a benign dictatorship centering in himself and his mechanical skills—a kind of technocrat's utopia. Dazzled by the wonders of applied science, Mark Twain always hoped for social as well as technological miracles from the dynamo.[8]

3. CLHUS

In what might be called the first of his dark works, A Connecticut Yankee in King Arthur's Court, Twain's larger reflection . . . led him to write one of the first parables of colonialization. In his novel he follows the journey from an advanced, confident civilization of a representative of modern technology and ideas who moves in time rather than in space into a historically backward, feudal society. Modernizing and destroying at the same time, Twain's enlightened cultural emissary is a slightly disguised version of his many contemporaries who were carrying what they called the White Man's Burden of colonial education and integration into the modern world system. The great fame of Rudyard Kipling, Twain's main rival as a popular author in his day, grew out of this colonial movement. The climactic barbarities of King Leopold's Congo, to which Joseph Conrad's Heart of Darkness as well as Twain's own journalism was a response, is already visible in Connecticut Yankee. Offering to develop the Arthurian world and rid it of superstition, Hank Morgan brings it war and destruction. Twain's book, like his great denunciations of the exploitation of the Congo in the early 1900s, was a thoughtful account of that most pressing of late nineteenth-century travel forms: the final mad scramble of the European powers to grab up and modernize whatever scraps were left of the underdeveloped world. Like his contemporaries Kipling and Conrad, Twain wrote, in A Connecticut Yankee, a parable of cultural arrogance and its self-destructive naiveté that has its place alongside Conrad's Heart of Darkness with its idealist turned savage, Kurtz.[9]

It should be clear how markedly each of these disparate readings reflects its historical moment: World War I, the Roosevelt era, and the contemporary era. The Yankee is first the patriotic American doing battle against old world tyranny, be it medieval or modern. Then he's the benevolent social engineer (also at one remove the scholar-elitist) handing his compatriots the New Deal that they're too inept to obtain for themselves. Then he's the ugly American imperialist. The transmogrification from benign Quixote to demonic exploiter is total and striking. It is additionally symptomatic that these reframings shift from depicting Twain as close to his protagonist but not in control of his text to fully in control of the text and completely ironic toward him. The shift, I take it, reflects on one hand the consolidation of Twain's status as a canonical writer and, on the other hand, the attitude toward mainstream American values on the part of the American intellectual establishment. With these shifts comes a reinvisioning of Twain from Yankee optimist to sardonic prophet whose last, dark phase was not a psychological crackup or aesthetic decline but a realization of the deeper potentials of his vision latent from the start.

But what do these readings say about literary history as a would-be discipline? Do they not discredit it, discredit anyhow its pretensions to historiographical authority in the ordinary sense, showing as they do such obvious presentism? They conjure up the spectacle of endless irreconcilable readings of *Connecticut Yankee* shifting according to the endlessly shifting position of the commentators.

Yet this shiftingness, which of course is a given in all historiography, does not invalidate the project, not even the project's "objectivity." To lack perfect objectivity is not to lose all contact with the object. Besides, and equally to the point, the passages are not in fact irreconcilable. Despite appearances, they share some basic approaches in common. To perceive what that is may restore faith in the presence of methodological if not doctrinal tradition.

All three, to start with, present strongly didactic readings of *Connecticut Yankee* as some sort of social parable. They collide on specifics but collude in reading *Yankee* as a symptomatic ideological artifact. In this respect they can be said to resemble not only each other but also most of the landmark works of American literary historiography from its beginnings in Tyler, Richardson, and Wendell, through Parrington and Miller and Matthiessen to the myth-symbol studies of the 1950s and 1960s, to contemporary criticism of American ideological patterns exemplified by Sacvan Bercovitch, Myra Jehlen, and other contributors to their critical anthology, *Ideology and Classical American Literature* (1986), to the most recent major collections of new work in American literary studies edited by Donald Pease and Philip Fisher.[10]

It is illuminating in this regard to juxtapose our three readings of *Yankee* to a very different one by Clarence Gohdes from the 1951 *Literary History of the American People*—another collaborative project that has been unjustly neglected since appearing in the shadow of the better-publicized *LHUS*.

Gohdes treats *Yankee* as a comic tour de force from which it is perverse to wrest a grave moral. Twain, he notes, has been called a "profound social critic railing against tyranny. The fact is that upon occasion he was, just as he was also a firm admirer of the German Emperor and a believer that the establishment of British rule was the best thing that ever happened to India."[11] This statement protests too much: one feels (perhaps because "one" is American?) that to read *Yankee* as mere spoof is to violate in some measure the scholar's implied covenant with a major canonical figure. However that may be, Gohdes's antireading highlights the shared convention of high seriousness that characterizes the American literary-historiographical mainstream.

But to move on to the more specifically historical aspect of the three passages. All employ the same fundamental structure, a structure that I take to be the single most fundamental analytic convention in national historiography: a convention so basic that it has not, to my knowledge, been isolated and held up for scrutiny but has remained transparent, rather. I refer to the encapsulated formulation of a work's significance as historical artifact and national product. The specific content of that statement changes, but the form does not, the form being to appraise the work as a microcosm or refraction of its era: in the first case, as an artifact of republican antimonarchicalism; in the second, as an artifact of the gospel of progressivist efficiency; in the third, as a late Victorian exposé of imperialist discourse. This convention of summary formulation of work into sociogram is altogether one of the most stable devices in the literary historiographical repertoire for interlacing text and context.

Regulating in some measure the deployment of the sociogram are several other fundamental structuring conventions, especially prominent in the first two histories. These might be called the conventions of *framing, chronology, proportion,* and *précis*: that is, the practice of framing discussions of literary texts with short accounts of historical events and/or biography; the practice of chronological treatment of materials within chapter units; the practice of proportional coverage of major and minor works; and the practice of summarizing the contents of works deemed major. These practices, like the sociogram, have traditionally been so embedded that they seem not to have been much thought about or discussed by practitioners. After a lecture version of this essay, for example, one *CLHUS* contributor in the audience told me that he had not conceptualized these devices but now realized he had employed them. The same was true for me. The coincidence is additionally striking given that individual contributors (especially in the first and third projects) seem generally to have worked in isolation from one another; critical fashions and prevalent conceptions of historicism have both greatly changed; and contributors to the later projects have probably often written without consulting their predecessors. (I have so far identified only two

CLHUS contributors who profess to have read the counterpart chapters of either predecessor's work specifically as a preparative for writing their own.) In short, we seem to have hit on a notable case of socialization by osmosis.

This is especially true in the case of the sociogram. For as we turn from *CHAL* and *LHUS* to *CLHUS*, we can see a certain attenuation of the other four conventions. For example, the *CLHUS* chapter on the "American Revolution as Literary Event" does not attempt even a cursory rundown of political or military highlights but confines itself to a series of genre studies of essays, verse, and narrative. Whereas the *LHUS* Thoreau chapter is strongly biographical, the *CLHUS* considers peripheral or irrelevant the literal details of the Walden experience, the memory of Thoreau's brother as a shaping force in the composition of *A Week*, and the history of Thoreau's love life. The *CLHUS* chapter on Cooper ingeniously complicates chronology by featuring a quartet of novels about the settlement process that "most clearly opens a view to the writer's inner life" (249), disclosing his career line in miniature, after which the chapter doubles back and reviews the progression in more detail. The chapter on Hawthorne lingers on a long analysis of "Young Goodman Brown" as the quintessence of Hawthorneism, and rushes past the full-length romances, saying little about *The Scarlet Letter* and almost nothing about other preceding works in the Hawthorne canon. All these choices, I think, pay off. All, however, are decidedly untraditional.

This list of contrasts overstates the formal innovativeness of *CLHUS*, some chapters of which are written much more conservatively than others, and which as a whole is far more traditional in its observance of conventional chronology, biography, and précis than, say, *A New History of French Literature*, which must be reckoned the masterpiece of experimental literary historiography to date.[12] So the contrast among our three American compendia is a relative one, a semidisruption rather than a distinct break: a shift within a set of practices still widely shared. Yet the partial erosion of the subsidiary structuring conventions makes the distinct retention of the sociogram (true of *A New History of French Literature* also) all the more striking.[13]

But now we must ask the "So what?" question. How much historical authority is there to the encapsulation device? Granted that it is heartening to be able to chart *some* constancy of practice at a time when all practices seem put under question; but perhaps this practice should be as well. Perhaps it has passed muster so far only because we have not been self-critical enough.

The sociogram's chief vulnerability is surely the ease with which it tempts us to accept a conveniently packageable assertion as if it were the result of a grounded argument about the relation between the work and its social frame. That may be an especially inviting temptation for Americanists, given how attracted our historical criticism has been to totalizing formulations of American literary culture in terms of major thematic patterns—from D. H. Lawrence to Vernon L. Parrington, Perry Miller to myth-symbol criticism of the 1950s and 1960s, from the consensus American Studies historiography to 1980s critiques of its "cold war" ideology. The sociogram enacts the programmaticism of the thesis book at the microlevel, its structure conducing to represent the literary work as inhabiting a single unitary macrocosm. The convention of high seriousness, remarked on earlier, mystifies the structure further.

The problem both subsides and increases as we move from traditional literary history to the modest experimentalism of the *CLHUS*. In *CLHUS*, the extraliterary is seen much more from the standpoint of the intraliterary. This is effected by the erosion of the four subsidiary conventions and by a narrowing of the agenda of featured text types. *CLHUS* concentrates much more than its predecessors on the fictive genres. Long gone are the *CHAL* chapters on the discourse of economics, education, and post-1800 theology. Radically foreshortened are the accounts of history, oratory, and exploration narrative, which were already trimmed down in the *LHUS*. (Also dropped from the *CLHUS*, interestingly, is oral literature—except for the opening chapter on Native American writing—and discussion of the Americanization of the English language.)

Consequently, once *CLHUS* moves past the colonial period, historical events and nonfictional genres are scantly dealt with. This has the virtues of concentrating on what most American literature specialists mostly read and teach, and of acknowledging the necessarily interpretative nature of the analysis, as against the older style that is less reflexive about the haphazardness and sometimes irrelevance of its set-piece background expositions. On the other hand, the more interiorized approach increases the susceptibility to desultory treatment of the contextual that is inherent in the sociogram to start with. Of our three readings of *Yankee*, the *CLHUS*'s is at once the most innovative and the most speculative in its evidential base. The *CHAL* appeals to Twain's known reading of Malory as well as his prior observation of and reading about Europe. *LHUS* appeals to Twain's known fascination with machines and machine shops. *CLHUS*, by contrast, appeals primarily to the intertext as a key to interpretation: to the precedents of Kipling and Conrad. With respect to Twain's life-record, *CLHUS* rests chiefly upon his later attack on King Leopold, a more circuitous route back to Camelot than its predecessors', since Twain might not even have known the work of Kipling or Conrad when he wrote *Yankee*, and *Heart of Darkness* was published a decade later.

It may be significant in this regard that the *CLHUS* passage is the only one not explicitly to call attention to its own moment and thus overtly betray the historically situated basis of its reading. Here again the explanation may lie in the passage's, indeed the whole volume's, frankly interpretative character. As the volume's preface forewarns us: "It is no longer necessary or desirable for the critic to argue that one reading is truer than any other, for the aim of historical criticism is to provide the reader with an interesting and feasible approach to a text, informed by a relevant interpretation of historical material" (xviii). The *CLHUS* passage certainly does fulfill this restricted notion of historical accountability, as I'll show more fully; and it signals at least to the informed reader that it aims at interpretative power rather than minute factical accuracy when it anachronizes by reversing causality in asking us to read *Yankee* through the eyes of the fiction that today stands as the touchstone Euro-American critique of colonialism.[14] This speculative cast of the *CLHUS* passage is of course veiled by a rhetoric that seems to presume that the anticolonial parable reading is *the* reading, not just *a* reading.

But to return to the issue of the sociogram's power to represent history. The fact that we can contrast our passages with regard to types and degrees of historical representation should warn us from dismissing it as unhistorical. If we look more closely at what each passage is doing we shall see that the appearance of impressionism is misleading.

The disciplined quality of the sociogram begins to become clear as we recognize that the interpretations pressed by the three commentators are not atomistic set-pieces but make sense in terms of the larger wholes in which they are embedded. The *CHAL* expresses the commentator's vision of Twain as the apostle of democratic man. In the case of the *LHUS*, a more programmatically unified work, the reading of *Yankee* not only applies the argument of the Twain chapter but the editors' overarching theory about major American authors, also the by-then-dominant scholarly view, that major American writers are critics and instructors of mainstream America from the standpoint of the democratic ideals that mainstream America has either betrayed or not yet realized. The *CLHUS* reading, in turn, reflects one of the distinctive emphases of that volume, namely that American literary history needs reinterpretation in light of the degree to which it registers division and interaction of race and class. For the *CLHUS*, the macropattern unifying Twain's work is cultural crossing and collision—the pattern of the traveler to the unfamiliar land who is increasingly seen as destabilizing it through his intrusion. In short, our three passages are not idiosyncratic or ad hoc but exemplary: all manifest the underlying historicist orientations of their respective volumes.

Each discussion, furthermore, invokes at least three specific historical contexts for its reading: the context of the specific moment and circumstances of composition, the broader context of the author's life and times, and the commentator's context. One explanation of the difference among our three readings is that each assigns different relative weights to these three contexts. *CHAL* regards the first as crucial; *LHUS* is equally interested in the second; *CLHUS* gives the second and third priority over the first, from which standpoint it would follow that for Twain not to have associated *Yankee* with Congo imperialism at the time of composition is inconsequential given that he did so retrospectively. These differences are likely related to the difference in the way the commentator's context is signaled in the three cases: in the first, with much self-consciousness of living at a moment other than Twain's; in the second, also self-consciously, but assured of a convergence of views between the two moments; in the third, without overt indication of representing a post-Vietnam ethos. The shift bespeaks a lessening regard for the claims of the unique historical instant at which *Yankee* was composed.

This shift toward a more thoroughgoingly presentist allegiance in rendering history does not, however, mean that the nineteenth century has been left behind; rather, the different readings rest on different bodies of historical/biographical evidence. *CHAL* rests on Twain's ex cathedra comments at the time of writing: he *did* have Malory in mind; he *did* describe *Yankee* to his English publisher as "a Yankee mechanic's say against monarchy and its several natural props." Even the Cervantes comparison can be found in the original publisher's blurb, which Twain approved.[15] *LHUS* appeals to Twain's known fascination with the apparatus of technocracy as well as to his known ambivalence toward the capacities of ordinary people. Finally, *CLHUS* picks up on Twain's Conrad-like denunciation of Congo exploitation in 1905–1906 (e.g., Twain's pamphlet *King Leopold's Soliloquy: A Defense of His Congo Rule*), a denunciation that Twain's own *Autobiography* links directly to his critique of feudalism in *Connecticut Yankee*.[16]

That the three encapsulations don't marshall their evidence in detail should not be held against them. One must allow for selectivity when the canvas is large. The form the sociogram takes, of a snapshot rather than a sifting of all pertinent evidence, is on pragmatic grounds a pardonable reductionism, especially given that reductionism is itself a convention of the genre that must be more or less recognizable to readers as well as authors. Surely neither the authors of the three passages nor the readers of the three volumes attempts to present or expect to find therein a complete exegesis of *Yankee*. Even an uninformed reader must have at least a subliminal sense when picking up such a volume of entering into a contract one stipulation of which is that anything written here is a beginning, not an end.

Yet our passages also point to how codified literary history might be strengthened historiographically. To offset the hazards of necessary simplification it is well to bring to the surface the awareness of how one's discourse is perforce bricked together from different historical strata—to recognize, that is, that one's discourse is inevitably a hybrid of biography, text, and larger historical forces understood as different but interacting domains and thus never to be seamlessly interwoven. Here the *CHAL*, for all its quaintness, is especially noteworthy in its distinctions between the specific stimulus of Malory, Twain's chronic bumptious Yankeeism, and the commentator's position of writing with the Great War freshly in mind. But a more ambitious model of discursive possibility would be the ordering of the *New History of French Literature* in terms of 199 chronologically-ordered literary/social "events" from "778: Roland dies at Roncevaux" to "1985: The 500th Program of 'Apostrophes' Is Broadcast on Antenne 2." This device— which permits a more centrifugal, discontinuous, and recursive treatment of literary history—beautifully announces at once the necessity and the haphazardness of placing literary texts within historical settings and sequences.

II

Several prescriptive conclusions seem to follow from my analysis. First, we need to resist the understandable suspicion that codified literary history is a bankrupt enterprise. The truth is that we cannot escape from it and even if we could we should not try. It is a pedagogical and market imperative that will keep on speaking for us whether we like it or not and whether we hedge it about with disclaimers like the *CLHUS* preface. This may not simply be a necessary evil, but a positive value in forcing us to specify our commitments in the face of our fastidious hesitancy to self-define.

Second, there is more continuity between older and newer literary historicizing than we might at first realize. That continuity is overstated by focusing on a subgenre that American scholars have so far handled conservatively, but not at our site of particular concentration. The sociogram is proving to be a resilient, persistent device even in the most experimental work, and will likely continue prominent as long as literary history considers examination of individual texts to be of major importance to its endeavor.

Third, and consequently, although today we practice a more interiorized form of literary history, it still rests on claims about the relation between literature and history, claims that are embedded even if not overtly articulated or argued through the device of the sociogram, as well as the four ancillary structuring devices that persist at least vestigially even in experimental work. Furthermore, we have seen that it is possible to make defining, differentiating statements about the historicity of particular literary histories.

Fourth, such being the case, we should not scorn the hybridity of old-style literary history, but recognize our investment in the same enterprise: that, for example, as Americanists we continue to frame our texts within myths of American civilization that rest in good part on evidence external to the belletristic artifacts we discuss. Old-style collaging of paraphrase, biographical cameos, public events, and so forth was prolix and incoherent; but it did have the merit of representing the jagged way we in our capacity as historians go about building our conceptual artifacts, whether we confess it or not.

That is why the sociogram will likely continue to be a staple of literary-historical method: because of its power to express a vision of the text's intrinsic-extrinsic relation in epitome. And that is also why it should be read warily: because the sociogram can be made to look so innocently formalist as to disguise literary history's continuing dependence on extraliterary knowledge. To stress literary history's irreducibly hybrid nature at this historical moment may help us avoid exchanging an older epistemological innocence for a newer innocence that we are engaging in a hermeneutics no longer vulnerable to empirical disconfirmation.

NOTES

1. See, however, Robert Johnstone, "The Impossible Genre: Reading Comprehensive Literary Histories," *PMLA* 107 (1992): 26–37, an illuminating comparatist study that places special emphasis on the utopian character of such compendia.

2. H. Aram Veeser, ed., *The New Historicism* (London and New York: Routledge, 1989), is a valuable critical anthology of appraisals of the new historicism movement by both insiders and outsiders. For participants' definitions, see especially the first three essays, by Stephen Greenblatt, Louis Montrose, and Catherine Gallagher. J. R. de J. Jackson, *Historical Criticism and the Meaning of Texts* (London and New York: Routledge, 1989), thoughtfully appraises the issues, problems, and resources of historical literary scholarship written from a more traditional historicist standpoint than those of most of the contributors to the Veeser anthology.

3. René Wellek, *The Rise of English Literary History* (Chapel Hill: University of North Carolina Press, 1941), pp. 200–201.

4. Wellek and Austin Warren, *Theory of Literature* (New York: Harcourt, 1949), pp. 241–60. It seems clear that Wellek was not trying to discredit literary history so much as to preserve it by envisaging a literary history that would be critical rather than antiquarian: cf. his *Concepts of Criticism*, ed. Stephen G. Nichols, Jr. (New Haven and London: Yale University Press, 1963), particularly the first and third essays.

5. The British literary histories are Peter Conrad, *The History of English Literature: One Indivisible, Unending Book* (London: Dent, 1985); W. W. Robson, *A Prologue to English Literature* (Totowa, N.J.: Barnes and Noble, 1986); Alistair Fowler, *A History of English Literature* (Cambridge, Mass.: Harvard University Press, 1989); Pat Rogers, *An Illustrated History of English Literature* (New York and Oxford: Oxford University Press, 1989). The American literary history is Peter Conn, *Literature in America: An Illustrated History* (Cambridge: Cambridge University Press, 1989).

6. *The Cambridge History of American Literature*, ed. William Peterfield Trent et al. (1917–1921; repr. New York: Macmillan and Cambridge: Cambridge University Press, 1946); *Literary History of the United States*, ed. Robert E. Spiller et al. (New York: Macmillan, 1948); *The Columbia Literary History of the United States*, gen. ed. Emory Elliott (New York and London: Columbia University Press, 1988). For a history of the first two of these compendia, see Kermit Vanderbilt, *American Literature and the Academy* (Philadelphia: University of Pennsylvania Press, 1986).

7. *CHAL* 3:17–18 (by Stuart Sherman).

8. *LHUS* 2:935 (by Dixon Wecter).

9. *CLHUS*, p. 643 (by Philip Fisher).

10. See Philip Fisher, ed., *The New American Studies: Essays from "Representations"* (Berkeley: University of California Press, 1991); Donald Pease, ed., special issue of work by "New Americanists," *boundary 2* 17.i (1990).

11. *The Literature of the American People*, ed. Arthur Hobson Quinn (New York: Appleton, 1951), pp. 718–19.

12. *A New History of French Literature*, ed. Denis Hollier (Cambridge, Mass. and London: Harvard University Press, 1989). It should be added that in *CLHUS* as in all other literary histories, *interpretative* experimentalism may or may not be accompanied by *formal* experimentalism, and vice versa.

13. For a range of instances in *A New History*, cf. the discussions of Racine's *Esther* (370), Montesquieu's *Lettres Persanes* (410–11), the intertwined discussions of Prevost's *Manon Lescault* and Tencin's *Memoires du comte de Comminges* (438–42), and Laclos's *Les liaisons dangereuses* (561–62).

14. Of course *Heart of Darkness* can also be seen as preempted *by* colonialism, and so can *Yankee*. But that's another story: the story we may look for when a team of African scholars writes *its* version of (Euro)American literary history. For the most influential statement to date, see Chinua Achebe, "An Image of Africa: Racism in Conrad's *Heart of Darkness*," *Massachusetts Review* 18 (1977): 782–94.

15. Henry Nash Smith, "Introduction" to *A Connecticut Yankee*, ed. Bernard L. Stein (Berkeley, Los Angeles, and London: University of California Press, 1979), p. 3; Albert Bigelow Paine, *Mark Twain: A Biography* (1912; repr. New York and London: Harper, 1929), 3:893; *A Connecticut Yankee*, p. 541n.

16. *The Autobiography of Mark Twain*, ed. Charles Neider (New York: Harper, 1959), p. 271.

CHAPTER TEN

Blackface, White Noise:
The Jewish Jazz Singer Finds His Voice

MICHAEL ROGIN

MOVIES AND THE BLACK QUESTION*

Each transformative moment in the history of American film has founded itself on the surplus symbolic value of blacks, the power to make African-Americans stand for something besides themselves.[1] There have been four such moments. Edwin S. Porter's *Uncle Tom's Cabin* (1903), bringing the most performed theatrical spectacle of the late nineteenth century into the movies, marked the transition from popular theater to motion pictures that characterized the prehistory of classic Hollywood cinema. The most lavish and expensive film to date, and the first to use intertitles, *Uncle Tom's Cabin* was the first extended movie narrative with a black character and, therefore, since African-Americans were forbidden to play African-Americans in serious, dramatic roles, the first substantial blackface film. Porter's one-reeler straddles the border between the most popular form of nineteenth-century entertainment, blackface minstrelsy, and the most popular entertainment form of the first half of the twentieth century, motion pictures. Undercutting Stowe's novel, Porter introduced the plantation myth into American movies.[2]

D. W. Griffith's *The Birth of a Nation* (1915) originated Hollywood cinema in the ride of the Ku Klux Klan against black political and sexual revolution. Its technique, cost, length, mass audience, critical reception, and influential historical vision all identify *Birth* as the single most important American movie ever made. *Uncle Tom's Cabin*, with Porter at the camera, derived from the artisanal mode of film production; *Birth* confirmed the period of directorial control.[3]

The Jazz Singer (1927), founding movie of Hollywood sound, introduced the blackface performer, Al Jolson, to feature films. Jolson was the most popular entertainer of his day, and *The Jazz Singer's* souvenir program (unlike critical attention since) devoted far more attention to blackface than to Western Electric's new sound and film projection system, Vitaphone. *The Jazz Singer* was a pure product of the studio producer system; the Warner brothers were in charge. Finally, David O. Selznick's *Gone With the Wind* (1939), an early example of the producer unit system that would come to dominate Hollywood, established the future of the Technicolor spectacular by returning to American film origins in the plantation myth. *Birth* was the most widely seen movie of the silent period, *The Jazz Singer* broke all existing box office records, and Jolson's blackface sequel, *The Singing Fool* (1928) became the leading money-maker of the 1920s. All three were eclipsed by *Gone With the Wind*, classical Hollywood's top box office success.[4]

American literature, as critics from D. H. Lawrence to Richard Slotkin have argued, established its national identity in the struggle between Indians and whites; American film was born from white depictions of blacks.[5] The white male hero of our classic literature frees himself from paternal, old-world constraints and establishes his independence against Indians; he rises from black/white conflict in film. These alternative racial roots are not arbitrary, for just as the frontier period in American history generated the classic literature (beginning with captivity narratives), so American film was born from the conjunction between southern defeat in the Civil War, black resubordination, and national reintegration; the rise of the multiethnic, industrial metropolis; and the emergence of mass entertainment, expropriated from its black roots, as the locus of Americanization. If, as Leslie Fiedler suggested, the white male literary hero replaces the white woman with his red brother, then *Birth* and *The Jazz Singer* (the former in the psychological subtext of the film, the latter on screen) use black men for access to forbidden white women. *The Jazz Singer* makes its subject that which is buried in *Birth*, that the interracial double is not the exotic other but the split self, the white in blackface.

Birth and *The Jazz Singer* ostensibly exploit blacks in opposite ways. *Birth* makes war on blacks in the name of the fathers; *The Jazz Singer's* protagonist adopts a black mask and kills his father. *The Birth of a Nation*, climaxing the worst period of violence against blacks in southern history, lynches the black; the jazz singer, ventriloquizing the black, sings through his mouth. *Birth*, a product of the progressive movement, has national political purpose. *The Jazz Singer*, marking the retreat from public to private life in the jazz age, and the perceived pacification of the (fantasized) southern black threat, celebrates not political regeneration but urban entertainment.

These historical contrasts in the use of blackface arise from an underlying identity. Griffith used blacks not to restore plantation patriarchy but to give birth to a new nation. The immigrants absent from his screen were present in his audience, as *Birth* used black/white conflict to Americanize them. The jazz singer also escapes his immigrant identity through blackface. Miscegenation as well as assimilation energizes both movies. White identification with (imaginary) black sexual desire, powerfully unconscious in *Birth*, comes to the surface in *The Jazz Singer*. The black desire for white women, enacted in blackface in *Birth*, justifies not only the political and sexual repression of blacks but also the marriage of Civil War enemies, North and South. Blackface promotes interracial marriage in *The Jazz Singer*, by apparent contrast with *Birth*, but it facilitates the union of gentile and Jew, not white and black.

Celebrating the blackface identification that *Birth of a Nation* denies, *The Jazz Singer* does no favor to blacks. The blackface jazz singer is neither a jazz singer nor black. Blackface marries ancient rivals in both movies; black and white marry in neither. Just as *Birth* offers a regeneration through violence, so the grinning, *Jazz Singer*, minstrelsy mask kills blacks with kindness.

The original reviews of *The Jazz Singer* responded as much to Jolson's blackface as to Vitaphone.[6] On the film's fiftieth anniversary, with *The Jazz Singer* securely established as the first talking picture and blackface an embarrassment, the four film journal commemorative articles barely mentioned blackface. But each reprinted movie stills that unavoidably made visible what their texts had repressed; all the articles showed Jolson in blackface. Critics in the 1980s, stimulated in part by Neil Diamond's self-consciously Jewish 1981 remake, downplayed sound in favor of the story, generational conflict, and Jewish assimilation.[7] *The Jazz Singer*, however, actually gives equal weight to all three stories: the conversion to sound, the conversion of the Jews, and the conversion by blackface. Far from being separate but equal, so that one story can be rescued from its contamination by others, the film amalgamates all three. Substituting racial masquerade for the mixing of bodily fluids, *The Jazz Singer* speaks from racial desire, not simply racial aversion. As immigration and technological innovations were creating American mass culture, the film announced old-world, patriarchal defeat to obfuscate new-world power, and appropriated an imaginary blackness to Americanize the immigrant son. White masks fail to hide black skin, in Franz Fanon's analysis, and turn African into European. But if the shift from bodily interior to beholder's eye inflicts an epidermal consciousness on the black masked as white, it allows the blackface performer to speak from his own, authentically felt, interior.[8]

TALKING PICTURES AND THE JEWISH QUESTION

Although it is always problematic to identify revolutionary innovations with a single achievement, *The Jazz Singer* can legitimately claim the status of the first talking picture. No feature film before *The Jazz Singer* had either lip-synchronized musical performance or dialogue. None used sound to cut away from and yet retain the previously visible action, and none incorporated words and music into the story.[9] These innovations are still electrifying because they are preceded within the film by the earlier forms this movie would destroy—silent, documentary, lower East Side scenes, pantomime gestures, and intertitles. When young Jakie Rabinowitz sings in Muller's café bar, he announces a cinematic revolution.

The second sound interval is even more startling. When the grown Jack Robin (formerly Jakie Rabinowitz) sings "Dirty Hands, Dirty Face" at Coffee Dan's, for the first time in feature films a voice issues forth from a mouth. Jack then breaks free of both the intertitles that have carried the dialogue and the musical accompaniment that has carried the sound, and speaks his own words. "Wait a minute. Wait a minute. You ain't heard nothing yet," says Al Jolson, repeating the lines he'd already made famous in vaudeville.[10] These first words of feature movie speech, a kind of performative, announce—"you ain't heard nothing yet"—the birth of sound movies and the death of silent film. The vaudeville performer, Al Jolson, has killed silent movies.

Jolson paid for his triumph, however, a sacrifice to what Andrew Sarris has called "the cultural guilt of musical movies." Although *The Jazz Singer* and *The Singing Fool* were box office hits, Jolson's career did not prosper in the 1930s. Vaudeville and silent movies complemented each other; talking pictures displaced both. Sarris writes, "Al Jolson became the first scapegoat for the cultural guilt assumed by movie musicals as the slayers of silent cinema."[11]

The jazz singer may have killed silent movies; within the film, however, he kills his father. Sarris's extraordinary formalism ignores the connection on which the film insists, between the death of silent movies and the death of the Jewish patriarch. Cantor Rabinowitz expects Jakie to become a cantor, like generations of Rabinowitzs before him. Jakie wants to sing jazz. Familially and musically, Cantor Jakie Rabinowitz would lose his own voice. Kol Nidre, the chant on the Day of Atonement for the forgiveness of sins, takes the place of Jakie's singing in the movie's opening scenes. But Jakie does not want to submerge his individual identity in ancient, sacred community; the result is family war. His father beats him for singing "raggy time" songs. He throws the grown Jack Robin out of his house. Jazz was the emblem of generational revolt in the jazz age; critics charged it with destroying the family.[12] Jakie's decision to become a jazz singer kills his father. The cultural guilt of the first talking picture is assimilation and parricide.

The Jazz Singer links its twin killings of silent movies and the Jewish patriarch since Vitaphone carries the generational conflict in its three, revolutionary scenes—the first, character-embedded, singing voice; the first lip-synchronized singing and first lines of speech; and the first dialogue. Together these scenes form an oedipal triangle—antithesis, thesis, synthesis—with the Jewish mother at the center. Cantor Rabinowitz stops Jakie's singing in the first scene, returning the film to silence, when he drags his son from the stage. Jack talks for the first time in the second scene, after the heroine admires his song. Jack's first spoken words introduce the Jewish/gentile romance.

Jewish father stops the voice (antithesis); gentile woman elicits it (thesis).

But there is no dialogue at Coffee Dan's; Jack only speaks from the stage to announce his next number. When he returns home, in the climax at the center of the film, he sings and speaks to his mother. Sara Rabinowitz frantically caresses her son and murmurs an embarrassed few words as she and Jack play a love scene. Jack sings "Blue Skies" to his mother, tells her he'd rather please her than anyone he knows, steals a kiss from her, promises to buy her a new dress, will hug and kiss her in the dark mill at Coney Island, returns to the piano to play a "jazzy" version of "Blue Skies," and asks her if she liked "that slappin' business" on the keyboard. *Slapping* was the jazz term for pizzicato playing; the sexual origins of the word "jazz" (in copulation) have never been more spectacularly, inappropriately present. A small door opens in the background, the tiny figure of the patriarch appears, the camera isolates his menacing head and shoulders, and a voice from the mouth shouts, "Stop!"[13] (See Figure 14.)

In stopping at the same time the music and the romance between son and mother, Cantor Rabinowitz ends speech. For the first and only time in the film there is an extended period of silence, before mournful, east European music, replacing "Blue Skies," returns. Jolson's singing will as well, but "Stop!" is the last spoken word in the film. Mother and son try to placate the father, in gestures and intertitles, and fail. Cantor Rabinowitz sends Jack from the house in silence, but the damage to silent pictures and the father has been done. Jack's father may have the power to stop speech in this film, but it will cost him and silent movies their life.[14]

In choosing *The Jazz Singer* as the first talking picture, "the itinerant peddlers, junk-dealers, and sweatshop entrepreneurs who had parlayed their slum-located storefront peepshows into" one of the country's major industries were telling their own story.[15] Neal Gabler has recently shown how the Jewish moguls created Hollywood against their paternal inheritance. Doting on their mothers, in rebellion against their failed, *luftmenschen* fathers, the moguls Americanized themselves by interpreting gentile dreams. *The Jazz Singer*, loosely based on Jolson's own life, suggests the history of the men who made Hollywood.[16]

Perhaps because its parricidal implications disturbed them, however, Harry, Al, Jack, and Sam Warner stressed the harmonious generational cooperation that had produced *The Jazz Singer*. As the souvenir program explained, "The faithful portrayal of Jewish home life is largely due to the unobtrusive assistance of Mr. Benjamin Warner, father of the producers, and ardent admirer of 'The Jazz Singer'" (*SP*, 9). Paternal approval, as J. Hoberman writes, was enlisted for paternal overthrow.[17] The Warner brothers patriarch, moreover, was being implicated in a Jewish home life of shouting, beating, exile, and death. But the Warner who paid for generational rebellion in *The Jazz Singer* was not Benjamin Warner, but his youngest son, Sam.

14. Still from *The Jazz Singer* ("Never saw the sun shinin' so bright—").

Benjamin Warner was poor and devout. Sam was antireligious, however, and after his older brothers married Jewish women uninvolved in show business, Sam chose in 1925 a gentile dancer. As his wife, Lina Basquette, recalls, Sam's brothers were furious at him for marrying "a little eighteen-year-old shiksa."[18]

Sam Warner had brought his brothers into the motion picture business, was the enthusiast for sound, and was in charge of the Vitaphone project. (His brothers called it "Sam's toy phonograph" ["GG," 57].) Since the Warner brothers' investment in sound was part of a coordinated strategy to expand their small studios market share and challenge the preeminence of Hollywood's big three (and not, as was once thought, a desperate attempt to stave off bankruptcy), Jack Robin was enacting Sam Warner's upward mobility through Vitaphone. Sam did not normally make movies, but he came west to supervise *The Jazz Singer*'s production. After Jolson ad libbed his famous line at Coffee Dan's, Sam reshot Jack Robin's homecoming, added dialogue, and thereby created the love scene with the mother.[19]

Jack faces the crisis of his life after his father forces him to choose between his mother and jazz. In the film's climax, he is torn between replacing his dying father to sing Kol Nidre on Yom Kippur eve, the holiest night in the

Jewish calendar, or going on with the vaudeville show. Since Kol Nidre is sung on the one night each year when the "skies open" and Jews can speak directly to God to ask for forgiveness of sins, Jack's sin would be to choose vaudeville stardom ("Blue Skies") over Kol Nidre; the Warner brothers, also flirting with blasphemy, premiered *The Jazz Singer* on the night before Yom Kippur, the night Jack learns that his father is dying and that he must choose between show business and filial piety. Mixing movie with worldly time, the studio wanted Cantor Rabinowitz's death and Jack's Kol Nidre to fall as close as possible to the actual Jewish holiday. But this evocation of the Jewish anarchic "Yom Kippur Ball," a satanic night of feasting during the holy fast, could not be enjoyed by the Warner brothers. The night before Cantor Rabinowitz was to die in New York, Sam Warner died in Los Angeles (of a brain abscess at the age of thirty-nine). The "screaming and wailing" mother at his deathbed—quoting Basquette ("GG," 58)—appeared again the next night on screen at the deathbed of the Jewish patriarch. Sam's dream of bringing together Jewish mother and gentile wife, fulfilled by the dying Cantor Rabinowitz, happened first over his own deathbed. Sam was buried on Yom Kippur eve, and his three brothers, all in Los Angeles to arrange the funeral, missed the movie premiere.[20]

Reflection and perhaps agent of generational war to the death, *The Jazz Singer* can hardly be accused of glossing over family conflict. *The Jazz Singer* exemplifies the hysterical text, in recent readings of film melodrama, exposing the familial conflicts buried in the name of realism. Because *The Jazz Singer* depicts the costs of assimilation to family and immigrant community, Hoberman calls it "the bluntest and most resonant movie Hollywood ever produced on the subject of American Jews."[21]

But *The Jazz Singer*'s ending and its overall, family frame, link this hysterical Jewish melodrama to flight rather than exposure. At the film's most hysterical moment, Jack sings first Kol Nidre at the synagogue over his father's dying body, and then "My Mammy" to his mother and girlfriend at the Winter Garden Theater. The movie was promising that the son could have it all, Jewish past and American future, Jewish mother and gentile wife. That was not what happened in Hollywood. The moguls left their Jewish wives for gentile women in the 1930s and eliminated Jewish life from the screen. They bid farewell to their Jewish pasts with *The Jazz Singer*. Americanized Jews ultimately would retain Jewish identities, but there was no going back to the lower East Side.[22]

The Jazz Singer's happy ending hardly wipes away the conflict that dominates the film. Jack is a "cultural schizophrenic," in Peter Rose's phrase;[23] the movie allows no easy, harmonious reconciliation between Jewishness and America. But to weigh the costs displayed within the movie against its happy ending accepts *The Jazz Singer* on its own terms, transforming Jewish history in the United States into family melodrama.

The struggle of sons against fathers was an immigrant social fact, but the documents that chronicle that story join generational conflict within the community to hostile, external pressure upon it, the context wished away by the first talking picture. All Jack's problems are with his father; none are with the gentiles. Cantor Rabinowitz's hostility to American entertainment is not balanced by any American hostility to Jews. *The Jazz Singer* culminates the tradition of ethnic films that emplotted generational conflict over intermarriage rather than racial prejudice. The *Judenfreiing* of the Rabinowitz name, so central to the story as we shall see, responds only to the attractions of Americanization, not to the prejudices against Jews.[24]

Also excised from *The Jazz Singer* are the social struggles that united Jews, often across generations, in trade unions, radical movements, businesses, and community organizations. Instead of pitting Jews against nativism, *The Jazz Singer* pits father against son. Domesticating the problem of the Jewish son, as critics of family melodrama would predict, *The Jazz Singer* lets America off the hook and fragments Jewish community. Shifting from ethnocultural to generational conflict, the film celebrates not the Jew as pariah, united with other outcast groups, but the Jew as parvenu.[25]

Two historiographies interpret the 1920s, an older approach by way of ethnocultural conflict and a newer one stressing the alliance between youth revolt and the culture of consumption. Provincial, backward-looking, nativism triumphs in the former view, which makes the 1920s the last decade of the nineteenth century. Urban, entertainment-centered self-fulfillment triumphs in the latter view, which makes the 1920s the harbinger of the future. *The Jazz Singer*, visible data for the more recent historiography, supports the older by what it hides, for its protagonist rises from the defeat not only of his cantor father but of radical, ethnic-based politics as well.[26]

F. Scott Fitzgerald, who "claimed credit for naming" "the Jazz Age," understood that it "extended from the suppression of the riots of May Day 1919 to the crash of the stock market in 1929."[27] The shift from radical protest to popular culture, enforced by continuing nativism, made possible *The Jazz Singer*. The jazz age introduced modern anti-Semitism into American politics, as traditional rivalry between immigrant and old-stock Americans coalesced with ideological racism. The anti-Semitic, anti-Catholic Ku Klux Klan (legacy of *Birth of a Nation*) flourished in the 1920s. Three years before *The Jazz Singer*, the racist immigration law of 1924 pretty well closed immigration from southern and eastern Europe. ("By far the largest percentage of immigrants [were] peoples of Jewish extraction," the U. S. House of Representatives Committee on Immigration and Naturalization had warned; the Jewish percentage of net migration to the United States, 21.2 percent in 1920, was reduced by the law to close to zero.) *The Jazz Singer* premiered six weeks after the judicial murder of Sacco and Vanzetti, the final victims of the postwar red scare.[28]

Nativist pressure created *The Jazz Singer*'s invisible frame. The movie emerged from the moguls' wish to evacuate anti-Semitism from the Jewish question. That wish derived not from Jewish power, Henry Ford's ravings about "Jewish supremacy in the motion picture world" notwithstanding,[29] but from just the context of gentile sufferance that the moguls did not want to acknowledge on film. Wishing away anti-Semitism required the disappearance of the Jews. Anti-Semitism is *The Jazz Singer*'s structuring absence. The visible cost it leaves behind is borne by Jolson as he plays not a Jew but a black.

A large image of Al Jolson in blackface rises above Sarris's title, "The Cultural Guilt of Musical Movies." (See Figure 15.) That picture, returning to haunt the text that represses it, insists that one can understand neither the cultural guilt of slaying silents nor the cultural guilt of slaying the father without harkening to yet a deeper layer, the cultural guilt of exploiting blacks. Riveting sympathetic attention on parents and son, united by the movie's affect as they are divided by its plot, *The Jazz Singer* blacks out the non-Jewish group behind the blackface mask. White painted mouth and white gloved hands sing and gesture in blackface performance. Black holes in space fragment, stand in for, and render invisible the broken-up, absent black body. The lips that speak Jack's personal voice are caricatured, racist icons.[30] Jack Robin rises through blackface, as vaudeville entertainer, lover, and Jewish son. Jolson's blackface performance dominates the crisis and resolution of the film. Blackface carries *The Jazz Singer* backward to the origins of mass entertainment and forward to American acceptance. The sign of what has been left behind appears not in collective Jewish identity but in the instrument of the jazz singer's individual success, the pasteboard mask that points to another American pariah group, African-Americans.

JEWS AND THE BLACKFACE QUESTION

"This is the turning point represented by Griffith," writes Pascal Bonitzer:

> What we have here is a cinematic revolution. With the arrival of montage, the close-up, immobile actors, the look (and its corollary—the banishment of histrionics) an entire facade of the cinema seems to disappear and be lost forever; in a word, all the excrement of vaudeville. The cinema was 'innocent' and 'dirty.' It was to become obsessional and fetishistic. The obscenity did not disappear, it was interiorized, moralized and passed into the register of desire. . . . As the body became more or less immobilized and the look was enthroned, morality, perversion and desire intervened for the first time in the cinema.[31]

But Griffith did not banish histrionics forever from film. *The Jazz Singer* revived them, innocent and dirty, with blackface. Blackface was the legacy of vaudeville entertainment and the silent screen; *The Jazz Singer*'s success

THE CULTURAL GUILT
OF MUSICAL MOVIES

THE JAZZ SINGER, Fifty Years After
by Andrew Sarris

15. Illustration to Andrew Sarris's "The Cultural Guilt of Musical
Movies," *Film Comment* 13 (Sept.–Oct. 1977): 39.

would begin to bring it to an end. The first talking picture went backward in
order to go forward and enter the era of sound. It revived the roots of movies
one more time.

Vaudeville, which succeeded blackface minstrelsy as the most popular
American entertainment form, was in turn displaced by movies. Each of
these spectacles, however, was linked to its predecessor. Vaudeville absorbed minstrelsy, as Jewish vaudeville entertainers like George Burns,
Eddie Cantor, George Jessel, and Jolson himself (Heywood Broun called
him "the master minstrel of them all" [quoted in *SP*, 15]) gave blackface a
new lease on life. One-reelers, in turn, were originally run in vaudeville
shows, and live vaudeville coexisted with silent movies in the 1920s motion
picture palace. Silent films, however, could not reproduce vaudeville noise
(musical numbers, sound effects, jokes, patter). Early sound movie shorts
returned to film origins—newsreel documentaries (mainly Fox) and vaudeville performances (mainly Warner Brothers)—to show they could improve

on silent pictures. The silent versions of these shorts had exposed the limitations of the stage; the sound versions revealed the shortcomings of the silents.[32]

The Jazz Singer condensed into a single feature film the entire history of American popular entertainment, from minstrelsy through vaudeville to silent films to talking pictures, for the first feature film to bring sound into the *diegesis* incorporated vaudeville minstrelsy as well. The "desire" that carries forward this "interiorized, moralized" oedipal narrative, to recall Bonitzer's words, is Jack's "innocent and dirty" desire—sung as "Dirty Hands, Dirty Face"—to become a histrionic, vaudeville performer. Classical movies, culminating in sound, may have replaced stock vaudeville caricatures with individuated, interior characters, but Jack develops his character, expresses his interior, finds his own voice by employing blackface caricature. Blackface reinstated the exaggerated pantomime that restrained filmic gestures had supposedly displaced. Characterization, to use David Bordwell's oppositions, employed restless movement rather than replacing it. The closeup, montage, and shot/reverse-shot editing (rudimentary and centered on the jazz singer's performance as the latter is) establish the register of desire between Jack and Mary, but after their initial encounter, Jack plays all their love scenes in blackface.[33] Blackface supports its antithesis, the film techniques, character development, and triumph of sound that will destroy it. It does so by splitting the protagonist into forward- and backward-looking halves. The jazz singer rises by putting on the mask of a group which must remain immobile, unassimilable, and fixed at the bottom.

Jack Robin and his black double emerge as split halves of a single self when Jakie Rabinowitz changes his name. "Last time you forgot and addressed me Jakie Rabinowitz," the vaudeville performer writes his mother. "Jack Robin is my name now." Before it was changed in production, the next scene was to show him in blackface for the first time, with the intertitle, "Orchard Street would have some difficulty recognizing Jakie Rabinowitz of Beth-El choir under the burnt cork of Jack Robin" (*JS*, 80). The scene brings Jack and Mary into intimate contact, however, and "playing a romantic scene in blackface" proved too risky "an experiment," as the scriptwriter, Alfred Cohn, feared it might (*JS*, 83). Jack in his dressing gown and a black maid in the wings are residues of the original plan, as Jack courts Mary in whiteface, but blackface's source in split Jewish identity remains. "It talks like Jakie but it looks like a nigger," says the old Jew, Yudleson, in the shooting script when he first sees Jack in blackface; the intertitle changed "a nigger" to "his shadow" (*JS*, 136; for Jack's blackface shadow, see Figure 16.)[34] Two Al Jolson heads dominate *The Jazz Singer*'s souvenir program, one a grinning black face, the other in white floating slightly above and in front. (See Figure 17.) When blackfaced Jack looks in the mirror, he sees his father before the congregation. *The Jazz Singer* is, and knows that it is, a doubles movie.

16. Still from *The Jazz Singer* ("Jakie—this ain't you?").

Other films that employ the magical doubling device also fail completely to conform to models of the classic narrative film. Compare *The Jazz Singer* with two examples, one, *The Student from Prague* (1913, 1926; the brief analysis here conflates the two versions) from German expressionist cinema, and the other, Charlie Chaplin's *The Idle Class* (1921) from the vaudeville comic legacy.

Blocked mobility, writes Thomas Elsaesser, generates the doubles on the German silent screen. These films typically signal a social obstacle in their openings and then shift to the fantastic. *The Student from Prague*, for example, begins with infantilized student life from which the protagonist is estranged, and then introduces the old (Jewish-looking) Scapinelli. Scapinelli arranges for the student to rescue a young countess, magically produces gold, and then takes payment by splitting the student in two. Scapinelli seizes the student's mirror image; out of ego's control, it comes between the student and his love. The double interrupts one kiss in the countess' bedroom, another at the Jewish cemetery. Interrupting eros, it enacts forbidden aggression, killing the aristocratic rival the student has promised not to harm in a duel. Liberation of his shadow side finally destroys the student; shooting into the mirror (in the 1926 version), he kills himself. Scapinelli, apparent permission-giving alternative to the countess' father, turns out merely to reproduce him.[35]

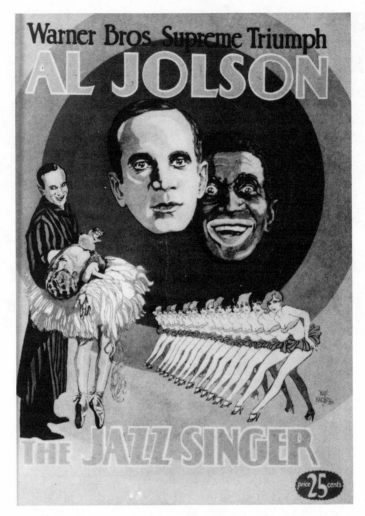

17. Illustration to souvenir program for *The Jazz Singer*. In *"The Jazz Singer," Souvenir Programs of Twelve Classic Movies 1927–1941*, ed. Miles Krieger (New York, 1977).

Like Jakie Rabinowitz, the student from Prague splits in two to fulfill transgressive desires. But there is no Scapinelli in *The Jazz Singer*. Whereas a black magician controls the student's double, Jack Robin controls his own black double. It does his bidding; it brings him success. Jack is the "master minstrel" in the souvenir program's words; his blackface double is his slave. Instead of W. E. B. DuBois's "two souls . . . warring . . . in one dark body," two bodies, one blacked and one white, heal Jack's single, divided soul.

Contrast the cooperation between the two Jack Robins with the conflict between the tramp and the man of the leisure class, both played by Chaplin in *The Idle Class*.[36]

Mistaken identity at a fancy dress ball gives the tramp temporary access to the rich man's wife and authorizes slapstick violence by the poor Chaplin against his rich double. This anarchic, rebellious, gestural residue of nickelodeon silent shorts makes fun of the rich, to be sure. But it requires that the classes end where they began, that the tramp return to the road and not displace his double in the family. Otherwise there would be no difference between them, and the film would lose its humor and its social point.

Blackface functions in precisely the opposite way in *The Jazz Singer*. Rather than fixing him in the one where he began, it allows the protagonist to exchange selves. Blackface is the instrument that transfers identities from immigrant Jew to American. By taking on blackface the Jewish jazz singer acquires that which is forbidden to the tramp and the student: first his own voice; then assimilation through upward mobility; finally women.

First his voice. Young Jakie Rabinowitz never appears in blackface, to be sure, but he gets the first individual voice in feature films by singing (as the shooting script puts it) "in the most approved darkie manner" (*JS*, 62). As Jakie shuffles on stage (see Figure 18), Yudleson reports to Cantor Rabinowitz (in an intertitle) that he is singing "raggy time songs"; the original shooting script had called them "nigger songs" (*JS*, 61, 136).[37]

Second, assimilation. Jakie finds his voice through black music; Jack will succeed as a blackface singer. But if the movie insists on the black origins of jazz (I will return to its use of that claim), it also wants the music to have Jewish roots, and so represents jazz as the link between Jews and America. The texts—original short story, play, movie shooting script, and intertitles—transfer Jewish sacred music to American jazz. The images put blacks into the picture.

"In seeking a symbol of the vital chaos of America's soul, I find no more adequate one than jazz," wrote Samson Raphaelson in the preface to his published play, reprinted in the souvenir program of the movie. The intertitle that follows the movie credits, "Jazz is prayer," appears to a background of mournful, east European music. "Distorted, sick, unconscious of its destination," Raphaelson explained, jazz linked polyglot, new world, America to the ancient, wandering Jews (*SP*, 14). "Carrying on the tradition of plaintive religious melody of his forefathers," as the narrator puts it in "The Day of Atonement," the short story from which *The Jazz Singer* derived, "Jakie was simply translating the age-old music of the cantors—that vast loneliness of a race wandering 'between two worlds, one dead, the other powerless to be born.' "[38]

"You taught me that music is the voice of God," Jack tells his father in the movie. "My songs mean as much to my audience as yours to your congrega-

18. Still from *The Jazz Singer* ("See them shuffle along—").

tion." "He sings like his Poppa, with a tear in his voice," says Sara when she hears him in blackface as the cantor is about to die. "He's not my boy any more. He belongs to the world." In blessing Jack's movement from cantor's son to jazz singer, Sara sustains his claim that entertainment was the new American religion. When the white-robed and skull-capped Jack replaces his father on Yom Kippur (see Figure 19; "a jazz singer singing to his God," says the intertitle; the shooting script had "stage's greatest blackface come-dian" [JS/133]) and then puts on wool cap and burnt cork to sing "My Mammy" (see Figure 20), he is exchanging one religious robe of office for another. The island communities of traditional America would be homoge-nized by idols of consumption. If political progressivism had failed to regen-erate America, the jazz age would bring the younger generation of classes and ethnic groups together around the performer as commodity fetish.[39]

Insisting on the shift from Hebraic particularism to American universal-ism, neither Raphaelson nor the intertitles acknowledge blackface as the instrument of that transformation. One would never know from Raphael-son—any more than from Henry Ford's accusation that the "Jewish song trust makes you sing"[40]—that African-Americans and not Jews had created jazz. Blackface gives back to the racial shadow the music taken from its substance.

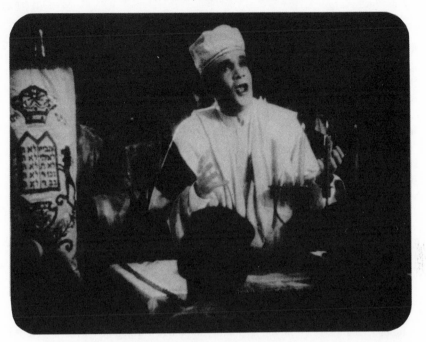

19. Still from *The Jazz Singer* ("—a jazz singer—singing to his God.").

20. Still from *The Jazz Singer* ("Mammy").

Much of the early success of Jolson's generation of Jewish entertainers was, as Irving Howe puts it, "gained from acts done in blackface," and Jews had almost entirely taken over blackface entertainment by the early twentieth century. Jewish song writers also turned to black derived music to create the uniquely American, melting pot sound of the jazz age. Irving Berlin (with whose "Blue Skies" Jack Robin seduces his mother) scored his first big hit in 1911 with the minstrel number, "Alexander's Ragtime Band." (Berlin had written "Yiddle on Your Fiddle Play Some Ragtime" two years earlier.)[41] "Originating with the Negroes," as John Tasker Howard expressed the consensus of enthusiasts and detractors alike, jazz "has become a Jewish interpretation of the Negro." "There is one vocation, all the known members of which could pass a synogogue door unchallenged," announced *Variety* in 1920, because those who made up "The Syncopated Symphony" were Jews.[42]

"We speak of jazz as if it were the product of the Negro alone," wrote Isaac Goldberg the month before *The Jazz Singer* premiere.

> True enough, its primary associations, like its rhythms, are black, deriving ultimately from the African southland. . . . It reaches from the black South to the black North, but in between it has been touched by the commercial wand of the Jew. What we call loosely by the name is thus no longer jet black; musical miscegenation set in from the beginning, and today it would be a wise son if it knew its own father.

Jews had made more than a commercial impact on jazz, Goldberg continued; although the "Negro ancestry" of Irving Berlin, Jerome Kern, and George Gershwin was "certainly questionable," the "musical amalgamation of the American Negro and the American Jew" had given birth to jazz. The *Baltimore Afro-American* excerpted Goldberg's essay under the headline, "Jazz Indebted to the Jews."[43]

"Musical miscegenation" was only part of the uniquely cooperative relationship between Jewish and African-Americans in the first decades of the twentieth century. Nativist coalescence of race and ethnic stereotypes into a single, monstrous alien pushed Jews to think of themselves as allied with other minorities. The Yiddish press, protesting against lynchings and other antiblack violence, compared race riots against blacks to pogroms against Jews. Wealthy German Jews made common cause with "talented tenth" Negroes in the struggle for civil rights; Jewish clothing unions organized black workers while American Federation of Labor craft organizations excluded them; and Jewish philanthropy and legal services supported black civic institutions and court fights. In fighting for our rights, Jews also fight for their own, explained the black writer, James Weldon Johnson.[44]

It is against that background of interracial cooperation that Irving Howe accounts sympathetically for the Jewish attraction to blackface. "Black became a mask for Jewish expressiveness, with one woe speaking through the voice of another," writes Howe. "Blacking their faces seems to have enabled

the Jewish performers to reach a spontaneity and assertiveness in the declaration of their Jewish selves" (W, 563).[45] This filial piety to the blackface
Jewish fathers makes Howe, himself, an easy target for a Jew from the next
generation, who risks imitating by reversing *The Jazz Singer*. For to attack
blackface (who would now defend it?) may simply be another way of putting
it on, as this (graybearded) Jewish son, like Jolson before him, uses blacks to
declare his independence from the patriarch, Irving Howe—and thereby,
like the blackface singer, pretends to speak for blacks as well.[46] Still, even at
the risk of contaminating the questioner, it is necessary to ask, after Howe,
what Jewish "woe" and which "Jewish selves" the jazz singer's blackface
ventriloquizes?

Blackface may seem not to express Jewishness at all but to hide it, so that
even your own mother wouldn't know you. "Jakie, this ain't you," says Sara
when she first sees her son in blackface.[47] But why should the member of
one pariah group hide his identity under the mask of another? Where Howe
sees only solidarity, I see transfer as well. Switching identities, the jazz
singer acquires exchange value at the expense of blacks. Miscegenation was
regression, in racialist theory, because the dark drove out the light. Blackface mimed that process in order to reverse it. Stereotypes located within
both pariah groups were exteriorized as black, embraced as regenerative,
and left (along with actual blacks) behind. Put Yiddish and black together,
wrote Goldberg, "and they spell Al Jolson" (quoted in W, 563).[48] Take them
apart and their doubling supports the flight of Jack Robin above them both.

Like the Jewish struggle for racial justice, the black-inspired music of
urban Jews was a declaration of war against the racial hierarchy of Protestant, genteel culture. Urban entertainment created an alternative, polyglot
world, in which the children of Jewish immigrants found new, cosmopolitan
identities among Jews, other immigrants, children of old-stock Americans—
Randolph Bourne, Hutchins Hapgood, Carl Van Vechten—and African-
Americans as well. The jazz singer's parricide spreads, from that perspective, out to the paternal cultural guardians of the dominant society. But *The
Jazz Singer* refuses that self-interpretation. Screening out the polyglot metropolis of the second generation, it confines rebellion within the Jewish
family. Substituting blackface doubling for ethnic and racial variety, the
movie points in spite of itself to another truth about the melting pot, not the
cooperative creation of something new but assimilation to old inequalities.
Blacks may have seemed the most distinctively American people, the fur-
thest from the old-world identities of Americanizing immigrants, but inte-
gral to that distinctiveness was their exclusion from the ethnic intermixture
that defined the melting pot. For Jews and blacks were not moving in the
same direction in the 1920s. When the historian of Jewish support for racial
justice calls Jews "mouthpieces" for the more powerless blacks, she inadver-
tantly invokes the cultural form, blackface, that spoke for assimilating Jews
and silenced African-Americans.[49]

A common set of racial stereotypes, that bore fruit in the 1924 immigration restriction bill, bound together Jews, Asians, and blacks under the orientalist umbrella. But Orientalism also had a redemptive meaning in the jazz age; it signified racially alien, primitivist qualities, embraced by Jewish and black musicians, that would revivify American life.[50] The conflation of racial minorities into a single, Orientalist alien, moreover, at the same time that it allied Jews with blacks, also provided the movie jazz singer with his way out. Unlike the hero of the short story, Al Jolson plays a person of color instead of being confused with one. By painting himself black, he washes himself white. "The cry of my race" pulls Jack back to his family, as he sees his father behind his own blackface, mirror reflection. Blackface, by contrast, liberates the performer from the fixed, "racial" identities of African-American and Jew. Freeing Jack from his inner blackness, blackface frees him from his father.

Blackface also gives Jack access to allegedly black qualities, intense emotionality and its form of musical expression. In part these were white fantasies, in part black achievements (jazz), and we will be turning to *The Jazz Singer*'s relation to both. The blackface singer makes those qualities his own. His "musical miscegenation" produces the excitement of racial contact without its sexual dangers, for Jack's child is his music and his own reborn self. As disguise, blackface capitalizes on identity as sameness; as expression it creates identity as difference. Interiority generated and repressed by the culture of origin finds public form through the blackface mask. Evoking an imagined alternative communal identity, blackface frees the performer from the pull of his inherited, Jewish, communal identicalness. The depersonalizing mask reaches a substrate of emotional expression out of which a new selfhood is born. *Variety* explained, "As soon as [Jolson] gets under the cork, the lens picks up that spark of individual personality solely identified with him." Supplying his spontaneity and freeing him to be himself, blackface made Jolson a unique and therefore representative American.[51]

Freeing the son from the Jewish father on the one hand, the black pariah on the other, blackface is racial cross-dressing. Just as the white man in classic American literature uses Indians to establish an American identity against the Old World, so the jazz singer uses blacks. If regeneration through violence against Indians won the West, then rebirth through mass entertainment (expropriating black music) won the city. Just as Leatherstocking can put on and take off the signs of nature and remain without "a cross of Indian blood," so the jazz singer acquires transformative black qualities by masquerade instead of miscegenation. Cross-dressing, says Sandra Gilbert, allows the white man to acquire the envied (fantasized) qualities of the other sex (here race) and yet reassure himself of his own identity: I am not really black; underneath the burnt cork is a white skin. Cross-dressing, says Elaine Showalter, allows the white man to speak for women (here blacks) instead of to them, and show the actual members of the stigmatized group how best to play themselves.[52]

Blackface does not simply substitute racial for sexual cross-dressing, for the movie's romance unites the two. The blackface shadow points to forbidden women. But whereas the double usually signifies sexual catastrophe, as for the Prague student and the tramp,[53] Jack's double gives him access both to his mother and to her gentile rival. Blackface takes Jack from his mother to Mary, expresses their conflicting demands on him, and finally acquires them both. Miming the most tabooed romance in American culture, that between black man and white woman, blackface disempowers both threatening participants.

Blackface is not the instrument of aggression, however, which is how doubling functions in its comic (tramp) and gothic (student) forms. The student from Prague is a passive, gender-destabilized, half a man whose double takes charge. The double's aggression blocks access to the higher status woman, whereas the aggressive tramp temporarily gets her; by contrast to both, however, the aggressive, self-confident Jack Robin (at Coffee Dan's and in the love scene with his mother) is feminized in blackface. He plays not the black sexual menace of reconstruction, progressive, and *Birth of a Nation* fantasy, but the child Negro of the restored 1920s plantation myth. In a decade that feared Jewish aggression and kept blacks securely in their place, and when white collegians considered blacks less aggressive than Jews, the black mask of deference enforced on one pariah group covered the ambition attributed to the other.[54]

Enacting submission made Jolson, as the souvenir program put it, "the master not only of laughter but of pathos" (*SP*, 77). Prominent teeth and grinning mouth had established the minstrel as a needy, greedy, oral self. Minstrelsy made African-Americans into lazy, boastful creatures of physical need, the underside of hardworking, ambitious, white Protestants. Jolson played blackface trickster on Broadway, but not in his movie hits, *The Jazz Singer* and *The Singing Fool*. Drained of the sexuality and aggression that were permitted only as self-ridicule, *The Jazz Singer* left behind a pure figure of longing. (See Figure 21.)[55]

Jack appears between Sara and Mary in two scenes, the two in which he wears blackface. The first scene, displaying the singer's divided loyalties, flirts with racial as sexual cross-dressing. Neither Jack nor Mary appears in the everyday clothes that signify sexual difference. Jack wears black skin as his costume; in tightfitting pants and shirt, he is blacking his face and putting on a black wool wig. Mary, undressed in scanty dance costume, is all white. Her visible limbs convey a phallic power that, her availability for the male gaze notwithstanding, accentuates the blackface performer's passivity. To complete the disorientation, Mary wears a giant tiara on her head. Standing as Jack sits in the scene's opening, Mary towers above him. (See Figure 22 for the three protagonists; I have no reproduction of Jack beneath Mary.)

21. Illustration to souvenir program for *The Jazz Singer*. In *"The Jazz Singer," Souvenir Programs of Twelve Classic Movies 1927–1941*, ed. Miles Krieger (New York, 1977).

As one sexual signifier floats from Jack to Mary, another slides from Sara to Jack. When his mother enters, "he starts to kiss her," the published shooting script explains, "then remembers her [*sic*] makeup" (*JS*, 120). Jack actually remembers *his* burnt cork; the editorial *sic* underlines the fact that the makeup is on the wrong sex; and it is Mary, as a production still from the souvenir program indicates, who first showed Jack how to use it (see Figures 23 and 24).

22. Still used as illustration to souvenir program for *The Jazz Singer*. In *"The Jazz Singer," Souvenir Programs of Twelve Classic Movies 1927–1941*, ed. Miles Krieger (New York, 1977).

23. Still from *The Jazz Singer* ("Maybe your Papa is dying—maybe he won't ever hear you sing again.").

24. Production still used as illustration to souvenir program for *The Jazz Singer*. In *"The Jazz Singer,"* *Souvenir Programs of Twelve Classic Movies 1927–1941*, ed. Miles Krieger (New York, 1977).

Eddie Cantor played *Salome* in blackface and drag. Ike Levisky, the clothing salesman in *Levisky's Holiday* (1913), disguises himself as a bearded lady to enter the circus without a ticket. Discovered, he is made the target in a "Hit the Nigger" booth, and his son sells the rotten eggs.[56] Neither menacing nor comic, neither anti-Semitic nor consciously antiblack, Jack's racial cross-dressing nevertheless has a transvestite component. It masks self-assertiveness in racial *cum* sexual drag. Whether as woman-identified or merely (some viewers may think) as child, blackface allows Jack to leave home and have it too. Putting on the mask of weakness, the upwardly mobile immigrant acquires the American girl without losing the Jewish mother.

Whiteface enforced a choice on Jack Robin, either Mary ("Toot, Toot, Tootsie") or Sara ("Blue Skies"). The two women come together in blackface, when Jack first sings the agony of choosing, then the ecstacy of double possession. As Jack sings "My Mammy" at Jolson's Winter Garden Theater, the camera cuts from the blackface performer on stage to the two adoring women, one in the audience and the other in the wings. Doubles are traditionally fraternal rivals for a single woman,[57] as in *The Student from Prague* and *The Idle Class*. The blackface shadow, doubling the mother instead, acquires two women for his white substance.

Emblematic of division in short story, play, and shooting script, blackface performs ecstatic synthesis in the movie's finale. The fadeout on Jolson with his arms outstretched surely means, in the *Uncle Tom's Cabin* tradition, to evoke Christ on the cross. Blackface Jack's sacrifice empowers the man behind the mask, however, as the singer moves from Sara to Mary, from the Jewish woman with an earthly husband to the Christian woman without one. At the same time, the plot diminishes Mary from career woman who gets Jack his break, to suppliant and admirer, and the powerful erotic bond remains that between mother and son. Maternal hysteria in the "Blue Skies" scene, in Martha Fineman's view, expresses less incestuous desire and more the anxiety of maternal loss; Sara wants to hold her family together. It is hard from the son's point of view not to feel the intermixture of Oedipus and separation in the maternal home. Jack sings on bended knee at the Winter Garden Theater, but this staged, blackface courtship ritual frees Jack from the sexualized mother at home to give him back at a safe distance—"I'd walk a million miles, for one of your smiles"—the purely nurturing one. The body in motion of "Blue Skies" reduces not to *Birth of a Nation*'s castrated black phallus but to exaggerated white lips that give and ask for nurture. Blackface expresses the "Jewish . . . woe" of leaving the maternal home.[58]

Blackface allows Jack to play the *fort/da* game, losing his mother and getting her back, by linking the black mammy to the Jewish mother. Sophie Tucker (born to Jewish parents in Poland, though Sartre thought she was black), who'd begun in New York vaudeville doing blackface in the afternoon and whiteface at night, and who learned "Some of These Days" from her black maid, introduced "My Yiddishe Momma" in 1925. Singing Yiddish on one side of her record and English on the other, Tucker's record sold a million copies. But if Tucker was also a "Red Hot Mamma," indebted to such classic blues mamas as Ma Rainey, Ethel Waters, and Ida Cox, the kneeling jazz singer reduces his Jewish mammy to passivity. No response comes from her like that Ethel Waters gave a year later to another man who thinks he can come and go at will: "Stand up when you're making your pleas / No use wearing out your knees / Get up off your knees, papa / You can't win me back that way."[59]

As a song of repentance for sins he knows he will repeat, "My Mammy" is a blackface Kol Nidre, but it no longer asks forgiveness from the Jewish Father God. The Lithuanian Jew who has lost his mother (Jolson's died when he was eight), and longs in blackface for a mammy, is giving up his

Jewish for an American dream. For this blackface inversion of Hortense Spiller's "Mama's Baby, Papa's Maybe" uses a surrogate black mammy to escape a real white father. In a sinister version of the psychoanalytic phrase, blackface is a regression in the service of the ego.[60]

Blackface exteriorizes Jewishness, embraces the exteriorized identity as regenerative, and leaves it behind. The linguistic ambiguity of that "it" has a cultural referent, for however thoroughly blackface relinquishes the Jewish past, it more thoroughly abandons blacks. Yankee, frontiersman, and black, wrote Constance Rourke, were the three humorous masks for establishing a uniquely American identity; urban Jews, racially stigmatized, chose the black.[61] But a sinister paradox inheres in this choice. Assimilation is achieved through the mask of the most segregated; the blackface that offers Jews mobility keeps the blacks fixed in place. By wiping out all difference except black and white, blackface turns Rabinowitz into Robin, but it does so by retaining the fundamental binary opposition. That segregation, imposed on blacks, silences their voices and sings in their name. Replacing the Jew, blackface also replaces the black.

The most obvious fact about *The Jazz Singer*, unmentioned in all the critical commentary, is that it contains no jazz. Al Jolson may have saved minstrelsy from extinction by giving it a syncopated beat, as Hoberman claims, but he rescued minstrelsy by blocking out jazz. The "jazz" of the jazz age, to be sure, was not the music of King Oliver, Louis Armstrong, Jelly Roll Morton, and Fletcher Henderson. Paul Whiteman, who led the most popular band of the 1920s and sold millions of records, was the acknowledged "King of Jazz." "Mr. Jazz Himself" is a 1917 Irving Berlin song, and Jolson gave Boston's first jazz recital in 1919. "Jazz is Irving Berlin, Al Jolson, George Gershwin, Sophie Tucker," proclaimed Raphaelson (*SP*, 14); Tucker's billing changed in the course of her career from "World Renowned Coon Shouter" to "Queen of Jazz."[62] As Amiri Baraka puts it, "Jazz had rushed into the mainstream without so much as one black face."[63]

Blackface did the work of black faces, standing not for what is now called jazz but for the melting-pot music of the jazz age. Almost without exception, popular culture writing in the 1920s treated Negro primitivism as the raw material out of which whites fashioned jazz. Jazz was identified with freedom as emotional release rather than as technical prowess. Improvisational skill, instead of being recognized in African-American musicians, was overlooked as central to jazz, and attributed to such performers as Jolson instead. It took a decade before a critic linked jazz improvisation to the act of speech, and that delayed insight suggests both why the first talking picture wanted to lay claim to jazz (sensing the link between jazz, speech, and individual freedom), and why (in a racially hierarchical society) *The Jazz Singer* assigned freedom to blackface ventriloquist rather than to an African-American jazz musician.[64]

An "industrialized folk music," jazz allegedly combined the sounds of the jungle and the metropolis. But Jolson's success, contemporaneous with Ulrich B. Phillips's celebratory *Life and Labor in the Old South*, points to the importance of slavery for the new music as well.[65] Blackface began under slavery, when blacks were forbidden access to the stage. *The Jazz Singer* returned them to the plantation. Jakie sings "Waiting for the Robert E. Lee" to begin the sound revolution in talking pictures; Jack sings "My Mammy" to end the movie. African-American jazz was the music of the urban, "New Negro," from New Orleans to Chicago to Kansas City, Harlem, and San Francisco. Blackface minstrelsy in the jazz age, by contrast, ventriloquized blacks as rural nostalgia. Domesticating the primitive, in the renderings of Jolson and other song writers and performers, the plantation supplied the lost-and-longed-for, innocent origins of jazz. Joining a lost southern to a lost Jewish to a lost maternal past, blackface "jazz" restored them all.[66]

The *Jazz Singer*'s blackface facilitated upward mobility in the competitive, urban present by symbolizing the peaceful, rural past. As Raymond Williams has argued for England and T. J. Clark for France, urban parvenus required the myth of the stable countryside.[67] The plantation played that function in the postbellum, industrializing United States, an American agrarian myth that imprisoned blacks. *The Birth of a Nation* invented black, reconstruction aggression to unite North and South against it. *The Jazz Singer* emasculated revolutionary, black modern music in the name of paying it homage. Like the other doubles movies, *The Jazz Singer* is also about blocked mobility. But whereas the tramp and the student from Prague are defeated by their doubles, blackface blocks mobility for the black double (and the woman) so that his white alter ego can rise.

Jazz may have been the jazz age's name for any up-tempo music, but that no more excuses *The Jazz Singer*'s missing sound than blackface compensates for its absence of blacks. Signifying the omitted referent claims possession of it, as urban mass entertainment let it be known it was capitalizing on its origins. Just as African-American performers introduced the cabaret songs that first underlay modern urban night life, and then were replaced by whites, so they invented jazz. And just as the first sound picture returned to and domesticated the "slum" origins of movies, so it expropriated jazz.[68] In the thematized, generational, Jewish story, the white noise of my title is the sacred chant that silences the jazz singer's voice. In the silenced, racial, black story, Jolson's white noise obliterates jazz.

BLACKFACE AND THE TALKING PICTURES QUESTION

The Jazz Singer retains its magic because, like no picture before or since, it is a liminal movie. It goes back and forth not only between sound and silence, music and intertitles, blackface and white, but also between Kol Nidre and "The Robert E. Lee," Jew and gentile, street and stage, male and female. Jack's putting on and taking off blackface is synecdochical for the movie's reversibility, its promise that nothing is fixed or lost forever.[69] Going back to the innocent, dirty origins of movies in order to go forward into sound, blackface was talking pictures' transitional object. It gathered together the shift from gesture to look, pleasure to desire, vaudeville to Hollywood, immigrant community to mobile individual, silence to sound, and only then became dispensable.

Blackface emancipated the jazz singer from Jews and blacks, I have been suggesting, by linking him to the groups he was leaving behind. It bears the same paradoxical relation to speech. The more primitive, histrionic technique displaces the more advanced, interiorized one during the course of the movie. Jack never appears in blackface before his father's prohibition stops speech. Blackface, in silent scenes and song, dominates the rest of the film. Jack sings in whiteface before the paternal "Stop!"—in blackface thereafter. But speech drove out blackface in the movies that followed *The Jazz Singer*. Blackface was the victim of the technological revolution for which it had fronted. Sarris's cultural guilt of movie musicals thus returns, pointing not only to the slaying of silent pictures in general but to the specific destruction of blackface. In what sense did the talkies kill blackface, and how can cultural guilt attach to the destruction of that vicious practice?

The dominant form of nineteenth-century entertainment, blackface, withdrew from center stage and finally disappeared from the twentieth-century motion picture. The first talking picture, making blackface its subject and not merely its method, is central to that trajectory. Blackface condensed two meanings, I have argued: heightened authenticity and American acceptance for the (Jewish) individual, subordination for the anonymous (black) mass. *The Jazz Singer*'s self-awareness about the former called attention to the role of performance in creating individuality. The first movie musical, *The Jazz Singer* was also the first movie to work musical numbers into its plot.[70] This conjunction of narrative and spectacle did not simply serve realism, however, and the "My Mammy" climax abandoned verisimilitude entirely for a utopian plenitude of feeling.

"My Mammy"'s pleasure principle set the precedent for production numbers in talking-pictures Hollywood, which occasionally also featured blackface. Without encompassing *The Jazz Singer*'s social and technological spread, minstrels under cork (like Fred Astaire in *Swingtime*) sang and danced with the emotional intensity enabled by blackface performance. World War II Hollywood featured blackface, in *Babes in Arms*, *Dixie*, and *Holiday Inn*, patriotically to celebrate its own origins in the minstrel show, and the USO called minstrelsy "the one form of American entertainment which is purely our own." *The Jolson Story* and *Jolson Sings Again* revived Jolson's popularity after the war; the latter was the top grossing picture of 1949. But in the wake of the post–World War II embarrassment about racial

subordination and stereotyping, and with the beginnings of the movement
for civil rights, these backward looks finally brought movie blackface to
an end.[71]

Musicals were an important talking pictures' genre; for the most part,
however, sound intensified the aspiration to verisimilitude that had defined
movies since Griffith. White actors might perform under cork in musicals,
but to play blackface dramatic roles violated cinematic conventions of realism. Calling attention to the figure behind the mask, blackface would then
expose the illusion that the individual was in charge of his or her voice, that
it issued forth from an authentic interior. Better to bequeath blackface to the
African-Americans who played the parts minstrelsy had prepared.[72]

But blackface was not only left behind for production numbers, nostalgia,
and African-Americans; it was universalized as well. During the period
when it was perfecting Vitaphone, Western Electric was also conducting an
experiment at the site of production. The "Hawthorne experiment" is as
germinal in industrial sociology as The Jazz Singer is in the history of film,
and the two have speaking in common. Getting workers to talk and feel
listened to, the company discovered, increased productivity more than did
the effort to create silent, efficient human machines. Talk, encouraged as
inner self-expression, functioned as social control. In production as in consumption, in work as at play, the company stood behind the workers' words,
Jolson to their blackface.[73] "Master Minstrel" Al Jolson models the dreams of
his fans, dreams produced socially for private consumption and ventriloquized as one's own. Freed from traditional cultural and communal re-
straints, the jazz singer becomes a component part of standardized organizations and standardized dreams. To cover up that mode of production, blackface had to go. For it exposed the illusion that the individual was speaking
and not being spoken for—whether by language, capital, the mass consumption industries, or the locus of all three for thirty years after The Jazz Singer
(returning to haunt us in the 1980s), by talking-pictures Hollywood.

That, at least, is the conclusion suggested by an extraordinary picture
published as part of the fiftieth anniversary celebration of The Jazz Singer.[74]
The picture is captioned with the first words of speech in a feature movie,
Jolson's "wait a minute, I tell ya. You ain't heard nothing. You want'a hear
'Toot Toot Tootsie?' " The photo (see Figure 25) shows a white man sitting
on a throne-like chair, with rows of identical-looking, blackface drummers
seated around and behind him. One figure in blackface stands front and
center, his arms outstretched in song. A blowup reveals that the singer is
Jolson himself.[75] But Jolson sang "Toot, Toot, Tootsie" alone in whiteface in
The Jazz Singer; the photograph reabsorbs him back into a minstrel troupe.
He represents the rows of blackface automatons, themselves synecdochical
for the reproduction of identical identities in film technology and mass society. The image thus undercuts the caption that misidentifies its picture.

25. Illustration for fiftieth anniversary celebration of *The Jazz Singer*.

Unmentioned, like blackface itself, in the article that prints it, the photograph makes visible the link between blackface and sound repressed in the text. For this silent picture assigns control over speech not to democratic, individual, or collective voices, but to the unidentified king of blackface, his authority sustained by the interchangeable identities of those who sing his song.

NOTES

* A slightly different version of this essay appeared in *Critical Inquiry* 18 (Spring 1991): 417–53. Copyright is held by the author.

1. Fred Schaffer assembled the materials from which this analysis began. I am greatly in his debt. Thanks also to the Center for Twentieth Century Studies, University of Wisconsin, Milwaukee (particularly Gordon Hutner, Patrice Petro, and Kathleen Woodward); the Interdisciplinary Group for Historical Literary Study at Texas A&M University; the Center for the Humanities, Johns Hopkins University; the Program in Liberal Studies, Emory University; the English department, Indiana University; the Social Thought and Ethics Program and the Conference for the Study of Political Thought at Yale University; and to Elizabeth Abel, Ann Banfield, James E. B. Breslin, Kim Chernin, Norman Jacobson, Charles Wolfe, and the readers for *Critical Inquiry*.

2. See William L. Slout, "Uncle Tom's Cabin in American Film History," *Journal of Popular Film* 2 (Spring 1973): 137–52; Donald Bogle, *Toms, Coons, Mulattoes, Mammies, and Bucks: An Interpretive History of Blacks in American Films* 2d ed. (New York: Continuum, 1989), p. 3; Charles Musser, *Before the Nickelodeon: Edwin S. Porter and the Edison Manufacturing Company* (Berkeley: University of California Press, 1991); Thomas Cripps, *Slow Fade to Black: The Negro in American Film, 1900–1912* (New York: Oxford, 1977), pp. 12–14; Robert C. Toll, *Blacking Up: The Minstrel Show in Nineteenth-Century America* (New York: Oxford, 1974), pp. 1–5; Edward D. C. Campbell, Jr., *The Celluloid South: Hollywood and the Southern Myth* (Knoxville: University of Tennessee Press, 1981), pp. 12–14, 37–39; David Bordwell, Janet Staiger, and Kristen Thompson, *The Classical Hollywood Cinema: Film Style and Mode of Production to 1960* (New York: Columbia University Press, 1985), p. 183. Eric Lott, " 'The Seeming Counterfeit': Racial Politics and Early Blackface Minstrelsy," *American Quarterly* 43 (June 1991): 223–54, and "Love and Theft: The Racial Unconscious of Blackface," *Representations* (forthcoming) came to my attention after this article was completed. These important essays suggest, for example, that what I call surplus symbolic value derived from surplus labor value under slavery, and from a white attraction to black bodies for which the term symbolic is too ethereal.

3. See Michael Rogin, " 'The Sword Became a Flashing Vision': D. W. Griffith's *The Birth of a Nation*," in *"Ronald Reagan," the Movie and Other Episodes in Political Demonology* (Berkeley: University of California Press, 1987), pp. 190–235; and Bordwell, Staiger, and Thompson, *The Classical Hollywood Cinema*, pp. 90–142.

4. See J. Hoberman, "Is 'The Jazz Singer' Good for the Jews?" *The Village Voice*, 7–13 January 1981, p. 32; Steve Whitfield, "Jazz Singers," *Moment* 6 (March–April 1981): 20; *"The Jazz Singer," Souvenir Programs of Twelve Classic Movies 1927–1941*, ed. Miles Krieger (New York: Dover, 1977), pp. 1–20, hereafter abbreviated *SP*; Harry M. Geduld, *The Birth of the Talkies: From Edison to Jolson* (Bloomington, University of Indiana Press, 1975), pp. 138, 213n.; and William K. Everson, *American Silent Film* (New York: Oxford, 1978), pp. 373–74. I am indebted to Peter Wollen for first adding *Gone With the Wind* to the sequence.

5. See D. H. Lawrence, *Studies in Classic American Literature* (New York: Viking Press, 1923); Leslie A. Fiedler, *Love and Death in the American Novel* (New York: Viking Press, 1960); Henry Nash Smith, *Virgin Land: The American West as Symbol and Myth* (Cambridge, Mass.: Harvard University Press, 1950); Richard Slotkin, *Regeneration through Violence: The Mythology of the American Frontier (1600–1860)* (Middletown, Conn.: Wesleyan University Press, 1973). The claim about the formative significance of black/white relations to film speaks to transformative moments; African-Americans were marginalized or absent from the routine Hollywood product until very recently. In the 1920s westerns were the single most common film genre. See the table in Lary May, *Screening Out the Past: The Birth of Mass Culture and the Motion Picture Industry* (New York: Oxford, 1980), p. 215.

6. See Mordaunt Hall, "Al Jolson and the Vitaphone," *New York Times*, 7 October 1927, p. 24, and "The Jazz Singer," *Variety*, 12 October 1927, p. 16.

7. See Jonathan D. Tankel, "The Impact of *The Jazz Singer* on the Conversion to Sound," *Journal of the University Film Association* 30 (Winter 1978): 21–25; Larry

Swindell, "The Day the Silents Stopped," *American Film* 3 (October 1977): 24–31; Andrew Sarris, "The Cultural Guilt of Musical Movies," *Film Comment* 13 (September–October 1977): 39–41; Audrey Kupferberg, "The Jazz Singer," *Take One* 6 (January 1978): 28–32; Hoberman, "Is 'The Jazz Singer' Good for the Jews?" pp. 1, 31–33; Neal Gabler, *An Empire of Their Own: How the Jews Invented Hollywood* (New York: Crown, 1988), pp. 134–45; "Jews on the Screen," special section of *Film Comment* 17 (July–August 1981): 34–48; Whitfield, "Jazz Singers," 19–25; Lester D. Friedman, *Hollywood's Image of the Jew* (New York: Ungar, 1982), pp. 48–53; Patricia Erens, *The Jew in American Cinema* (Bloomington: University of Indiana Press, 1984), pp. 70–110; Mark Slobin, "Some Intersections of Jews, Music, and Theater," in *From Hester Street to Hollywood: The Jewish-American State and Screen*, ed. Sarah Blacher Cohen (Bloomington: University of Indiana Press, 1983), pp. 36–69.

8. See, for example, Frantz Fanon, *Black Skin, White Masks*, trans. Charles Lam Markmann (1952, repr., New York: Grove Press, 1967) and Jean Genet, *The Blacks: A Clown Show*, trans. Bernard Frechtman (London: Faber and Faber, 1960) for the asymmetrical inversion of whites in blackface.

9. See Tankel, "The Impact of *The Jazz Singer* on the Conversion to Sound," 23, and Gabler, *An Empire of Their Own*, p. 143.

10. See Swindell, "The Day the Silents Stopped," 28.

11. Sarris, "The Cultural Guilt of Musical Movies," 41.

12. See Paula S. Fass, *The Damned and the Beautiful: American Youth in the 1920s* (New York: Oxford, 1977), p. 22.

13. See *The Jazz Singer*, ed. Robert L. Carringer (Madison: University of Wisconsin Press, 1979), pp. 144–45; hereafter abbreviated *JS*. See also Francis Newton [Eric J. Hobsbawm], *The Jazz Scene* (Harmondsworth: Penguin, 1961), p. 275. Hobsbawm, putting on blackface, borrowed his nom de plume from an African-American jazz trumpeter.

14. Cf. R. E. Sherwood, "The Jazz Singer," *Life*, 27 October 1927, p. 24, and Gabler, *An Empire of Their Own*, p. 150. See also Friedman, *Hollywood's Image of the Jew*, p. 48.

15. Hoberman, "Is 'The Jazz Singer' Good for the Jews?" p. 32, is the first to make this point.

16. See Gabler, *An Empire of Their Own*, pp. 3–4; and also May, *Screening out the Past*, pp. 167–79.

17. See Hoberman, "Is 'The Jazz Singer' Good for the Jews?" p. 31.

18. Quoted in Barry Paris, "The Godless Girl," *The New Yorker*, 13 February 1989, p. 57; hereafter abbreviated "GG." See also Gabler, *An Empire of Their Own*, pp. 3–4, 123–24, 140.

19. See Gabler, *An Empire of Their Own*, pp. 124–37; Herbert G. Goldman, *Jolson: The Legend Comes to Life* (New York: Oxford, 1988), pp. 101, 151; Kupferberg, "The Jazz Singer," 30; *JS*, pp. 18, 140; and Doublas Gomery, "The Coming of Sound: Technological Change in the American Film Industry," in *The American Film Industry*, ed. Tino Balio, rev. ed. (Madison: University of Wisconsin Press, 1985), pp. 236–39.

20. See Ronald Sanders, *The Downtown Jews: Portraits of an Immigrant Generation* (New York: Dover, 1987), pp. 99–100; Hasia R. Diner, *In the Almost Promised Land: American Jews and Blacks 1915–1935* (Westport, Conn.: Greenwood, 1977),

p. 33; and Gabler, *An Empire of Their Own*, pp. 142–43. Thanks to Aliza Bresky for the characterization of Yom Kippur.

21. Hoberman, "Is 'The Jazz Singer' Good for the Jews?" p. 1. See also Christine Gledhill, "The Melodramatic Field: An Investigation," in *Home is Where the Heart is: Studies in Melodrama and the Woman's Film*, ed. Gledhill (London: British Film Institute, 1987), pp. 9, 30.

22. See Gabler, *An Empire of Their Own*, pp. 142–49; Carlos Clarens, "Moguls— That's a Jewish Word," *Film Comment* 17 (July–August 1981): 35; Otto Friedrich, *City of Nets: A Portrait of Hollywood in the 1940s* (Glasgow: Headline Books, 1986), pp. 220–21, 354–56; Erens, "Mentshlekhkayt Conquers All: The Yiddish Cinema in America," *Film Comment* 12 (January–February 1976): 48; Hoberman, "Yiddish Transit," *Film Comment* 17 (July–August 1981): 36; Erens, *The Jew in American Cinema*, pp. 138, 162. Generational-conflict Jewish films continued to appear occasionally, particularly in the few years after *The Jazz Singer*, but that film marks the apogee of the immigrant film in Hollywood.

23. Peter Rose, *Mainstream and Margins: Jews, Blacks and Other Americans* (New Brunswick, N.J., Transaction Books, 1983), p. 67.

24. See Friedman, *Hollywood's Image of the Jew*, pp. 46–47, and Erens, *The Jew in American Cinema*, pp. 54–57, 73. For an academic study in *The Jazz Singer* tradition, compare Werner Sollors, *Beyond Ethnicity: Consent and Descent in American Culture* (New York: Oxford, 1986), another celebration of the melting pot that frees ethnic history from nativism and makes music its central metaphor. Although Sollors complicates *descent* by showing one can choose one's grandfather, he simplifies *consent* to cover all adaptations to the dominant culture.

25. Compare Hannah Arendt, "The Jew as Pariah: A Hidden Tradition," in *The Jew as Pariah: Jewish Identity and Politics in the Modern Age*, ed. Ron H. Feldman (New York: Grover Press, 1978), pp. 67–90, and Robert A. Burt, *Two Jewish Justices: Outcasts in the Promised Land* (Berkeley: University of California Press, 1988).

26. For the older historiography, see John Higham, *Strangers in the Land: Patterns of American Nativism, 1860–1925* (New Brunswick, N.J.: Rutgers University Press, 1955); William Leuchtenberg, *The Perils of Prosperity, 1914–1932* (Chicago: University of Chicago Press, 1958); William Preston, *Aliens and Dissenters: Federal Suppression of Radicals, 1903–1933* (Cambridge, Mass.: Harvard University Press, 1963); Robert K. Murray, *Red Scare: A Study in National Hysteria, 1919–1920* (Minneapolis: University of Minnesota Press, 1955). Newer interpretations include Fass, *The Damned and the Beautiful*, and *The Culture of Consumption: Critical Essays in American History, 1880–1980*, ed. Richard Wightman Fox and T. J. Jackson Lears (New York: Pantheon Books, 1983).

27. Quoted in Arnold Shaw, *The Jazz Age: Popular Music in the 1920s* (New York: Oxford, 1987), p. 14. See also, F. Scott Fitzgerald, "May Day," *Tales of the Jazz Age* (New York: Scribner's, 1922), pp. viii, 61–125. For a comparable shift from radical politics to aesthetics, encapsulated in the changed meaning of the term, *the new Negro*, see Henry Louis Gates, Jr., "The Trope of a New Negro and the Reconstruction of the Image of the Black," *Representations* 24 (Fall 1988): 129–155.

28. See Lee J. Levinger, *The Causes of Anti-Semitism in the United States* (Philadelphia: Lippincott, 1925), pp. 9–15, 94; David Levering Lewis, *When Harlem Was In Vogue* (New York: Oxford, 1981), p. 44; *"Kike!" A Documentary History of Anti-*

Semitism in America, ed. Michael Selzer (New York: World Publishing, 1972), p. 117; Higham, "American Anti-Semitism Historically Reconsidered," in Charles Herbert Stember et al., *Jews in the Mind of America* (New York: Basic Books, 1966), pp. 240–51.

29. Quoted in David H. Bennett, *The Party of Fear: From Nativist Movements to the New Right in American History* (Chapel Hill: University of North Carolina Press, 1988), p. 205.

30. The description of Jolson in blackface is indebted to Lemuel Johnson and Anne Norton. On the black hole as problematic ground for black artists, see Houston A. Baker, Jr., *Blues, Ideology, and Afro-American Literature: A Vernacular Theory* (Chicago: University of Chicago Press, 1984), pp. 3–6, 144–54. For black interpretations of and responses to blackface minstrelsy, see Ralph Ellison, "Change the Joke and Slip the Yoke," *Shadow and Act* (1964; New York: Vintage, 1972), pp. 45–59; Gates, *Figures in Black: Words, Signs, and the "Racial" Self* (New York: Oxford, 1987), pp. 50–60; Henry T. Sampson, *Blacks in Blackface: A Sourcebook on Early Black Musical Shows* (Metuchen, N.J.: Scarecrow Press, 1980).

31. Quoted in Thomas Elsaesser, "Film History and Visual Pleasure: Weimar Cinema," in *Cinema Histories, Cinema Practices*, ed. Patricia Mellencamp and Philip Rosen (Frederick, Md.: University of Maryland Press, 1984), p. 58.

32. See Toll, *Blacking Up*, p. 274; Robert C. Allen, *Vaudeville and Film, 1895–1915: A Study in Media Interaction* (1916, repr., New York: Dover, 1980); Whitfield, "Jazz Singers," 20; Hugo Munsterberg, *The Film: A Psychological Study; The Silent Photoplay in 1916* (New York: Dover, 1970), p. 7; and Gomery, "The Coming of Sound," pp. 229–51, and "Problems in Film History: How Fox Innovated Sound," *Quarterly Review of Film Studies* 1 (August 1976): 315–30.

33. See Bordwell, Staiger, and Thompson, *The Classical Hollywood Cinema*, pp. 177, 189–93, and Charles Wolfe, "Vitaphone Shorts and *The Jazz Singer*," *Wide Angle* 12 (July 1990): 58–78. Wolfe's splendid article, which emphasizes frontal performance, denies there is shot/reverse-shot editing in the scene where Jack meets Mary. Repeated viewings support, I believe, my language in the text.

34. I have quoted Jack's letter from the movie intertitle, which differs slightly from the version reprinted in the shooting script.

35. See Elsaesser, "Social Mobility and the Fantastic: German Silent Cinema," *Wide Angle* 5 (1982): 15–17, 24–25; Heide Schlüpmann, "The First German Art Film: Rye's *The Student of Prague*," in *German Film and Literature: Adaptations and Transformations*, ed. Eric Rentschler (New York: Methuen, 1986), pp. 9–24; and Otto Rank, *The Double: A Psychoanalytic Study*, trans. and ed. Harry Tucker, Jr. (1925, repr., New York: New American Library, 1979), pp. 4–7.

36. W. E. B. Du Bois, *The Souls of Black Folk: Essays and Sketches* (Chicago: A. C. McClury, 1903), p. 2.

37. See also Gabler, *An Empire of Their Own*, p. 136. *SP* has Jakie singing in "his best darkey manner" (4).

38. Sampson Raphaelson, "The Day of Atonement," in *JS*, p. 151.

39. My summary comes from the actual movie. On the moving picture cathedral in the 1920s, see May, *Screening Out the Past*, pp. 147–66; on island communities, see Robert H. Wiebe, *The Search For Order, 1877–1920* (New York: Hill and Wang, 1967); on the jazz singer as religious figure, see Slobin, "Some Intersections of Jews, Music, and Theater."

40. Quoted in Bennett, *The Party of Fear*, p. 204.

41. Irving Howe, *World of Our Fathers* (New York: Simon and Shuster, 1976), p. 562; hereafter abbreviated *W*. See also Friedman, *Hollywood's Image of the Jew*, p. 19; Goldman, *Jolson*, p. 40; Cripps, *Slow Fade to Black*, pp. 223–24; Gary Giddins, *Riding on a Blue Note: Jazz and American Pop* (New York: Oxford, 1981), pp. 5–17; Marilyn Berger, "Irving Berlin, Nation's Songwriter, Dies," *New York Times*, 23 September 1989, pp. 1, 7–8; and Shaw, *The Jazz Age*, p. 47.

42. John Tasker Howard, quoted in MacDonald Smith Moore, *Yankee Blues: Musical Culture and American Identity* (Bloomington: University of Indiana Press, 1985), p. 160; see also pp. 1–3, 70–71, 131–60; *Variety*, quoted in Michael Freedland, *So Let's Hear the Applause* (London: Vallentine, 1984), pp. 22–23.

43. Isaac Goldberg, "Aaron Copland and His Jazz," *American Mercury* 12 (September 1927): 634; *Baltimore Afro-American*, 10 September 1927, p. 9. Compare Diner, *In the Almost Promised Land*, pp. 112–15.

44. See Higham, "American Anti-Semitism Historically Reconsidered," pp. 250–51; Diner, *In the Almost Promised Land*; Lewis, *When Harlem Was in Vogue*, pp. 100–102, 148.

45. Ralph Ellison accused Howe of "appearing . . . in blackface," as the good son reminding Ellison and James Baldwin of their debt to their social protest father, Richard Wright (Ralph Ellison, "The World and the Jug," *Shadow and Act*, p. 111).

46. Sollors, dismissing sensitivity to distinctive cultural perspectives as the status-seeking of "biological insiders," unwittingly mimics American nativism; for Sollors attributes biological racism not to nativists but to members of minority groups. Infatuated by the power of the melting pot, he confuses the experience of varying cultures with the claim of different natures. See Sollors, *Beyond Ethnicity*, pp. 11–12.

47. Compare Ruth Perlmutter, "The Melting Pot and the Humoring of America: Hollywood and the Jew," *Film Reader* 5 (1982): 248.

48. The full discussion is in Goldberg, *George Gershwin: A Study in American Music* (New York: Simon and Shuster, 1931), p. 41.

49. Diner, *In the Almost Promised Land*, p. 239.

50. See Edward W. Said, *Orientalism* (New York: Pantheon, 1978); Michael Rogin, "The Great Mother Domesticated: Sexual Difference and Sexual Indifference in D. W. Griffith's *Intolerance*," *Critical Inquiry* 15 (Spring 1989): 527–28; Lewis, *When Harlem Was In Vogue*, pp. 29, 187–88; Rudolph Fisher, "The Caucasian Storms Harlem," *American Mercury* 11 (August 1927): 393–94; Goldberg, "Aaron Copland and His Jazz," 63; Moore, *Yankee Blues*, pp. 131–36; and Hutchins Hapgood, *The Spirit of the Ghetto: Studies of the Jewish Quarter in New York* (1902, repr., Cambridge, Mass.: Harvard University Press, 1967), p. 155.

51. See Goldman, *Jolson*, pp. 35–36; Gilbert Seldes, "The Daemonic in the American Theatre," *The Seven Lively Arts* (1924, repr., New York: Harper, 1957), pp. 175–77; and "The Jazz Singer," *Variety*, p. 16. Compare Giddins, *Blue Note*, p. 17.

52. See Slotkin, *Regeneration through Violence*, pp. 466–516; Sandra M. Gilbert, "Costumes of the Mind: Transvestitism as Metaphor in Modern Literature," in *Writing and Sexual Difference*, ed. Elizabeth Abel (Chicago: University of Chicago Press, 1982), pp. 199–201; and Elaine Showalter, "Critical Cross-Dressing: Male Feminists and the Woman of the Year," *Raritan* 3 (Fall 1983): 130–49. Compare Robert J. Stoller, "A Contribution to the Study of Gender Identity," *International Journal of Psycho-Analysis* 45, no. 2–3 (1964): 220–26, and "The Sense of Maleness," *Psychoan-*

alytic Quarterly 34, no. 2 (1965): 207–18; Fred Schaffer, "Male Political Hysteria," unpublished seminar paper, 1987. To identify appropriative desire in blackface is not to espouse a racial essentialism in which white should remain white and black, black, but rather to interpret racial cross-dressing as generated and contaminated by the rigid boundary, itself. Nonetheless, in relying on hostile accounts of cross-dressing, I am neglecting an important strand in feminist theory, whose bearing on blackface must be explored elsewhere. Compare Judith Butler, *Gender Trouble: Feminism and the Subversion of Identity* (New York: Routledge, 1990); Carol J. Clover, "Her Body, Himself: Gender in the Slasher Film," *Representations* 20 (Fall 1987): 187–228; Lott, " 'The Seeming Counterfeit.' " On the relation between mixed gender and mixed genre, see W. J. T. Mitchell, *Iconology: Image, Text, Ideology* (Chicago: University of Chicago Press, 1986), pp. 104–15.

53. See Rank, *The Double*, pp. 4–7, 11, 33, 73. The student's rescue of the count's daughter on a runaway horse, which initiates their tragic romance, is replayed as the tramp's comic fantasy.

54. See Patrice Petro, *Joyless Streets: Women and Melodramatic Representation in Weimar Germany* (Princeton: Princeton University Press, 1989), pp. 110–21, 155–58; Jim Pines, *Blacks in Film: A Study of Racial Themes and Images in the American Film* (London: Vista, 1975), pp. 17, 19; Joel Williamson, *The Crucible of Race: Black/White Relations in the American South since Emancipation* (New York: Oxford, 1984); and Fass, *The Damned and the Beautiful*, p. 482.

55. See Goldman, *Jolson*, pp. 65, 69, and Nathan Irvin Huggins, *Harlem Renaissance* (New York: Oxford, 1971), pp. 251–56.

56. See Friedman, *Hollywood's Image of the Jew*, pp. 23, 50.

57. Rank, *The Double*, p. 75.

58. Martha Fineman believes that there is unwarranted sexualization of the homecoming scene in my interpretation. On the safe distance between mother and son, compare Perlmutter, "The Melting Pot and the Humoring of America," 249.

59. Sophie Tucker, *Some of These Days: The Autobiography of Sophie Tucker* (Garden City, New York: Doubleday, 1945), pp. 2, 112; Jean-Paul Sartre, *Nausea*, trans. Lloyd Alexander (1938, repr., New York: New Directions, 1969), pp. 22, 178; Denis Hollier, *Politique de la Prose: Jean-Paul Sartre et l'an quarante* (Paris: Gallimard, 1982); W, p. 561; Shaw, *The Jazz Age*, pp. 168, 176, 203; Whitfield, "Jazz Singers," 20, 22; and Ethel Waters, "Get Up Off Your Knees," *The Blues 1923–1937*, BBC RFB 683. Self-identifications of the blues mama, which demand comparison with the mammy in mainstream popular culture, include Sara Martin, "Mean Tight Mama," *The Immortal King Oliver*, Milestone MLP 2006; Bessie Smith, "Reckless Blues," *Bessie Smith, The Collection*, CBS 7461–44441; Ma Rainey, "Oh Papa Blues," *Blues: Ma Rainey*, Riverside RLP 12–108. Compare Rosetta Reisz, liner notes to *Mean Mothers*, and *Women's Railroad Blues*, Rosetta Records RR 1300, 1301; Hazel Carby, "It Just Be's Dat Way Sometime: The Sexual Politics of Women's Blues," *Radical America* 20 (April 1986): 6–13; and Daphne Duval Harrison, *Black Pearls: Blues Queens of the 1920s* (New Brunswick, N.J.: Rutgers University Press, 1988). For the *fort/da* game, which Freud interprets as the child's play with the loss and return of the mother, see Sigmund Freud, *Beyond the Pleasure Principle*, vol. 17, Standard Edition of the Complete Psychological Works of Sigmund Freud, ed. James Strachey (London: Hogarth Press, 1955).

60. Hortense J. Spillers, "Mamma's Baby, Papa's Maybe: An American Grammar Book" *Diacritics* 17 (Summer 1987): 79–80; Ernst Kris, *Psychoanalytic Explorations in Art* (New York: International Universities Press, 1952), and Goldman, *Jolson*, pp. 4, 74. For the link between Kol Nidre and "My Mammy," as for so much in my approach here, I am indebted to Norman Jacobson; however, he would (I am pretty sure) like to be held no more responsible for the analysis than Cantor Rabinowitz for Jack's music.

61. Constance Rourke, *American Humor: A Study of the National Character* (New York: Harcourt, Brace, and Co., 1931), pp. 95–104.

62. See Hoberman, "Is 'The Jazz Singer' Good for the Jews?" p. 31; Shaw, *The Jazz Age*, pp. 41–44; Goldman, *Jolson*, p. 102; Slobin, "Some Intersections of Jews, Music, and Theater," p. 35; and Tucker, *Some of These Days*, pp. 62, 139.

63. Leroi Jones [Amiri Baraka], *Blues People: Negro Music in White America* (New York: William Morrow, 1963), p. 99.

64. See, among many other examples, Seldes, *The Seven Lively Arts*, pp. 67–109; "King Jazz and the Jazz Kings," *Literary Digest*, January 30, 1926, pp. 37–42; Don Knowlton, "The Anatomy of Jazz," *Harper's*, 152 (April 1926): 578–85; Henry O. Osgood, *So This Is Jazz* (Boston: Little, Brown, 1926); and, most egregiously, the lavish 1930 Paul Whiteman film, *King of Jazz*. Compare also Moore, *Yankee Blues*. For the jazz/speech analogy, see Reed Dickerson, "Hot Music: Rediscovering Jazz," *Harper's* 172 (April 1936): 567–74. James Lincoln Collier's revisionist interpretation of the reception of jazz, valuable as it is, ignores the racial question in the 1920s. See James Lincoln Collier, *The Reception of Jazz in America: A New View* (New York: Brooklyn College, 1988).

65. See William T. Shultz, "Jazz," *The Nation*, 25 October 1922, p. 438, and Ulrich B. Phillips, *Life and Labor in the Old South* (Boston: Little, Brown, and Company, 1929).

66. See Gunther Schuller, *The History of Jazz* (New York: Oxford, 1968), and Lewis, *When Harlem Was in Vogue*, pp. xv, 171.

67. See Raymond Williams, *The Country and the City* (London: Chatto and Windus, 1973), and T. J. Clark, *Image of the People: Gustave Courbet and the Second French Republic 1848–1851* (Princeton: Princeton University Press, 1973), pp. 140–54.

68. See Lewis Ehrenberg, *Steppin' Out: New York Nightlife and the Transformation of American Culture, 1890–1930* (Chicago: University of Chicago Press, 1981). Adolph Zukor's desire "to kill the slum tradition in the movies" is quoted in Miriam Hansen, "Early Silent Cinema: Whose Public Sphere?" *New German Critique* 27 (Spring–Summer 1983): 151.

69. Thanks to Michael Fried and Ruth Leys for this perception.

70. Compare Jane Feuer, "The Self-Reflective Musical and the Myth of Entertainment," in *Genre: The Musical*, ed. Rick Altman (London: Routledge, 1981), p. 160.

71. For the emphasis on performance in *The Jazz Singer*, see Wolfe, "Vitaphone Shorts and *The Jazz Singer*," 12. See also *Genre: The Musical*; Joseph Boskin, *Sambo: The Rise and Demise of an American Jester* (New York: Oxford, 1986), p. 88 (for the USO quote); and Gomery, "Al Jolson," in *Actors and Actresses*, ed. James Vinson (Chicago: St. James Press, 1986), pp. 335–36. Movies no longer employ traditional

blackface, of course, but one can hardly overstate the importance of blackface more broadly understood in contemporary American culture, from Elvis Presley to Vanilla Ice.

72. See Bogle, *Toms, Coons, Mulattoes, Mammies, and Bucks*, pp. 20–90; Evan William Cameron, introduction, *Sound and the Cinema: The Coming of Sound to American Film*, ed. Cameron (Pleasantville, N.Y.: Redgrave, 1980), pp. xii–xiii; Bordwell, Staiger, and Thompson, *The Classical Hollywood Cinema*, pp. 245–48, 257–58, 302; Gledhill, "The Melodramatic Field," p. 39; Sarris, "The Cultural Guilt of Musical Movies," 41; Noël Burch, "Narrative/Diegesis—Thresholds, Limits," *Screen* 23 (July–August 1982): 19–20; André Bazin, "The Myth of Total Cinema," in *What is Cinema?* trans. Hugh Gray, 2 vols. (Berkeley: University of California Press, 1967), 1:17–40; and Gomery, "Hollywood Converts to Sound: Chaos or Order?" in *Sound and the Cinema*, pp. 26–33.

73. See Gomery, "The Coming of Sound," pp. 234–35; Geduld, *The Birth of Talkies*, pp. 100–101; and Elton Mayo, *The Social Problems of an Industrial Civilization* (Boston: Division of Research, Graduate School of Business Administration, Harvard University, 1945).

74. See Kupferberg, "The Jazz Singer," 29.

75. Credit Adrienne MacLean for discovering Jolson under the blackface.

CHAPTER ELEVEN

Black, White, and in Color, or
Learning How to Paint:
Toward an Intramural Protocol of Reading

HORTENSE J. SPILLERS

I

IN A FOOTNOTE IN RESPONSE TO highly contested passages from Paule Marshall's *The Chosen Place, the Timeless People*,[1] I discuss "an epistemological ground for locating centers of interpretation." The central query here is not only if Marshall's work might be read in some of its lights as "homophobic," but also how the latter criticism is muted, or assumes a different perspective, if the ideology and practice of race are thrown into the mix. From the vantage of power relations, wherein race admittedly situates, the claims of "homophobia" on this novel are both misleading and inadequate. If we are right to look for the "science of a general economy of practices,"[2] then no single aspect/event of the socionom (the web of identity) can be perfectly isolated, nor can it occupy, from its local and particular site, the sovereign position. The ground for "locating" competing interpretive interests—Barbara Herrnstein Smith calls them "communities"[3]—for placing them in relation to one another is made up of one's leanings and inclinations toward one system, or logics of representation, and not another. This much must be admitted. It seems to me that the repertoire of isolated strands of subject-effect, which characterize our current critical inquiries, are interpenetrating and incontrovertible and that they are at play, first and last, in the realm of history and its key moments of power relations. One might attempt to forge, realizing this, a "critical pertinence" that would mobilize, at least implicitly, its own ideological biases, perhaps even *use* them, that would recognize the play of contradiction and difference as an aspect of her own critical project. What we posit as a "thereness" in any given surface of a text is as much our conjuring with one's own social positionality, as it is with a repertory of practices designated "author." The rupture of certainty, of the "colonization" of discourses by a mighty and irrevocable gesture of appropriation is the promise of a fairly new reader's tale, the outcome of which cannot be anticipated. But this jamming of the expectations, we grow accustomed to think, constitutes an intervention that could render the new attitude *serviceable*, I would dare say, to what we might think of as an "intra-mural protocol of reading," how to see, really, when what you're looking at is perceived to be some of your own stuff—a subject history, a historical subjectivity. Or, to put the matter somewhat differently, how do "look alikes" behave toward one another?

Marshall's *The Chosen Place, the Timeless People* systematizes a response, and how I think it is done lends focus to this essay. The conflated allusion of my title to film[4] and to painting offers a visual metaphor: one would try to negotiate, across a plurality of seeing, numerous and subtle coordinations, as if pieces of identity as different from each other as the nerve endings of the fingers and the sense of aspiration and desire were all groping toward an exercise of attention and memory as precise as the mathematical. Heaven forbid that the reader/critic must now learn to paint and do numbers, but the protocol of reading that I would imagine is now called upon to disabuse us of the unacknowledged tyrannies of our own involvement in dominative forms. "Black," "white," and "in color" are precisely the figurative stops that I would invoke in arriving at an adequate examination of a different inter-pretive practice for an African-American readership in particular.

In preparing to reread moments of Marshall's novel[5] and assay another writing concerning it, I was especially interested in Roland Barthes's *S/Z* and its five codes of reading: the hermeneutic, semic, symbolic, proairetic, and cultural codes (and we should add a sixth here, the "translative," since the "Barthes" I mean is "in English") inscribe a work of severe fragmen-tation—93 sections, 561 items, to be exact, in which the most brilliantly bizarre textual calculus is hurtled against Balzac's *Sarrasine*—*to cite*, for instance, given its "tauromachian" emphasis, implies the *citar*: "the stamp of the heel, the torero's arched stance which summons the bull to the bande-rilleros,"[6] or the career of the signifier as a *citing*, or *siting*. Items of textuality treated as lexical instances, followed by a running, seamless commentary that made up Barthes's own metacritical gesture, *S/Z* demonstrates the criti-cal project as a subversion of the proper name, just as it celebrates the proper name to be undetermined in the first place—"BARTHES" as a gath-ering of decided critical and cultural forces and as a dispersion of energies that replicate themselves pitilessly, as though to say that the transparent utterance of the bourgeois text must be laboriously revealed as the distance between itself and the opaque lie that transforms "culture" into "nature." The Barthesian performance meets our own purposes here in the most gen-eral sense: looking at a carnival scene from Marshall's work, I will attempt to recover whatever pluralities of meaning the text might lead us to consider. Barthes's work filters through my own understanding of reading as an elab-oration and complication of competing, overlapping, and complementary discourses.

II

I will forgo the usual courtesy of providing, here and now and all at once, a plot summary of the novel, though doing so is barely avoidable. Instead, my observations start "in the middle," where the carnival scenes fall in the midst of an orientation and a conclusion. We are concerned with a character named Vere and a female figure, who, for all intents and purposes, remains anonymous, except for a tribal marker in a last name called "MacFarland." Though the events to which I refer are traversed and crosshatched several times, they come to focus in Book III, "Carnival," chapter 1, 267–77.

I have isolated this ten-page sequence because its riddle stands out from the surrounding narratives at the same time that it serves to reinforce the latter by (a) specifying carnival in the fictitious community as a hyperbolic function, (b) articulating "namelessness" as the central dread of an impoverished culture, whose fictional limits are traced in the novel, and (c) "metaphorizing" the uncanny at the crossroads of cultural exchange, or the excessively unfamiliar as a quite familiar aspect of all social choreographies. In other words, this chapter, in its terrible centrality, situates the problematics that the novel retraces as an interrogation into the *interior* dynamics of otheredness: If "I" is another, then "I" will never know Other than this Otherness, even if the texts of my history call upon me to think and act as if it were not so. This ambivalence in both the fictional and historical text is neither permissible, nor near the surface, but it might explain, at heart, the peculiar texture of hostilities that prevail, both openly and covertly, over the social economies of Bourne Island. But that is a tentative conclusion. What steps have induced it?

By these signs you shall know them . . .

1. Through a principle of convergence and enumeration, Marshall's narrators range between and within scenes as the subtle admixture of omniscient and local narrative properties. Four of the actors of the plot converge on Book I, chapter 1: Vere, Allen Fuso, and Saul and Harriet Amron, each, in turn, observing the other and self in an inward narrative movement, confer on the plot the gifts of their sharply divergent points of view. In more than one instance, we see aspects of Bourne Island from an aerial vantage through their eyes. But the magic of seeing here is that one is also observed in a ruthless democracy of the specular: even before Allen Fuso knows Vere, the motherless, he recognizes, on board the small twin-engine plane, "Farm Labor Scheme" in Vere's "high-crowned, wide-brimmed sharpie's hat of blue velour, the same light powder-blue as his suit"—the passenger and stranger a few seats ahead of him (14–15).

Vere comes to be associated, then, with vivid color, a wild, delightful impertinence of taste (which signal his youth and lack of exposure to a broader world), and an excess of the dramatic, which aggressive indulgence leads to a spectacular moment of carnival on the one hand and his death on the other. In the first instance, only the reader oversees the event, in the second, the "world" looks on. But in any case, we experience this character in sharp alignment with the breathtaking and the rending, the decorative and the exaggerated.

The inference of associations that we make belies the "real" Vere, who maintains, outwardly, a virtual silence of manner and the unobtrusive arrogance of an "essential immunity" (30). If the ironical is the chief trick of a reversal of intention, then Vere, under its sign, is not so much a "bad guy" as hardly the good one that everybody loves—toward whom Allen Fuso entertains homoerotic ambitions, for whom Merle Kinbona weeps interminably, and over whom great-Aunt Leesy Walkes suffers soundlessly.

2. This character, who draws the reflexes of pathos to his *persona* like a moth to flames—the death of his mother in birthing him, his disappointment and betrayal in America, the loss of his child at the hands of the anonymous woman—is paired with an agent observed through the filter of scattered and ephemeral impressions. Her "crime" is never clarified in the course of things, except that it appears that various narrators indict what we take to be her incestuous origins and nasty skin color. But more than that, this character without name comes from "up Canterbury" that remains somewhere beyond and peripheral to the primary demographic centers of the fiction—New Bristol, Bournehills, and Spiretown. She is estranged and without defenders, or a legitimate "citizenship" in a novel of impeccable ceremony and belonging. Her membership, however, in a clan of "Backra," or "red people" flings the possibilities of kinship and filiation outward, in the direction of the chaotic and uncontainable.

That the Canterbury woman is indigenous to this fictive Caribbean island sounds the thematic of estrangement all the more intently because it would suggest that the metaphysics of the social and political body has little to do with "color," but everything concerning any arbitrary basis for determining "near" and "far," "inner" and "outer," "licit," and "illicit," whose bondings and manipulations hold in place the cultural necessity of order and degree. The breach of it, embodied in the female figure's irrupture on the textual surface, creates the crisis that is punishable by whipping and banishment. The tall, red-boned female instantiates the novel's puzzle and nightmare because she is not only unoriginated, but also, like the classically marked figure, the bearer of a secret contamination, on par with the "sins" of Merle Kinbona in her London years, or the "touch" by black Lyle Hutson that would turn the inward dread of white Harriet Amron outward.

"Those red people from up Canterbury are all cross-bred and worthless," Leesy speaks in despair to Vere (upon his return to Bourne Island from

Florida) (31). And several pages later, in Sugar's Nightclub at the tip of New Bristol, Merle introduces Saul to aspects of local society by dramatic enumeration—the finger point—Bourne Island is a nation of diabetics, to a man and woman: " 'Take for example that young miss yonder . . .' a tall, thin, indifferently pretty girl in a colorful skirt puffed up by a score of can-can petticoats":

"Everyone up there has the *same name* and *looks the same*. We call them Backras, meaning more white than black and poor as the devil. This one had a nice boy liking her, but when he went to America on the labor scheme she turned wild. She wouldn't even take care of the child she had for him and it died." (85; emphasis mine)

A third narrator traverses the same semantic field, as though these characters were, pointedly, the repetition of certain rhetorical symptoms: working behind the counter of the store of Delbert's Rumshop in Spiretown, there is this woman, who duplicates the figure of the female anonymity:

The woman, a large, raw-boned Backra, was from Canterbury, a hill southeast of Westminster where everyone in the small settlement there was related and shared the same crinkled, snuff-colored hair, rough reddish near-white skin and the same name, "MacFarland." (157)

The very notion of duplication, of the human look-alike, is stirring, because it suggests the absence of discriminating genetic features at the level of the eyesight. The manipulations of sameness, or twinness open the door to the potential for comic error and confusion and posit an excess in the already-powerful stuff of life itself. But "sameness" here, raised to the level of the clan and the pervasive last name that does not "conjugate" in difference through the vertical and spatial timeline of generations, evokes a fable of inheritance that is not permissible. We would also assume that this shadow of illegitimate endogamous mating implicates the fathers, since other last names of the novel, "Vaughn," "Walkes," "Pollard," "Kingsley," "Bryam," capable of endless modification by a Christian name and the prerogatives of patriarchal marriage, are the marks of a proper cultural function.

But two dramatic features here seem overwhelming: (1) that the Backra "tribe" of Bourne Island, peripheral to the fiction's central culture, is already fabled, or "written" as an exotic history, in which case nobody knows their name, but only their sign and (2) the sign "MacFarland," contiguous with other traits, that is, skin color, hair texture, body type, loses its efficacy to name precisely because it becomes preponderant indiscriminate naming; in that regard, "MacFarland" imitates the status of a geographical site. It *is* a place, of taboo, to be avoided.

In Harlem Heights, the figure of anonymity makes a new home for her-self neighboring the city of New Bristol, with its shops, hotels, nightclubs; to her "ramshackle house," in the hills above New Bristol's wealthy, Vere will track her down and inflict on her the terrible whipping with his *family's* Malacca cane.

We observe as an aspect of her estrangement that she is seldom cast with other characters, except for cameo figures—young officers from a tracking station near Sugar's, who appear to have a purely commercial function in relationship to her, buying her body for the course of a night. But we only guess as much, since the activities that define her *persona* remain shrouded in mystery. This enigmatic person, difficult to envision, with her "can-can petticoats" and a physiognomy fractured by descriptive details, assumes a centrality to the novel by virtue of her marginal status. The narrator can only point to her, can only suggest an iconographic value, whose integrity is im-pure. We are offered a cluster of traits whose aspects of identity split up in contiguous elements. To my mind, this is not an enigmatic property known only to the text, or to the author, but invokes a repertoire of unresolved, ambiguous issues that cannot be "answered," or even said with ease. Per-haps the Canterbury woman is meant to "say" that Bourne Island, in its tenacious clinging to the very elements of human oppression that it would undo, reinforces its own appropriative violence. "MacFarland" is no longer a "person," or a "character," but in this instance, the emptiness and abstrac-tion of a "thing."

A Mirror Stage

John T. Irwin in his study of William Faulkner's *Absalom, Absalom!* and *Sound and Fury*[7] points out, after Otto Rank, that "the brother and the shadow are two of the most common forms that the figure of the double assumes." We might conclude, after Irwin, that the sister and the double, or the woman in the mirror, are not as well known; in this case, the subject indentifies with the object thrown before her, at the same time that she recognizes that she is not one with it. Nevertheless, no amount of recogni-tion forestalls the peculiar and unique pleasure that the looker derives from seeing *in*, if not *through* the glass. That Marshall's narrator introduces a mirror to the scene of Vere's and the female figure's encounter claims its entire dramatic import *for* difference, *as* difference.[8]

We are amazed that the communicative exchange between the pair has been conducted up to the moment of their would-be face to face meeting in an exquisitely terrifying silence. It is as though the two figures have agreed beforehand to "act" themselves, to mime this pre–text through dramatic ges-tures that keep strictly to an already-assumed outcome. Though one might explain these scenes to herself as if they were a rational whole of fiction—and that they are rational is the trouble—there is no explaining what we sense, what is insinuated in the absolutely self-contained dreadfulness that is trapped in the rationally ordered syntax of these paragraphs of narrative. There *are* other things, and this extra, immured in the folds of the rational, erupting as an unspecified irrational content that can only be *signaled*, is the secret of Bournehills, looking in the direction of first traumas. If psychoanalytic theory offers the analysand a narrative, a text in the "place" of a dropped-out content, or a content that was never there, then what is the relationship between a fictional text and the historical, or the community in history, both *inventing* and *invented* by its texts?

Imagine this: Vere soundlessly tracks the woman (again, "a tall, thin, sharp-boned girl of perhaps twenty with snuff-colored hair and the eyes and the coarse mottled skin typical of those from up Canterbury" [190]), several times before he enters the house in Harlem Heights. "Her petticoats fussing around her knees," she leads him nightly, "down Whitehall Lane past the bawdy sailor clubs and rumshops lining the street to Sugar's at the tip of the long finger of land that marked the extremity of the deep bay upon which New Bristol stood" (191). He never announces himself, but simply falls in behind her as she "moves up the narrow cobblestone street." Eventually, she sees him, as he exerts no effort to hide. Head snapping around suddenly, she looks "over her shoulder to where he had come to a halt under a street lamp some yards behind to wait for her to continue on." Knowing all along that he has been there, she simply stares at him, "one bony arm akimbo," determined to brazen it out, if need be, but does not speak.

Replete with bodily tensions and haltings, this scene could be scored as a hunter stalking his quarry, an appropriate figure for city streets, but Vere also stages the "haunter," a sort of poltergeist that neither reveals itself, nor goes away. In effect, the narrator implies that he is the female agent's "shadow"—"She had known all along, it was clear, that he had been shadowing her, but for reasons of her own had waited until this moment to acknowledge it" (191). Terror and dread do not here consist in the lack of knowledge that would make surprise inevitable, but in the acquaintance that boomerangs, when one's own projected shadow falls down, abruptly, in her path, between herself and the light. Though the Freudian view of the "uncanny" does not indicate this version of the dramatic as a case in point, we could very well place these haunting scenes under its auspices and say that the shadow—a "not-me," as the mirror image is not—is so apt an analogy on the living body, so remarkable a trace of its occurrence, that the shadow's sudden projection can take a body out, so to speak, destroy it. It would appear, then, that the male agent, in the outward overlap between the city's terrors and the psyche's dread, entertains just such ambition regarding this fictive female body.

Thus, the scene is set, precisely "staged," for even greater and matured agitations of the spirit. The preceding scenes concerning Vere and his prey, dispersed along the line of intervening fictions, have opened the door to the "funhouse" that is ironically misnamed. Carnival itself, though a celebration, marks the social body turned inside out: the preserved, secreted fantasies, from which the ego shrinks, or about which it quietly boasts, erupt into play. That the scene to come takes place without witness, except that of the read-ers', heightens its bizarre import, lends it a purity of narrative and dramatic function that parodies the solitude of lone readers and narrators.

When Vere enters the woman's place unannounced, the streets of Harlem Heights and New Bristol are virtually deserted. Everyone has gone, or will go shortly to Carnival Monday Night dance at the Sports Oval outside New Bristol. This is the interrupted destination of the lone female figure in the mirror when Vere bears down upon her with his streamlined black self and his family's Malacca cane, snugly secured to his spine: "She was busy apply-ing the make-up to her neck and throat, having finished her face, when the door behind her opened, and as she saw Vere suddenly well up in the mirror to the makeshift vanity table at which she was sitting, her hand paused half-way to her raised chin. But she did not start. She made no outcry. Nothing crossed her eyes as they encountered his in the glass" (272).

This tight space brims over with her bed, her clothing, and most astonish-ingly, her dolls,

> to be seen everywhere in the packed untidy room—large, expensive boudoir dolls with deeply lashed, painted blue eyes and painted smiles and pink brushed lightly over their white cheeks. . . . They lazed amid the tumbled sheet on the unmade bed, where they obviously served as the girl's sleeping compan-ions. . . . And they were all dressed, even the ones lounging in bed, in an exact copy of her lavish gown; and their spun-gold hair, piled in the same elaborate tower of curls as her wig, was studded with fake jewels also. (272, 273)

Vere watches the reflection in the glass, and the image trapped there watches him watching her. In this tenacious play of replication, we suddenly enter a factitious world of invariably contrived and counterfeit identities. One might say that we are aware of our self-conscious involvement in a fictional moment that bares its props, that names its game as the falsehood: "a heavy stark-white pancake make-up that looked like grease paint," or "her white mime's face, [that] of a sullen, intractable child" (272). The duplicitous mirror participates in the transaction as a source of enrichment, making, in effect, *two* of everything that catches in the frame. But in this simple scheme of multiplied images, the dolls and the woman increase multifold in a hid-eously curious spectacle of undifferentiated objects on a scale of impres-sions. The dolls are grand, but a miniature version of the woman, and the woman an outsized instance of the dolls. If we imagine that at any quirky

moment in the "life" of objects, the dolls might move—there is that astonishing moment for the spectator looking through the glass of the wax museum
at figures that seem just on the verge of movement, or to have completed a
nuance that the eye just missed—then we recognize the cunning of dolls
and manikins (should we add the corpse?), or even the Buckingham Palace
guard, as the threat of life in still things, or the menace of death in the living.
The tension that shudders across the moment between properties and their
energies in a potential exchange and transfer of "stuff" reveals a suppressed
contradiction—we have just missed the passing of a distinction between
things and human that *almost* collapses into a single identity. The "almost"
mimics the Freudian "uncanny."

We must concede to the Canterbury woman a superior imagination: she
knows that in her selection of a carnival costume in tulle, which copies the
boudoir dolls exactly, that she has not achieved "beauté," nor is that her
purpose. She appears to aim, instead, at the reconstitution of a protocol
whose iconographic significance/signal has already been established. (And
what else is "beauty" or "unbeauty" "in the West," if not an *unspontaneous*
perception of a spontaneously emergent female body?) Even if we decide
that "stark-white pancake make-up" (even difficult to get off the tongue) and
the look of grease paint are displeasing to the eye, we must admit that the
special occasion of ritual, or of a designated event of the hyperbolic, lends
costuming/signifying a certain immunity. We suspend judgment on the
clown, for instance, or the character of the masque, deciding that the grotesque—a human deficiency on the one hand and an excess on the other—
holds a crucial place in the order of things. Our acceptance of the extraordinary look comes to rely on the tease. The actor suspects that, beyond the
mask, the actor looks different, or "all too human." But the embodied lie,
which the costume and makeup achieve, creates the illusion that outruns
the "truth." It is appropriate, then, that the Canterbury woman never turns
her face, in effect, to Vere, or to the audience of this scene and that we see
her as Vere does (and as we see him as well), through the mediations of the
glass.

Seeing thus, we decide that the woman in the mirror is not what she
appears to be, though we could say that "what you see is what you get." And
what of the male figure conjured up in *her* mirror? The figure "wells up," we
are told, *gushes* to the surface, as if by magic. The fluid verbal metaphor that
takes its cue from dream work tempts us to read Vere as a superimposed
image on an image that, in the revisionary ratio of dreams, produces multiple
characters who collapse into one. Does Vere become, in effect, the woman's
own dream stuff—induced by guilt—that spontaneously appears in her
looking glass? How else might we explain: (1) Vere's obsessive potential for
her mind (as he has literally put himself there in order to "mature" at some
later moment); (2) her incapacity to shake him, or even turn around from the

mirror to confront the interrogation; (3) the failed magic of her words to dispel the intruder?

The dreamer is trammeled up—on "being shot," pulls a "gun" that doesn't fire, or that miraculously transforms itself into an umbrella; locks do not secure doors and electrical switches click on blown-out lights; hurled insults do not send the pursuer flying—but waking, in anguished astonishment, discovers that it wasn't so. But somehow, it is the recall of disempowerment that provides waking with its own brand of trouble in mind. Even if the agent who inflicts the "blow" is only a proxy, an alibi for Vere, the dream and the waking for the Canterbury woman are charged with the same unrelieved tensions of lack, of insufficiency, so that "truth" and "illusion" come to share the same place. This entire scene is truly illusory for actors and spectators, occurring as it does in the radical alterity of makeup and mirrors. In the intersection of personae, both characters, having become the centrally embodied deferment and evasion that neither can any longer forestall, discover each other as the realized aspect of a self-alienation.

But is such an explanation sufficient for the man who "wells" up in the woman's mirror? In more than one way, Vere has no "business" there, even though, in his "essential immunity" (and *what*, or *who* has immunized *him*?), he takes it as his right. We could say that the woman who stays in man's company keeps alive the possibility of one day having an unwanted guest, the one who decides to "hump the hostess." It is surely more than coincidental that her involvement with the dolls, of her carrying out a program of the dolls, is essentially contextualized in a male eyeball. (We cannot imagine, for instance, that these scenes could ever reverse locations.) It is *she* who presents to *him* a passive, inert female back, in the fetal curve, as he flails away. How far removed are we from a notion of sexual use/abuse, recalling the telling symbolism, caught by the Malacca cane? And it is only *he* whose realizations are both *writ* and *written*:

> And then suddenly he was angry. Perhaps it was the sight of that hardened back which sent the blows rebounding his way so that he almost felt he was whipping himself. Or the realization that no matter how long he flailed away at her he would never be able to convey to her what it was he had been seeking in having her as his woman and giving her the child, and how deeply she had wronged him by denying him both. (275)

And so, we discover that the male agent here has gained entry into the female house and the female mirror by *breaking in*, by intruding himself in the split between the woman and her other, content not yet specified. It is precisely this *process of obtrusion* that stands between Bournehills and the texts of its own invention. Never mind what the texts are, never mind that they might, in fact, tell a "lie." But the freeing gesture would be that they

ARE. In other words, the Island's coming into possession of its own material resources—its sugarcane crop, for instance—and the modes of production sufficient to transform them would undo Bournehills' bondage to its absentee landlords. This strategic rewriting of the practices of political economy in the local instance would yield revised social relations: not only would the cane farmers, for example, have the assurance of benefiting, *themselves*, from the annual harvest, but also the conditions of work would be so restructured that Gwen, in another instance, could feed her children and no longer have to perform labor's tediums under conditions of pregnancy.

The economic oppression of Bournehills is, at once, the novel's most implicit and obvious feature of travail. Its effects must be reckoned with at all times, beginning with the hierarchy of social being and value that situates the Canterbury woman on the bottom. It is certainly not "written" that the Bournehills collective, freed from its neocolonial trap, would uplift the woman's status by much. But the point is that the well-rehearsed *excuse* could be jettisoned, as the "authors" of modes of reconfigured social relations are now none other than the local citizenry itself. Fallen between the gaps of her culture, the Canterbury woman, whom the text refuses anything beyond a vain and parodic movement, remains the unspoken. But *that* is also a text.

The Paradox of the "Non-Dit"

In order to say the "not-sayable," I must say—must enter the chain of significant differences inscribed by the sentence. One almost "gets" what theorists of female representation mean in their insistence that "the woman," "the female" escape representability,[9] or what I mean when I claim that the Canterbury woman remains "unspoken." Not absolutely certain what the theorists have in mind, since, by their own various witness, key historical moments "in the West" are *based on* "the female" and its ascribed symptoms of lack, we might conclude that "unrepresentability" and "un-sayable-ness" are the preeminent features of a paradox. For Julia Kristeva, the "maternal body," specifically, locates the meeting place of "nature" and "culture." This point of intersection, to which Lévi-Strauss tracked the incest taboo, also marks the explosion of grammatical and logical purities. In this "atmosphere," we cannot think of things as simply differentiated. Each "haunts" and "shadows" the other as meaning moves into radical abeyance.

For Kristeva, the *"non-dit"* and the maternal body are twinned:

> The weight of the "non-said" (*non-dit*) no doubt affects the mother's body first of all: no signifier can cover it completely, for the signifier is always meaning (*sens*), communication or structure, whereas a mother-woman is rather a

strange "fold" (*pli*) which turns nature into culture, and the "speaking subject" (*le parlant*) into biology. Although it affects each woman's body, this heterogeneity, which cannot be subsumed by the signifier, literally explodes with pregnancy—the dividing line betwen nature and culture—and with the arrival of the child—which frees a woman from uniqueness and gives her a chance, albeit not a certainty, of access to the other, to the ethical. These peculiarities of the maternal body make a woman a creature of folds, a dialectic of the trinity or its supplements.[10]

That the Canterbury woman has had a child, according to Kristeva's theory, would heighten the contradictions surrounding her. Having undergone pregnancy, or straddled the line, she now has nothing to "show" for her pains. From this angle, she has been restored, theoretically, to the unique, to the "heterogeneity" of the female body. But this outcome is hardly felicitous, since both mothers and not-mothers on Bourne Island can neither forge their access to others—the ethical vocation that Kristeva suggests belongs to maternity—nor rehearse their uniqueness, dependent as it is on a degree of freedom. In the situation of neocolonialism, which the novel mimics, motherhood is really *not* available as a *choice*. The *fruits* of mother-labor set the children's teeth on edge.

Under these conditions of work and living, we would not be shocked to have "forgotten" that Vere's mother died in childbirth and that the infant of the Canterbury woman did not live for very long. According to her own angered outburst, thrown in the direction of Vere's feet, the dead child was already fated:

> 'But I bet none of them told you that from the day that child was born you could tell it wasn't going to live any time. It was a sickly something!' she shouted at the floor. 'And t'besides,' she cried at the same defiant pitch, all the silver dust and sequins on her dress shimmering amber in the dull amber light as she stuck her arms akimbo, 'who told you the child was even yours? Who said you was man enough then to be giving anybody a baby . . . ?' She sucked her teeth in scorn."
> (274)

It is, of course, harmful to the female—she will be beaten with many "stripes"—to laugh at, to traduce paternity, both in the specific occurrence of fatherhood (as with Vere) and in the mythical notion of the father who bestows culture on the child. Is it that a woman who "does away" with her children (abortions here included)—unlike a father who abandons them—not only meets with particular violence, but also encounters the generalized opprobrium of the community-at-large?

That the Canterbury woman is *just* a woman would make her *the* woman of this fiction. "Arms akimbo," a repeated gesture, modified by "skinny," isolates her within a special category of contempt and apartness. It seems that the narrator(s) chooses sides here and speaks *for* Bournehills society. In doing so, the implied narrative judgments contradict Canterbury and its tribe of women who *look* different, *do* different. These females live alone, prostitute their bodies, and do not (cannot?) maintain their children at all cost. I am not suggesting that we make a heroine of the woman from "up Canterbury," but that we recognize in her antiheroic stress provocation to the hierarchical arrangements of father-law. The latter, as we know, are difficult, if not impossible, to escape. We may even wonder if such arrangements are as desirable to release as we might publicly acknowledge and privately imagine. For instance, the "lesson" for me is that aspects of my own readerly, sentimental, and ideological biases *agree* with Vere's. Because she has been disobedient to the female's vocation, she *should* be dishonored and unveiled. But on second thought, that conclusion does not quite add up, inasmuch as the "Rat" in Bournehills is only *partially* "Western man" in so simplistic a guise.

If, as in Kristeva's view, the maternal body straddles the "nature/culture" split, then what might be said of the Canterbury woman, who is situated on the line, but retreats from it with a different story?

Made to approach the gateway to madness, the Canterbury woman turns her own body into a symptom of fetish-adoration. The dolls serve in complementary ways, insofar as they restore her body to her, by reflecting it, amended and corrected. When Vere, in ecstatic rage, looking for something to destroy, turns on the dolls, the woman, for the first time, "veers" toward him with the ferocity of the mother protecting her child. In what seems a hideous caricature of the protecting mother, the woman, suddenly mobilized and animated beyond recognition, releases the mask, figuratively speaking, in order to play out quite a different role:

> She looked up then, her face emerging from the safe hollow between her shoulders like a bird's head from under its wing, and seeing the doll swinging by a leg from his hand, its gown already torn and hair in disarray, its blue painted eyes terrified, a look of horror came over her face, and she leaped from her stool, screaming "Leave that! Put it down! God blind you in hell, leave my doll baby. . . ." (276)

Anticipating the reader, the narrator even describes her movements in the ensuing tussle as that of someone struggling "with the strength of a mother who sees her child murdered before her eyes" (276). In this "furious pantomime dance," the body of the doll is "ripped wide, and all its sawdust and cotton innards" explode in her face. The rhetorical thrust of the passage slides toward human description: the cry of the woman, " '. . . give it to me, I beg you, don't you see you're hurting it,' " and the finishing gestures of Vere, "[He] flung the remains of the mangled doll at her and strode from the room."

I think we would do well to recognize in this furious dance a not-very-amusing parody of a killed infant and all the stirrings of emotion that might accompany such an event. If the pantomime "acts" the unspoken, then the scene before us goes far to explore the dynamics of maternal helplessness. But here such outcome is *staged*; the props are dolls, after all. In the historical outline that subsumes Bournehills culture, however, mangled bodies describe the irrevocable circumstance from which little distance can be struck. It is plausible, then, that the Canterbury woman, in her ceremonial and dramatic features, "makes meaning," but in a way that riddles sense.

If we think of the mangled doll and her companions as an *investment* and as the objects in which the woman is *invested*, then we bring together two related components of desire. As items of investment, the dolls not only close the distance successfully overcome between the desiring subject and the something desired,[11] but also reconfigure and analogize the woman's location of exchange in the sexual economies of Bournehills. That the dolls are "bought," just as the woman is, replicates the mirror's imaging on yet another level, while it is clear that the circulation of desire in this case involves very different stakes for desiring subjects. On the other end of the sailors' casual, body-for-money transaction, a woman eats, adorns herself, and brazenly indulges her fantasies. That there are several such "investments" in the crowded room might argue that the Canterbury woman experiences at least a certain amount of success at her "trade," though it is likely not enough, since her house is "ramshackle." Unlike Enid, the barrister's wife, the Canterbury woman has not yet breached that class of male clients whose cash and cachet might improve her status of prostitution. But in any event, the prostitute and the sailors demonstrate, in their economic relatedness, the primacy of "cold hard cash" in the Island's human and social nexus.

As invested objects, the dolls are laden with an emotional weight that focuses their subjective value. "The girl's sleeping companions," they might well embody and express "all the things she had ever wanted and been denied." Empty themselves of value, the dolls are "assigned" it by the desiring subject, whose disrupted unity[12] reveals nothing less than the deepest hunger. In that case, the equation between money and dolls concretizes anguish beyond its theoretical and psychoanalytic import. Anguish now courses the blood vessels, just as surely as money is "eaten."

We might assume as well that desire subtended by a "foreign code of conscience" marks the needs of strangers in pathetically memorable ways. Thinking about the locus of these particular objects on the grid of Bournehills society invites decided pause, inasmuch as they "look like" none of the characters who may so invest them. The "white mime's face" interjects a startling note of physiognomy onto a fictional site whose critical populace is black, but it is carnival in Bournehills, when the extraordinary is normal, and the normal disappears. That the Canterbury woman apes a *boudoir* doll brings several things to mind, but preeminent among them is that she embraces the "import" as *masked* desire. (The traveler in erstwhile colonized societies recognizes right away that the former are glutted markets for the discarded, expensive junk of the metropolitan cultures. These protuberances on the landscape of the new capitals stand out like a bulging eyeball. In the case of the Canterbury woman, the "foreign products" are taken to bed and strike as discordant a note in the brimming-over room as old abandoned Chevrolets in the midst of kiosks and houses of slatted windows.) We might say that the "domestication" of the "foreign," its *inculcation* "where we live," offers the subtle complexity that stalls most radical change. In other words, revolutions are not very well equipped to recognize, or even acknowledge, the "unscientific" errancy of *want*, or the stringent demands of the unconscious.

Desiring, therefore, runs along the strangest channels, the "farther away" the point of origin, the more powerfully seductive the pull. Europe's and North America's "goods" provide a "table of contents" not-at-home with the Island's material culture, from Merle's beat-up Bentley, to Vere's raggedy Opel; from Lyle Hutson's costly Savile Row suits, to the Canterbury woman's expensive boudoir dolls. Subsequently, Bournehills is bereft of a correct history of its material layers, inasmuch as the latter are buried in the earth. In other words, the dolls, for instance, do not "grow" out of an embedded memory of evolved, or related, forms. For example, changing moments of a body-politic might be mirrored in altered stages of diminutive objects. In considering how so, we gain a different angle on the historical sequence: perhaps in recognition of the rising human rights movement of African-Americans, my best doll "Patti Jo" was special-delivered "black and beautiful" from Lincoln, Nebraska sometime during the 1950s. "Walking" on cue from the constant up and down motion of either arm, Patti Jo was adorned in pink silk-taffeta. U.S. involvement in Vietnam evoked a great deal of national ambivalence perhaps reflected in one of my nephews' "G.I. Joe," the dismembering, falling-apart doll. Then, in anticipation of the strict sexual neutralities of the contemporary period, the interchangeable female/male "cabbage patch" doll was neither here nor there. With a touch of realism, dolls are made even larger now, nicely modeled after one's relatives and friends.

If we studied this cross section of time, technique, and material, we might be able to write a piece of U.S. history in its interstate trade relations, small-industry factors and output, the concatenation between "home grown" and "made in Taiwan," the glamour of the toy, and the desiring games that adults hint to their children.[13] In other words, we could discover and make sense of certain continuities in changes of national taste. What I am suggesting about boudoir dolls in Bournehills is that they are quite literally plucked from a divergent cultural semantics. As a result of transactions like this one across the society and without the benefit of a "favorable balance of trade," either real or symbolic, the local culture swims the broken currents of its own time's flow.

In an uneven cross-cultural exchange, the Canterbury woman desires what comes to hand. Reinventing self-image in play, she reverts to the emotional doll-stage of the child. For her, the dolls not only symptomatize the "return" of the baby (as the latter is the child's anticipation), but also mark a "return" with perfection, minus the contingencies of the material world. Whatever the sickly, living infant might have lacked, the dolls provide. At the same time, the objects of play repeat none of the "mistakes" of "his/her majesty, the baby," or what some observers speak of as the nursery's messiness.

We might say that the boudoir dolls are the surrogate baby body. At the site of a fantastic displacement, whose living subject has dropped out, so to speak, the dolls are both "themselves" and repression's symptom. In manipulating this double inscription, the narrator shows both the lapsed maternal body and its outright reversion into the fantastic realm of childhood. In that sense, the Canterbury woman contains and contained not only the baby, but also the embedded child, whose traces stay. The maternal body here is dramatically configured as the sign of the female child-become-adult and child-at-play in the fantasies that "answer."

That the woman can "have her cake and eat it too," in playing out the real and symbolic capabilities of the female body, places her at odds with some of the novel's other female figures. Pregnancy for them is the mortal debt that must be paid in eternal and endless child care. As I observed before, the fatality of multiple births, under conditions of impoverishment, bears down on Gwen, Stinger's woman, with unrelieved harshness. It would be absurd, consequently, to compare these social positionalities in the fiction against some putative ideal of maternal behavior. But it does appear that the Canterbury woman is being punished for "playing" in all the nuances of the term: "playing" her sex for monetary gain; "playing" mother against the real thing; "playing" at a kind of self-indulgence that partially determines its own movement; "playing" out the assumptions of carnival in taking on the mask, albeit a "borrowed" one. Though we view her behavior through the distortions of the *reflected*, we do not have much choice but to conclude that the fictional world we are in is twisted entirely by the political logics of foreign occupation.

III

Once the doll loses its innards, exploding in the woman's face, the character is permitted a prolonged cry that the ear cannot quite register. It is a "sudden shrill atonal scream . . . with the regularity of a siren," and it calls to mind "in its almost ritualistic fluting, the high-pitched, tremolant keening of

Arab women mourning their dead" (276). Well beyond the point of contact, it travels the "length and depth of the Heights," continues long after Vere has departed, and signals the reader that perhaps we have touched an edge of mimetic behavior. This "loud ululation" in italics runs approximately: . . . oh God oh God Oh God oh god Oh God oh god Oh God for thirty-seven such intervals, in what seems to be the rising and falling motion of the voice and arms. Trying to accurately record the recurrence for citation obliges the reader *to count*, but it does little good to do so, since, it seems, enumeration is not the point, though *repetition* is. The decisive punctualities of the lines, determined by their spacing and the simple manipulation of small and capital letters, suggest a ritualized dance, so that the passage might also be "read" as a version of labanotation, or notes for a dance score.

The lines cannot be spoken, or "naturally" spoken, but only read and gazed at. Perhaps they might satisfy what Robert Scholes describes as "phatic," or that utterance whose primary urge is contact itself.[14] Could we also include in the phatic dimension processes of learning a language? It is striking that the Canterbury woman, in the synthesis of displacements "spoken" by her body, "answers" effectively both programs of action.

IV
AFTER WESTMINSTER: COMING TO CONCLUSIONS

Marshall's exquisite lyrical talent evinces mastery of multiple discursive orders. A culture code, for example, specific to a fictionalized Caribbean instance, draws on a repertoire of linguistic, historical, ethical, geophysical, geopolitical, ritualistic, decorative, satorial, gustatory, amorous, and celebrative elements. Even the Canterbury woman's "Oh God," in the general category of imprecation, seemingly based in the removal of the Christ-Body from the eye of the human, bears the distinctive inflections of Caribbean English. Or so it seems to my ear. But the dispersed commingling of an ecclesiastical density with specific elements of a contrasting cultural landscape creates a rhetoric of dissonance. From one point of view, this disjuncture serves the narrative purposes of the novel quite well since it situates the economies of conflict and ambivalence inside decided dramatic goals. From another angle, however, this clash of tongues, so effectively mediated that we catch the binarity only on studied reflection, would appear to make peace with traces of a dominant order precisely *because* this rapprochement is rendered perfectly natural. The symbolic density that I specify as "ecclesiastical" is embedded in imagery adopted from the hierarchical church. Its subtle weave of textures accounts for one of the most skillfully handled elements of narrative that the work affords.

Merle Kinbona, for instance, wears a pair of "pendant silver earrings carved in the form of those saints to be found on certain European churches." The earrings, fixed as a continuous dramatic prop on Merle's person, sustain an impressively rich history and destination: copied for Merle from "the saints on the outside of Westminster Abbey," which also lends its name to an overwhelming hill that bears down on Bourne Island, the earrings are a gift from the wealthy and mysterious Englishwoman, whose relationship to Merle remains ambiguous (4, 327).

That an object the dimensions of an earring carries its weight in gold, both literally and figuratively, embodies a synecdochic echo that reverberates through various "nerve centers" of the novel. The saints on "certain European churches," now "reduced" on a pinpoint in the ear lobe, are no longer just "gaunt with piety." In the symbolic power that they have come to assert over European imagination, the saints suggest that indeed a "world" of cultural exchanges, which includes unsaintly lives, unseemly tales, is immured within their intricate handiwork. That the Atlantic slave trade originated in and proceeded with the blessings of the hierarchical church of Europe never leaves the reader's mind. The idea lends a subtext to every reference that slips and slides between a symbolic modulation and its outright pointing back toward the past. In that sense, the saints' past, here standing in for the European cultural complexity, reconfigures the future of what is already known.

The "ironizing" possibilities of agreement between African-Caribbean things and European things are not at all lost for the novel's narrative strategies. But while irony apparently offers a superior interpretive model, it can also accommodate to a "domestication of dissent": Merle, for instance, wears not only the earrings of the saints, but also the bracelets of the enslaved. Heavy, clangorous, crudely made, the bracelets create an ambiance of sound in which she moves and "like a monk's beads or a captive's chains," the sound "announced her" (5). The symbolic equivalent of another kind of silver working, these "numerous bracelets," similar to the monk's prayer beads, present a choice between items no longer sharply antithetical by virtue of their adherence to the coordinate conjuncton. Read another way, "or" outlines two radically divergent crossways, as in "life" or "death." In either case a conflicted movement runs through the semantic chain, which marks uncertainty for character in the narrative's psychological work.

This symbolic structure, working its way through the gaps of the novel, meets on every hand the semantics of a particular historical order. These texts-before-hand, subtly encoded as the novel's given, rapidly oscillate between two unspecified political ends, except that we know them both all too well. The narrators brilliantly proceed to frustrate any program of Manichaean investment. By endowing each situation and character who responds in its context with sufficiently sullied, corrupt, unclear, naive, and self-interested motives, the narrative strategies force the reader to rethink whatever certainties of outcome she had wagered. To put it crudely, we cannot choose

"Africa" over "Europe," or "Europe" over "Africa," inasmuch as we recognize that not a little of our own emotional/cultural capital is tied up in an international currency whose profoundest grammars are "pidgin," the impurities that fall between the cracks of "STANDARD." Yet, in this high and impressive adventure in irony, everybody has a place, not always certain, but nonetheless the symptoms of a place, with the vexing exception of the Canterbury woman. Apparently a sign of Bournehills' Other, she marks, in effect, a tribal limit, and all her kin follows her status. Neither absorbed nor absolved by the structure of irony, this character without a *first* name, or a *last* one that would claim precise differentiation, enters the fiction and leaves it—is *abandoned* by it, more appropriately—as the single figure who is not exhausted by the work's rhetorical resources.

First names in the novel are the origin of a narrative repletion or saturation: Merle, Vere, Saul, Harriet, Leesy, Gwen, Stinger, Ferguson, Lyle, Enid are not only the names of characters, but the characters' naming suggests a site of traits founded on the *assumption* of completeness; the characters' movement between an "inner" and "outer," or the tension that arises between an interior and exterior function. What we recognize as "act" consists in the cross-traversing of these rhetorical lines that conventionally gesture when we have moved into a character's "brain" and when the character has moved, so to speak, "out" of it into the broader circumstances of the narrative. Without an "inner," the Canterbury woman discovers no fictional "autonomy" that would "explain" the mode of narrative chosen for her.

However, the clues to the Canterbury woman's identity converge on a lucidly specified place: "MacFarland" equals "Backra" (play on "Buckra," a West African term for the "white man"), which equals Merle's "more white than black." The Canterbury woman stands for a local version of "mulatta," who, from the standpoint of a humiliating past, may be described as a "black" masquerading as a "white." There is never a political need for the proposition or practice to reverse itself; reversal occurs as a ruse of entertainment: the minstrel's blackened face not only parodies the African person, but actually erases him or her as a human possibility. From the angle of strategem and disguise, the Canterbury woman cannot turn round from the mirror to either the audience of the fiction, or the one outside it, since *to turn* would bring this figure into the one symbolic confrontation that all the parties have not engaged systematically, cannot engage at all, except in the most violent manner, as the scene depicts: *Who* is the "European" in me that the "African" in me need fear?

At this point, the strangeness of the stranger is far clearer: it is the stranger in the house, reading that formulation in its figurative emphasis as fictional Bournehills society. The woman at the threshold of meaning has no name, and how could she, if the conditions that engendered her cannot be spoken, say nothing of bragged about, if such conditions inscribe the impermissible—the "white man" in a black woman's house, in her mirror, in her "boudoir," *in* her? And whose *fault*? For that reason, the Canterbury woman involves us in the *intramural dynamics of alterity*, and it is, doubtlessly, the *interior*, in this historical instance, that counts far more than we credit or acknowledge; that would account for the "secret" text of the African-American fictional text in a world of keen ears, of decisively configured discursive interests. By interior, we mean, of course, that chain of *intracommunal* enactments, reenactments, and engagements yoking members of the same "natal community." Even though the Canterbury woman "belongs" to Bournehills, she is situated decisively at its borders, at the limit.

In this fictional instance, we are compelled to read "race" as an *outcome*, rather than an originary source of power relations. It seems quite clear that this figure of anonymity carries about her all the traits of "race," but does not embody one. "Otherness," therefore, cannot be asserted simply as the condition in *others* from the vantage of a dominant community. "Otherness" declares itself instead as the infectious cultural property that bears a secret contamination, an impurity showing itself "in the blood."

The Canterbury woman, however, is not the sole "mulatta" figure of the novel: Enid Hutson, of the Vaughan paternity, shares membership in a similar category of kinship alignment, but with a crucial difference, as we have observed before. The wife of a charming, corrupt, successful man, Enid lives on her own private hill *looking down on* New Bristol. The demographic and figurative distance places her in proximity to a symbolic order that takes in Lyle's Oxonian accent and manners appropriate to the Inns of Court. To the contamination of the blood, we might add the privations of the flesh in order to understand more precisely the dreadful exposure of the Canterbury woman to the wolves of namelessness.

Under the influence of Old Testament scripture, we are accustomed to think "chosen people" in specific reference to the historic Jewish community and to confront "timelessness" with an idea of spatial dispersion. In fact, "saying" the title, the reader often gets it wrong, transposing "timeless" with "place," "chosen" with "people." This inversion and reversal of semantic destinies invite the reader to "splice" disparate cultural expectations, as we bend the attention away from certain inherited cultural properties. Opening the way to contrastive and antithetical possibilities, the epigraph that inscribes *The Chosen Place, the Timeless People* is "copied" from another Book (not of Christian origin) attributed to the Tiv people of West Africa:[15] "Once a great wrong has been done, it never dies. People speak the words of peace, but their hearts do not forgive. Generations perform ceremonies of reconciliation but there is no end." Right away, we perceive a combat of culture codes in the making, without announcing itself as such. This opposition between cultures of the fiction and the operations of antithesis within the mimetic frame that grounds it offer but a single route of critical maneuver.

Within the intricacies of the structure, however, this clear route to combat is continuously demolished in the interest of greater ironic subtlety.

The force of anonymity in the Tiv epigraph, its ahistorical drive and appeal, as if words spoken from an undated past are being spoken still, in a contemporary fictional mode, represents an unimpeachable authority, on par with biblical scripture in its annulment of local contexts. "An epistemological ground for locating centers of interpretation" would attempt to move among the novel's various centers of authorities that manipulate quite successfully the reader's own divided allegiance among diverse processes of appeal. To read "race" alone, or "sexual preference" by itself bogs down in one of several possibilities. "Namelessness," for instance, is configured in the novel along various lines of stress: (1) Caribbean/ritual versus U.S. and European capitalist machinery; (2) agents as bearers of these moments of cultural production; (3) an interiorized apparatus that throws "male" against "female," "blood" against "blood," a heterosexual synthesis of sexuality and desire against unspecified, barely-hinted different possiblities of sexual congress; (4) a "natural" landscape that performs its own semiotics in relationship to the semantic chains of character. At no point does any single cluster of these modalities *exhaust* the fiction, though any one might metaphorize it, may substitute for the whole in its partialness. In fact, I have privileged a single one of these, aspects of interiority, that gathers up "critical pertinences" that move off in different directions.

In positing a "ground" of any sort, one is not only attempting to clear floor space, but also to ascertain that there *is* a floor, or some basic point of structure that would grant the free flow of movement among various appointments. I am suggesting that an interpretive ground for this novel, perhaps *any* text of fiction, rests on a thematics that falls completely *outside* its expressed boundaries. The historical basis is not totally exhausted by "race," "class," "gender," "previous state of servitude," "sexual preference," "last name," "region of birth," "religious faith," etc. These elements of social modality come to bear on the historical situation of the text, the writer, and various constituent reader-groups that "choose" the text, but I mean *historical situatedness* primarily as the *enunciative conditions* that surround a particular act of speaking/writing and the textual densities ("writings" that precede) flowing back against it. In that regard, African-American fictional texts declare, by definition, a subversive move: not empowered to speak in the historical instance by any act of morality, legislation, or rule of cultural precedence; by tradition, the subject of speaking in others, but not a speaking subject itself, the "largest poet" (who has far less to do with particular writers' identities than I personally like) of writings by black persons inscribes a fugitive condition. She or he is history's "runaway" person, the missing commodity of the gross national product, whose whereabouts were top secret (from about A.D. 1619, Jamestown, the colonial South, to the present).

The "fugitive poet" bears a fundamental obsession, and that is, *to speak*, even though the "law" at one time did not allow it, and to break the equation between her or his flesh and any nation's £30 sterling. It is axiomatic that the "fugitive poet" takes up the vocation of the enunciative/enunciating in certain danger by "revealing" her or his whereabouts and that of significant others, *the interior landscape*. It seems to me that any critical act of reading and interpretation, with reference to this community of texts and whatever *conclusions* it reaches, must begin with *that* story, as assumptive ground, in the fundamental ambience of the fugitive man and woman *against the law*.

Because particular poets must pit themselves against texts written long before, we engage in their works the peculiar tensions established between a priority and a succession. In fact, we observe Marshall's writing against this current of the inexorable as she mobilizes the offices of irony. But can the particular poet set in motion a new structure of enunciative rules? *The Chosen Place, the Timeless People* offers just such possibilities by insisting that the politics of culture are not solely made by the logics of domination; the dominated have some say, especially "where we live." This perspective forecasts essentially a critical ways and means that must situate itself not only in opposition to the expectations of critical behavior, but also in self-service to one's own ideological investments. "Black, white, and in color" promises one thing for certain: that the reader shall be discomfited.

NOTES

1. See note 6 in "Chosen Place, Timeless People: Some Figurations on the New World," in *Conjuring: Black Women, Fiction, and Literary Tradition*, ed. Marjorie Pryse and Hortense J. Spillers (Bloomington: Indiana University Press, 1985). The dispute here primarily concerns one reading of Marshall's novel as "homophobic." My position is that "homophobia" as interpretive/critical device for this, or any other novel, represents a single constituent reading of the work, but that there are others. For me to call the "homophobic" claim "racist" would simply proliferate the name-calling, even if I do think so. That our various readings replicate today's fractured political scene will not come as news, but as *citizens* who are also *critics*, I think we owe it to the "business" of our work to do more than simply impose our particular prejudice on forms of art. The point is to *use* one's view in a way that is rigorous, responsive, and contextualized according to the *situations of the work before us*. Not to accout for the *narrative positionalities* of *Chosen Place, Timeless People* is to imagine that the work was derived in a vacuum of politics and history and that we can impose whatever discursive fashions and passions of the moment reflected in our *own* historicity. It seems to me that doing so would be an *error* that "criminalizes" any viewpoint that is not our own.

2. Pierre Bourdieu, *Outline of a Theory of Practice*, Cambridge Studies in Social Anthropology, gen. ed. Jack Goody (Cambridge: Cambridge University Press, 1977). Articulating the relatedness between "economism" (in the narrow and traditional

sense) and noneconomic topics of appeal, Bourdieu suggests that the former might be understood "as a particular case of a *general science of the economy of practices . . .*" (183). In abandoning the dichotomy, we are in position to derive, then, a discursive practice that is "capable of treating all practices, including those purporting to be disinterested or gratuitous, and hence non-economic, as economic practices directed toward the maximizing of material or symbolic profit." Somewhat relatedly, I would contend that a "general science of the economy of practices" in its literary critico-theoretical moment might urge a more forceful articulation between, or among, divergent constituencies of cultural claims. Any reading project, or discipline, will, of necessity, leave "something out," but its doing so need not occasion celebration, or the arrogance of a moral rightness. In fact, the abounding "absences"—collateral with the emergent discourse—*enable* a particular interpretive economy by "shaping" it as *this* choice and not *that*, or *the other*. In short, the critico-theoretical text attempts to identify and mark its investments as a single site of contestatory urgencies and commitments (cf. Stanley Fish, *Is There a Text In This Class?: The Authority of Interpretive Communities* (Cambridge, Mass.: Harvard University Press, 1980).

3. Barbara Herrnstein Smith, "Contingencies of Value," "Canons" in *Critical Inquiry* 9 (September, 1983): 1–36. (Cf. *Contingencies of Value: Alternative Perspectives for Critical Theory* [Cambridge, Mass.: Harvard University Press, 1988]).

4. The title of this essay is based on two punctualities: Joanna Field's *On Not Being Able to Paint* (Los Angeles: J. P. Tarcher, Inc., 1957) and Jean-Jacques Annaud's 1976 film, "Black and White In Color." A film from the Ivory Coast, "Black and White," coauthored by Annaud and Geores Conchon, bears the French title "La victoire en chantant." Produced by Arthur Cohn, Jacques Perrin, and Giorgio Silvagni, the film—which focuses post-colonial intersubjectivities in the Francophone sphere— won the Motion Picture Academy's best foreign film award in 1976.

5. Reprint, New York: Vintage Contemporaries, 1984. (All references to the novel and quotations from it are taken from this edition, page numbers noted in the text.)

6. Roland Barthes, *S/Z*, trans. Richard Miller, preface by Richard Howard (New York: Hill and Wang, 1974), p. 22.

7. John T. Irwin, *Doubling and Incest: Repetition and Revenge: A Speculative Reading of Faulkner* (Baltimore: Johns Hopkins University Press, 1980), pp. 31–33.

Jacques Lacan's discussion of the significance of the "mirror stage" ("stade du miroir") in the development/deployment of the cultural agent, alienated in language, is provided in "The Mirror Stage as Formation of the Function of the I, in *Écrits: A Selection*, trans. Alan Sheridan (New York: W. W. Norton and Company, 1977), pp. 1–8.

For critique, see, among numerous other sources: Anthony Wilden, trans. with notes and commentary, *The Language of the Self: The Function of Language in Psychoanalysis* by Jacques Lacan (New York: Delta Books, 1968), "Lacan and the Discourse of the Other," pp. 157–313; and Fredric Jameson, "Imaginary and Symbolic in Lacan," in *The Ideologies of Theory: Essays: 1971–1986* by Fredric Jameson, foreword by Neil Larsen, *The Ideologies of Theory*, Vol. 1: *Situations of Theory* (Minneapolis: University of Minnesota Press, 1988), pp. 75–119.

In Lacanian epistemology, the mirror becomes the primary hodological (self-mapping) instrument of ego-identity, which arises in critical deception, in *méconnaissance*. Imbricated between and in the midst of the imaginary and symbolic dimensions of the Lacanian project, the "mirror stage" inscribes the tiny subject's "interpellation" in the self-alienating dynamics of self-image and representation. If we could risk such imprecision, we would say that the subject's involvement in the prelinguistic realm of undifferentiated objects demarcates the "beginning" of its crucial destiny in, its traverse (and travail?) through the Symbolic Order and the Name (and the Law) of the Father. See also: Julia Kristeva, *Desire in Language: A Semiotic Approach to Literature and Art*, ed. Leon S. Roudiez; trans. Thomas Gora, Alice Jardine, and Leon S. Roudiez. (New York: Columbia University Press, 1980).

Marshall's characters "mimic" the "mirror stage" insofar as they register the necessary "coupledness" of self-gazing, a process that occurs *because* there is a witness (in Lacan's scheme, a parental caretake) *against* whom the unknowing and primary subject "sees" itself for the first time. The characters in the novel *aggressively* engage parodies and illuminate the identitarian and the egoistic as a *rupture* in the apparent unity of perception and desire.

8. Among recent works of feminist theory that devote all, or some significant portion of their conceptual apparatus to an investigation of female representability, are included: Teresa de Lauretis, *Alice Doesn't: Feminism, Semiotics, Cinema* (Bloomington: Indiana University Press, 1982); Alice A. Jardine, *Gynesis: Configurations of Woman and Modernity* (Ithaca: Cornell University Press, 1985), Susan Rubin Suleiman, ed., *The Female Body in Western Culture: Contemporary Perspectives* (Cambridge, Mass.: Harvard University Press, 1986); Teresa De Lauretis, ed., *Feminist Studies/Critical Studies* (Bloomington: Indiana University Press, 1986); Teresa De Lauretis, *Technologies of Gender: Essays on Theory, Film, and Fiction* (Bloomington: Indiana University Press, 1987).

9. Julia Kristeva, "Stabat Mater," in Suleiman, *The Female Body in Western Culture*, p. 115.

10. Georg Simmel, *The Philosophy of Money*, ed. David Frisby, trans. Tom Bottomore and David Frisby (London: Routledge and Kegan Paul, Ltd., 1978), pp. 61–66. Simmel's discussion of desiring subjects and objects of desire occurs within the context of his elaboration of "value" and "money" in chapter 1 of *The Philosophy*. Independent of natural order, valuation and its conceptual apparati inscribe the "whole world viewed from a particular vantage point" (60). Over and against what Simmel calls "objective qualities and determinations," "the great categories of being and value, inclusive forms that take their material from the world of pure contents," stand arrayed (61). The sharp distinctions that Simmel draws between "objective determinations" and subjective valuation omit the intermediary stages that decide how the repertoire of value/desire arises; such a question is posed by psychoanalytic theories of language, specifically, Lacan's itinerary of the "unconscious" as that which is structured "like" a language.

Getting to money as value's signifier and signification—terms which Simmel does not specifically deploy—the author "reduces" value and the desiring ego to the same temporality, or contemporaneity (67). The latter constellation, therefore, situates the tension that disrupts and interrupts the unity of subject-effect and its lost, or receding, or interchangeable, objects and "makes us conscious of each in relation to the other." "In desiring what we do not yet own or enjoy, we place the content of our desire outside ourselves" (66). Characterized by its separation and distance from subject, object is posited as that which desire seeks to *overcome*. By way of this transitivity, object is situated, therefore, as a *value* (66).

11. Ibid., p. 66.

12. Ibid.

13. Toni Morrison, *The Bluest Eye* (New York: Washington Square Press, 1970), p. 21. Claudia MacTeer, one of the adult-as-child narrators in Morrison's first novel, comments on "desire" as oppressive imposition: "But I did know that nobody ever asked me what I wanted for Christmas. Had any adult with the power to fulfill my desires taken me seriously and asked me what I wanted, they would have known that I did not want to have anything to own, or to possess any object. I wanted rather to feel something on Christmas day . . . to sit on the low stool in Big Mama's kitchen with my lap full of lilacs and listen to Big Papa play his violin for me alone." Even though Claudia's notion of authentic desire is nonetheless as staged and melodramatic as the customary baby doll for girls at Christmas time, her narrative at least points up the adopted and adaptive *fictionality* of *wanting* as adults "author" it in this novel.

14. Robert Scholes, *Structuralism in Literature: An Introduction* (New Haven: Yale University Press, 1974), p. 26.

15. Basil Davidson identifies the Tiv as a West African family that moved into southern Nigeria of the Niger Delta around A.D. 1500. Grouped with the Fulani, the Tiv came into the area from distant regions to the north of Nigeria. *A History of West Africa to the Nineteenth Century*, with F. K. Buah and the advice of J. F. Ade Ajayi (New York: Doubleday Anchor, 1966), p. 145.

CHAPTER TWELVE

Exiling History: Hysterical Transgression in Historical Narrative

ROBERT D. NEWMAN

I

I have been a sojourner in a foreign land.
(Exod. 2:22)

This essay is an attempt to explore the dynamics of narrative engagement by considering the interplay of erotic and tragic elements implicit in that engagement.* I am interested in what goes on in the privacy of our minds as we illuminate the grids of black marks on white pages—what in the "Proteus" episode of *Ulysses* Stephen Dedalus terms signs on a white field—and in how our perspective adjusts and is adjusted by transactions with narrative. I contend that this illumination is an ongoing process of vision and revision that approximates the authorial experience, thereby narrating the narrative with which it is engaged. Furthermore, this engagement empowers and reveals the narrative as a complex mind in itself, like the mind of the reader, governed by the revelations and displacements of memory. I therefore assume memory to be the shaping power of narrative and will establish analogies between the interpretive processes of reading and psychoanalysis. The psychoanalytic case history is no less a history or a story than the narrative of historical events or the interpretation of a work of fiction, art, or film. I consider both reader and narrative as texts in that they are both composites of messages and codes to be unraveled. I also maintain that the loss engendered by the invasion of the Imaginary by the Symbolic Order in the individual's psychic life motivates the reading process in an attempt to recover the ideal Imaginary state while narrative memory inevitably recapitulates this loss.[1]

The narrative recreation of the exile reveals the fluidity of genre between biography and history as symptomatic of a more profound unsettling of fixed binarism. Exiles continually define themselves in relation to what is absent, their homeland, which they simultaneously embrace and deny. Their recreation of that homeland, necessarily infused with irony, demonstrates memory as a revisionary act and history as an exercise in narrative memory.

Exiles' memories of homeland are not constants but are constantly changing due to their experience as exiles. Their mental returns are guided by the necessity of making that home, which was once an extension of Self, Other, in part to preserve the home that now is. This necessitates alienation from oneself, the Self that was and that still is present as an influence upon and aspect of the present Self. Hence, irony is a natural vehicle for the writer as exile. The authorial Self is extended into the character functioning within a setting that recalls a previous self of the author through a present interpretation, and thus must be ironically distanced as Other.

Readers engaged by a text function much like exiles, viewing the narrative as a type of homeland in which they can no longer live. They are shifted between narrative and metanarrative constructions while each construction adjusts continually the readers' perspective on the other. However, because metanarratives (both those explicit in the text and those implicitly erected by the readers' engagement with the text) depend to a large degree upon narratives for their subject matter, readers need to visit this homeland often. Metanarratives remind readers of their actual distance from the narrative which is seducing them. They are conflicted by opposing urges to yield and to resist while metanarratives, as polemics, also seduce through the illusions they create.

At the level of metanarrative, readers adopt the comfortable pose of omniscience, joining the narrator in the interpretive act through the discourse of rational analysis. Playing critic, readers exile themselves from vicarious participation in the narrative to observe and judge it. However, this omniscient pose is another spell conjured by their desire for autonomous order and a means by which the self-conscious authors may tweak their deluded confidants. The rational construct created by the seemingly objective stance may be exposed as ephemeral, the metanarrative as necessarily contaminated by the narrative, thereby revealing the metanarrative itself as no more than a story. Irony similarly highlights the perspectivity of the exile's mnemonic visions, and reveals ideas of home and return as fictional constructs. The exile, who chooses the ironic mode or is chosen by it, creates a mirror for the reader's experience while infiltrating and modifying that experience.

In posing readers as exiles whose desire for return shapes their journey through the narrative memory of the text and whose desire is in turn shaped by that narrative memory, I offer a paradigm which describes the fragmented experience of narrative engagement. The dynamics of this paradigm, yearning and loss, appropriately are shifting contingencies. The reading of literature, history, art, film, or personal narrative is by no means limited to a singular text or event. Instead the engagement occurs primarily in the margins. We do not read or observe without the flood of memory continually relating present to past experience. Events and the images they conjure bleed from the immediate focus of the text into other events and images both from within and outside the text. The desires which motivate memory arrange these links, but the recognition that similarity is infused with difference and repetition with change constitutes a trauma, an awareness by the exile that origin is recoverable only through mnemonic traces that blend into phantasm.[2]

We might view memory as a narrative of homecoming just as we see narrative as an act of memory. In either case, readers function as wanderers, perpetually exiled by their desire for the order of metanarration which both obstructs and enters into their engagement with the narrative. Just as they wander the text in search of the illusion of unity, smoothing its folds to meet the contours of their present desires, the margins of the text invade and alter the path they wander. Their return home can never be completed because their image of home changes.

In a letter to Jacob Burckhardt, Nietzsche wrote, "Every name in history is I."[3] Much contemporary literary theory has encouraged us to view reading and writing as based in the inevitable self-referentiality of language or in its blocking of its own significations. Historical interpretation has often become transhistorical. The binary conventions used by traditional historiography are attacked and linear history is replaced by concepts of systematic rupture. Subjectivity is seen as a culturally constituted category, an extension of an ideology which the interpreter must expose. However, one problem we risk in adapting literary theory to history is an interpretive hegemony where unraveling the master code of language is performed through an equally exclusive model. Edward Said has attempted a way out of this impasse by promoting a broader cultural criticism that transcends disciplinary boundaries. His opposition of "filiation" and "affiliation" reveals how political power molds the perceptions of individual writers while pragmatically situating structure so as to avoid overly general models.[4]

In choosing the re-creation of the exile as my paradigm for narrative engagement and the interpretive experience, I am proposing a model of *disaffiliation*. In this model, structure is situated as a perpetually sliding signifier, generated by the revisionary mix of desires and repressions at work in the interaction between the narrative memories of text and reader (or events and interpreter).[5] Disaffiliation, however, assumes prior affiliation, and the exile as model offers the memories of that affiliation, its loss, and the conflict between the liberation of wandering and the desire to return as primary constituents in the dynamics of narrative engagement.

In collapsing the distinction between the fictional and the factual, I am drawing on Roland Barthes's merging of *mimesis* and *diegesis* and on Paul Ricoeur's assumptions concerning the allegorical equivalence of structure in historical and narrative events.[6] I do so to set up an equivalence between the reader of a novel, the historian composing a narrative about the past, the viewer of a film or visual narrative, and the psychoanalyst constructing a case history (all of whom I have labeled above as readers both for the purpose of simplicity and to indicate the commonality of their endeavor). Like Hayden White, particularly in his analysis of the tropological basis of historiography, I contend that all narratives of interpretation are involved with extended figures that generate representation. I focus on the reader or viewer rather than the author, filmmaker, or artist both to demonstrate the effects of that mediation and to show that such mediation is an ongoing dynamic whereby the reader assumes the role of creator.[7]

In *One Hundred Years of Solitude*, Gabriel García Márquez describes an insomnia plague that has seized the village of Macondo and José Arcadio Buendía's attempts to protect the town against the resultant loss of memory by labeling everything with its name and function. However, Buendía's well-intentioned system cannot anticipate the vagrant desires of many of his fellow townspeople:

> In all the houses keys to memorizing objects and feelings had been written. But the system demanded so much vigilance and moral strength that many succumbed to the spell of an imaginary reality, one invented by themselves, which was less practical for them but more comforting. Pilar Ternera was the one who contributed most to popularize that mystification when she conceived the trick of reading the past in cards as she had read the future before. By means of that recourse the insomniacs began to live in a world built on the uncertain alternatives of the cards, where a father was remembered faintly as the dark man who had arrived at the beginning of April and a mother was remembered only as the dark woman who wore a gold ring on her left hand, and where a birth date was reduced to the last Tuesday on which a lark sang in the laurel tree. Defeated by those practices of consolation, José Arcadio Buendía then decided to build the memory machine that he had desired once in order to remember the marvelous inventions of the gypsies. The artifact was based on the possibility of reviewing every morning, from beginning to end, the totality of knowledge acquired during one's life. He conceived of it as a spinning dictionary that a person placed on the axis could operate by means of a lever, so that in a very few hours there would pass before his eyes the notions most necessary for life.[8]

García Márquez presents a situation where the past becomes as fictionalized as the future. Furthermore, Buendía's spinning dictionary, like the mystical consolation he rejects, is based upon personal selection, upon infinite permutations, albeit from a finite source. Attempts to reconstruct the past require the reconstruction of memory, a selective and partial remembering necessarily accompanied by massive forgetting. The reconstruction can never be comprehensive because it is ordered by desires that are situational and personal as well as by ones that are universal. Desire itself can never be fully satiated, although the quest to do so motivates our yearning for the illusory comforts of narrative closure and theoretical totalization.

Like Buendía's memory machine, readers' desires to render objective, complete judgments regarding their object of study rest upon a faith in the provisional suspension of the subjectivity implicit in the inevitable dialogic relationship between interpreter and object of interpretation. Interpretive discourses consist of a dynamic dialogue, an ongoing interchange between Self (interpreter) and Other (object of interpretation), whereby Otherness is consistently internalized by the Self as well as projected with codes of desire and repression inherited from the Self back onto the Other. The psychoanalytic analogy is relevant here. Lacan links Freud's processes of displacement and condensation in dream interpretation to the literary tropes of metonymy and metaphor, respectively. For Lacan, desire is manifested by our attempts to integrate metaphorically the metonymy of disconnected serial events, attempts that cannot fully be satisfied. This metaphoric urge can be related to Freud's view of transference whereby the patient transfers unconscious wishes onto the analyst:

> The content of the wish had appeared first of all in the patient's consciousness without any memories of the surrounding circumstances which would have assigned it to a past time. The wish which was present was then, owing to the compulsion to associate which was dominant in her consciousness, linked to my person, with which the patient was legitimately concerned; and as the result of this *mesalliance*—which I describe as a 'false connection'—the same affect was provoked which had forced the patient long before to repudiate this forbidden wish.[9]

The shift in the analogy where the patient (text) is imposing a sense of order upon the analyst (interpreter), however, suggests not only the dialogic nature of the psychoanalytic relationship but also the oscillations involved in the interactions between interpreter and text.[10] The illusions of objectivity and totality neglect these oscillations and the transference that catalyzes them.

Lacanian psychoanalysis holds that the unconscious always speaks in response to the desire of the Other and that its Symbolic Order lies in a "transindividual" space between Self and Other.[11] Freud's definition of hysteria makes pantomime the symptomatic locus of the Imaginary.[12] In the hysterical, discourse achieves its etymological intent ("dis" plus "currere" = "to run in different directions"). Furthermore, it continually internalizes and projects the presence of Otherness and therefore is most effectively presented in forms of the grotesque. In the grotesque, the illusion of an integrated autonomy of self is transgressed and repressions and fetishes are projected in exaggerated forms. Bodies are expressed as being synecdochic or being multiple, their lower parts emphasized over their heads with more attention to openings and orifices than to images of closure or completion.[13] When the grotesque dominates in a narrative, traditional hierarchies are upset.

An ending seldom occurs without the dissipation of hysteria or the hysteric unless it is an ending that does not resolve the tensions it has aroused, but causes them to extend beyond the physical confines of the narrative. These tensions are presented within apocalyptic events where the horrific dominates and order has collapsed. Readers come face to face with the presentation of their repressions and an uneasy conflict of identity occurs. The pleasure of narrative engagement, the participation in the acting out of repressions through identification with the Other, is accompanied by a quest for the restoration of order through the eradication of the Other. The desire for an end joins the resistance to ending. In Freudian terms, Eros battles Thanatos as the need for narration encounters the necessity to remedy it.

Peter Brooks argues that the master trope in making sense of narrative is an anticipation of retrospection where the past is read as present and the present past in relation to a future we know to be already in place waiting for us to reach it. In other words, narrative constitutes an effort to reach origins through endings. Structural and imagistic repetitions, recognized by memory, inform the narrative and metanarrative structures and rehearse this desire for closure and return. However, these repetitions also interrupt the movement forward that will lead to the satisfaction of that desire. Repetition therefore can be seen as an expression of the conflicting desires of narrative memory—the exile's wish to return home and the need to wander. The journey toward the ideal Imaginary state as an end to the alienation from unity and order and the pleasure of deviance realized in the journeying both persist through repetition.

In hysterical discourse, transgressions of order intensify readers' experiences of deviance. The Other appears exaggerated because it is no longer safely contained. Rather than being dictated by the direction of events, it dictates them and does so by destabilizing. While a yearning for a return to containment is consequently aroused in readers, so too is their recognition of identity, and a dynamic between their internalization and their projection of the Other occurs. Again, repetition offers an indication and an expression of this dynamic, but repetition with a difference. In the hysterical, repetition becomes compulsive, demonic.[14] And the need for alleviation on the part of hysterics, a need with which readers also identify, is indicated by the prevalence of the apocalyptic in their discourse and the discourse concerning them. Thus, the annihilation of order which hysterics and their discourse effect becomes also a revelation of the desire for self-annihilation, for a final transgression that will end all transgressions.

I wish to apply these ideas to two texts, one a reconstruction of actual events, the other a fiction. I will examine the story of Jim Jones, exiled patriarch of the People's Temple, who, in a grotesque parody of Moses, brought his people to the Promised Land of Guyana. I will look at his story through the narrative constructed by James Reston, Jr. in *Our Father Who Art in Hell* after the mass suicide of 911 of Jones's followers. I will also use Chilean exile Ariel Dorfman's first novel written in English, *Mascara* (1988), in which the protagonist and narrator, who is literally faceless, focuses on the secretive and the obscene while the narrative considers the betrayals of memory. Although these two narratives are vastly dissimilar from the perspective of genre, the engagement between reader and text in both cases has fascinating correspondences. Both convey the transgressive and the hysterical discourse which informs their respective histories. Furthermore, this discourse derives from and motivates the conflicting desires and mnemonic revisions of the exile, thereby creating a mirror for the interpreter as well.

II

I became my own obituary.
(Sartre, Les Mots*)*

The news reports of the assassination of Congressman Leo Ryan and of mass suicide at Jonestown on November 18, 1978, were both chilling and fascinating. Each day boldfaced headlines declared the new body count, and each day the number increased. Our attention fixed on that number as if its magnitude could somehow offer us a means of measuring, of quantifying this macabre event, of putting it on some scale by which we could assess the weight of tragedies. An exiled cult seeking a Promised Land in Guyana, proclaiming its principles with the fervor of a tent meeting, and finally protecting its purity against unknown and unseen persecutors by a self-induced Armageddon; here was our biblical consciousness hyperbolically dramatized. Here was Moses and Masada, the Garden of Eden and the Fall, the mesmerizing preacher and Satan subsumed into one story. And, most traumatizing, here were our cultural myths, our universal narratives, confronting us as gruesome revelations.

The protagonist of this story, Jim Jones, was savior, God, and angel of death to his followers. Addicted to alcohol, antidepressants, and barbiturates, having eliminated his body's natural defenses through massive doses of antibiotics, Jones would have died from natural causes within ten days after the apocalypse at Jonestown according to his doctor. His monstrous power and twisted passion are most fully revealed in the nine hundred hours of tapes he made at Jonestown—his attempt to preserve the holy word, his words. Jones's contradictions underscore our paradoxical reactions to the Jonestown calamity. Like Hazel Motes preaching the Church of Christ without Christ, Jones used his ministerial zeal to convert his followers to atheism. A crusading socialist who practiced capitalism, his sermons in the swamps of Guyana mixed the rhetoric of faith healing, political revolution, and paranoia.

To strengthen his followers' bonds to him, Jones worked to eradicate their blood ties with relatives in the States. Sometimes White Nights (a name chosen by Jones to counteract the racism he felt inherent in the term "black night"), all-night mass meetings during which Jones whipped his followers into hysterical frenzies, became testimonials in which Jonestown residents would take turns spinning stories about how they would like to maim and torture their fallen relatives. Jones exhorted them, applauding the most inventive with his high-pitched squeals of laughter. The tapes give us one little girl explaining to a delighted Jones how she would cut up her father's body and then invite her other relatives over to eat it.

Jones promised death, murder, and suicide to his followers. He heaped doses of profanity on his religious phrases while vocalizing imagined apocalyptic scenes. Inventing snipers and warning against an imminent invasion by Fascist troops who would torture the Jonestown babies and elderly first, Jones rehearsed his self-proclaimed "Greatest Decision in History." And indeed it was the children, followed by the elderly, who lined up first to receive the toxic sacrament. Their savior, unable to steel himself sufficiently with a fistful of barbiturates to take the poison, asked a nurse to shoot him in the temple.

Yet Jones's voice cannot be summarily dismissed as lunatic. His professed cause was just, the elimination of racism and the elevation of the oppressed. His followers numbered in the thousands. He was appointed by Mayor Moscone to the San Francisco Housing Authority Commission in 1976 and was frequently feted and lauded by local politicians. Walter Mondale courted him to deliver the votes of his followers to the Carter campaign. Even during the last months of Jonestown, when the rantings of the White Nights would pierce the jungle, representatives of the Soviet government negotiated with Jones to bring his settlement to the Soviet Union. Jones calculated his appeal and his deviousness well beyond the capacities of the irrational madman. And because of this, our need as interpreters to distance him as merely crazy is frustrated. On some level we recognize that, in different circumstances, we might have been among Jim Jones's followers and therefore our involvement in the tragedy of Jonestown is enhanced.

Attempts to interpret the story of Jim Jones are attempts to exorcise complicity in his story, attempts to play patient and analyst, priest and confessor, simultaneously. Yet we unconsciously recognize this complicity in our initial attraction to the story. With Jim Jones we reenact and transgress cultural myths, achieve vicarious pleasure in his power to command and manipulate them, and can punish ourselves for this delight by participating in his demise.

Making Sense of the Jonestown Suicides by Judith Weightman and *Jesus and Jim Jones* by Steve Rose present sociological and religious perspectives, respectively, on the People's Temple.[15] Rebecca Moore, whose sisters,

Carolyn and Annie, and nephew Kimo died at Jonestown, proposes to offer a history of "the believers, rather than of the non-believers, or the ex-believers" in *A Sympathetic History of Jonestown*, but her history understandably tends to focus on the betrayal and manipulation by Jones of these believers.[16] I find James Reston's account, *Our Father Who Art in Hell*, the most intelligent and compelling in its effort to attach allegorical significance to the events at Jonestown. Also, Reston is both a novelist and a historian and is therefore sensitive to the links between these two genres.

Reston views the deaths at Jonestown as a consequence of the "spiritual floundering of post-Vietnam America":[17]

> Before I left for Guyana the first time, I saw Jones and his demise as a novel in real life, one of those rare public events which possess the essential elements of compelling fiction: mystery and horror, a primeval setting, a theme close to the raw, primordial instincts of man, a plot stretching belief and imagination, and a villain of satanic power who had used arguments I cared about on race and Vietnam and social progress to produce this ghoulish spectacle. The story tapped my morbid fascination, but it also questioned my political rootedness. Was the Jonestown calamity simply the *reductio ad absurdum* of 1960s thinking and practice? (150)

This "novel in real life" was a contemporary *Heart of Darkness*, and Reston plays Marlow to Jones's Kurtz. Jones was the brilliant leader whose mission warped in the primal jungle, a cultural hero who unleashed that culture's dark, repressed urges when he freed it of its constraints. He would "exterminate the brutes," and his uncanny legacy, "the horror, the horror," would echo in his chronicler's mind as he recognized a cultural, and by extension a personal, doppelgänger.

Reston tells us the Jonestown community was founded upon the three qualities for which Dostoevski's Grand Inquisitor said humankind thirsted: miracle, mystery, and authority (58). Jones's followers called him "Father" or "Dad," titles whose implications convey these three qualities. He demanded their idolatry, fostering allegiance through public humiliation, and he stoked this idolatry by staging dramatic proof of his healing powers, even faking an assassination attempt from which he miraculously healed himself. He promulgated a doctrine of Christian atheism that placed himself as the realization of God in man:

> In *me*, the twain have been married. In this dispensation, I have taken on the body, the same body that walked in the plains of Palmyra, of whom Solomon said his hair is black as a raven, and, who, as Isaiah said, 7:20, would shave with a razor. I *do* shave with a razor. My hair *is* black as a raven's. I came as the God to eliminate all your false Gods. Men have dastardly distorted the spirit that I have, but it was necessary for me to come upon the scene and I have. From time to time, I shall show you proofs, so that you will have no further need of religion.

I have repeatedly resurrected the dead before your eyes. You have never seen anyone shot down before your eyes and heal themselves, yet I, the socialist leader, have done it. I am the only God you've ever seen, with blood gushing out of his chest, who, after the nurses put their fingers in the bullet holes, just wiped his hand across his chest, and closed them. Your God is one of the people. He is the instrument of all you've ever desired, all that freedom embraces, all that justice embodies, all that sensitivity involves. That is what your God is.

I must say that it is a great effort to be God. I would lean upon another, but no other in the consciousness we are evolving in has the faculties that I possess. When they do, I will be glad to hold his coat. In the meantime, I shall be God, and beside me, there shall be no other. If you don't need a God, then fine, I'm no problem to you. But if you need a God, I'm going to nose out that other God, because it's a false God, so you can get the right concept in your mind. If you're holding onto that Sky God, I'll nose him out ten lengths every time.

And when all this has been done, I shall go into the obscurity of the conscious collective principle of socialism, and I shall have no further intrusion into the affairs of man.

"With that," Reston reports, "he would take the Bible and fling it before him, spit on it, and stamp on it with his feet. He would raise his bare arm to the roof of his Temple and shout, 'If there is a God in the sky, I say, FUCK YOU,' and when he was not struck dead on the spot, this was his proof of the silliness of the Sky God and proof of their superstition" (56–57). As Father, Jones became the God that his followers lacked and created meaning for their disenchanted lives. He offered a panacea for disillusionment and, in a culture full of disillusioned people, his appeal was magnetic, not least of all to the narrator of his story.

Reston's account begins much like Marlow's, waiting for his ship to depart for a journey down a jungle river. He also quickly establishes the motif of the double that dominates *Heart of Darkness* and infiltrates his narrative. Since Caucasian travelers are scarce, one of the deckhands jokingly calls Reston "Jim Jones":

> It was a joke that time, but two days later, as I boarded the *Pomeroon* again for the return, the same thing happened, but with an edge to it. "You Jim Jones?" a muscular, unsmiling Oriental shouted over to me, and before I could answer he said, "If you Jim Jones, you a skunk. Jump overboard, I say," and he turned away angrily. The report had just been published in the *Guyana Chronicle*, the government newspaper, that seventeen of the children at Jonestown had been adopted Guyanese. Many still believed that Jim Jones had a double in Jonestown, that he was still alive. (4)

Just as Marlow discovers the repressed disease of his culture and of himself in Kurtz, we witness Reston's discovery of the same in his narration of Jones's story:

Jim Jones was the singular product of the last thirty years of American history, and his following was the blend of disaffected blacks and whites for whom modern America provided no answer in religion, political action, or education. His overwhelming success in California, where he built the single largest Protestant membership of any church in that state in little more than four years, dramatizes the void he filled. His success was deeply rooted in the general failure of the 1970's. Without Richard Nixon, without the Vietnam War, without the demise of the civil rights movement or the departure of the traditional church from social action, without the current trend toward self-concern and hedonism, there would have been no Jim Jones. (228)

Reston's personal and political investment had been subverted by 1970s America's abandonment of the social mission of the sixties and by its immersion in narcissism and cynical forgetfulness. "It could have been different," he laments, "the 1970s could have been the Second Reconstruction in American history, an active, inspiring attempt to bind up the nation's wounds, to care for those who had borne the pain and the defeat of Vietnam and for those who had resisted it as immoral, to ensure that those for whom the civil rights struggle had been waged were not left in a void after the gains of the sixties" (229). Reston's resultant alienation explains his and the cultists' attraction to Jones, whom Reston characterizes as "the true Alienated Man in an age when alienation had ceased to be fashionable" (230). It also explains the disconnected images—quotes from the Bible tacked to rafters, Santayana's famous epigram "those who do not remember the past are condemned to repeat it" emblazoned above Jones's chair, a Smile sign—he recalls from his trip to Jonestown on November 27, 1978, deeply tinged with irony in the aftermath of a holocaust. Reston's narrative reveals the dynamic interplay of attraction and repulsion at work in his memory. It is an attraction to a restoration of purpose, a historical telos, an Imaginary ideal which he found so profoundly absent in contemporary cultural life. And it is a repulsion from the perversion of that ideal, the recognition of the Other intruding into that most precious domain—the illusory unity of Self—in this instance projected onto an integrated social mission. In other words, Reston recognizes the cultist in himself, and through this recognition he achieves the status of both analyst and analysand. Rather than becoming dominated by the mystique of Jones so that the repetitions of his narrative memory become the compulsive repetitions of the cultist, continually acting out his enthrallment in the power of that mystique, Reston can respond critically to that power. In this sense his narrative becomes a dialogue, a reciprocal relationship between the analyst and analysand whose collaboration determines its shape.

The story of Jim Jones and the People's Temple, Reston's "novel in real life," bears comparisons to stories as diverse as those of Manson, Hitler, Kurtz, or Sutpen. All of these, whether "historical" or "fictional," contain a generic plot structure—that of the exile or outcast who forges a Promised Land out of an obsession with loss, thereby dooming the dream to destruction. The exile as wanderer can only realize the object of his or her search through self-annihilation, so that the wish to return to an origin becomes the desire for an ending. And this plot of identity suicide usually includes a Manichaean quest to eradicate the Other as unconscious projection of the Self. The return to the ideal Imaginary is premised on the death of the Real; the object of history becomes the end of history.

Jameson's theory of expressive causality presents one model for approaching the exile as protagonist and metacode. Jameson draws on Althusser's concept of history as an absent cause in which the causes of present social effects can be approached only through perceptions of functions that we experience as "Necessity."[18] Expressive causality places a sequence of historical events into an underlying interpretive allegory. This exercise of narratological will views the present as a satisfaction of genealogical desire, a realization of the past rather than simply an effect. In *The Content of the Form*, Hayden White interprets Jameson's narratological causality in the following manner:

> The seizure by consciousness of a past in such a way as to define the present as a fulfillment rather than as an effect is precisely what is represented in a narrativization of a sequence of historical events so as to reveal every thing early in it as a prefiguration of a project to be realized in some future. Considered as a basis for a specific kind of human agency, narrativization sublimates necessity into a symbol of possible freedom.
>
> The narrativization of history, for example, transforms every present into a "past future," on the one side, and a "future past," on the other. Considered as a transition between a past and a future, every present is at once a realization of projects performed by past human agents and a determination of a field of possible projects to be realized by living human agents in their future.[19]

In this sense, interpreters of history function like characters in a novel in that their mission is to realize the inherent potentialities of the plot in which they are engaged. In doing so, they tie events together so that they lead to conclusions which, retrospectively, subsume beginnings as part of their process.

Expressive causality helps to define the shape of narrative memory, but its view of genealogical desire fails to consider sufficiently the degree to which simultaneous attraction to and repulsion from loss informs narrative memory's dynamics. Readers as exiles from an ideal Imaginary state seek to recover that state by wandering the text, only to continually wander into recognitions of their exiled condition. Although genealogical desire empowers them to assign direction and purpose to their wandering, the return to homeland is still not accomplished. While the search for an ending motivates their journey, the fear of ending that journey, of finding the Imaginary unrestored, impels them to resist conclusion. Once again, the transgressive, particularly in hysterical discourse in which repetition becomes compulsive, offers us insight into the flirtation with the death drive. The master text for understanding this is Freud's *Beyond the Pleasure Principle*.

In this work Freud views repetition as the essence of drives, but paradoxically he views the individual's basic need to reproduce his or her earliest states as indicative of the desire to abolish all drives, a death instinct (Thanatos). Like the pleasure principle (Eros), Thanatos is an internal force. Indeed, Freud considers it the supreme form of the pleasure principle in its complete reduction of tension, and at times terms it the "Nirvana principle," thereby linking pleasure with annihilation.[20] According to Freud, all living beings possess an internal tendency toward the end of life as the end of life's drives and the restoration of an original, tension-free state. Life's ambiguities, intensified by traumas and subsequent repressions, represent detours, wanderings from this path. Ironically, Freud's expression in *Beyond the Pleasure Principle* lacks his usual clarity and logic. As if resisting his proclamation of the primacy of a death drive, Freud fills the text with contradictions and blurred references. His conclusions seem uncertain, and we might take this groping not as indicative of Freud's lack of a comprehensive understanding of his subject but rather as an unconscious resistance to that understanding.

Narrative engagement with a fictional text or with events in history, characterized as it is by yearning and resistance, recapitulates the narrative of life. Our engagement with literary and historical texts becomes the arena in which the contest between Eros and Thanatos is performed. We are exiles from our origin, yearning for return and possessed by our sense of loss of that origin while simultaneously resisting that yearning because of the pleasures of wandering and our fear of the loss of those pleasures. Interpretation, as an act of memory, is controlled by these opposed urges. We travel a text in quest of an ending that will retrospectively impose order by relieving the tensions generated by the plot, thereby returning us to a beginning. In doing so, we seek the beginning of history in its end.

The discourse of repetition, signaling the death drive, catalyzes and is catalyzed by narrative memory. It functions as an indication of ending while, ironically, it tentatively halts progress toward the end. Freud termed repetition a "demon," and we witness the demonic aspect in the cadences of Jim Jones's orations. Repetition in the transgressive discourse of the hysteric becomes compulsive, transgressing the normal function of repetition within discourse. Rather than relaxing tension, it contributes to it. Rather than coalescing to augment order, it disperses order and destabilizes through its constancy. Hysterical transgression combines Eros and Thanatos, bringing erotic excitement to loss. It fetishizes memory, inducing sexual frenzy in infinite repetition, and undermines narrative by collapsing beginnings and endings while eliminating middles. Exiles have nowhere to wander but must spin endlessly in the same place. They have found a home, an Imaginary ideal, but it is no resting place. And Father has castrated their memories.

III

> The new historian, the genealogist, will know what
> to make of this masquerade. He will not be too
> serious to enjoy it; on the contrary, he will push
> the masquerade to its limits and prepare the great
> carnival of time where masks are constantly
> reappearing. Genealogy is history in the form of
> a concerted carnival.
> (Michel Foucault, "Nietzsche, Genealogy, History")

Ariel Dorfman adopts the language of the land to which he is exiled to give voice to memories of the land from which he is exiled.[21] In doing so, he offers an example of the movement from filiation to affiliation although his focus remains on disaffiliation, on the fact that his identity will always be predicated on his exilic status. Indeed, this act underscores the gap between experience and representation of experience and demonstrates language to be but part of the makeup that constitutes the mask. Mascara deals with acquiring and losing identities, with self-possession through the possession of others, with the deceptions of memory. The text becomes a mirror in which the narrator's facelessness reveals the reader's face.

Dorfman presents the story of an unnamed character who is born without a recognizable face. No one, not even his parents, remembers who he is, and therefore he is able to become the perfect voyeur. To enhance this vocation, he destroys all records of his identity, including his fingerprints. Unable to forget a face, he perceives the hidden faces of others and captures them in photographs, thereby acquiring power over them by possessing evidence of their secrets. Photography as an act of erotic possession is more satisfying to him than sex: "A photograph: now, you can fuck a photograph forever"; "to own another human being, the only thing necessary is to kidnap her intimacy, to deflower with my camera what my eyes had already explored."[22] His employment as assistant to the archivist of photography files at the Department of Traffic Accidents enables him to acquire a collection of photographs that depicts its subjects in their most private and grotesque moments. For this featureless narrator, all faces are false. By putting on their socially authorized masks, they respond to a historical rather than a genetic imperative:

The first face a little one sees is not something far away, outside, like a mirror in the sky. Not so. The first thing any child sees is the inside of his father's face, he sees the maneuvers that his own features must start rehearsing and that are constantly being sewn onto him like an umberella of skin against the rain. In order to keep out other, possibly worse, invaders, he adopts his father's shell. Human beings are trapped inside the dead faces of their remote ancestors, repeated from generation to generation. (32)

Mascara's narrator finds his perfect love, his twin, in Oriana, an amnesiac whose memory past the age of four is nonexistent. This child-woman with no past mirrors his lack of a face and permits him the opportunity to dictate the parameters of her identity and thereby substitute his authority for society's:

For her, every day shall be as a first birth, with all the fresh air that came at the beginning of Creation. And the person who accompanies her, the person who can show her the perpetually recent contours of the universe, will be as a god. . . . I can rewrite and recapture the whole of human history. We can be each of the past's lovers, each character in each novel: and it will always be my narrating her, a thousand and one times if that is necessary. (80–81)

However, the narrator fears the disruption of his Edenic situation by the reemergence of Oriana's past, an adult Oriana, "normal: someone with a past, with a mask" (77), hiding within the child Oriana and waiting to reclaim her face. In order to prevent this, he seeks the skills of the plastic surgeon, Dr. Mavirelli, whom he addresses in the sections of the novel which he narrates. While he attempts to blackmail this remaker of faces to unmake Oriana's past, the narrator intentionally and ironically misremembers Mavirelli's name, offering instead a panoply of variations.

Mavirelli responds to him in the third section of the novel and reveals himself as a double of the narrator. He has achieved professional prominence by reconstructing the faces of important public figures to match public desires as expressed in opinion polls, even recreating the face of one popular victim of sudden death on the face of his successor. Like the narrator's photography, Mavirelli's surgery functions as a means of erotic possession; penetration constitutes control:

All right, I admit it, I start to think that I am possessing that face: that small apparatus is like a metallic clitoris, which I am inserting into the precise intersecting line of the brain. . . . Tell me, of what use is it to change somebody's twisted nose if his memory persists in remembering the old one and, therefore, continues to twist the new one until it resembles the nose that will not vanish from that memory? That is why my operations have such an incredible degree of success: because along with the old skin, they eliminate the old habits, the past. (140)

In the epilogue, we discover that Mavirelli has given his face to the narrator and can die smiling, having conferred his identity rather than having had identity conferred on him.

From the narrator's Kafkaesque job to the Gestapo-like repossessors of the hands of the dead to the two unidentified investigators who become rude interrogators in the epilogue, Dorfman's references to the political oppression in his native Chile are clear. Totalitarian authority renders memory a fraud. Like the plastic surgeon, its "efforts are made in order to suppress a revelation" (35), to enforce the repetition of sameness, and to erase the personal. Social identity is predicated on the loss of the Self, and resistance to that loss ironically is fostered through anonymity. But aside from a political allegory, *Mascara* also presents an allegory of the reading process.

As faceless voyeur, the narrator functions like a generic reader. His vicarious pleasure derives from subsuming the Other and using its sameness or difference to affirm his ideal projection of the Self. In the wish to attain that imaginative ideal, to revise memory so as to eliminate the recognition of an exilic condition, the reader, like the narrator, desires privation rather than plenitude, return rather than journeying, and manipulates whomever and whatever is encountered in order to conserve the fixed center of desire. By focusing on origins and elevating them to myth, the reader represses the knowledge of loss and willfully attains the status of amnesiac. In effect, the reader ends history in order to recreate it.

Dorfman uses first person narration to better convey the obsessive quest, the death drive toward the Imaginary. Even though the section narrated by Mavirelli revises those of the faceless narrator, the tone and perspective of the narrative voice remain consistent until the epilogue. The faceless narrator and the plastic surgeon, like the social Gestapo they resist, are thieves of memory. However, their figurative and tonal parallels, the propensity of their discourse toward the grotesque and the cynical, inject repetition into the text and activate its readers' narrative memories while suggesting metanarrative constructions to them. Their similarities are reified as the novel concludes with the initial narrator putting on Mavirelli's face, thereby compelling its readers, like Narcissus, to stare into their own reflections. Whether or not they drown depends on the extent to which they have established a reciprocal dialogue with the narrative or have been possessed by it.

Hysterical transgression again fetishizes memory and eroticizes loss. Just as the faceless narrator loses his voyeuristic distance in his obsession with Oriana, allowing himself to become possessed by her in his wish to possess her, Mavirelli gives up his life to impress his identity without first having to erase a prior image. Both wish to invade the insides of another and father a new individual who is a replication of themselves. In *Mascara*, they combine to succeed, and this merging catalyzes their readers' identifications. The narrative reaches into their private recesses and affirms their fetishes, fusing Eros and Thanatos, while they participate in its conclusion. Chameleon-like, they permit the novel to stamp its face upon their own. This yielding constitutes a transgressive act, one which the narrative endorses and which its readers compulsively repeat, deriving pleasure from their loss of Self.

Yet readers wish to play Dr. Mavirelli to the text as much as they desire to be molded by it and therefore are impelled to resist the compulsion to be subsumed, which hypnotically promises to lessen the tension produced by their journey through the novel. Instead, readers make their own incisions into the face of the text and stitch it back together in the image of their own narrative memories. Furthermore, they must refashion their handiwork to accord with the mutable demands of that memory. By oscillating between yielding and resisting, readers again perform the role of exile.[23] Their conflicting impulses to journey and to return are regulated by the desires of memory which assert themselves only to fade and to be replaced by another assertion, like so many applications of makeup.

We have seen the discourse of the hysteric, the pantomimic language of the Imaginary, at work in both a historical narrative and a work of fiction. Both types of narrative are conditioned by the judgments inherent in description, and the descriptions in both cases contain a complex of symbols that relate to universal patterns. The engagement of the historian or reader with the narrative of events is continually mediated by a dialogic process akin to psychoanalytic transference where Otherness is internalized and projected. Repetition offers the means and the evidence for this process and, as the foundation of memory, refers backward in the narrative to propel it forward. This paradox mirrors and is dictated by readers' conflicting desires for excitement and stasis. However, hysterical discourse transgresses this dialogic process by rendering repetition compulsive, thereby destroying the movement forward and freezing the narrative memory in trauma.

Lacan contends that Freud made distinctions between repeating (*wieder-holen*) and reproduction (*reproduzieren*). While reproduction consists of the actual reexperiencing of the original traumatic event, repetition confronts this past event in symbolic form.[24] Hysterical discourse reproduces the tragic vision inherent in the end product of narrative—its temporality. The aspiration to be liberated from history inherent in the quest for the Imaginary is undercut by the historical underpinnings of the Imaginary. Interpreters or readers, who are subsumed by the thanatotic urge of hysterical discourse, become fixated on trauma. They lose the critical distance necessary for a dialogue with the text so that their narrative memories endlessly replicate the trauma reproduced in the narrative memory of the text.

By searching out origins, one becomes a crab.
The historian looks backward, eventually he
believes backward.
(Nietzsche, Twilight of the Idols)

To conclude this discussion, I wish briefly to examine what amounts to a work of fiction that masquerades as a history. Originally titled *The Man Moses: A Historical Novel*, Freud's *Moses and Monotheism* attempts to extend the principle of primal forfeiture that he presented in *Totem and Taboo* to Jewish monotheism. Its discussion of the archetypal exile, Moses, however, succeeds more as a narrative of its author's psyche. Freud argues that Moses was actually an aristocratic Egyptian who descended from his position to side with the children of Israel and imposed the monotheistic religion that revolved around the Egyptian sun god, Aten, on the Semitic tribes. Freud contends that Moses was subsequently killed by his people and that the worship of the god of Moses melded with the worship of a volcano god, Yahweh, through whom the Jewish people repressed their guilt for murdering their leader. However, this repressed trauma returned as the Jewish prophets advanced a religion based on ethics by focusing on the Mosaic god and enhancing the guilt of the people.[25]

Although Freud's assertions have not been given much credence by historians and biblical scholars, *Moses and Monotheism* does offer much material by which to analyze its author's engagement with the events he narrates.[26] As James Strachey's editorial note informs us, its construction is extremely unorthodox for Freud. It consists of three essays of greatly varying lengths and contains two prefaces, one located at the beginning of the third essay and another halfway through that essay. What is perhaps most striking is the sputtering quality of the argument, again uncharacteristic of Freud. The work is full of parenthetical remarks, repetitions, and recapitulations, and contains several apologies by Freud for these distractions. These features begin to make sense when we place Freud's history of Moses in the context of Freud's own desires.

Moses and Monotheism was four years in composition (1934–1938), well above Freud's standard for a work of this length. During these four years, Freud witnessed increasingly ominous signs in Austrian politics that were to climax in the Nazi occupation of Vienna and force his departure to London with the manuscript of *Moses and Monotheism* among his possessions. Freud's attention to the prototypical exile therefore is symptomatic of his anxiety over his own imminent exile. His argument that Moses was an aristocratic Egyptian who left his country because of its oppressive tactics toward the Jews dramatizes his own dilemma as a member of Austria's intellectual elite who could no longer tolerate its country's slide into anti-Semitic hooliganism. Freud viewed the rejection of psychoanalysis by the political establishment as the symbolic murder of himself as the lawgiver of psychoanalysis just as he argued that Moses, the lawgiver of his people, was slain by them. His contention that the Jewish prophets brought about the return of the Mosaic god indicates his desire that his disciples, the Jewish prophets of psychoanalysis, reinstate his teachings. The consequent guilt suffered by the children of Israel from the return of repressed trauma constitutes Freud's secret wish for retribution.

The fits and starts that characterize the narrative are symptomatic of Freud's ambivalence concerning the entire notion of exile. His attachment to Vienna was as extreme as the attachment to Egypt he manufactures for Moses. Unconsciously he recognized that the departure from his homeland would preserve that homeland only in the postures of his memory and would be manifested only through condensation and displacement. His reconstructions therefore would be informed by the very methodology of the law he had preached—the law of psychoanalysis. The stone tablets into which Freud had engraved that law had suffered numerous cracks and crumblings during the 1930s, a period during which some of his disciples, in his eyes, became infidels. Perhaps their proposed revisions to his law secretly tested his own faith. Perhaps his narrative of Moses represented his working out his anxiety concerning both exile and living by the very law he dictated.

Freud writes of his interpretation of the story of Moses:

> Its evidential value seems to me strong enough for me to venture on a further step and to posit the assertion that the archaic heritage of human beings comprises not only dispositions but also subject-matter—memory-traces of the experience of earlier generations. In this way the compass as well as the importance of the archaic heritage would be significantly extended.[27]

What he is arguing is a universal history based on a universal memory of trauma. Ricoeur draws on this argument to posit all narrative, whether historical or fictional, as an allegory of temporality.[28] I have attempted to demonstrate that the fear of loss generated by awareness of the corrosive power of time embodies the tragic underpinnings of all narratives. Although methods of historiography, like techniques of fiction, vary, the dynamics of narrative engagement always involve conflicting desires to yield to and to resist this traumatic recognition. While repetitions within narrative reproduce and enhance the function of memory by offering signs of origin, hysterical repetition, like hysterical memory, arouses trauma by excising the marginalia that typically accompany the encounter with origin. The tragic experience in this instance is not diminished by the mediative intrusion of signs, symbols, or other projections. Instead, the reflection of the Self encountered is an absent

Self, and the subsequent reverberations of this perception constrict any future encounters.

As interpreters, we function as exiles. Our desires and our denials, our masks and our absences, our alienation and our yearning for omniscience all come into play as we seek and resist our origins in our narrations of narrative. Our visions of home altered by the revisions of memory, we are condemned to wander our texts eternally, recreating history in our quest to conclude it.

NOTES

* This essay appears in a slightly different form in Robert D. Newman, *Transgressions of Reading: Narrative Engagement as Exile and Return* (Durham, N.C.: Duke University Press, 1993).

1. I am referring to the three essential orders Lacan constructs for the psychoanalytic field: the Imaginary, the Real, and the Symbolic. The Imaginary constitutes a narcissistic relation of the subject to its ego. It evolves out of the mirror stage in which the infant first perceives its bodily unity through encountering its reflection in a mirror, thus forming the outline of what is to become the ego. This order extends into adult relations through fantasies and images. The Symbolic contains language and therefore is the order through which the subject can represent desires and feelings. These representations, however, are culturally conditioned and therefore become expressions of oneself through the Other. The Real is the domain outside the subject, a persistent and intrusive realm, that exists outside symbolization. Malcolm Bowie writes, "Each of Lacan's orders is better thought of as a shifting gravitational centre for his arguments than as a stable concept; at any moment each may be implicated in the redefinition of the others." "Jacques Lacan," *Structuralism and Since*, ed. John Sturrock (New York: Oxford University Press, 1979), pp. 132–33.

2. Trauma for Freud is not brought through the original event in isolation but through repetition. An event becomes traumatic retrospectively when it is recalled by a later event in trauma. In *Project for a Scientific Psychology* (1895), Freud writes: "Here we have the case of a memory arousing an affect which it did not arouse as an experience, because in the meantime the changes [brought about] by puberty had made possible a different understanding of what was remembered. . . . We invariably find that a memory is repressed which has only become a trauma by *deferred action* [*nachträglich*]." *The Standard Edition of the Complete Psychological Works of Sigmund Freud*, trans. and ed. James Strachey, 24 vols. (London: Hogarth Press, 1953–1974), 1:356. Hereafter abbreviated as *SE*.

3. *Selected Letters of Friedrich Nietzsche*, trans. Christopher Middleton (Chicago: University of Chicago Press, 1969), p. 347. Letter of January 5, 1889.

4. Said writes,

The contemporary critical consciousness stands between the temptations represented by two formidable and related powers engaging critical attention. One is the culture to which critics are bound filiatively (by birth, nationality, profession); the other is a method or system acquired affiliatively (by social and political conviction, economic and historical circumstances, voluntary effort and willed deliberation).

This movement from filiation to affiliation "can be considered an instance of the passage from nature to culture." *The World, the Text, and the Critic* (Cambridge, Mass.: Harvard University Press, 1983), pp. 24–25, 20. For intelligent analytical summaries of recent trends in applications of narratology to historiography, see David Simpson, "Literary Criticism and the Return to 'History,' " *Critical Inquiry* 14 (1988): 721–47 and John Kucich, "Narrative Theory as History: A Review of Problems in Victorian Fiction Studies," *Victorian Studies* 28 (1985): 657–75.

5. Certainly Harold Bloom's work on revisionism, particularly *Agon: Towards a Theory of Revisionism* (New York: Oxford University Press, 1982), is a primary influence on this model.

6. Here I am interested chiefly in Barthes's essay "The Discourse of History," trans. Stephen Bann, *Comparative Criticism: A Yearbook*, vol. 3, ed. E. S. Schaffer (New York: Cambridge University Press, 1981), and in Ricoeur's three volume *Time and Narrative*, trans. Kathleen McLaughlin and David Pellauer (Chicago: University of Chicago Press, 1984–1989).

In *The Philosophy of History*, Hegel states,

In our language the term History unites the objective with the subjective side, and denotes quite as much the *historia rerum gestarum*, as the *res gestae* themselves; on the other hand it comprehends not less what has happened than the narration of what has happened. This union of the two meanings we must regard as of a higher order than mere outward accident; we must suppose historical narrations to have appeared contemporaneously with historical deeds and events. It is an internal vital principle common to both that produces them synchronously. Family memorials, patriarchal traditions, have an interest confined to the family and the clan. The uniform course of events which such a condition implies is no subject of serious remembrance; though distinct transactions or turns of fortune may rouse Mnemosyne to form conceptions of them— in the same way as love and the religious emotions provoke imagination to give shape to a previously formless impulse. But it is only the state which first presents subject-matter that is not only adapted to the prose of History, but involves the production of such history in the very progress of its own being.

The Philosophy of History, trans. J. Sibree, (New York: Dover, 1956).

7. My concern with textual erotics, with the view that narrative engagement constitutes an act of desire, leans heavily on the work of Jacques Lacan, particularly on Lacan's applications of Freud to narrative, and on Freud himself. I am also heavily indebted to Peter Brooks's applications of psychoanalysis to narrative, *Reading for the Plot: Design and Intention in Narrative* (New York: Knopf, 1984), and to Hayden White's tropological readings of historiography: *The Content of the Form: Narrative Discourse and Historical Representation* (Baltimore: Johns Hopkins University Press, 1987), *Tropics of Discourse: Essays in Cultural Criticism* (Baltimore: Johns Hopkins University Press, 1978), and *Metahistory: The Historical Imagination in Nineteenth-Century Europe* (Baltimore: Johns Hopkins University Press, 1973).

8. Gabriel García Márquez, *One Hundred Years of Solitude*, trans. Gregory Rabassa (New York: Avon, 1971), pp. 53–54.

9. "The Psychotherapy of Hysteria," *Studies in Hysteria* (1895), *SE* 2:303. For the development of the concept of transference in Freud's works, see J. Laplanche and J. B. Pontalis, *The Language of Psycho-Analysis*, trans. Donald Nicholson-Smith (New York: Norton, 1973), pp. 455–62. For a discussion relating the historian's disavowal of transference to Freud's suppression of the seduction theory, see Dominick La Capra, "History and Psychoanalysis," *The Trials of Psychoanalysis*, ed. Françoise Meltzer (Chicago: University of Chicago Press, 1987), pp. 9–38.

10. Donald P. Spence argues that the psychoanalytic process is not one of archaeological reconstruction, but is rather an interaction between patient and analyst to construct a narrative about the patient's past, *Narrative Truth and Historical Truth: Meaning and Interpretation in Psychoanalysis* (New York: Norton, 1982).

11. In "Analysis and Truth or the Closure of the Unconscious," Lacan writes:

> It is in the space of the Other that the subject sees himself, and the point from which he looks at himself is also in that space. Now this is also the point from which he speaks, since in so far as he speaks, it is in the locus of the Other that he begins to constitute that truthful lie by which is initiated that which participates in desire at the level of the unconscious.

The Four Fundamental Concepts of Psycho-Analysis, trans. Alan Sheridan (New York: Norton, 1981), p. 144.

12. "Fragment of an Analysis of a Case of Hysteria" (1905), *SE* 7:1–122.

13. Peter Stallybrass and Allon White convincingly explore the grotesque as transgressive and apply it to the concept of carnival:

> Social historians who have charted transformations of carnival as a social practice have not registered its displacements into bourgeois discourses like art and psychoanalysis: adopting a naively empirical view they have outlined a simple disappearance, the elimination of the carnivalesque. . . . Part of that process was the disowning of carnival and its symbolic resources, a gradual reconstruction of the idea of carnival as the culture of the Other. This act of disavowal on the part of the emergent bourgeoisie, with its sentimentalism and its disgust, made carnival into the festival of the Other. It encoded all that which the proper bourgeois must strive not to be in order to preserve a stable and correct sense of self.

The Politics and Poetics of Transgression (Ithaca: Cornell University Press, 1986), p. 178. See also Allon White, "Pigs and Pierrots: The Politics of Transgression in Modern Fiction," *Raritan* 2 (1982): 51–70.

14. In "The 'Uncanny'"(1919), Freud writes,

> In the first place, if psycho-analytic theory is correct in maintaining that every affect belonging to an emotional impulse, whatever its kind, is transformed, if it is repressed, into anxiety, then among instances of frightening things there must be one class in which the frightening element can be shown to be something repressed which *recurs*. This class of frightening things would then constitute the uncanny; and it must be a matter of indifference whether what is uncanny

was itself originally frightening or whether it had some *other* affect. In the second place, if this is indeed the secret nature of the uncanny, we can understand why linguistic usage has extended *das Heimliche* ['homely'] into its opposite, *das Unheimliche*; for this uncanny is in reality nothing new or alien, but something which is familiar and old-established in the mind and which has become alienated from it only through the process of repression.

SE 17:241.

15. Judith Mary Weightman, *Making Sense of the Jonestown Suicides: A Sociological History of the People's Temple, Studies in Religion and Society*, vol. 7 (New York: Edwin Mellen Press, 1983). Steve Rose, *Jesus and Jim Jones* (New York: Pilgrim Press, 1979).

16. Rebecca Moore, *A Sympathetic History of Jonestown, Studies in Religion and Society*, vol. 14 (Lewiston: Edwin Mellen Press, 1985).

17. James Reston, Jr., *Our Father Who Art in Hell* (New York: Times Books, 1981), p. 57. Subsequent references are noted parenthetically.

18. Fredric Jameson, *The Political Unconscious: Narrative as Socially Symbolic Act* (Ithaca: Cornell University Press, 1981), p. 35.

19. *The Content of the Form*, p. 149.

20. *SE* 18:3–64. In his analysis of the death drive, Jean Laplanche considers three recurring elements: (1) the reflexive phase in which "Eros, the force that maintains narcissistic unity and uniqueness, can be deduced as a *return to a prior state* . . . "; (2) "the priority of zero over constancy," in which Laplanche cites Freud's "economic principle" in *Beyond the Pleasure Principle*, the tendency of the psychical apparatus "to maintain as low as possible the quantity of excitation present within it, or at least to maintain it at a constant level"; and (3) "the necessity of inscribing the two preceding priorities within the domain of the vital." *Life and Death in Psychoanalysis*, trans. Jeffrey Mehlman (Baltimore: Johns Hopkins University Press, 1976), pp. 115–17.

21. In a letter to me, dated October 24, 1989, Dorfman writes,

I wrote *Mascara* first in Spanish, then rewrote it in English, and then, with that English version, rewrote the Spanish version again. I had it edited by my (North) American editor, and then, with her corrections and my rewriting parts to make some things clearer, I worked over the Spanish text (which was published by Sudamericana in Buenos Aires under the title *Mascaras*, though it should have been called *Mascara* in Spanish as well). In a sense, then it is my first English novel—and I was able to do this because the material seemed so alien to me, so *exiled* [my emphasis] from my contingent reality as a Chilean. It is a step further than *The Last Song of Manuel Sendero*, in the sense that rather than dealing with exile directly, it does in fact project my experience of distance and evil and "transgression" in a different way. So I seemed to control the text hardly at all—or was, at least, extremely surprised as it made its way into the world (word).

22. Ariel Dorfman, *Mascara* (New York: Viking, 1988), pp. 16, 42. Subsequent references are noted parenthetically.

23. In a December 1986 interview, Dorfman states,

I see exile as a terrible loss, the pain of being distanced from everything that gives you a meaning. There are two basic myths that come out of humanity's experience of that loss. One is the foundational myth. You break the past, you rupture the umbilical cord of the past to found a new society. . . . And the other myth of exile, the other form of redemption that exile offers, is the opportunity to go back, to return and with what you have learned outside, to renew your original society. One myth speaks of birth, the other of rebirth.

Peggy Boyers and Juan Carlos Lertora, "Ideology, Exile, Language: An Interview with Ariel Dorfman," *Salmagundi* 82–83 (Spring–Summer 1989): 142–63.

24. See Freud, "The Dynamics of the Transference" (1912), *SE* 12:97–108, and "Remembering, Repeating and Working Through" (1914), *SE* 12:145–56. See also Lacan, *The Four Fundamental Concepts of Psycho-Analysis*, pp. 49–50. Peter Brooks has elucidated and applied these principles in *Reading for the Plot*, especially pp. 113–42, in a manner that has profoundly influenced my argument.

25. I have found Paul Ricoeur's explanation of Freud's text extremely useful for my analysis. See *Freud and Philosophy*, trans. Denis Savage (New Haven: Yale University Press, 1970), pp. 243–54.

26. For example, Yosef Hayim Yerushalmi's recent *Freud's Moses: Judaism Terminable and Interminable* (New Haven: Yale University Press, 1991) quickly dismisses the credibility of Freud's thesis from a factual or scholarly standpoint. Yerushalmi cogently presents *Moses and Monotheism* as Freud's celebration of the Jews as agents of civilization, and of psychoanalysis as an extension of Jewish monotheism.

27. *SE* 23:99.

28. Ricoeur develops this line of thinking in *Time and Narrative*. See especially 1:77–80 and 2:100–101. See also White's brilliant analysis of Ricoeur's theory of narrative in *The Content of the Form*, pp. 169–84. Louis O. Mink claims that the concept of universal history is as old as Augustine's *City of God* and was introduced in modern thought in Vico's *Scienza nova*. According to Mink, "Universal History did not deny the diversity of human events, customs, and institutions; but did regard this variety as the permutations of a single and unchanging set of human capacities and possibilities, differentiated only by the effects of geography, climate, race, and other natural contingencies." "Narrative Form as a Cognitive Instrument," *The Writing of History: Literary Form and Historical Understanding*, ed. Robert H. Canary and Henry Kozicki (Madison: University of Wisconsin Press, 1978), p. 138. Furthermore, Mink states that the claim to historical objectivity presupposes the idea of a universal history. Ricoeur writes of Freud's contention in *Moses and Monotheism*, "For Freud, 'the universality of symbolism in language' is far more a proof of the memory traces of the great traumas of mankind than an incentive to explore other dimensions of language, the imaginary, and myth." See *Freud and Philosophy*, p. 247.

CHAPTER THIRTEEN

Figures, Configurations, Transfigurations

EDWARD W. SAID

THE MOST POWERFUL ASPECT of all the "new" communities and forms of non-European literatures that we both celebrate and study today is that they are for the most part postcolonial and in a few instances actively anti-imperial. None of us would disagree, I think, if in the first instance we were to interpret the great mass of recent non-European literature as expressing ideas, values, emotions formerly suppressed, ignored, or denigrated by, and of course in, the well-known metropolitan centers. For in the decades-long struggle to achieve decolonization and independence from European control, literature has played a crucial role in the reestablishment of a national cultural heritage, in the reinstatement of native idioms, in the reimagining and refiguring of local histories, geographies, communities. As such then literature not only mobilized active resistance to incursions from the outside but also contributed massively as the shaper, creator, agent of illumination within the realm of the colonized.

What gives the actuality of literature in English its special force is that of all languages today English is, properly speaking, *the* world language. I say this as someone who grew up outside the commonwealth orbit and, still outside the Commonwealth, who now lives at the center of what has become the new English-speaking empire. This gives a particular and perhaps even eccentric perspective on what to an outsider like myself appears as the privileged historical centrality of English within the British Isles Commonwealth grouping. I do not for a moment wish to minimize the hardships, violence, or horrors endured by enormous numbers of people on whom the rule of English was impressed with sometimes catastrophic force, even as English also brought the many advantages of a prosperous culture. But I do think that it might serve a purpose here to begin by talking about the relationship between the dominance of English on the one hand and, on the other, resistances to it that come from cultural spheres and practices where English is either adjacent to the main English speaking dominions, or is still confined to specialized status. This will enable us to understand better the place of English in the global environment.

Let me impose a little more autobiography on you. I grew up in what in effect were two British colonies, Palestine and Egypt, but which remained

principally non-British culturally as well as politically. In addition to interests requiring a commanding British presence there, Egypt and Palestine
were of importance to the French, were technically within the Ottoman
Empire until the end of World War I, and of course went their own ways
after World War II. One can get some sense of the dynamics of that now
almost forgotten prewar world from Olivia Manning's *Levant Trilogy*, a
somewhat more lurid version of which (mainly concentrated in Alexandria,
for whom better guides are E. M. Forster, Cavafy, and Ungaretti) turns up
in Durrell's *Alexandria Quartet*. Very recently, a young English writer Anthony Sattin in his book *Lifting the Veil* produced an elegant history of British society in Egypt from the middle of the eighteenth through the middle
of the twentieth centuries.

From such works one concludes that the kind of culture embodied in the
notion of a British Commonwealth surrounded, but remained confined to
minority status within, the Arab world. One result of this is that unlike the
Caribbean, India, or Anglophone Africa, the Arab world that fell under British control for at least a century and a half never produced any literature to
speak of in English. This is strikingly different from the experience of the
French Muslim-Arabic imperial realm, where a thriving Francophone literature continues until this day, with eminent writers and critics in it like Ben
Jalloun, Kateb Yacine, Mohammed Dib, el Khatibi who are true cultural
amphibians at home both in metropolitan France and in their own societies.
In the world in which I was a boy, English was either the language of the
ruler, of tiny administrative elites, or of even smaller Christian minorities.
Thanks to the researches of a number of historians, we have come to understand the dynamics of national and Islamic resistance by which British institutions (which were unlike their French counterparts and not designed for
the assimilation of natives) made their selective incursions on native society,
and yet were kept at bay while schools of native reformers harnessed tribes,
guilds, fraternities, and schools to the mobilizing cause of what would later
become full-fledged independence.

Jump now to the middle 1980s. Asked a few years ago by a national university in one of the Gulf States to visit there for a week, I found that my
mission was to evaluate the English program at the university and perhaps
offer some recommendations for its improvement. I was flabbergasted to
discover that in sheer numerical terms English attracted the largest number
of young people of any department in the university. I was disheartened to
find, however, that the curriculum was divided about equally between what
was called linguistics (that is, grammar and phonetic structure) and literature. The literary courses were, I thought, rigorously orthodox, a pattern
followed pretty much, I think, even in older and more distinguished Arab
universities like those of Cairo and Ain Shams. Young Arabs read up dutifully on Milton, Shakespeare, Wordsworth, Austen, and Dickens as they

might have studied Sanskrit or medieval heraldry; no emphasis at all was placed on the relationship between English and the colonial processes that brought the language and its literature to the Arab world. I could not detect much interest, except in private discussions with a few faculty members, in the new literatures of the Caribbean, Africa, or Asia. The result seemed to me an anachronistic and odd confluence of rote learning, uncritical teaching, and (to put it kindly) very haphazard results.

On the other hand, I found out two additional things of some concern to me as a secular intellectual and critic. The reason for the large numbers of students taking English was given to me quite frankly by a somewhat disaffected instructor: they take English in droves, he said, because many of them proposed to end up working for the airlines, or for banks, in which English was the worldwide lingua franca. This all but terminally consigned English to the level of a technical language almost totally stripped not only of expressive and aesthetic characteristics but also of any critical or self-conscious dimension. You learned English to use computers, respond to orders, transmit telexes, decipher manifests, and so forth. That was all. The other (to me alarming) thing I discovered is that English such as it was existed in what seemed to be a seething cauldron of Islamic revivalism. While I was there, for instance, elections to the university senate were being contested; everywhere I turned, Islamic slogans were plastered all over the walls and, I later found out, the various Islamic candidates won a handsome, if not ultimately decisive, plurality. In Egypt where I observed much the same thing earlier this year, it is amusing to mention that at a lecture to the English faculty at Cairo University, after having spoken for an hour about nationalism, independence, and liberation as alternative cultural practices to imperialism, I was asked about "the theocratic alternative." (I had mistakenly supposed she was asking about "the Socratic alternative," and was put right very quickly.) The question came to me from a well-spoken young woman whose head was covered by a veil and who obviously was asking the question because religion constituted the main alternative concern to her as a citizen in a largely secular society. I had simply overlooked *that* in my heedless anticlerical and secular zeal. I nevertheless proceeded boldly to my attack!

Thus the very same English whose users in the Commonwealth can aspire to literary accomplishments of a very high order and for whom, in the notion of Ngugui Wa Thiongo, a critical use of the language might permit a decolonizing of the mind, coexists with very different new communities in a less appealing new configuration. On the one hand, in places where English was once present as the language of ruler and administrator its residue today is a much diminished presence. Either it is a technical language with wholly instrumental characteristics and features; or it is a foreign language with various implicit connections to the larger English-speaking world, but where its presence abuts on the much more impressive, much more formidable emergent reality of organized religious fervor. And since the language of Islam is Arabic, a language with considerable literary community and hieratic force, English seems to me to have sunk quite low, and to a quite uninteresting and attenuated level.

To gauge this new subordination in an era where in other contexts English has acquired remarkable prominence and many interesting new communities of literary, critical, and philosophical practice, we need only briefly recall the quite stunning acquiescence of the Islamic world to the overall prohibitions and proscriptions as well as threats pronounced against Salman Rushdie because of *The Satanic Verses*. That the novel dealt with Islam in English and for what was believed to be a largely Western audience was its main offense. I certainly do not mean that the entire Islamic world acquiesced, but that its official agencies, spokespeople, secular as well as religious, took what appeared to be a united stand either blindly rejecting or vehemently refusing to engage with a book which the enormous majority had never read. (The Khomeini threat of course went a good deal further than mere rejection but the Iranian position was a very isolated one.) On the other hand, it is equally important to note two things about the English-speaking world's reaction to *The Satanic Verses*. One was the relative (although with the usual caution and squeamishness) unanimity of condemnations of Islam marshaled in a cause that appeared to most of the writers and intellectuals at the time both safe and fashionable. As for the many writers either murdered, imprisoned, or banned in places where either American allies like Israel or irremediably anti-American "terrorists" like Libya, Iran, and Syria *could* have been condemned for such reprehensible practices, nothing was said. And second of all, there seemed to be little further interest either in the Islamic world as a whole or in the conditions of authorship where once the ritual phrases in support of Rushdie and denunciatory of Islam were pronounced. Whereas in fact I had hoped that some greater enthusiasm and energy would be expended in dialogue with those considerable literary and intellectual figures from the Islamic world (Mahfouz, Darwish, among others) who occasionally defended (and occasionally attacked) Rushdie in much more trying circumstances than those prevailing where writers protested Rushdie's fate in Greenwich Village or Hampstead.

None of this, however, takes very much away from my main point here, which is that there are highly significant *deformations* within the new communities that now exist alongside and partially inside the recently coherent outlines of the world-English group, a group that includes the heterogeneous voices, various languages, hybrid forms that give the Commonwealth its distinctive and still problematic identity. Thus, the emergence since the late 1970s of a startlingly sharp construction called "Islam" is, I think, one such deformation; others are "Communism," "Japan," and the "West," (there are still others) each of them possessing styles of polemic, a whole battery of discourses, and an unsettling profusion of opportunities for dissemination. Only if we try to map and register the vast domains commanded by these gigantic caricatural essentializations can we more fully appreciate and interpret the relatively modest gains made by smaller literate groups that are bound together not by insensate polemic but by affinities, sympathies, and compassion.

Few people during the exhilarating heyday of decolonization and early third-world nationalism were watching or paying close attention to what would later happen to the presence of a carefully nurtured nativism in the anticolonial ranks, how it would grow and grow to inordinately large proportions. I will concede that it is quite easy now to play the role of a retrospective Cassandra, but one still ought to be a little surprised that all those nationalist appeals to pure or authentic Islam, or to Africanism, negritude, or Arabism, were joined by so many without sufficient consciousness that precisely those ethnicities and spiritual essences would come back to exact a very high price from their successful adherents. To his credit Fanon was one of the few to remark on the dangers posed by an untutored national consciousness to a great sociopolitical movement like decolonization. Much the same could be said about the dangers of an untutored religious consciousness. And so the appearance of various mullahs, colonels, and one-party regimes who pleaded national security risks and the need to protect the foundling revolutionary state as their platform, foisted a new set of problems onto the already considerably onerous heritage of imperialism.

In intellectual and historical terms I do not think it is possible to name many states or regimes that are exempt from active participation in the new postcolonial international configuration. National security and identity are the watchwords. Along with the authorized figures of the ruler, the pantheon of national heroes and martyrs, the established religious authorities, the newly triumphant politicians seemed to require borders and passports first of all. What had once been the imaginative liberation of a people—Aimé Césaire's "inventions of new souls"—and the audacious metaphoric charting of spiritual territory usurped by colonial masters, were quickly translated into and accommodated by the world system of barriers, maps, frontiers, police forces, customs, and exchange controls. The finest, most elegiac commentary on a dismal state of affairs was provided by Basil Davidson in the course of a memorial reflection on the legacy of Amilcar Cabral (published in the Winter 1986 issue of *Race and Class*). Rehearsing the questions that were never asked about what would happen after liberation, Davidson concludes that a deepening crisis brought on neoimperialism and put petty-bourgeois rulers firmly in command. But, Davidson continues, this brand of "reformist nationalism continues to dig its own grave. As the grave deepens, fewer and fewer persons in command are able to get their own heads above the edge of it. To the tune of requiems sung in solemn chorus by hosts of foreign experts or would be *fundi* of one profession or another, often on very comfortable (and comforting) salaries, the funeral proceeds. The frontiers are there, the frontiers are sacred. What else, after all, could guarantee privilege and power to ruling elites?" (43). Chinua Achebe's most recent novel *Anthills of the Savannahs* is a compelling survey of this enervating and dispiriting landscape.

Davidson goes on to rectify the gloom of his own description by pointing to what he calls the people's "own solution to this carapace accepted from the colonial period."

> What the peoples think upon this subject is shown by their incessant emigration across these lines on the map, as well as by their smuggling enterprises. So that even while a 'bourgeois Africa' hardens its frontiers, multiplies its border controls, and thunders against the smuggling of persons and goods, a 'peoples' Africa works in quite another way. (44)

The cultural correlative of that audacious but often extremely costly combination of smuggling and emigration is, of course, familiar to us as exemplified by that new group of writers referred to as cosmopolitan recently in a perceptive analysis by Tim Brennan (Summer 1989 issue of *Race and Class*). And the subject of crossing borders as well as the representative deprivations and exhilarations of migration have become a major theme in the art of the postcolonial era.

Although it is possible to characterize these writers and themes as comprising a new cultural configuration and to point with considerable admiration to regional achievements not only in Europe but also in the Caribbean, in Africa, North and South America and the subcontinent, I believe the configuration ought to be looked at from a somewhat less attractive but, in my opinion, more realistic and political point of view. While we should quite correctly admire both the material as well as the achievements of, say, Rushdie's work, as part of a significant formation within the general field of Commonwealth literature, we should be just as willing at the same time to note with what it is encumbered or, to put it more precisely, how the particularly aesthetically valuable work of our time is strikingly also a part of threatening, or coercive, or deeply antiliterary, anti-intellectual formations. "There is no document of civilization which is not at the same time a document of barbarism." Those other darker connections, those sinister relationships and partnerships alluded to by Benjamin are where in political and cultural terms today's interesting conjunctures are to be found. They beseech our individual and collective critical work no less than the hermeneutic and utopian work we feel better about doing when we read, discuss, and reflect on valuable literary texts.

Let me be more concrete. It is not only tired, harassed, and dispossessed refugees who cross borders and attempt acculturation in new environments;

it is also the whole gigantic system of the mass media that is ubiquitous, slipping by most barriers and settling in nearly everywhere. Anyone who has read the work of Herbert Schiller and Armand Mattelart is aware of the practically total encroachment of a handful of multinationals on the production as well as the distribution of journalistic representations; Schiller's most recent study attempts to describe how it is that all departments of culture, not just those having to do with news, have been invaded by or enclosed within the ever-expanding circle of this relatively small number of privately held corporations.

There are too many consequences of this for me to list and discuss here, so I shall limit myself to two or three things. First is that the international media system has in actuality done what idealistic or ideologically inspired notions of collectivity or totality aspire to do. I mean by this that when, for instance, we speak about and research a theoretical entity called Commonwealth or world literature in English, our efforts remain pretty much at the level of (in Lukacian terms) a putative wholeness; for example, discussions of magic realism in the Caribbean and African novel allude to and in the most successful cases sketch the possible contours of a postmodern field that binds these works together. Yet we know at the same time that the works and their authors and readers remain concretely specific to and articulated in their own local circumstances, circumstances that are usefully kept separate when we analyze the contrasting conditions of reception in the metropolitan center (London or New York) on the one hand, the peripheries on the other. Yet compared to the way in which the four major Western news agencies operate, or the mode by which television journalists from CNN or NBC select, gather and rebroadcast pictorial images from India or Ethiopia, or the way programs like "Dallas" and "Dynasty" work their way through even the Lebanese civil war, we not only have in the media system a fully integrated practical network, but there also exists within it a very efficient *mode of articulation* knitting the world together.

I know of no detailed theoretical balance sheet that lays out what the power of this gradually universal system of articulation truly is. I do know, however, that a monument to an attempt by the less developed world to regulate and in other ways to influence it can be found in the McBride Report on the New World Information Order published by UNESCO in 1980. But that was in the days before UNESCO was first attacked and then restructured to suit the interests of the major Western powers. Thus the NWIO has ended, and market forces rule unchecked. Reinforcing this system is the map of patronage and monetary power elucidated in the North-South Report (the so-called Brandt Commission) in which the old imperial demarcations have reappeared both in the form of the predictable economic discrepancies as well as in the lamentably skewed interrelationships between the debtor nations of the peripheries and the creditor nations of the metropolis.

Lastly, the world system map articulating and producing culture, economics, and political power along with their military and demographic coefficients, has also developed an institutionalized tendency to produce out-of-scale transnational images that are now in the process of reorienting international social discourses and processes. Take as a case in point the emergence of terrorism and fundamentalism during the 1980s. For one, you can hardly begin (in the public space provided by international discourse) to analyze political conflicts involving Kurds and Iraqis, or Tamils and Sinhalese, or Sikhs and Hindus—the list is infinitely extendable—without having to resort to categories and images of terrorism and fundamentalism. For another, these images derive entirely from the concerns and from the intellectual factories in metropolitan centers like Washington and London. Moreover, they are fearful images that seem to lack discriminate contents or definitions, and they signify moral power and approval for whomever uses them, moral defensiveness and criminalization for whomever they designate.

During the past decade these two gigantic reductions have mobilized armies as well as dispersed communities. Neither the official Iranian reaction to Rushdie's novel, nor the unofficial or semiofficial enthusiasm of expatriate Islamic communities in the West, nor the public and private expressions of Western outrage is intelligible, in my opinion, without reference to the minute logic of articulations, reactions, and large-scale movements enabled by the overbearing system I am trying to identify. For in the relatively open environment postulated by communities of readers interested in emergent postcolonial Commonwealth or Francophone literature, the underlying configurations on the ground are directed and controlled not by processes of hermeneutic investigation, nor by sympathetic and literate intuition, nor by informed reading, but by much coarser and instrumental processes whose goal is the mobilization of consent, the eradication of dissent, the promotion of an almost literally blind patriotism. By such means is the governability assured of large numbers of people whose potentially disruptive ambitions for democracy and expression are held down (or narcotized) in mass societies.

The fear and terror induced by the overscale images of terrorism and fundamentalism—call them the figures of an international or transnational imaginary made up of foreign devils—contribute to hastening the individual's subordination to the dominant norms of the moment. This is as true in the new postcolonial societies as it is in the West. Thus to oppose the abnormality and extremism embedded in terrorism and fundamentalism—I provide what is only a small degree of parody with my example—is also to uphold the moderation, rationality, executive centrality of a vaguely designated "Western" (or otherwise local and patriotically assumed) ethos. The irony is that far from simply endowing the Western ethos with the confidence and secure "normality" we tend to associate with privilege and rectitude, this dynamic imbues "us" with a righteous anger and defensiveness in which all "others" are seen as enemies, bent on destroying our civilization and way of life. A perhaps exaggerated instance of what I mean is to be found in a *Wall Street Journal* editorial in May 28, 1988, by the eminent Orientalist Bernard Lewis. Addressing the simmering controversy at Stanford University and elsewhere concerning changes in the reading list of courses on Western civilization, Lewis notes that to tamper with these venerable canons of great books is in fact to threaten "the West" with a good deal more than a modified reading list containing black or female writers. It is, he says portentously, no less than to threaten us with the return of the harem and polygamy, with child marriages, with slavery and the end of political freedom, self-consciousness, and the disinterested pursuit of truth. Only the West, according to Lewis, abolished slavery on its own—one would have thought that slave revolts added some measure of persuasion—abolished polygamy on its own, studied itself and other societies for no other reason than the purest scientific curiosity untainted by profit or the exercise of power.

What I have rapidly sketched here furnishes, I think accurately, a sense of how these patterns of coercive orthodoxy and self-aggrandizement further strengthen the hold of unthinking assent and unchallengeable doctrine. Their slow perfection over time and after much repetition is answered, alas, with corresponding finality by the designated enemies. Thus, Muslims or Africans or Indians or Japanese, in their idioms and within their own, constantly threatened local enclosures, attack the West, or Americanization, or imperialism with little more attention to detail or to critical differentiation, discrimination and distinction than is lavished on them by the West. This cannot unfortunately stop or inhibit an ultimately senseless dynamic. For to the extent that what we might call the border wars have aims, those aims are wholly impoverishing. One must either join the primordial or constituted group; or one must as a subaltern Other accept inferior status; or one must fight to the death.

To characterize what I have been calling border wars as a regime of essentializations—Africanizing the African, Orientalizing the Oriental, Westernizing the Western, for an indefinite time and with no alternative because African, Oriental, Western essences can only remain essences—immediately raises the question of what resists this pattern, and the systems that serve it. One obvious instance is identified by Immanuel Wallerstein as what he calls antisystemic movements whose emergence is a consequence of historical capitalism. There have been enough cases of these latecoming movements in recent times to hearten even the most intransigent pessimism: the democracy movements on all sides of the socialist divide, the Palestinian *intifada*, various social, ecological, and cultural movements throughout North and South America. Yet few of these movements seem (to me at least) to be interested in, or have the capacity and freedom to generalize beyond, their own regionally local circumstances. If you are part of a Philippine, or Palestinian, or Brazilian oppositional movement you are necessarily circumscribed by the tactical and logistical requirements of the daily struggle. But, on the other hand, I do think that there is developing here, if not a general theory, then a common discursive readiness or, to put it in territorial terms, an underlying world map for efforts of this kind. Perhaps we can start to speak of a common counterarticulation, a phrase which best catches this somewhat elusive oppositional mood and its emerging strategies.

But what new or newer kind of intellectual and cultural politics does this call for; what important transformations and transfigurations are there in our ideas of such traditionally and eurocentrically defined identities as the writer, the intellectual, the critic, and so forth? Because English is a world language and because the logics of borders and or warring essences are so totalizing, we should begin with acknowledgments of a world map without divinely or dogmatically sanctioned spaces, essences, or privileges. It is necessary therefore to speak of our element as secular space and humanly constructed and interdependent histories that are fundamentally knowable, but not through grand theory or systematic totalization. These formulations sound much more impressive and ponderous than they really are. I am trying to say that human experience is finely textured, dense, as well as accessible enough *not* to need the assistance of extra-historical or extra-world agencies to illuminate or explain it. What I am talking about is thus a way of regarding the whole world we live in as amenable to our investigation and interrogation quite without appeals to magic keys, or to special jargons and instruments, or curtained-off practices. As one example of how we would proceed having acknowledged these things, there is the pattern implicit in Hobsbawm and Ranger, *The Invention of Tradition*, which suggests that it is a coherent intellectual undertaking to consider that all parts of human history are available to understanding and elucidation because they are humanly constructed and designed to accomplish real tasks in the real world. History and geography are susceptible to inventories in other words.

What this and, to mention other examples, Martin Bernal's *Black Athena*, or *Subaltern Studies*, or Colls's and Dodd's anthology *Englishness*, or Paulin Hountoudji's *Sur la "Philosophie Africaine"* all suggest is a different paradigm for humanistic research than those that have reigned for about a century now. The scholar in these innovative works is frankly engaged in the politics and interests of the present, engaged with open eyes, rigorous analytic energies, and with the decently social values of someone whose main concern is not the survival of a disciplinary fiefdom or guild but the improvement and noncoercive enhancement of life in a community struggling among other communities. One must not, however, minimize the inventive excavations that constitute the center of such work. No one here looks for uniquely original essences, either to restore them or to set them in a place of unimpeachable honor. The study of Indian history is viewed by *Subaltern Studies* as an ongoing contest between classes and their disputed epistemologies; similarly Englishness for the contributors to the Colls and Dodd volume is not given before history, any more than Attic civilization in Bernal's important study can be extracted from history and made easily and simply to serve as an ahistorical model for superior civilizations.

Nor is this all. The conception of history enabling such work is that official, orthodox, authoritatively national and institutional versions of history tend principally to designate provisional and highly contestable attempts to freeze these versions of history into identities for use. Thus the official version of British history embedded, say, in the durbars arranged for Queen Victoria's visit to India in 1872 pretends that there is an almost mythical longevity to British rule over India; traditions of Indian service, obeisance and subordination are implicated in these ceremonies so as to create the image of an entire continent's transhistorical identity pressed into compliance before the image of a Britain whose own constructed identity is that it has and must always rule both the waves and India. Whereas these official versions of history attempt to capture it for, in Adornian terms, identitarian authority, the disenchantments, disputations, and systematically skeptical investigations in the innovative work I have cited submit these fabricated identities to a negative dialectic which dissolves them into variously constructed components. What matters a great deal more than the stable essence or identity kept in currency by an official discourse is the contestatory force of a historical method whose material is made up of disparate, but intertwined and interdependent, and above all, overlapping streams of historical experience.

A major set of corollaries derives from this. For if the chief, most official, forceful, and coercive identity is the State with its borders, customs, ruling parties and authorities, and if that is questioned, then it must also be the case that other similarly constructed identities need to be similarly investigated and interrogated. For those of us involved in literature, our education has for the most part been organized under various rubrics—the creative writer, the self-sufficient and autonomous work, the national literature, the separate genres—that have acquired almost fetishistic presence. Now it would be insanity to argue that individual writers and works do not exist, that French, Japanese, and Arabic are really the same thing, or that Milton, Tagore, and Carpentier are only trivially different variations on the same theme. Neither would I want to be understood as saying that writing an essay about *Great Expectations* and *Great Expectations*, the novel that Dickens wrote, are the same thing. But I do want to be understood as saying that a focus on identity need imply neither the ontologically given and eternally determined stability of that identity, nor its uniqueness, its utterly irreducible character, its privileged status as something total and complete in and of itself. I would much prefer to interpret a novel as the selection of one mode of writing among many others, and the activity of writing as one social mode among several, and the category of literature as something created, made to serve various worldly aims. Thus the focus that corresponds with the destabilizing and investigative attitudes I have mentioned in connection with active opposition to states and borders is to look at the way a work, for instance, begins *as* a work, begins *from* a political, social, cultural situation, begins *to do* certain things and not others.

Yet the modern history of literary study is strictly bound up with the development of cultural nationalism, whose aim was first to distinguish the national canon then to maintain it in a place reserved for eminence, authority, and aesthetic autonomy. Even where discussions concerning culture in general seemed to rise above national differences in deference to a universal sphere, it is very apparent that hierarchies (as between European and non-European cultures) and ethnic preferences were held to. This is as true of Matthew Arnold as it is for twentieth-century cultural and philological critics whom I revere—Auerbach, Adorno, Spitzer, Blackmur. For them, their culture was in a sense the only culture. The threats against it were largely internal, like fascism and communism, so that what they upheld after a long period of siege, was European bourgeois humanism. Neither the ethos nor the rigorous training required to install that *bildung* and the extraordinary discipline it demanded has survived, although occasionally one hears the accents of admiration and retrospective discipleship without anything resembling work of the order of *Mimesis*. Instead of European bourgeois humanism, the basic premise of what literary scholars now do is provided by the residue of nationalism with its various derivative authorities, in alliance with professionalism, which divides material into fields, subdivisions, specialties, accreditations, and the like. Insofar as it has survived, the doctrine of aesthetic autonomy has dwindled to the formalism associated with one or another professional method like structuralism, deconstruction, etc.

A look at some of the fields that have arisen since World War II, and especially as a result of the newer non-European nationalism struggles with which I began these remarks, reveals a different topography and a different set of imperatives. Most students and teachers of non-European literatures today must take account of the politics of what they study right at the outset; one cannot postpone discussions of slavery, colonialism, racism, in any serious investigations of modern Indian, African, Latin American, Caribbean, and Commonwealth literature. Nor strictly speaking is it intellectually responsible to discuss any of these literatures without specific reference to their embattled circumstances either in postcolonial societies or as subjects taught in metropolitan centers where, for example, the study of what are marginalized and/or subjugated literatures is confined to secondary spots on the curricular agenda. By the same token, discussion of literature today cannot hide inside positivism or empiricism and offhandedly require the weapons of theory. On the other hand I think it is a mistake to try to show that the "other" literatures of Africa and Asia, with their more obviously worldly affiliations to power and politics, can be studied respectably, that is, as if they were in actuality as high, as autonomous, as aesthetically independent and satisfying as French, German, or English literatures. The notion of black skin in a white mask is no more serviceable and dignified in literary study than it is in politics. Emulation and mimicry never get one very far.

Contamination is perhaps the wrong word to use here, but some such notion—of literature as hybrid and encumbered, or entangled with a lot of what used to be regarded as extraneous elements—strikes me as *the* essential idea adequate for the revolutionary realities that face us today, in which the contests of the secular world so provocatively inform the texts we both read and write. Moreover, I believe that we can no longer uncomplainingly afford conceptions of history that stress linear development or Hegelian transcendence, any more than we can accept geographic or territorial assumptions assigning centrality to the Natopolitan world, and ontogenetic peripherality to the non-Western regions of the world. If configurations like Commonwealth or world literature are to have any meaning at all it is, therefore, because by their existence and actuality in the late twentieth century they first testify to the contests and continuing struggles by virtue of which they have emerged not only as texts but as experiences, and second, because they interact ferociously not only with the whole nationalist basis for the composition and study of literature, but also with the lofty independence and indifference with which it has become customary Eurocentrically to regard the metropolitan Western literatures.

What this means for Commonwealth no less than for English, French, or American literatures classically differentiated is that once we accept the more actual configuration of literary experiences overlapping with one another, and interdependent despite national boundaries and coercively legislated national autonomies, history and geography are transfigured into new maps, new and far less stable entities, new types of connections. Exile, far from being the fate of those nearly forgotten unfortunates who have been dispossessed and expatriated, becomes something closer to a norm, an experience of crossing boundaries and charting new territories in defiance of the classic canonic enclosures, however much the loss and sadness of exile may also need acknowledgment and registering. Thus, changed models and types jostle the older ones. The reader and writer of literature—which itself loses its perdurable forms and accepts the testimonials, revisions, notations of the postcolonial experience, including underground life and prison—no longer needs to tie him or herself to an image of the poet or scholar in isolation, secure, stable, national in identity, class, gender, or profession, but can think and experience with Genet in Palestine or Algeria, with Tayib Saleh as a black man in London, with Jamaica Kinkaid in the white world, with Rushdie in India and Britain, and so on.

I suppose what I am getting at is how we might expand the horizons against which the questions of *how* and *what* to read and write are both posed and answered. To paraphrase from a remark made by Auerbach in one of his very last essays, our philological home is the world, and not the nation or even the individual writer. For those of us who are professional students of literature, for whom the literary life is principally teaching and research, there are a number of quite astringent things to take account of here, at the risk both of unpopularity and accusations of megalomania. For in an age of the mass media and what has been called the manufacture of consent it is little short of Panglossian to assume that the careful reading of a relatively small number of works designated as humanistically, professionally, or aesthetically significant is much more than a private activity with some slender public consequences. Texts are protean things; they are tied to circumstances and to politics both large and small, and these require attention and critique. No one can take stock of everything of course, just as no theory can possibly explain or account for the connections between texts and societies. But to read and write texts cannot ever be neutral activities: there are interests, powers, passions, pleasures entailed no matter how aesthetic or entertaining the work. Media, political economy, mass institutions: in fine, the tracings of secular power and the influence of the State are now part of what we call literature. And just as it is true that we cannot read literature by men without also reading literature by women—so transfigured has been the shape of literature—it is also true that we cannot deal with the literature of the peripheries without also attending to the literature of the metropolitan centers.

Instead of the partial analysis offered by the various schools of national or systematically theoretical approaches, I propose finally the contrapuntal lines of a global analysis, in which texts and worldly institutions are seen working together, in which Dickens and Thackeray as London authors are read also as writers informed constitutively by the colonial enterprises of which they were so aware, and in which the literature of one commonwealth is involved in the literature of others. Separatist or nativist enterprises strike me as exhausted, since the ecology of the new and expanded meaning of literature that I have been discussing cannot at all be attached only to one essence, or to the discrete idea of one thing. I do not think, however, that global and contrapuntal analysis can itself be modeled (as earlier notions of comparative literature were modeled) on the notion of a symphony; rather we have more to do with atonal ensembles, and with such spatial or geographical and rhetorical practices as inflections, limits, constraints, intrusions, inclusions, prohibitions, all of them tending toward elucidations of a complex and uneven topography. While it remains of value in the work of a gifted critic, the intuitive synthesis of the type volunteered by hermeneutic or philological interpretation (whose prototype is to be found in Dilthey) strikes me as the poignant restoration of a serener time than ours.

This brings us round in the end to the question of politics. No country is exempt from the debate about what is to be taught, written or even read. I've often felt envious of theorists for whom either a radical skepticism or deferential reverence before the status quo have been real alternatives. I don't feel them to be, perhaps because my own situation prevents any such luxury, any such detachment and satisfaction. Yet I do believe that some literature is actually good, and that some is of a bad quality, and I remain as conservative as anyone when it comes to, if not the redemptive quality inherent in reading a classic rather than staring at a TV screen, then the potential enhancement of one's sensibility and consciousness by it, and by the exercise of one's mind in dealing with it. I suppose the issue reduces itself to what the relatively humdrum and pedestrian daily work of what we do as readers and writers is really about, if on the one hand, professionalism won't serve and on the other, a belief in waiting for apocalyptic change won't either. I keep coming back—simplistically and idealistically—to the notion of opposing and alleviating coercive domination, transforming the present by trying rationally and analytically to lift some of its burdens, situating the works of various literatures with reference to each other and to their historical modes of being. What I am really saying is that readers and writers in the configurations and by virtue of the transfigurations taking place around us are now in fact secular intellectuals with the archival, expressive, elaborative, and moral responsibilities of that role.

Index